JAY HALEY REVISITED

JAY HALEY REVISITED

EDITED BY Madeleine Richeport-Haley AND Jon Carlson

Routledge
Taylor & Francis Group
New York London

Routledge
Taylor & Francis Group
270 Madison Avenue
New York, NY 10016

Routledge
Taylor & Francis Group
27 Church Road
Hove, East Sussex BN3 2FA

Routledge is an imprint of Taylor & Francis Group, an Informa business

10 9 8 7 6 5 4 3 2 1

International Standard Book Number: 978-0-415-80531-5 (Hardback) 978-0-415-80533-9 (Paperback)

Library of Congress Cataloging-in-Publication Data

Haley, Jay, 1923-2007.
[Selections. 2010.]
Jay Haley revisited / edited by Madeleine Richeport-Haley and Jon Carlson.
p. cm.
Includes bibliographical references and index.
ISBN 978-0-415-80531-5 (hardback : alk. paper) -- ISBN 978-0-415-80533-9 (pbk. : alk. paper)
1. Family psychotherapy. I. Richeport-Haley, Madeleine. II. Carlson, Jon. III. Title.

RC488.5.H32122 2010
616.89'156--dc22 2009036282

Visit the Taylor & Francis Web site at
http://www.taylorandfrancis.com

and the Routledge Web site at
http://www.routledgementalhealth.com

ARTICLES BY JAY HALEY

Dedication

To my husband, Jay, with all my love forever and ever.
—Madeleine Richeport-Haley

To Jay Haley for his timeless inspiration and wisdom.
—Jon Carlson

Contents

Acknowledgments

It was Jay Haley's idea to publish a book of some of his published and unpublished essays that he called *Papers Pleasant and Unpleasant*. All of these essays are included in this volume. We want to thank Dr. George Zimmar, editor of behavioral sciences at Routledge, for his support and for suggesting that we add leading experts in the field to introduce each paper. We are grateful to Braulio Montalvo, who worked with Jay Haley for so many years, for suggesting additional articles to be included and for valuable discussions about ideas in the articles. We are indebted to the many experts who wrote the introductions in this volume. We thank each of them for their thoughtful comments on these essays and on the therapy field in general.

Our appreciation to Scott Woolley, systems-wide director of the Marital Family Therapy Program at the California School of Professional Psychology, Alliant International University, where Jay Haley worked for 10 years, for his administrative wisdom and friendship. Alliant performed the arduous task of putting all the papers in digital form. Yukiko Hishiya accomplished this task with attention to every detail. There are countless numbers of colleagues and students, too numerous to mention here, who contributed to Jay Haley's ideas throughout the years.

A special acknowledgment to the Erickson family and to Elizabeth Erickson, who passed away earlier this year, for her encouragement, love, and generosity to Madeleine Richeport-Haley and Jay Haley throughout so many years.

Madeleine Richeport-Haley
La Jolla, California

Jon Carlson
Lake Geneva, Wisconsin

About the Editors

Madeleine Richeport-Haley, PhD, is currently senior research faculty, California School of Professional Psychology, Alliant International University. She is an anthropologist filmmaker who trained with Milton Erickson. She collaborated with her husband, Jay Haley, for 18 years, and coauthored with him *The Art of Strategic Therapy* and *Directive Family Therapy*. They also produced documentaries and training films on therapy, including *Milton H. Erickson: Explorer in Hypnosis and Therapy*; *Whither Family Therapy?*; and the series *Learning and Teaching Therapy by Jay Haley* and *Family Therapy in Bali*. She has served as mental health consultant to the Pan American Health Organization–World Health Organization (PAHO-WHO) in Brazil; the Department of Mental Health in Puerto Rico; the Department of Psychiatry, University of Miami; and *National Geographic*. Her numerous publications have added a cross-cultural healing perspective to the therapy field. http://www.jay-haley-on-therapy.com.

Jon Carlson, PsyD, EdD, ABPP, is distinguished professor, psychology and counseling at Governors State University and a psychologist at the Wellness Clinic in Lake Geneva, Wisconsin. Jon has served as editor of several periodicals, including the *Journal of Individual Psychology* and *The*

Family Journal. He holds diplomas in both family psychology and Adlerian psychology. He has authored 150 journal articles and 45 books, including *Time for a Better Marriage*, *Adlerian Therapy*, *Inclusive Cultural Empathy*, *The Mummy at the Dining Room Table*, *Bad Therapy*, *The Client Who Changed Me*, and *Moved by the Spirit.* He has created more than 250 professional trade videos and DVDs with leading professional therapists and educators. In 2004 the American Counseling Association named him a Living Legend. Recently he syndicated an advice cartoon, *On the Edge*, with cartoonist Joe Martin.

About the Contributors

George Burns, PhD, is an Australian clinical psychologist, adjunct senior lecturer at Edith Cowan University, and director of both the Milton H. Erickson Institute of Western Australia and the Hypnotherapy Centre of Western Australia. In addition, he runs a busy private practice and has authored seven books along with numerous journal articles and book chapters. He teaches internationally and leads study tours in places such as the Himalayan Kingdom of Bhutan. george-burns@iinet.net.au.

William J. Doherty, PhD, is professor of family social science, former director of the Marriage and Family Therapy Program, and founding director of the Citizen Professional Center at the University of Minnesota. He has authored 14 books and many journal articles on clinical and research topics. He is cofounder of the National Registry of Marriage Friendly Therapists. http://www.drbilldoherty.org.

Mony Elkaim, MD, is a neuropsychiatrist, family therapist, and honorary professor at Brussels Free University (ULB). He was founder and president of the European Family Therapy Association (EFTA), and is currently president of the European Association of Psychotherapy (EAP). He is the author of several books, including *If You Love Me, Don't Love Me* (Basic Books, 1990).

Leslie Greenberg, PhD, is professor of psychology, York University in Toronto; director of the Psychotherapy Research Clinic; and conducts a private practice and training. He has authored the major texts on emotion-focused therapy. He received the Society for Psychotherapy Research (SPR) Distinguished Research Career Award and the Carl Rogers Award of the American Psychological Association (APA) Society for Humanistic Psychology.

David Grove, LISW, has published two books on family therapy, *Conversations on Therapy* (with Jay Haley) and *Invisible Men* (with Rhonda Burnaugh). He is a former regional faculty of the Family Therapy Institute of Washington, DC. Currently Mr. Grove is researching home-based therapy and is one of the cofounders of Integrative Family and Systems Treatment, an in-home therapy approach aimed at preventing the removal of children from their families. d.grove@sbcglobal.net.

Kenneth V. Hardy, PhD, is professor of family therapy at Drexel University in Philadelphia, Pennsylvania, and is also director of the Eikenberg Institute for Relationships in New York City, where he maintains a practice specializing in working with traumatized children and families. Dr. Hardy serves on the editorial boards of several journals and has published prolifically in the areas of family therapy. He is the coauthor of *Revisioning Family Therapy: Race, Class, and Culture in Clinical Practice*; *Teens Who Hurt: Clinical Interventions for Breaking the Cycle of Youth Violence*; and *Minorities and Family Therapy*. kvhardy@syr.edu.

Michael F. Hoyt, PhD (Yale '76), is a senior staff psychologist at the Kaiser Permanente Medical Center in San Rafael, California. Dr. Hoyt is the author of *Brief Therapy* *and Managed Care, Some Stories Are Better Than Others, Interviews With Brief Therapy Experts, The Present Is a Gift*, and *Brief Psychotherapies: Principles and Practices*; he is also the editor of several volumes. He is a Woodrow Wilson fellow and has been honored as a Continuing Education Distinguished Speaker by both the American Psychological Association and the International Association of Marriage and Family Counselors, and was the 2007 recipient of the prestigious APF Cummings Psyche Prize for lifetime contributions to the primary role of psychologists in organized health care.

Jay Lebow, PhD, is clinical professor of psychology at the Family Institute at Northwestern University. He has conducted clinical practice, supervision, and research on couples and family therapy for over 30 years. He is board certified in family psychology by the American Board of Professional Psychology and an approved supervisor in the American Association for Marriage and Family Therapy. He is the author of 100 book chapters and articles, most of which focus on the interface of research and practice of integrative couple and family therapy. His published books include *Research for the Psychotherapist* and four edited volumes, including *The Clinical Handbook of Family Therapy*. He is a past president of the Division of Family Psychology of the American Psychological Association and is involved in the Family Institute's Psychotherapy Change research project.

Judith Mazza, PhD, has been teaching, writing, and practicing in the area of brief therapy for more than 30 years. She trained with Jay Haley, and served as a supervisor and clinical director of the Family Therapy Institute of Washington, DC. She teaches marriage and family therapy at the National Naval Medical Center, and has written *Strategic and Brief Therapy*. Currently, she is director of the Center for Problem

Solving in Bethesda, Maryland, where she continues her clinical practice and teaching. http://familytherapy.com.

Braulio Montalvo, MA, is a family therapy consultant in private practice. Until recently, he was affiliated with the Geriatric Evaluation Clinic at the University of New Mexico Medical School and at the Veterans Readjustment Center in Albuquerque, New Mexico. He collaborated with Salvador Minuchin and Jay Haley at the Child Guidance Clinic in Philadelphia (1965–1975). He has coauthored *Families of the Slums*, *The Difficult Divorce*, and numerous articles in the field. He also made some of the first family therapy videos. montcom@aol.com.

Michael P. Nichols, PhD, is professor of psychology at the College of William and Mary, Williamsburg, Virginia. He also teaches and practices family therapy. Among his many books are *Family Therapy: Concepts and Methods*; *Family Healing* (with Salvador Minuchin); and *The Lost Art of Listening*. mpnich@wm.edu.

Bill O'Hanlon, MS, LMFT, has written and published 29 books, the latest being *A Guide to Trance-Land* (Norton, 2009). He studied directly with Milton H. Erickson, MD, and admired Jay Haley's work and writings, through which he was introduced to Erickson. Bill travels and teaches workshops regularly around the world and also coaches people on getting published and doing public speaking. His primary Web site is http://www.billohanlon.com.

Neil P. Schiff, PhD, is a psychologist in private practice in Washington, DC, and Maryland. He is a consultant to the Office of Medical Services, U.S. Department of State. He trained, supervised, and taught strategic therapy with Jay Haley at the Family Therapy Institute of Washington, DC. From 1986 until 1995, he collaborated with Jay Haley on a project dealing with difficult cases, which included clients with severe diagnoses such as schizophrenia, to produce training tapes that were used to teach family therapy. Dr. Schiff has presented workshops to professional audiences throughout the United States and abroad. He has published in the field of brief, strategic family therapy.

Carlos E. Sluzki, MD, is professor, Department of Global and Community Health and Institute for Conflict Analysis and Resolution, George Mason University; and clinical professor, Department of Psychiatry and Behavioral Science, George Washington University. He was director of the Mental Research Institute (1980–1983), and editor-in-chief of *Family Process* and of the *American Journal of Orthopsychiatry*. He has authored 200 papers and several books in the fields of family therapy, social networks, community mental health, victims of violence, migration, and human rights. csluzki@gmu.edu; http://www.sluzki.com.

Len Sperry, MD, PhD, is professor of mental health counseling at Florida Atlantic University, and clinical professor of psychiatry at the Medical College of Wisconsin. He is board certified in clinical psychology, psychiatry, and preventive medicine; has 500 publications, including 55 professional books; and is on 10 editorial boards. lsperry@fau.edu.

Michele Weiner-Davis, MSW, is an internationally renowned relationship therapist who specializes in helping people change their lives and improve important relationships. She is the author of seven books, including *Divorce Busting: A Step-by-Step Approach to Making Your Marriage Loving Again* (Simon & Schuster) and *The Sex-Starved Marriage: A Couple's Guide to Boosting Their Marriage Libido* (Simon & Schuster). She was the recipient of the American Association of Marriage and Family Therapy's prestigious Outstanding Contribution to the Field of Marriage and Therapy Award and Smart Marriages' Impact Award. Michele is the director of the Divorce Busting Center with offices in Boulder, Colorado, and Woodstock, Illinois. http://www.divorcebusting.com.

Robert E. Wubbolding, EdD, RTC, is professor emeritus of counseling at Xavier University; director of the Center for Reality Therapy in Cincinnati, Ohio; and director of training for the William Glasser Institute. He has authored more than 125 articles, chapters, and DVDs as well as the most comprehensive book on reality therapy, *Reality Therapy for the 21st Century*. He has conducted workshops throughout North America, Europe, Asia, and the Middle East. http://www.realitytherapywub.com.

Michael D. Yapko, PhD, is a clinical psychologist and marriage and family therapist residing in Fallbrook, California. He is internationally recognized for his work in clinical hypnosis, brief psychotherapy, and the strategic treatment of depression, routinely teaching to professional audiences all over the world. He is the author of 10 books, including *Breaking the Patterns of Depression*; *Hand-Me-Down Blues: How to Stop Depression From Spreading in Families*; *Treating Depression With Hypnosis*; and *Trancework: An Introduction to the Practice of Clinical Hypnosis*. He is the recipient of numerous awards for his innovative contributions in advancing the fields of hypnosis and brief therapy. michaelyapko@roadrunner.com; http://www.yapko.com.

Jeffrey K. Zeig, PhD, is the founder and director of the Milton H. Erickson Foundation. He has edited, coedited, authored, or coauthored more than 20 books on psychotherapy that appear in 11 foreign languages. Dr. Zeig is the architect of the Evolution of Psychotherapy Conferences, considered the most important conferences in the history of psychotherapy. He organizes the Brief Therapy Conferences, the Couples Conferences, and the International Congresses on Ericksonian Approaches to Hypnosis and Psychotherapy.

A psychologist and marriage and family therapist in private practice in Phoenix, Arizona, Dr. Zeig conducts workshops internationally (in 40 countries). He is president of Zeig, Tucker & Theisen, Inc., publishers in the behavioral sciences. http://www.jeffzeig.com.

Jay Haley: An Introduction

Madeleine Richeport-Haley, PhD, and Jon Carlson, PsyD, EdD

Jay Haley was a Renaissance man. He was a writer, filmmaker, anthropologist, painter, sculptor, playwright, teacher, lecturer, researcher, and librarian, and a revolutionary in therapy. This collection of Jay Haley's papers was taken from an exciting time in the history of psychotherapy. These papers were pivotal in creating psychotherapy's major paradigm shift from insightful long-term therapy to a family, problem-focused, brief strategic therapy. Jay Haley was one of the most influential thinkers in psychotherapy and revolutionized the field through his writings, teachings, research, and supervision for more than half a century. He was a pioneer in family therapy, as both a founder and editor for 10 years of *Family Process*, the first journal in family therapy. He was the chief architect of the brief strategic approach to therapy. His contribution is published in 21 books and more than 100 papers translated into 15 languages. He pioneered therapy recording, training, and supervision on film and video. His reputation spanned many years from being the most cited author in psychology in the 1970s to being voted the most valuable therapist in California in 2004.

Jay Haley's work can be divided into different periods. He held degrees from the University of California, Los Angeles and Berkeley campuses, and Stanford University. While at Stanford he met Gregory Bateson, and as a young member of the Gregory Bateson Research Project, he participated in the early research in family therapy and schizophrenia described in Chapter 18. His work on leading medical hypnotist Dr. Milton H. Erickson in *Uncommon Therapy: The Psychiatric Techniques of Milton Erickson, MD* (1973) influenced many people to become therapists. He elaborated and codified a brief strategic family therapy approach, which grew out of Erickson's work, and departed in many significant ways from the more traditional approach to therapy before the 1950s where, Jay stated, "Everything happened." It emphasized the present, not the past; a positive unconscious, not a negative unconscious; and a focus on action rather than developing insight, emphasizing the skills needed to change problems rather than diagnosis.

In the mid-1960s, Jay joined Salvador Minuchin and Braulio Montalvo at the Philadelphia Child Guidance Clinic as director of family therapy research for 10 years. They received a grant to train paraprofessionals in the community (poor

African Americans and Latinos). This innovative training and live supervision are published in *Problem-Solving Therapy*, a text for learning therapeutic skills. Jay always remembered these trainees as some of the best therapists he had known. He also served as clinical associate professor at the University of Pennsylvania. He cofounded the Family Therapy Institute of Washington, DC, and served as professor of clinical psychiatry at Howard University and at the University of Maryland, where he continued this pioneering work in training therapists from around the world in directive family therapy. In the early 1990s, he returned to California, joined the faculty of Alliant International University, and continued making training films, writing, and lecturing until his death in 2007.

His techniques stressed directives to produce change rather than social conversation. His focus was on the problem in the social context, not on the problem individual. His view was optimistic and that change was possible. He was a man with a cause. First, therapists should do no harm. He argued against psychotropic medication replacing therapy with schizophrenics because he believed that schizophrenia and addiction are curable with therapy. He also argued for training therapists through live supervision, giving them the tools to use for problem solving through an active, thoughtfully planned-out family therapy. For example, instead of advocating the *Diagnostic and Statistical Manual* (DSM; see, e.g., American Psychological Association, 2000), which stresses pathology and sickness, he advocated a DSM that stresses therapy techniques.

Jay Haley was a visionary. In addition to the major papers in this volume, we call your attention to a brief paper entitled "The Eastern Question," which appeared in *The New Yorker* in 1947. Haley shares a story of an encounter in Japan that clearly captures the importance of culture in human connection. It took another half century before professional associations caught up and drafted guidelines in this area.

When Jay Haley sat down to write, like Erickson, he did not quote what came before him. His ideas were broad and influenced many fields: psychology, psychiatry, hypnosis, communication, history of science, and anthropology. His ideas continue to trigger diverse reactions from mental health professionals. He forced the field to reexamine significant ideas in mental health. Haley said in his last book, *Directive Family Therapy* (Haley & Richeport-Haley, 2007), "As I look back I am amazed to see the ways in which directive and traditional approaches are opposite each other" (p. 1). Some of these significant differences include long-term therapy versus brief therapy; therapy focused on the past versus therapy focused on the present; negative unconscious versus positive unconscious; focus on the problem individual versus focus on the problem in the social context; focus on developing insight versus focus on action; diagnosis is stressed versus skills needed to change problems are stressed; memories bring up the truth versus memories can be false; hypnosis is not respected versus hypnosis is a valuable tool in psychotherapy; psychosis and addiction are considered incurable versus psychosis and addiction are considered curable; paradox is considered manipulative versus paradox is considered legitimate; and conversation cures versus directives produce change.

After Milton Erickson died in 1980, Jay delivered a moving address in which he described Erickson as "a man with class." This uncommon choice of words as the ultimate compliment for his respected mentor prompted Jeffrey Zeig (2001) to use the same phrase to return the compliment to Jay in the tribute organized by the Erickson Foundation. Since that time, Jay has also been referred to as "a man with class." Although I (M.R.-H.) never discussed this with him personally, more recently I thought of the countless times we watched the classic film *On the Waterfront* (Schulberg, 1980) with Marlon Brando. It was a film that impressed Jay all the more because as a young man he had a job working in the shipyards. He always joined in reciting the famous line, "I could'a had class, I could'a been a contender. I could'a been somebody." Perhaps this deep compliment for Erickson grew out of this line in the film. We will never know. But Jay worked his whole life for people to do good work. He was committed to teaching students therapy skills so they could be excellent therapists and have fun doing it. He had optimism that clients could change even in the direst circumstances.

This book brings together leading experts in the field of psychotherapy who introduce and comment on classic papers by Jay Haley. These are the papers that changed the field of psychotherapy. The papers capture the wit, the humor, and the ability to look at our field and offer a critique that leads to constructive change. In these papers, Haley teaches the therapist how to fail, the schizophrenic to remain schizoid, and the techniques for an awful marriage. We hope you will enjoy this "pleasant and unpleasant" collection.

References

American Psychiatric Association. (2000). *Diagnostic and statistical manual of mental disorders* (4th ed., text rev.). Washington, DC: Author.

Haley, J. (1973). *Uncommon therapy: The psychiatric techniques of Milton Erickson, M.D.* New York: Norton.

Haley, J., & Richeport-Haley, M. (2007). *Directive family therapy*. New York: Routledge.

Schulberg, B. (1980). *On the waterfront*. Carbondale: Southern Illinois University Press.

Zeig, J. K. (2001). Introduction. In J. K. Zeig (Ed.), *Changing directives: The strategic therapy of Jay Haley*. Phoenix, AZ: Milton H. Erickson Foundation Press.

1

The Art of Psychoanalysis

INTRODUCTION

Mony Elkaim, MD

Jay Haley's article "The Art of Psychoanalysis," which first appeared in 1958, was also published in his 1971 book *The Power Tactics of Jesus Christ and Other Essays*. Among other things, the book describes the extraordinary strength some people acquire thanks to their own weakness. In Haley's view, the patient's symptom is an adaptive strategy that allows him or her to control the definition of the relationship within a human system. The strategy is all the more effective in that the patient stresses the involuntary aspect of his or her symptom or behavior.

This sort of behavior leads to stability, a family homeostasis, and the patient is likely to recreate a similar relationship with the psychoanalyst or psychotherapist. By sustaining this way of interacting, the patient maintains control over the relationship.

For this reason, according to Haley, the therapist must try not to reinforce this stability, and in order to do this, he or she must be directive.

In the following article, Haley looks at the tactics of the ostensibly nondirective psychoanalyst who, from a position of apparent weakness, stops the patient from taking charge of the psychoanalytic situation and thus keeps control of the relationship.

Haley believes that one of these tactics "falls in the category of 'helpless' or 'refuse to battle' ploys. It is impossible to win a contest with a helpless opponent since if you win you have won nothing." Which makes silence an important ploy for the psychoanalyst.

For Haley, psychoanalysis ends when the patient "doesn't really care whether the analyst is in control of the relationship or whether he is in control." In other words, the analyst uses the tactics of her craft to not be where the patient would like her to be, without ever acting defensively. Tired of resisting, the patient will abandon his ploys and can then separate from the psychoanalyst.

At the same time as this article, Haley wrote another one that was published in 1959 (1959/1968) [1]. In "An Interactional Description of Schizophrenia," he went further than the Palo Alto group's definition of the double bind, introducing the idea of the reciprocal double bind. This time, it is no longer about a person sending out a double message—one at a verbal level, the other at a nonverbal level—but about two people responding to a double message with another double message. They are mutually trapped by their relationship. What matters is not "Who is trapping the other?" or "Who is doing what to whom?" but "What are both of them doing together?" The patient is no longer the individual but the relationship. How can psychotherapy prevent this from happening? Allow me to develop a hypothesis based on Haley's concept of the reciprocal double bind. Let us imagine that the patient under psychoanalysis or in psychotherapy is torn between what she officially wants to attain (the improvement of her symptom) and whatever protects her from disillusion. Her conviction is that the outside world can only reinforce her worldview, her way of conducting relationships, and that she would be foolish to attempt to think differently if she doesn't want to suffer again.

In this way, the patient sends a double message to the psychoanalyst. Officially, she is asking for help, but from the angle of her worldview, she doesn't believe the analyst can give it. Were things to change and were the patient to allow herself—against her better judgment—to believe that she can lower her defenses, the disillusion would be all the greater. If the psychoanalyst accepts the position the patient is inviting him to take and ostensibly attempts to help her, he is responding to one level of the double bind. But if he doesn't help the patient, then what is the patient doing in a psychoanalyst's office?

By refusing to engage in the request for help as the patient sees it, the psychoanalyst is responding to the patient's worldview ("No one can help me"). But at the same time, he is responding to the patient's official request ("Help me!") because the relationship is a psychoanalytical one, which by definition is about helping people. This is how the psychoanalyst squares the circle. He responds simultaneously to both levels of the double bind. The patient—tired of attempting to recreate a relationship that makes her suffer but that she can't abandon—finally lays down arms and accepts the end of a battle she no longer cares about. She is cured!

My hypothesis can only reinforce Haley's deeply held conviction that the psychotherapist must be in control of the therapeutic framework. If he isn't, he would end up repeating the forms of relationship the patient knows so well and apparently can't avoid. With brio and humor, as well as pertinence in his handling of the theme, Jay Haley reminds us in "The Art of Psychoanalysis" that he was not only an inspired therapist but a great writer as well.

Reference

Haley, J. (1968). An interactional description of schizophrenia. In D. D. Jackson (Ed.), *Communication, family and marriage.* Palo Alto, CA: Science and Behavior Books. (Original work published in *Psychiatry, 22*, 321–332 [1959])

THE ART OF PSYCHOANALYSIS

Jay Haley

Enough research has been done by social scientists to corroborate many of Freud's ideas about unconscious processes. Yet there has been surprisingly little scientific investigation of what actually occurs during psychoanalytic treatment. Fortunately this situation has been remedied by a scholar on the faculty of Potters College in Yeovil, England. Assigned a field trip in America, this anonymous student spent several years here studying the art of psychoanalysis both as a patient and a practitioner. His investigation culminated in a three-volume work entitled "The Art of Psychoanalysis, or Some Aspects of a Structured Situation Consisting of Two-Group Interaction Which Embodies Certain of the Most Basic Principles of Oneupmanship." Like most studies written for Potters College, the work was unpublished and accessible only to a few favored members of the clinical staff. However, a copy was briefly in this writer's hands, and he offers here a summary of the research findings for those who wish to foster the dynamic growth of Freudian theory and sharpen the techniques of a difficult art.

Unfamiliar terms will be translated into psychoanalytic terminology throughout this summary, but a few general definitions are necessary at once. First of all, a complete definition of the technical term "oneupmanship" would fill, and in fact has filled, a rather large encyclopedia. It can be defined briefly here as the art of putting a person "one-down." The term "one-down" is technically defined as that psychological state which exists in an individual who is not "one-up" on another person. To be "one-up" is technically defined as that psychological state of an individual who is not "one-down." To phrase these terms in popular language, at the risk of losing scientific rigor, it can be said that in any human relationship (and indeed among other mammals) one person is constantly maneuvering to imply that he is in a "superior position" to the other person in the relationship. This "superior position" does not necessarily mean superior in social status or economic position; many servants are masters at putting their employers one-down. Nor does it imply intellectual superiority as any intellectual knows who has been put "one-down" by a muscular garbage collector in a bout of Indian wrestling. "Superior position" is a relative term which is continually being defined and redefined by the ongoing relationship. Maneuvers to achieve superior position may be crude or they may be infinitely subtle. For example, one is not usually in a superior position if he must ask another person for something. Yet he can ask for it in such a way that he is implying, "This is, of course, what I deserve." Since the number of ways of maneuvering oneself into a superior position are infinite, let us proceed at once to summarize the psychoanalytic techniques as described in the three-volume study.

Psychoanalysis, according to Potter's study, is a dynamic psychological process involving two people, a patient and a psychoanalyst, during which the patient insists that the analyst be one-up while desperately trying to put him one-down, and the analyst insists that the patient remain one-down in order to help him learn to become one-up. The goal of the relationship is the amicable separation of analyst and patient.

Carefully designed, the psychoanalytic setting makes the superior position of the analyst almost invincible. First of all, the patient must voluntarily come to the analyst for help, thus conceding his inferior position at the beginning of the relationship. In addition, the patient accentuates his one-down position by paying the analyst money. Occasionally analysts have recklessly broken this structured situation by treating patients free of charge. Their position was difficult because the patient was not regularly reminded (on payday) that he must make a sacrifice to support the analyst, thus acknowledging the analyst's superior position before a word is said. It is really a wonder that any patient starting from this weak position could ever become one-up on an analyst, but in private discussions analysts will admit, and in fact tear at their hair while admitting, that patients can be extremely adroit and use such a variety of clever ploys[1] that an analyst must be nimble to maintain his superior position.

Space does not permit a review of the history of psychoanalysis here, but it should be noted that early in its development it became obvious that the analyst needed reinforcement of the setting if he was to remain one-up on patients more clever than he. An early reinforcement was the use of a couch for the patient to lie down upon. (This is often called "Freud's ploy," as are most ploys in psychoanalysis.) By placing the patient on a couch, the analyst gives the patient the feeling of having his feet up in the air and the knowledge that the analyst has both feet on the ground. Not only is the patient disconcerted by having to lie down while talking, but he finds himself literally below the analyst and so his one-down position is geographically emphasized. In addition, the analyst seats himself behind the couch where he can watch the patient but the patient cannot watch him. This gives the patient the sort of disconcerted feeling a person has when sparring with an opponent while blindfolded. Unable to see what response his ploys provoke, he is unsure when he is one-up and when one-down. Some patients try to solve this problem by saying something like, "I slept with my sister last night," and then whirling around to see how the analyst is responding. These "shocker" ploys usually fail in their effect. The analyst may twitch, but he has time to recover before the patient can whirl fully around and see him. Most analysts have developed ways of handling the whirling patient. As the patient turns, they are staring off into space, or doodling with a pencil, or braiding belts, or staring at tropical fish. It is essential that the rare patient who gets an opportunity to observe the analyst see only an impassive demeanor.

Another purpose is served by the position behind the couch. Inevitably what the analyst says becomes exaggerated in importance since the patient lacks any other means of determining his effect on the analyst. The patient finds himself hanging on the analyst's every word, and by definition he who hangs on another's words is one-down.

Perhaps the most powerful weapon in the analyst's arsenal is the use of silence. This falls in the category of "helpless" or "refuse to battle" ploys. It is impossible to win a contest with a helpless opponent since if you win you have won nothing. Each blow you strike is unreturned so that all you can feel is guilt for having struck while at the same time experiencing the uneasy suspicion that the helplessness is calculated. The result is suppressed fury and desperation—two emotions characterizing the one-down position. The problem posed for the patient is this: how can I get one up on a man who won't respond and compete with me for the superior position in fair and open encounter. Patients find solutions, of course, but it takes months, usually years, of intensive analysis before a patient finds ways to force a response from his analyst. Ordinarily the patient begins rather crudely by saying something like, "Sometimes I think you're an idiot." He waits for the analyst to react defensively, thus stepping one-down. Instead the analyst replies with the silence ploy. The patient goes further and says, "I'm *sure* you're an idiot." Still silence in reply. Desperately the patient says, "I said you were an idiot, damn you, and you are!" Again only silence. What can the patient do but apologize, thus stepping voluntarily into a one-down position. Often a patient discovers how effective the silence ploy is and attempts to use it himself. This ends when he realizes that he is paying a large sum each hour to lie silent on a couch. The psychoanalytic setting is calculatedly designed to prevent patients from using the ploys of analysts to attain equal footing (although as an important part of the cure the patient learns to use them effectively with other people).

Few improvements have been made on Freud's original brilliant design. As the basic plan for the hammer could not be improved upon by carpenters, so the use of the voluntary patient, hourly pay, the position behind the couch, and silence, are devices which have not been improved upon by practitioners of psychoanalysis.

Although the many ways of handling patients learned by the analyst cannot be listed here, a few general principles can be mentioned. Inevitably a patient entering analysis begins to use ploys which have put him one-up in previous relationships (this is called a "neurotic pattern"). The analyst learns to devastate these maneuvers of the patient. A simple way, for example, is to respond inappropriately to what the patient says. This puts the patient in doubt about everything he has learned in relationships with other people. The patient may say, "Everyone should be truthful," hoping to get the analyst to agree with him and thereby follow his lead. He who follows another's lead is one-down. The analyst may reply with silence, a rather weak ploy in this circumstance, or he may say, "Oh?" The "Oh?" is given just the proper inflection to imply, "How on earth could you have ever conceived such an idea?" This not only puts the patient in doubt about his statement, but in doubt about what the analyst means by "Oh?" Doubt is, of course, the first step toward one-downness. When in doubt the patient tends to lean on the analyst to resolve the doubt, and we lean on those who are superior to us. Analytic maneuvers designed to arouse doubt in a patient are instituted early in analysis. For example, the analyst may say, "I wonder if that's *really* what you're feeling." The use of "really" is standard in analytic practice. It implies the patient has motivations of which he is not aware. Anyone feels shaken, and therefore one-down, when this suspicion is put in his mind.

Doubt is related to the "unconscious ploy," an early development in psychoanalysis. This ploy is often considered the heart of analysis since it is the most effective way of making the patient unsure of himself. Early in an analysis the skilled analyst points out to the patient that he (the patient) has unconscious processes operating and is deluding himself if he thinks he really knows what he is saying. When the patient accepts this idea he can only rely on the analyst to tell him (or, as it is phrased, "to help him discover") what he really means. Thus he burrows himself deeper into the one-down position, making it easy for the analyst to top almost any ploy he devises. For example, the patient may cheerfully describe what a fine time he had with his girlfriend, hoping to arouse some jealousy (a one-down emotion) in the analyst. The appropriate reply for the analyst is, "I wonder what that girl *really* means to you." This raises a doubt in the patient whether he is having intercourse with a girl named Susy or an unconscious symbol. Inevitably he turns to the analyst to help him discover what the girl really means to him.

Regularly in the course of an analysis, particularly if the patient becomes obstreperous (uses resistance ploys), the analyst makes an issue of free association and dreams. Now a person must feel he knows what he is talking about to feel in a superior position. No one can maneuver to become one-up while free associating or narrating his dreams. The most absurd statements inevitably will be uttered. At the same time the analyst hints that there are meaningful ideas in this absurdity. This not only makes the patient feel that he is saying ridiculous things, but that he is saying things which the analyst sees meaning in and he doesn't. Such an experience would shake anyone, and inevitably drives the patient into a one-down position. Of course if the patient refuses to free associate or tell his dreams, the analyst reminds him that he is defeating himself by being resistant.

A resistance interpretation falls in the general class of "turning it back on the patient" ploys. All attempts, particularly successful ones, to put the analyst one-down can be interpreted as resistance to treatment. The patient is made to feel that it is *his* fault that therapy is going badly. Carefully preparing in advance, the skillful analyst informs the patient in the first interview that the path to happiness is difficult and he will at times resist getting well and indeed may even resent the analyst for helping him. With this background even a refusal to pay the fee or a threat to end the analysis can be turned into apologies with an impersonal attitude by the analyst (the "not taking it personally" ploy) and an interpretation about resistance. At times the analyst may let the patient re-enter the one-down position gently by pointing out that his resistance is a sign of progress and change taking place in him.

The main difficulty with most patients is their insistence on dealing directly with the analyst once they begin to feel some confidence. When the patient begins to look critically at the analyst and threaten an open encounter, several "distraction" ploys are brought into play. The most common is the "concentrate on the past" ploy. Should the patient discuss the peculiar way the analyst refuses to respond to him, the analyst will inquire, "I wonder if you've had this feeling before. Perhaps your parents weren't very responsive." Soon they are busy discussing the patient's childhood without the patient's ever discovering that the subject has been changed. Such a ploy is particularly effective when the patient begins to use what he has learned in analysis to make comments about the analyst.

In his training the young analyst learns the few rather simple rules that he must follow. The first is that it is essential to keep the patient feeling one-down while stirring him to struggle gamely in the hope that he can get one-up (this is called "transference"). Secondly, the analyst must never feel one-down (this is called "counter-transference"). The training analysis is designed to help the young analyst learn what it is like to experience a one-down position. By acting like a patient he learns what it feels like to conceive a clever ploy, deliver it expertly, and find himself put thoroughly one-down.

Even after seven or eight years in a training analysis seeing his weak ploys devastated, an analyst will occasionally use one with a patient and find himself forced into a one-down position. Despite the brilliant structure of the analytic fortress, and the arsenal of ploys learned in training, all men are human and to be human is to be occasionally one-down. The training emphasizes how to get out of the one-down position quickly when in it. The general ploy is to accept the one-down position "voluntarily" when it is inescapable. Finding the patient one-up, the analyst may say, "You have a point there," or "I must admit I made a mistake." The more daring analyst will say, "I wonder why I became a little anxious when you said that." Note that all these statements *seem* to show the analyst to be one-down and the patient one-up, but one-downness requires defensive behavior. By deliberately acknowledging his inferior position the analyst is actually maintaining his superior position, and the patient finds that once again a clever ploy has been topped by a helpless, or a refusal to do battle, ploy. At times the "acceptance" technique cannot be used because the analyst is too sensitive in that area. Should a patient discover that this analyst gets embarrassed when homosexual ideas are discussed, he may rapidly exploit this. The analyst who takes such comments personally is lost. His only chance for survival is to anticipate in his diagnostic interviews those patients capable of discovering and exploiting this weakness and refer them to analysts with different weaknesses.

The more desperate ploys by patients are also anticipated in analytic training. A patient will at times be so determined to get one-up on his analyst that he will adopt the "suicide" ploy. Many analysts immediately suffer a one-down feeling when a patient threatens suicide. They hallucinate newspaper headlines and hear their colleagues chuckling as they whisper the total number of patients who got one-up on them by jumping off the bridge. The common way to prevent the use of this ploy is to take it impersonally. The analyst says something like, "Well I'd be sorry if you blew your brains out, but I would carry on with my work." The patient abandons his plans as he realizes that even killing himself will not put him one-up on this man.

Orthodox psychoanalytic ploys can be highlighted by contrasting them with the more unorthodox maneuvers. There is, for example, the Rogerian system of ploys where the therapist merely repeats back what the patient says. This is an inevitably winning system. No one can top a person who merely repeats his ideas after him. When the patient accuses the therapist of being no use to him, the therapist replies, "You feel I'm no use to you." The patient says, "That's right, you're not worth a damn." The therapist says, "You feel I'm not worth a damn." This ploy, even more than the orthodox silence ploy, eliminates any triumphant feeling in the patient and makes him feel a little silly after awhile (a one-down feeling). Most orthodox analysts look upon the Rogerian ploys as not only weak but not quite respectable. They don't give the patient a fair chance.

The ethics of psychoanalysis require the patient be given at least a reasonably fair chance. Ploys which simply devastate the patient are looked down on. Analysts who use them are thought to need more analysis themselves to give them a range of more legitimate ploys and confidence in using them. For instance, it isn't considered proper to encourage a patient to discuss a subject and then lose interest when he does. This puts the patient one-down, but it is a wasted ploy since he wasn't trying to become one-up. If a patient makes such an attempt then of course losing interest may be a necessary gambit.

Another variation on orthodox psychoanalytic ploys demonstrates a few of their limitations. The psychotic continually demonstrates that he is superior to orthodox ploys. He refuses to "volunteer" for analysis. He won't take a sensible interest in money. He won't lie quietly on the couch and talk while the analyst listens out of sight behind him. The structure of the analytic situation seems to irritate the psychotic. In fact when orthodox ploys are used against him, the psychotic is likely to tear up the office and kick the analyst in the genitals (this is called an inability to establish a transference). The average analyst is made uncomfortable by psychotic ploys and therefore avoids such patients. Recently some daring therapists have found they can get one-up on a psychotic patient if they work in pairs. This is now called the "it takes two to put one down" therapy, or "multiple therapy." For example, if a psychotic talks compulsively and won't even pause to listen, two therapists enter the room and begin to converse with each other. Unable to restrain his curiosity (a one-down emotion) the psychotic will stop talking and listen, thus leaving himself open to be put one-down.

The master oneupman with psychotics is a controversial psychiatrist known affectionately in the profession as "The Bull." When a compulsive talker won't listen to him the Bull pulls a knife on the fellow and attracts his attention. No other therapist is so adroit at topping even the most determined patient. Other therapists require hospitals, attendants, shock treatments, lobotomies, drugs, restraints, and tubs, to place the patient in a sufficiently one-down position. The Bull, with mere words and the occasional flash of a pocket knife, manages to make the most difficult psychotic feel one-down.

An interesting contrast to the Bull is a woman known in the profession as "The Lovely Lady of the Lodge." Leading the league in subtle oneupmanship with psychotics, she avoids the Bull's ploys which are often considered rather crude and not always in the best of taste. If a patient insists he is God, the Bull will insist that *he* is God and force the patient to his knees, thus getting one-up in a rather straightforward way. To handle a similar claim by a patient, The Lady of the Lodge will smile and say, "All right, if you wish to be God, I'll let you." The patient is gently put one-down as he realizes that no one but God can *let* anyone else be God.

Although orthodox psychoanalytic ploys may be limited to work with neurotics no one can deny their success. The experienced analyst can put a patient one-down while planning where to have dinner at the same time. Of course this skill in oneupmanship has raised extraordinary problems when analysts compete with one another at meetings of the psychoanalytic associations. No other gathering of people exhibits so many complicated ways of gaining the upper hand. Most of the struggle at an analytic meeting takes place at a rather personal level, but the manifest content involves attempts to (1) demonstrate who was closest to Freud or can quote him most voluminously, and (2) [demonstrate] who can confuse the most people by his daring extension of Freud's terminology. The man who can achieve both these goals best is generally elected president of the association.

The manipulation of language is the most startling phenomenon at an analytic meeting. Obscure terms are defined and redefined by even more obscure terms as analysts engage in furious theoretical discussions. This is particularly true when the point at issue is whether a certain treatment of a patient was *really* psychoanalysis or not. Such a point is inevitably raised when a particularly brilliant case history is presented.

What happens between analyst and patient, or the art of oneupmanship, is rarely discussed at the meeting (apparently the techniques are too secret for public discussion). This means the area for debate becomes the processes within the dark and dank interior of the patient. Attempting to outdo one another in explanations of the bizarre insides of patients, each speaker is constantly interrupted by shouts from the back of the hall such as, "Not at all! You're confusing an id impulse with a weak ego boundary!" or "Heaven help your patients if you call *that* cathexis!" Even the most alert analyst soon develops an oceanic feeling as he gets lost in flurries of energy theories, libidinal drives, instinctual forces, and super ego barriers. The analyst who can most thoroughly confuse the group leaves his colleagues feeling frustrated and envious (one-down emotions). The losers return to their studies to search their minds, dictionaries, science fiction journals, and Freud for even more elaborate metaphorical flights in preparation for the next meeting.

The ploys of analyst and patient can be summarized briefly as they occur during a typical course of treatment. Individual cases will vary depending on what maneuvers the individual patient uses (called "symptoms" by the analyst when they are ploys no sensible person would use), but a general trend is easy to follow. The patient enters analysis in the one-down posture by asking for help and promptly tries to put the therapist one-down by building him up. This is called the honeymoon of the analysis. The patient begins to compliment the therapist on how wonderful he is and how quickly he (the patient) expects to get well. The skilled analyst is not taken in by these maneuvers (known as the "Reichian resistance" ploys). When the patient finds himself continually put one-down, he changes tactics. He becomes mean, insulting, threatens to quit analysis, and casts doubt upon the sanity of the analyst. These are the "attempts to get a human response" ploys. They meet an impassive, impersonal wall as the analyst remains silent or handles the insults with a simple statement like, "Have you noticed this is the second Tuesday afternoon you've made such a comment? I wonder what there is about Tuesday," or "You seem to be reacting to me as if I'm someone else." Frustrated in his aggressive behavior (resistance ploys), the patient capitulates and ostensibly hands control of the situation back to the analyst. Again building the analyst up, he leans on him, hangs on his every word, insists how helpless he is and how strong the analyst is, and waits for the moment when he will lead the analyst along far enough to devastate him with a clever ploy. The skilled analyst handles this nicely with a series of "condescending" ploys, pointing out that the patient must help himself and not expect anyone to solve everything for him. Furious, the patient again switches from subservient ploys to defiant ploys. By this time he has learned techniques from the analyst and is getting better. He uses what insight (ploys unknown to laymen) he has gained to try in every way to define the relationship as one in which the analyst is one-down. This is the difficult period of the analysis. However, having carefully prepared the ground by a thorough diagnosis (listing weak points) and having instilled a succession of doubts in the patient about himself, the analyst succeeds in topping the patient again and again as the years pass. Ultimately a remarkable thing happens. The patient rather casually tries to get one-up, the analyst puts him one-down, and the patient does not become disturbed by this. He has reached a point where he doesn't *really* care whether the analyst is in control of the relationship or whether he is in control. In other words, he is cured. The analyst then dismisses him, timing this maneuver just before the patient is ready to announce that he is leaving. Turning to his waiting list, the analyst invites in another patient who, by definition, is someone compelled to struggle to be one-up and disturbed if he is put one-down. And so goes the day's work in the difficult art of psychoanalysis.

Endnote

1. A ploy is technically defined as a move or gambit which gives one an advantage in a relationship.

2

The Art of Being Schizophrenic

INTRODUCTION

Braulio Montalvo, MA

Those who saw how Jay Haley worked do know that, in practice, he was as much related to the suffering of the schizophrenic as he was to the art of being schizophrenic. When "brain disease" was overemphasized by the mental health field as the fundamental issue, Haley went out of his way to convey—through humor—the "abilities" and "coping strategies" of the schizophrenic. He went on to parody not only the supposedly "causal" family constellations proposed at that time but also the misuse of the mental hospital.

"The Art of Being Schizophrenic" should be read along with Shankar Vedantam's report (2005) on the results of the 30-year follow-up study of the World Health Organization by Dr. Norman Sartorius (Vedantam, 2005). The International Pilot Study of Schizophrenia, launched in 1967, covered

3,300 patients in a dozen countries and discovered that patients who display hallucinations, disorganized thinking, and social withdrawal do better in undeveloped countries like India, Nigeria, and Colombia rather than in Denmark, England, and the United States. Researchers concluded that family ties in poorer countries have a profoundly positive effect on rates of long-range recovery.

European and U.S. psychiatrists refused to believe these findings. The study was repeated, and the results held up. Haley's basic notion that the family and the community's participation are crucial to the normalization process was amply confirmed. Across cultures, the communities that keep the schizophrenics somehow employed, despite their bizarre behavior, improve their long-range adjustment (for Haley's techniques in getting schizophrenics back to work, see Haley, 1997, pp. 283–298; Haley & Richeport-Haley, 2003, pp. 157–174). The study also revealed that undeveloped countries do not have service providers who rely exclusively on the altering of brain chemistry with drugs without drawing on the help of the family. Instead, their biological psychiatry is delivered with the family's collaboration.

In my opinion, had "The Art of Being Schizophrenic" been written after reflecting on the findings from the 30-year follow-ups, Haley would have dwelled on abilities such as the patients' art of involving the family—or some of its members—in a marathon-like relationship that was flexible and enduring. The art would consist of ways, obvious and not so obvious, of never exasperating the family so completely that it would finally cut you off or totally abandon you. In turn, the family's art would display ways of removing themselves before undergoing extreme exhaustion, and of stepping in when essential intervention was necessary.

Haley would see that the clinical material from the front lines of the 12 countries included in the international study offers no support for any antimedication bias, nor for any interpersonal model of etiology, nor of causation through communication dilemmas. However, he would underline the finding that the monitoring function of the family is able to modify the trajectory of the schizophrenic. This is the superseding finding of most consequence for improving treatment outcomes.

My guess is that Haley, a lifelong student of Eastern philosophies and of Asian families who immigrated to the U.S. west coast, would have been particularly interested in examining further the observations of Dr. Martin Gittelman regarding the unfolding of schizophrenia in rural China. Dr. Gittelman (Vedantam, 2005), a clinical professor of psychiatry at New York University, pointed out that in his study of rural China, the extended family and primary care workers constantly monitor patients and bump up the dosages of medications at the earliest signs of psychotic flare-ups. In his population, low doses of medication were as effective as high doses, and virtually eliminated side effects. He noted that older medications—which for the most part had been discarded in wealthier countries, where expensive, newer antipsychotic drugs are preferred—do an efficient job.

In such examples, I think Haley would see corroborating evidence for one of his leading ideas. He always thought that one of the most valuable skills of schizophrenics across cultures was the ability to engage service providers who are capable of focusing, not on producing a cure but on making relapses less likely and on facilitating longer periods of health between relapses. He would proclaim again that among the most important skills to have as a schizophrenic is the ability to avoid primary care providers and family members who believe that any long-range future is hopeless because of an incurable, chronic brain disease.

I think Haley's response to the findings of the international study would probably explore how the art of the schizophrenic could be used to make arrangements to live somewhere other than Denmark. There, according to Dr. William Carpenter (Vedantam, 2005), a psychiatrist at the University of Maryland in Baltimore who ran a wing of the World Health Organization study in the Washington, DC, area, "If you were psychotic you were on disability for life. Virtually nobody who had schizophrenia had a job."

References

Haley, J. (1997). A model therapy for psychotic young people. In *Leaving home: The therapy of disturbed young people* (2nd ed.). New York: Brunner/Mazel.

Haley, J., & Richeport-Haley, M. (2003). A positive approach with a psychotic couple. In *The art of strategic therapy*. New York: Brunner-Routledge.

Vedantam, S. (2005, June 1). Social networks, healing power is borne out in poorer nations. *Washington Post*, p. A01.

THE ART OF BEING SCHIZOPHRENIC

Jay Haley

It is common today to hear complaints that standards are falling in every field of endeavor. Like most generalizations, this one may not be true, but certainly standards are dropping in the field of psychiatric diagnosis. Where there was once neatness and rigor, one now finds a slipshod, lackadaisical, devil-may-care lumping together of the most diverse maladies as if the need for diagnostic precision no longer existed. The most shocking example is the diagnosis of schizophrenia. At one time it was clear that a person was either schizophrenic or not, and the several species were neatly catalogued and appreciated. Today we find that the label of schizophrenia is likely to be applied to just about anyone. A passing temper tantrum by an adolescent can earn a diagnosis of schizophrenia without providing the youth any opportunity to show his true nature and abilities in this line of endeavor. Not only are the wrong sort of people included in this category, but we also find ourselves drowning in the attempts to water down the diagnosis so that just about anyone can be classed in this way. Let us face facts: what on earth is a schizoid, or worse yet a schizo-affective state? Are not such labels merely absurd compromises showing an unwillingness to keep the diagnosis clean and pure in the European, particularly the German, tradition? At this time we should review what is required of a person who truly merits this diagnosis so that we can ruthlessly eliminate the false contenders and draw a sharp line between this and other maladies. To use the term "schizophrenic" loosely for anyone who wanders in the hospital door looking befuddled betrays those individuals who have worked long and hard to achieve the disease.

The Right Sort of Family

To say that not everyone can achieve schizophrenia is to say a great deal. Today any competent diagnostician who is sifting the true schizophrenic from the chaff will include in his observation the environment of the patient. After all, to be schizophrenic it is essential that one be born into the right sort of family and if one can manage that all else may follow. However, we cannot choose our parents, they are a gift of heaven. People who have attempted schizophrenia without the correct family background have universally failed. They can erupt into psychotic-like behavior in combat or when caught in some other mad and difficult situation, but they are unable to sustain that behavior when the environment seems to right itself. The same point applies to the variety of fascinating drugs which are falsely said to induce psychosis. Not only does the drug influence miss the essence of the experience, but the effect wears off rapidly. The occasional goat who manages to be a schizophrenic after the drug has left his system is easily separated from the sheep who go back to normal—he has come from the right sort of family and probably would have achieved schizophrenia even without the benefit of medical research.

The type of family one must come from to become schizophrenic has been extensively described in the professional journals. One can summarize these scientific reports by saying that as individuals the family members are unrecognizable on the street but bring them together and the outstanding feature is immediately apparent—a kind of formless, bizarre despair overlaid with a veneer of glossy hope and good intentions concealing a power-struggle-to-the-death coated with a quality of continual confusion.

Observing such a family one is struck by the central figure, the mother, and notes at once that the schizophrenic owes to her his flexibility and his exasperating skill in frustrating people who attempt to influence him. Just as the child in a circus family learns from his parents how to maneuver on a slack wire, so does the schizophrenic learn from his mother how to maneuver acrobatically in interpersonal relations. To achieve schizophrenia a man must have experienced a mother who has a range of behavior unequalled except by the most accomplished of actresses. She is capable when stung (which occurs when any suggestion is made to her) of weeping, promising violence, expressing condescending concern, threatening to go mad and fall apart, being kind and pious, and offering to flee the country if another word is said. This type of mother when faced with the dreadful child she has raised, is able to reply innocently that the fault lies elsewhere since she has done nothing in life for herself but everything for her child. This halo-effect is apparent in the comment of a mother who said, "A mother sacrifices, if you would be a mother yourself you would know this, like even Jesus with his mother, a mother sacrifices everything for her child."

It should be obvious that such mothers are not easy to find and probably don't represent more than 20 percent of the females born. Yet for the true flowering of schizophrenia, even such a mother is not enough. To balance the flexibility provided by mother, the schizophrenic must have a father who will teach him to remain immovable. The father of the schizophrenic has a stubbornness unequalled among men (as well as the skill to keep a woman in the state of exasperated despair which helps mother make use of her full range of behavior). On occasions when present and sober such a father can easily say, "I am right, God in heaven knows I cannot be proven wrong, black is not white and you know it too in your heart of hearts." This sort of father is not easily found in the general population, largely because he is rarely home.

When one considers the odds that this type of uncommon man will find such an uncommon woman, and the even more astonishing odds that two such people could copulate, it is clear at once that the incidence of true schizophrenia could not be high. (Often such parents report that the copulation only occurred when one or both was asleep and that is why they had to get married, but even granting this possibility the odds against schizophrenia being common do not change appreciably.)

Finally, it is important, although not essential, that a schizophrenic have as part of his environment a certain type of brother or sister. This sibling must be the kind of person who is hated on contact—a do-gooder, a good-in-schooler, a sweet, weak, kind bastard of a sibling who can provide the contrast for the future schizophrenic by showing him up to be the complete idiot his family expects him to be.

Given this array of talent around him, one might think the individual raised in such a family constellation would inevitably achieve schizophrenia. However, this is obviously not true since all children in such families do not go clearly mad. The schizophrenic must not only have such a family, but he must hold a certain position in it and serve certain vital functions over an extended period of time. Like any artist, several hours a day of practice over many years are necessary.

Regarding his position, he must be the child the parents choose to focus upon—that special child the parents expect to be remarkable for reasons related to their own dark pasts. Whatever this particular child does is of exaggerated importance to the parents, and he soon learns that touching his nose can set off an earthquake in the family. This parental focus is sufficiently intense that when it is turned from the schizophrenic to the sibling, the sibling begins to disintegrate like a match head placed under a burning glass.

It is the primary function of the schizophrenic to be the representative failure in the family, and in that sense to be remarkable. The parents feel themselves to be insignificant wretches, lost souls incapable of any human accomplishment (although many of them make rather good scientists). Therefore for their survival they must have before their eyes the schizophrenic child as an example of a worse failure so they can stand a little higher in the world by that fact. The child can fulfill this function rather easily since he need only fail at whatever he attempts. The average schizophrenic shows his artistry by achieving more than usual ability along this line, while also indicating at regular intervals that he could do quite a good job at succeeding if he wanted to, thus shining in the light of his parents' admiration while giving them sufficient cause for disappointment.

The schizophrenic is not only the focus of his parents' life, but he serves a key position in the wider morass that is the total family network. One is reminded of the vast array of tumblers who stand upon each other's shoulders, all constructed upon one man standing at the bottom holding up the entire edifice. Just as the child is caught up in the conflict between his parents, so is he in the middle of the triangular struggle between his mother and her mother, his father and his mother, and the many other cross-generational conflicts in this type of family. (When the schizophrenic sides with his mother against father, father can only protest weakly since he is joining *his* mother against his wife.)

The average schizophrenic has had a lifetime balancing conflicting family triangles, each one focused upon his every action, so that whatever he says and does in one triangle has repercussions in another. If he should please his grandparents, he will displease his parents, and should he agree with any one person he is certain to antagonize several others. Therefore the schizophrenic must learn to communicate in a way that satisfies everyone by saying one thing and disqualifying it with a conflicting statement and then indicating he didn't mean any of it anyhow. This complicated mode of adaptation makes his behavior appear rather peculiar.

The schizophrenic soon learns, of course, that he has a position of extreme power in manipulating triangles to his advantage. The importance of his skill in this essential game cannot be overemphasized. For example, one teenage schizophrenic, precocious as most schizophrenics are, said, "My parents and I are involved in the eternal triangle," and she showed her skill in this game by climbing into bed between her parents and kicking her mother out (while father protested weakly that mother should have locked the bedroom door). The schizophrenic also takes for granted what social scientists are only beginning to realize—the true disturbance in human life comes when secret coalitions occur across generations or other power hierarchies (this is The Second Law of Human Relations). The schizophrenic is, of course, the master at cross-generation coalitions. He may decline to join his peers, but he has even been known to provoke a great-grandfather to intrude into the parental conflict.

The primary responsibility of the schizophrenic is to hold the family together. Although social scientists, even family therapists, have not yet the vaguest idea how to prevent a family from disintegrating, the schizophrenic child accomplishes this with ease. It is his duty to use his keen perception and interpersonal skill to maintain the family system in a stable state, even if that state is a mood of constant despair. His importance in this function appears on those rare occasions when the schizophrenic abandons his disease and becomes normal, succeeding in life and leaving his family. His parents at once individually collapse, losing their sense of purpose in life, and they set about to divorce (weakly apologizing to *their* parents for being more successful as parents than they were).

The schizophrenic child prevents divorce and family dissolution in a rather simple way; he provides the parents an excuse for staying together by offering himself as a problem. With minor threats of separation, he merely looks unhappy to provide mother and father with an excuse to stay together. When the parents are constantly on the verge of leaving one another, the child must present himself as a more severe problem. Such children learn quickly how to behave; a few odd mannerisms and grimaces at inappropriate moments are helpful, as well as muteness and a kind of twisting, weird waving of the hands accompanied by an occasional idiotic squeal. If of school age, the child must show that he is incapable of existing outside the family and therefore his parents must stay together and comfort him since they are his only source of life. By becoming the family problem, the child requires his parents to stay together to save him, offers himself as an excuse for their misery with each other, and he also challenges them. These parents feel they must be perfect parents. When their child behaves oddly all their determination to cure him is aroused, thus giving them further reason to continue to associate as a family.

The schizophrenic must also act quickly if the parents threaten to come closer together and be more affectionate, thereby provoking a change in the family (as well as panic in the parents). Should father almost reach out a hand to mother, the schizophrenic must promptly wet his pants, or he must say, "Oh, I want to visit Granny," thereby bringing father's mother into the scene, which always provokes an argument between parents.

When the schizophrenic is old enough to perceive that his family is culturally defiant, he begins to function as the symbol of the family's differentness. The peculiar way he chooses to express himself on this matter will drive the parents closer together and at the same time attract community attention to provide some help for the family. His technique is to use parody. Schizophrenics have long been known as the most skilled people at parody in the world, and it has been said that they parody all the worst aspects of our society. This gives them too much credit; they are merely parodying their families. For example, if the parents insist that they are devoutly religious while behaving in a most unreligious manner, the schizophrenic son will begin to grow a beard and burn holes in the palms of his hands with cigarettes. Should this not attract sufficient attention—some of these parents will consider this only playful behavior—then the schizophrenic will take to strolling about the neighborhood carrying a large cross. The parents do not always take this as action in their best interest, particularly since they have a passion for secrecy about many matters, but in such a case they can hardly accuse the child of misbehavior when he merely is being more religious than they are. In a similar way, if the parents have unsavory minds while insisting that they are terribly puritan, the schizophrenic will loudly condemn dirty words, naming them and even writing them on the front sidewalk.

The skill with which a schizophrenic calls attention to a family problem while simultaneously declining responsibility for doing this is best illustrated by his verbal comments. The ideal comment is one which is as ambiguous as mother could offer—it must reach the parents in their souls but keep them uncertain whether an outsider gets the point. For example, a schizophrenic daughter listened to her parents describe how happy this family was except for this wretched daughter, and she said, "Yes, but wouldn't you and Daddy be happier if you didn't drink so much?" Granting that this calls attention to the parents' need for help, it was also a rather unskillful and crude thrust which does not merit being called schizophrenic. This rude directness might be attributed to the daughter's faulty control of her anger. The more experienced schizophrenic can completely control the expression of his feelings and offer flattened affect even when the doctors are sticking pins into him at medical demonstrations. One can only applaud a son who sent his mother a Mother's Day card which said, "You've always been like a mother to me," and a daughter who arrived with her mother and stepfather in a psychiatrist's office and said, "Mother had to get married and now I'm here."

When the family threatens to dissolve, the schizophrenic must be willing to go to any extreme, even insane activity which brings in the neighbors and the police. It is the willingness on his part to fulfill the function of holding the family together which explains why the schizophrenic—despite his skill, wariness, and keen perception—lets himself be cast into a mental hospital. His psychotic behavior is a last resort when a family crisis has reached the point where an unresolvable breach is about to take place. This final extremity drives the parents together because their common burden of a truly unfortunate child, forces the parents into a common front against the community which is protesting that something must be done, and lets the family make the schizophrenic the patsy for all past and present difficulties. The psychotic episode is merely a more extreme version of other behavior of the schizophrenic at times of family crisis, but this time it precipitates him into a situation which calls forth all his skill—the treatment situation. Before describing the talent necessary for the schizophrenic to survive in the hospital setting, let us summarize the training the schizophrenic has had when he arrives, his face unwashed and his hair uncombed, ready for entrance into the institution which will become his tomb.

In sum, the schizophrenic must have come from the right sort of family, with appropriate parents as models. He must have learned to manipulate and balance complicated, conflicting family triangles, and he must be perceptive enough to keep his feet in a morass of trickery and despair. He must also have learned to deal with intensive attention; other children are ignored at times by their parents, but with the schizophrenic every move and word is taken personally. As a consequence he must become skilled in concealing his emotions, he must learn to indicate that whatever he did just happened and he is not responsible for it, he must perceive the threats in every situation, and he must achieve skill in stabilizing whatever system he is in by being a willing scapegoat to support the inadequacies of those around him. It should be immediately evident that few people can meet the complicated requirements of the world of the average schizophrenic. There is one final requirement which eliminates most contenders. Only certain of the great political and religious leaders of the past have had the character structure, the determination of the schizophrenic. He has the will to devote his life to an absolute and stubborn crusade. His crusade is this: never to let his family off the hook. The hundred million affronts he has suffered are never to be forgiven to the end of his days.

Even if the law should force him to separate from his parents, he must continually remind them, by bizarre letters if necessary, that they have driven him mad and he plans to continue in that state. His one risk is cure because if cured this means he has forgiven his family, and the true schizophrenic, his will power forged in the fire of a billion conflicts, will not offer that forgiveness even in the face of the most pitiable pleas. Just as the Crusader tenaciously pursued the Holy Grail over the bodies of the infidels, the true schizophrenic will remain attached to his family at all costs and by any methods so that on their deathbeds his parents still have on their conscience this parental disaster.

The Right Sort of Hospital

Only in the mental hospital can schizophrenia achieve its full flowering. Just as a plant reaches its greatest growth in well manured ground, so does the schizophrenic achieve his full range on the closed wards of mental institutions. Yet oddly enough the first reaction of the schizophrenic to hospitalization is a stout objection. Only when he has been incarcerated for a period of time does he recognize the merit of the establishment. Then he is almost impossible to remove. Nowhere in the world can he find an environment so similar to life at home and yet with opponents so much less skilled than the members of his family.

The average mental hospital has been extensively described in the professional literature. One can summarize these scientific reports by saying that the outstanding feature of a mental institution is a kind of formless, bizarre despair overlaid with a veneer of glossy hope and good intentions concealing a power struggle to the death between patients and staff, coated with a quality of continual confusion. The basic art of schizophrenia lies in a genius for dealing with power struggles, and of course in a mental hospital the problem of power is central. It should not be thought that the struggle between patient and staff is unequal. True, the staff has drugs, tubs, cold packs, shock treatments (both insulin and electric), brain operations, isolation cells, control of food and all privileges, and the ability to form in gangs composed of aides, nurses, social workers, psychologists, and psychiatrists. The schizophrenic lacks all these appurtenances of power, including the use of gang tactics since he is essentially a loner, but he has his manner and his words and a stout and determined heart. He also has had extensive training in a family made up of the most difficult people in the world. A normal person might disintegrate or capitulate on any issue in the face of the organized assault by the staff of a mental hospital, but the schizophrenic at one glance can size up the situation and seize upon his opportunities. Even though disconcerted by being betrayed into the hospital, as he usually is, the schizophrenic can have family and staff embroiled in an argument before he has been stripped of his civilian clothes and had his money and driver's license confiscated.

The first lesson the schizophrenic learns in the hospital is that he must do what the aides tell him to do. His initial reaction is to decline, since he has never in his life done what he was told; it is against family tradition. However, the aides cannot permit recalcitrance since it is their duty to keep the hospital functioning. Therefore when the schizophrenic refuses to obey an order, the aide hits him as hard as he can in the gut. This astonishes the patient, and he muses over how to turn it to his advantage. He soon learns that he cannot, because being hit in the gut receives no publicity. Should the patient complain, the aide denies that it happens and the doctor pretends to believe him. That night the aide hits the schizophrenic as hard as he can in the gut twice more and calls him a squealer. From that time on the schizophrenic obeys the aide, although his courage is apparent even in these circumstances because he does what he is told in a desultory manner as if he has not heard a command and is only happening to follow it. In more modern and progressive mental hospitals the aides are not allowed to beat up on the patients. It is necessary for the aide to report that the patient cannot control his hostility so that the doctor can bang the patient in the head with a shock machine. This procedure maintains the proprieties for medical investigating boards who know medical treatment when they see it. Recently institutions have attempted to incapacitate the schizophrenic by pouring drugs into him until his eyeballs float and he is uncertain what is up and what down. Drowned in sufficiently powerful drugs, the schizophrenic's keen perception becomes impaired and he is less skillful in the hospital power struggle. However, over time, immunity to the drugs begins to set in, and recently there has been a trend in hospitals to return to the shock machine.

After his first encounter with the brute force of the hospital structure, the wise schizophrenic casts his dull and calculating eye upon the basic game he must play to survive and keep his self respect. He soon learns that little is new; all is like life at home.

The first weakness the schizophrenic discovers in the hospital structure is the same one he found in his family; the hospital can be hoisted on its own pretense of benevolence. Just as the parents defined all they did as done for his sake, so does the hospital define all it does to be for the benefit of the schizophrenic. Arrangements which suited parents' convenience were said to be for the child's best interests, and all hospital activity which is for efficient operation or convenience of the staff, whether forcing patients to rise at six in the morning or cutting out random portions of the brain, must be said to be for the sake of the schizophrenic. It is when he is offered such benevolence that the schizophrenic manifests his most skillful appearance of confusion, disorientation, and delusion. If he is told he must be in bed at nine in the evening because of his need for rest (and not the convenience of the ward staff) the schizophrenic will experience night terrors which keep the ward in turmoil until his more reasonable bedtime. Having forced the hard fist of the aide or the heavy hand of the psychiatrist on the shock machine to quiet him, the schizophrenic has won the acknowledgement that nine o'clock bedtime is a hospital convenience. Hanging a psychiatrist on his benevolence is best illustrated by the patient who was faced with a doctor who could not tolerate his patients milling about the ward indicting him for his inability to cure them. He therefore announced that for their sakes the patients must be out of the ward all day getting fresh air. This particular schizophrenic declined to leave the ward. When he was forced out the front door, he walked straight ahead until he bumped into a tree, remaining there outside the doctor's window with his forehead against the tree until the exasperated physician retrieved him later in the day.

The hospital also provides the schizophrenic with the comfortable feeling he is still at home with his family by the similarity in power structure. Just as mother maintained the pretense that father was in charge, while ignoring him, so does the nurse pretend the ward psychiatrist is in charge while running things herself. The schizophrenic soon finds that the ward psychiatrist is as unavailable as his father ever was, since of course the psychiatrist never has the time or inclination to talk to the patients. The schizophrenic finds too that his long training in stirring conflict between his parents is unusually valuable in the hospital where nurse and psychiatrist can be played off against each other with a minimum of maneuvers. The confusion between doctor and nurse over their official and actual power position can be touched off in quite simple ways. For example, when the doctor requires some activity of the patient, the schizophrenic can indicate that the nurse said he was not to do that. The doctor may reply that by God he is the one who makes such decisions, but he becomes uncertain in his dealings with the nurse, who feels in turn that she must have antagonized him in some inexplicable way. If necessary to go to extremes because of a dull-witted staff, the patient can begin to scream whenever a particular staff member comes near him, thus making the entire staff look upon that person with suspicion.

The schizophrenic's training in manipulating coalitions across generations comes in appropriately in the hospital. He can join psychiatrist against nurse, nurse against aide, social worker against ward doctor, ward doctor against hospital administrator, staff against family, and so on. More skillful schizophrenics will escape occasionally and join community and police against the hospital. On the rare occasions when the schizophrenic is provided with a psychotherapist, he has the entire confusion in the staff power structure to play upon. The therapist, like mother, can be persuaded to request that the schizophrenic be given special treatment or at least be more fully understood and the ward psychiatrist, like father, will bluster ineffectually that the patient must do what is expected of him, while the nurse protests that despite what the patient implied she wasn't out of her office for two hours leaving the ward unattended, and the aide will say that it's clearly a paranoid delusion when the patient says he was hit in the gut during the night. These periods of excitement alternate with long days of boredom for the schizophrenic, just as at home.

Whenever he is sufficiently bored, the schizophrenic can provoke action to enliven life on the ward. In fact, many schizophrenics have found they can provide some excitement by *not* doing anything. For example, they can stop eating. Just as mother went into a panic at home if her food was ignored and her poor child was wasting away to her shame, so does the hospital staff develop waves of anxiety if the patient ignores their food. Before reaching the point of no return, the schizophrenic will usually begin to eat again. Some clever schizophrenics will time their resumption of food to coincide with a new drug the doctor has given them. Since the staff is always hoping for a pill which will cure all the staff problems, they rejoice with each success of a new drug—only to discover later that other patients do not respond to it and schizophrenics have duped them again.

The position and function of the schizophrenic in the hospital is identical with his position and function at home. The staff of a mental institution feel themselves to be outcasts in the profession, insignificant wretches incapable of human accomplishment. Therefore it is essential for their survival that they surround themselves with people who are more incompetent than they are. Living among the experts in failure, the schizophrenics, the staff can stand a little higher in the world. From the top administrator of the hospital who kicks his assistant when irritated, down through the hierarchy to the aide who kicks the patient when irritated, the structure requires that final someone that all else can feel superior to—and there we behold the schizophrenic. As at home, the bad feelings and difficulties of the staff members with each other can be excused as a product of dealing with such a difficult person as the schizophrenic, so that his valuable function as a scapegoat binds the entire structure together like an adhesive.

It should not be thought that just anyone, including people with other psychiatric problems, could fulfill the schizophrenic's function. Training, persistence, and ingenuity are required. There is also a need for courage because of the risks. The schizophrenic not only faces the daily possibility of the aide's fist and the psychiatrist's shock machine, but he also lives under the threat of total isolation in solitary confinement as well as the threat that the doctors will plunge a scalpel into his brain as a last resort. Because of medical advances, he now lives with a 40% chance that his anti-psychotic drugs will give him irreversible brain damage. These dangers add spice to the schizophrenic's life, and they require a particular style of behavior from him. This style is known medically as symptomatic of the hospitalized person. Since clear rebellion or justifiable outrage against the institution provokes savage punishment for his own good, the schizophrenic must behave like a difficult person while indicating that it's not he who's doing it and besides he cannot help himself—this is the definition of mental illness. The staff is reluctant to give him the business since he cannot help himself and so they must flounder in dealing with him—this is called treatment of the mentally ill. The most basic way to behave in a difficult manner and deny that it is your own fault is to say that you are someone else and so aliases are common among schizophrenics. However, the mere alias is not enough, it should be one which is clearly an alias, such as a male patient calling himself "Miss United States." Alternatively, one can say that the behavior originated elsewhere, and therefore one should not be punished. A nice device to achieve this is to say that a "voice" told one to do it, therefore responsibility lies elsewhere. One can make any criticism of the staff, even accuse a puritanical nurse of unsavory thoughts, if one says that it is really the Lord speaking and one is merely an instrument for that voice. The nurse becomes uncertain about putting the Lord on the shock roster. Another procedure is to act clearly insane so that one is obviously not responsible for needling the staff. A way to do this is to appear to be disoriented in space and time, which is particularly effective if it carries within it an indictment of the staff. To say that the place is really a prison and it is the 17th century is to make it clear that one is too insane to be blamed for an act. Yet at the same time the resemblance to a 17th century prison is close enough to most hospitals to arouse the guilt feelings of the staff. One thereby can indict while disarming and escaping blame, all neatly in one maneuver. Sometimes the guilt can be aroused by more ironical disorientation; one can say, for example, that the hospital is a palace and the doctor a king, thereby dismaying the doctor with the comparison. A third procedure is to make caustic comments while giving a silly and dilapidated laugh—who can punish such an idiot, and yet the comments simultaneously reach home. One can also indict by actions without ever saying a word. When a schizophrenic stands against the wall with his head hanging down and his arms outstretched, the staff suspects that they are being told that they are crucifying the patient, yet they are told in a way that they cannot accept or deny the accusation, or blame the schizophrenic—here lies the true art of schizophrenia.

These few simple procedures may seem limited, but a skillful schizophrenic can provide tremendous variety in his use of them. Whenever he has finally driven the staff to bring brute force to bear, it could be expected that the staff does so with the guilty feeling that they are taking advantage of a poor, helpless victim who cannot control himself. However, to assume that the staff feels guilty is to underestimate their education. After all, psychiatrists have received a liberal college education, thorough medical training, and a full residency in the science of psychiatry. They are usually good-hearted men attempting to do their best, and they follow civilized rules in dealing with the human being. Because of their education and knowledge of the history of men, they are able to use a device which has always been used by civilized men caught in a death struggle for power with other men—they define the other men as not human beings, and therefore anything goes. The good-hearted Southerner can give the Negro his lumps and the good-hearted concentration camp guard in Germany can fling people into the gas chambers as long as he can define those people as subhuman. Knowledge of this tradition has helped the psychiatrist to define the schizophrenic as not a person but a thing, an organic hulk who is out of contact with reality. Therefore civilized rules do not apply. By adopting this point of view and building it into a theory of psychosis, the staff can agree that the patient is not responsible for the trouble he is causing because he is not really a person and therefore brain-damaging drugs are obviously necessary to point the beast in a more amiable direction. Only by arguing that civilized rules do not apply to the schizophrenic can the staff meet the patient on at least equal terms, because the schizophrenic too is unwilling to follow civilized rules. Driven by his terrifying despair, he will go to any extremity of self-abasement and therefore has a great advantage in such a struggle. The staff is faced with a person of extraordinary determination and skill in innovations. Even stripped nude and flung into a cell without furniture and soundproofed so that he cannot be heard, the schizophrenic is still not incapacitated. Ordinary people who must rely on friends, furniture to fling, or at least insults when they are in a power struggle would collapse in futile hopelessness in such a situation. Yet locked up alone and unheard, the schizophrenic still finds ways to express his opinion of the staff and arouse them further. He is willing to use the products of his own body and he will pee upon the door and crap upon the floor, cheerfully drawing pictures of the staff upon the wall in what he considers appropriate material.

Since there is some variety in the hospital environment, from reasonably pleasant wards for showing visiting dignitaries to the miserable back wards ruled by sadistic nurses and aides, it is important that the patient learn how to deal with the staff so that he forces them to behave badly to him but only if he has arranged it. He does not mind misery that he has provoked, but he does not like people to treat him badly on their own initiative. Therefore the schizophrenic must do a diagnosis of the staff to find the areas which are most suitable for provocations. The staff too must have an estimate of the range of skill of the schizophrenic so they can know what maneuvers to expect of any individual patient in this struggle. The need for a quick estimate of the schizophrenic has produced psychologists who are willing to do psychological testing so that the staff can diagnose the patient's weak points and thereby gain an advantage in dealing with him. Schizophrenics, however, are not put off as normal people would be by the aroma of pseudoscience exuding from the pores of the psychologist. The patients see immediately that this fellow who sits down pleasantly with them and asks them to look at blots of ink and talk about them is indeed a man who does not have their best interests at heart. In fact the schizophrenic knows what he says about the ink blot will be held against him and affect his career in the hospital in ways he cannot predict. Therefore the wise schizophrenic is guarded in his comments about the ink blots. Faced with the same kind of ambiguous situation he was raised in at home, with equally disastrous effects if he should say the wrong thing, the schizophrenic will avoid describing any coherent picture, because he knows this staff member may make ulterior use of the coherence. Instead he will point out little pieces of the ink blot here and there and make no connections between them. He will also avoid mentioning any of the human shapes he sees, even if they look like the psychologist, because he cannot be sure whether the human beings in power over him will take his comments personally. The more self-confident schizophrenic will toy with the test, reaching for bizarre points to see if he can shake the deadpan expression from the psychologist's face, playing with the idea of a bat since he is supposed to be bats, and occasionally making oblique references to violence to indicate that he knows that this threat lies behind the testing. Only indirectly will he indicate that looking at blots of ink seems rather silly and so he knows there must be some reason for it which is being kept from him. The psychologist is pleased with the schizophrenic's protocol because he can discover that the responses are not common, ignoring the fact that the situation of the schizophrenic is also rather uncommon. It is like the white man in the South who concluded that a Negro was ignorant because the fellow shuffled and scratched his head and said, "Yassah, Boss," ignoring the context which made it wise for the Negro to behave that way. Since psychologists have a trained incapacity to examine contexts, they write down in their reports that the patient is confused and loose in his associations, has distorted perception, deeply repressed hostility, and a sprained ego. This scientific description of test results is given to the staff, which uses it, as the schizophrenic knew they would, to determine where to place him and how to deal with him.

It would seem evident that schizophrenia can be a dangerous game, but it has its lighter side too. Occasionally, for example, the patient is given a chance to have psychotherapy. Although the ward psychiatrists are so flooded with patients they do not have time to talk with them, and would hardly know what to talk with them about if they did take the time, most hospitals report in their publicity brochures that they are not merely prisons because they have a therapy program. This consists of group therapy meetings led by social workers. It is the function of these meetings to (a) turn the schizophrenics upon each other so they will be less occupied with entrapping the staff (this is called the Keseyan function); and (b) provide the social workers with a feeling of being useful while also letting them vent upon the patients the feelings they have developed from attempting to deal with the patient's families. The schizophrenic usually uses these group meetings to sharpen and broaden his techniques of verbal comment. Often he uses them to practice subtle variations in his repetitious behavior; the schizophrenic is, of course, the master at repeating the same behavior until the staff is driven to distraction. A possible record is held by the schizophrenic who, in a period of only two years, said, "I think my thinking is not good," a total of two hundred million seventy three times.

Occasionally a hospital will have a psychiatrist training program, and here the schizophrenic might have an opportunity for individual psychotherapy with a resident. The profession considers it wise to start these young fellows out on schizophrenics so that anything they meet later when making their fortunes in private practice will be anticlimactic. Psychiatric residents are a peculiar lot. Either they chose psychiatry because they thought they were going mad and it might help, or they could not develop a passion for some other medical speciality, like proctology, and so they fell into psychiatry by default. Once in training they discover that little of what their teachers say is of any use to them in dealing with a schizophrenic. The instructors teach only part time and make their living in private practice where they entirely avoid schizophrenics (having had enough of them when they were residents). The basic problem of the resident is one of translation. His instructors talk in one bizarre language and the patients in another. While the instructors talk about dark Ids flooded with anxiety and the daffodil structure of ego syntonics, the schizophrenics talk about the influence of atomic energy upon the burontonic systems and the difference between he-cocks and she-cocks. It is forbidden for instructors or residents to talk directly about the central theme of hospital life, the power struggle among staff and patients.

A typical beginning interchange between patient and psychotherapist can be presented to illustrate the kind of skill required of the true schizophrenic. The patient is brought to a room by an aide who mumbles something about seeing a doctor and then shuffles away. The schizophrenic waits, uncertain what new tactic the staff is offering, and attempting to estimate its degree of savagery. At this point the door opens and a vacant-faced young man enters. He wears a suit and tie to distinguish himself from the patients. "Hello," he says with a false heartiness, "I'm Dr. Offgamay." The schizophrenic stares at the wall as if he has not noticed the intrusion. "Well," says the doctor, attempting to ignore being ignored, "I thought we might talk about things." This typical therapeutic gambit, the vague, ambiguous, open-ended statement interests the patient. It may even arouse his admiration since it is a degree of ambiguity he thought only his parents could achieve. He begins to test whether this man is really what he appears to be or is more dangerous by saying something like, "My taillight is on," or perhaps, "My head was bashed in last night."

"Well now," says the young man, uncertain what to do with that sort of statement, "I'd like to know a little bit more about you, won't you tell me about yourself?"

The schizophrenic, who knows perfectly well that his record has been carefully examined for his history, has already understood the situation and he decides on a further test for confirmation. He says, "I want to do what you do."

The doctor freezes—his status position shaken by this mild remark as if by an earthquake. "Oh," he says, his voice rather cool, "how long have you been a *patient* here?"

The schizophrenic has finished his testing, and he replies, "I was born here." He makes this statement with absolute sincerity, as if he fully believes it. "Born here?" says the doctor, so confused by the sincerity that he can only inquire, "How old are you?"

"A hundred and eighty-seven," says the schizophrenic. The doctor suddenly has that lost feeling of one who suspects he is being put on and has been provoked into making a fool of himself and yet cannot be sure. The result is continuing suppressed fury and desperation as the game goes on and the doctor finds himself constantly provoked into saying what he would rather not say. He can only grab onto his shaky status position as a passenger holds the door handle on a wild ride down a mountain road.

This illustration of a typical interchange demonstrates the quick perception and interpersonal skill of the schizophrenic. If they had competitions, schizophrenics would vie among themselves to see who could discover most quickly whether he was dealing with a worthy opponent.

Once the therapy is off to this fine start, the only skill required of the schizophrenic is to keep it going. After all, the therapist is usually the only one in the hospital who will speak to him, except for the aides, who have more muscle than wit. The schizophrenic must keep the therapy ongoing by not creating too much fear and despair in the therapist while at the same time not allowing anything which might approach success. Since residents change every few months, it is also good to give an impression of being almost cured so this resident can encourage one of the next crop of residents to continue the treatment. Some schizophrenics can achieve strings of eight to ten psychotherapists over time, each one feeling that he is almost able to "reach" this poor wretch and a few more interviews will bring about a breakthrough.

The skill of the schizophrenic comes into play in several ways in psychotherapy. He must provide stimulation for the therapist and keep him coming, but he must also provide sufficient exasperating difficulties to help the therapist feel that he faces a worthy challenge of his abilities. Keeping the therapist on the hook requires an avoidance of any direct confrontation of the therapist with his miserable incompetence, as part of a courtesy procedure. For example, if the therapist is late to an appointment and does not bother to apologize, it is not correct to directly confront him with his rudeness or he is likely to flee, as mother did when directly confronted with her misbehavior. Rather, the schizophrenic must tell a story which allows the therapist to correct himself if he chooses. For example, the patient can say, "I was out on my submarine this morning, and we were to meet the refueling ship off Madagascar, but unfortunately the ship had been struck by an atomic bomb and barely limped in late with its Chinese flagons at halfmast." This rather complex statement, which any schizophrenic can quickly devise, allows the therapist an out. He can say, "I'm sorry I was late today," or he can argue, "Now Sam, you know you weren't out on a submarine this morning, you were right here in the hospital." The therapist's recognition that there might be more here than meets the vacant eye is usually represented by his following such an argument with, "Now let's try to get an understanding of why you'd think you were on a submarine. What does a submarine mean to you?"

A further requirement of the schizophrenic is an ability to find out quickly what the current psychiatric ideology is so that he can provide the young therapist with support for the theories he is learning. If it is a period where genital symbolism is the order of the day, the patient must discuss kings being overthrown and virgin queens married and vaguely rub his crotch whenever he mentions his mother. If genital symbolism is out and oral symbolism is being emphasized in training, the patient must quickly adapt to oral metaphors. He will discuss the cement in his stomach and the whiteness of milk, he can offer drawings which vaguely resemble breasts to the keen psychiatric eye, and he may make occasional sucking motions with his lips to stimulate the therapist. The skillful schizophrenic can read the interests of therapists from minimal cues, such as lighting up of the eyes when some obvious symbol that makes sense in theory is mentioned. The more Sullivanian fads require more skill from the patient. As the therapist struggles to handle his interpersonal defenses and to help the patient discover how he deals with people, the patient must offer interpersonal behavior which is easily enough interpreted by even a novice therapist. For example, he must fold his arms and cross his legs and turn his head away so the therapist can point out that he is building a wall between them and interfering with their interpersonal relationship. However, the patient must not merely help the therapist, he also must occasionally show the novice that he still has a great deal to learn. When the young fellow is feeling rather confident in his therapeutic acumen, the schizophrenic can stare thoughtfully at him and then look away and say, "There are some people in the world who have a homosexual fix." Such a comment will shatter any sensitive resident and leave him dragging through the day wondering about his unconscious desires.

The odds against a schizophrenic in a hospital meeting a skillful therapist of schizophrenics are so great that in the memory of those who keep track of these matters the last time it occurred was in Buffalo in 1947. Should this happen, the full range of schizophrenic genius is necessary. He must play therapist against staff, make a thrust at every weak point in the man, pretend improvement when there is none, and generally fight for his life. After all, if he is inadvertently cured he must go out of the hospital to the family waiting for him at the gate. That family has discovered their child can be the burden which holds the family together while still being in the hospital with a hired staff to deal with the inconvenience, and so they protest how welcome he is without wishing him back. The occasional families who actually wish the patient to return home have marshaled their forces in his absence and plan to make up for lost time in giving him the business. Should the patient go mad and become normal, he also faces a society which will blacklist him for having accepted hospital treatment.

Psychiatry today is going through revolutionary changes, and we owe to the schizophrenic many of the advances being made. It is evident that the schizophrenic is responsible for the recent movement to close down all mental hospitals. The leaders of this movement, the more prominent psychiatrists in the field, have suggested that rest homes should be created for the aged and emergency wards be set up in general hospitals for people to stay for a few days during family crises. Mental hospitals would be discarded with a state law that psychotic patients could not be kept in custody more than a few days unless they had committed a crime. The proponents of this scheme argue that schizophrenics should be returned to the families who deserve them and psychiatrists should be forced to deal with the insane and not just drug them and avoid them.

Enthusiasts for the mental hospital, a group composed of families of patients, psychiatrists in peaceful private practice, and those people employed in such institutions, argue that such a radical change is fantastic. These patients are diseased and need medical care, they say, and besides they don't make sufficient income to pay psychiatrists for treatment. The moral wing of this faction also points out that it would be unfair to loose psychotics upon the profession of psychiatry. Just as one would not put a man who runs the mile in four hours in the same race with a man who runs it in four minutes, so it is unfair to face the average psychiatrist with a schizophrenic or his family.

However, enthusiasts for closing down the hospitals argue in turn that such an act is necessary because of the skills of the true schizophrenic. As one proponent put it, "When patients were confined at home, it was thought they would improve with hospital treatment. Now let us admit defeat. Despite all attempts at reform and promising new methods of approach, the schizophrenic has beaten us. We should concede that fact and find other ways to deal with him." More active advocates of closing down mental institutions have created a slogan which can be seen on the signs they carry as they picket mental hospitals, "Let's get the patients off the back wards and back home into the back rooms!"

3

An Ordeal for Pleasure: A Story

INTRODUCTION

Michael F. Hoyt, PhD

> If one makes it more difficult for a person to have a symptom than to give it up, the person will give up the symptom. Over the years I have made use of this type of intervention in a variety of ways, and in this book I will describe the range of variations.
>
> —**Jay Haley**
> *Ordeal Therapy: Unusual Ways to Change Behavior (1984, p. 5)*

"An Ordeal for Pleasure: A Story" is drawn from *Ordeal Therapy*, one of Haley's (1984) finest books. Written with his typical clarity, full of humor, and shorn of obfuscating jargon, "This is a book about the absurd dilemmas people find themselves in and the absurd solutions offered them in therapy. The reports are accurate descriptions of cases" (Haley, p. xi). Before turning to the case under consideration, which concludes the book, some general remarks are in order.

In the book's introduction, Haley quoted Erickson's description of his famous case of a man with insomnia who was given the task of polishing the floor all night if he wasn't asleep within 15 minutes—the man soon chose the "lesser of two evils" and was sleeping soundly throughout the night! (Viewers of the 1993 Haley and Richeport-Haley videotape can watch Erickson tell the story himself.) He noted that ordeal therapy is different from some of the other techniques originated by Erickson (such as the use of metaphors and geometric progression), then outlined the ordeal technique:

> With the ordeal technique, the therapist's task is easily defined: It is to impose an ordeal appropriate to the problem of the person who wants to change, an ordeal more severe than the problem. The main requirement of an ordeal is that it causes distress equal to or greater than that caused by the symptom, just as a punishment should fit the crime. Usually, if an ordeal isn't severe enough to extinguish the symptom, it can be increased in magnitude until it is. It is also best if the ordeal is good for the person. Doing what's good for you is hard for anyone and seems particularly difficult for people who seek therapy.
>
> Examples of what's good for people are exercise, improving the mind, eating a healthy diet, and other self-improvement activities. Such ordeals may also include making a sacrifice for others.
>
> The ordeal must have another characteristic: It must be something the person *can* do and something the person cannot legitimately object to. That is, it must be of such a nature that the therapist can easily say, "This won't violate any of your moral standards and is something you *can* do." There is one final characteristic of a therapeutic ordeal: It should not harm the person or anyone else....
>
> One final aspect of the ordeal: Sometimes the person must go through it repeatedly to recover from the symptom. At other times the mere threat of an ordeal brings

> recovery. That is, when the person lays out the ordeal as a procedure and the person agrees to experience it, he or she often abandons the symptom before the ordeal even goes into effect. (Haley, 1984, pp. 6–7)

Haley (1984) described different types of ordeals:

Straightforward Task, such as having a person exercise, preferably in the middle of the night, each time the problem occurs. He emphasizes the importance of securing the patient's ironclad agreement to do the task, and notes that "the exercise should be sufficient so that it can be felt in the muscles the next day" (p. 10).

Paradoxical Ordeals, such as interventions like having a depressed patient schedule specific times to be depressed, having a phobic patient repeatedly imagine that which he or she fears, or requiring a quarreling couple to quarrel. "It is a question whether a paradoxical intervention can be anything but an ordeal insofar as individuals are asked to go through what they'd rather recover from" (p. 10).

The Therapist as an Ordeal, including interventions in which the therapist reframes, confronts, or interprets the patient's behavior such that the patient is forced to face or think about the problem in ways they would rather avoid.

Ordeals Involving Two or More Persons, such as having a mother check a child's bed at dawn and, if the bed is wet, having her help him practice handwriting.

He cautioned,

> [T]he therapist need only provide something the person would rather give up the symptomatic behavior than do. However, a sharp distinction needs to be made between therapeutic, benevolent ordeals and those ordeals that cause a person to suffer either for the advantage of a therapist or for social control reasons. Simply to lock someone in jail when he or she steals does not fall into the category of ordeal therapy but is a method of social control. All therapists should be on guard against persecution of the

> public under the guise of therapy. To make it quite clear, the ordeal should be voluntary by the person and good for the person experiencing it but not necessarily for the person imposing it except insofar as there's satisfaction in successfully helping someone to change when he or she wishes to. (Haley, 1984, pp. 12–13)

(As Burns [2001] has noted, Haley also wrote in *Uncommon Therapy* [1973] about "providing a worse alternative" [Haley, p. 25] but made it clear that it should be a "benevolent ordeal" [Haley, p. 155]. In my words, we erect an impediment that makes the problematic behavior not worth continuing. We don't quite "make them an offer they can't refuse," but we help patients to give up a symptom by offering them a chance to take an easier way out, "a path of less resistance.")

Haley (1984) also outlined the stages of ordeal therapy:

1. *The problem must be defined clearly.*
2. *The person must be committed to getting over the problem*:

   > One way to motivate a client is to say that there is a cure that is guaranteed, but the client will not be told what it is until he or she agrees in advance to do it. Sometimes clients are asked to come back next week only if they're willing to do whatever is asked. (p. 15)

3. *An ordeal must be selected.*
4. *The directive must be given with a rationale*:

   > [The therapist] must make clear that the task is to occur only with symptomatic behavior and that there is a set time for it. Exactly what is to be done must be described. If appropriate, the task must be given with a rationale that makes it seem reasonable.... For some people, it is best to not explain but simply to tell them to do it. This more magical approach is best for the intellectuals among the clientele who can undo or explain away any rationale and find the whole thing not necessary. (pp.15–16)

5. *The ordeal continues until the problem is resolved.*
6. *The ordeal is in a social context*:

> The therapist needs to be aware that symptoms are a reflection of a confusion in a social organization, usually a family. The existence of a symptom indicates that the hierarchy of an organization is incorrect.... Sometimes, just as the ordeal is proving effective, the client will telephone the therapist and say that something strange is happening. The therapist must reassure him that what is occurring is part of the expected change and help him [or her] through the reorganization of his life. (pp. 16–17)

A dozen case reports, each an interesting, well-written chapter, then comprise the main body of the book. Based on verbatim audio and video recordings, each merits careful study to enjoy the subtleties of the strategies and artful clinical interaction, including various nuances and adjustments. The book's final case, "An Ordeal for Pleasure: A Story," appears as an epilogue. (Haley, who got his undergraduate degree at UCLA in theater arts and spent a year in New York aspiring to be a playwright, noted [p. xi] that this last report is "a piece of fiction ... [but] is based on an actual case.") I don't want to give anything away, so suffice it to say that the therapy is successful. The problem is clearly defined, the client's cooperation secured, an ordeal selected and presented in a way that gains the client's compliance, the ordeal is continued until the problem is resolved, and the ordeal and desired solution are integrated into the social context of the client's life. The therapist gives voice to Haley's view that a change in action, not a putative insight, is the way to resolve a problem. Readers will enjoy watching how the therapist intensifies the work when the client pledges his fealty too easily, how he utilizes the client's moral character and growing desperateness to set the hook, and how he addresses various issues that could otherwise vitiate the effectiveness of the intervention. Good judgment and clinical skill are brought to bear. As Haley (quoted in Crenshaw, 2004, p. 46) said when asked how he knew to use a certain intervention at a certain time, "You wouldn't use it on someone it wouldn't work on!"

The theory and techniques of ordeal therapy—making it too hard (or at least not worth it) to continue a problematic behavior—are still relevant, of course, although in today's therapy climate (doctors seen less as ultimate authority figures, informed consent procedures, an emphasis on medications and cognitive-behavioral interventions rather than systemic and strategic-interactional approaches, etc.), one might have more difficulty getting clients to comply with some of the ordeals that Erickson and Haley constructed. Indeed, the hassle of dealing with insurance companies and HMO limits can be an ordeal in itself that may encourage some people not to dawdle but to resolve their problems as soon as possible (J. Frykman, 2009, personal communication). One time (reported in Hoyt, 1995), a woman with bridge phobia (no small problem for someone living in the San Francisco Bay area) came to see me. Because she wanted the best treatment, I persuaded her that more data would be necessary about her reactions at different times and locations, and so under my direction she began driving—sometimes quite anxiously—across several bridges at varying times of day and night. This experiment both promoted her desensitizing exposure and convinced her that she could drive with reasonable comfort as long as she could avoid the ordeal of rush-hour traffic. Another time I persuaded a couple, after getting them to agree that they would do whatever I suggested, that they would send a political contribution to a candidate they hated if they failed to spend the money on something enjoyable together. Sometimes just quoting to people the old saying, "If you don't change directions, you're going to wind up where you're heading!" is enough to make them expect an unending ordeal if they don't do something different. My wife and I were once sitting in a marriage counselor's office spending $100 an hour arguing about whether to spend $50 a week on a housecleaner—I did the math, *cha-ching!*, and realized how to end the ordeal.

Consistent with the theme of *Revisiting Jay Haley*, I'd like to conclude this commentary with a couple of brief stories. I remember when I first read Haley's (1973) book *Uncommon Therapy: The Psychiatric Techniques of Milton H. Erickson, M.D.* a few years after it had come out. A world of *utilization* and *reframing* and *metaphor* and *strategy* and *therapeutic artistry* opened before me. I eagerly read some of Haley's other books—*Strategies of Psychotherapy* (1963), *The Power Tactics of Jesus Christ and Other Essays* (1969), and *Problem Solving Therapy* (1976)—and heard him give brilliant keynote speeches, but had not met him personally. Finally, I contacted Jay, by letter and telephone, asking him to participate in an interview for a book I was working on at the time (as reported in Hoyt, 2004, p. 243). He indicated his preference not to do a formal interview, but then graciously added, "How about if we just get together for a drink?" And so we did, at the Fifth International Congress on Ericksonian Approaches to Hypnosis and Psychotherapy, held in Phoenix in December 1992. He was 25 years my senior. When we first met at the elevator, I called him "Mr. Haley" as we shook hands. He replied, "Please, call me Jay." Sitting atop the Hyatt-Regency, we visited and got a bit acquainted. I had no specific agenda, other than to enjoy the pleasure of his company. Finally, however, an important issue came to my mind. "Jay, may I ask you a question?" "Sure," he replied. I then asked, "What do you feed your twinkle?" He smiled and hit it back: "Well, you have one, too, don't you?" I paused, "Well, yeah ... but yours is older—I want to make sure I'm feeding mine the right stuff!" We both laughed.

Over the years we stayed in touch and saw each other at various conferences. He was one of the "first generation" participants I quoted in my report (Hoyt, 1997) of the 1995 Unmuddying the Waters conference we attended. On behalf of my colleagues in the Japanese Brief Therapy Association, I invited him to Japan to receive a lifetime achievement award. He was honored but had to decline the arduous trip because of health reasons; but we had a couple of long, fascinating phone conversations about his observations about Japanese families and culture. I wrote admiring reviews (Hoyt, 2000, 2001, 2002, 2009) about his work and some of his excellent teaching videotapes. We had a drink together at the 2005 Evolution of Psychotherapy Conference.

When I heard that Jay had passed away, a few days after his death, I called my good friend John Frykman, who had known Jay for many years. John lives in San Francisco, across the Golden Gate Bridge a few miles from my home. We made a plan, and a week later got together at John's place to hold our own little private remembrance. We had lunch and revisited some of our memories of Jay: his many professional contributions, his keen intelligence and trenchant wit, his commitment to patients and students, his compassion and concerns about human rights. He was a gentleman, with a sharp sense of irony and a great twinkle in his eye. True to the definition of *strategic therapy* ("Therapy can be called strategic if the clinician initiates what happens during therapy and designs a particular approach for each problem"—Haley, 1973, p. 1), he liked the power of giving people directives and having them obey them for their own good. John reminded me that it was Haley's suggestion that John call Erickson "Milton" (rather than the more formal "Dr. Erickson" that everyone else used) as a way of fostering the special relationship John and Erickson eventually developed. I recalled standing in the back of the room at a workshop I was teaching (in Santa Fe) when Haley walked in (he was teaching in the room next door and was on a break) and together watching and discussing his videotape *Milton H. Erickson: Explorer in Hypnosis and Therapy*. John and I laughed when we recalled Jay's quip, when he was asked how he would like to be remembered: "As the world's oldest living teacher of therapy" (Klein, 2001, p. xiv; Wylie, 2007, p. 54)! We were also both touched by his tender remark, when asked what memorial he would like when he did pass, that he would prefer that people should spend the time together with their families.

I had left my dog in the car while John and I met. When we finished, I took Ranger over to the beach a few blocks from where John lives. I let him off leash so he could play with the other dogs. There was one he especially took a liking to. They romped up and down, into the water and back, having a great time. Finally, when we were getting ready to go, I asked the dog's owner (who didn't know me or what I had been doing that day), "Hey, what's your dog's name?"

He smiled and replied, "Haley."

(Hey, you can't make up stuff like this!!)

References

Burns, G. W. (2001). Jay Haley: The man who made therapy an ordeal. In J. K. Zeig (Ed.), *Changing directives: The strategic therapy of Jay Haley* (pp. 154–170). Phoenix, AZ: Milton H. Erickson Foundation Press.

Crenshaw, W. (2004). *Treating families and children in the child protective system*. New York: Brunner-Routledge.

Haley, J. (1963). *Strategies of psychotherapy*. New York: Grune & Stratton.

Haley, J. (1969). *The power tactics of Jesus Christ and other essays*. New York: Avon.

Haley, J. (1973). *Uncommon therapy: The psychiatric techniques of Milton H. Erickson, M.D.* New York: Norton.

Haley, J. (1976). *Problem solving therapy: New strategies for effective family therapy*. San Francisco: Jossey-Bass.

Haley, J. (1984). *Ordeal therapy: Unusual ways to change behavior*. San Francisco: Jossey-Bass.

Haley, J., & Richeport-Haley, M. (1993). *Milton H. Erickson, M.D.: Explorer in hypnosis and therapy* [videotape]. New York: Brunner/Mazel.

Hoyt, M. F. (1995). Managed care, HMOs, and the Ericksonian perspective. *Ericksonian Monographs, 10*, 25–36. Reprinted in M. F. Hoyt (1995), *Brief therapy and managed care* (pp. 163–176). San Francisco: Jossey-Bass.

Hoyt, M. F. (1997). Unmuddying the waters: A "common ground" conference. *Journal of Systemic Therapies, 16*(3), 195–200. (Reprinted in Hoyt, M. F. [2000]. *Some stories are better than others* (pp. 195–200). Philadelphia: Brunner/Mazel).

Hoyt, M. F. (2000). Video review of J. Haley & M. Richeport-Haley's *Family Therapy at a Distance: A Case of Depression. The Milton H. Erickson Foundation Newsletter, 20*(3), 17.

Hoyt, M. F. (2001). Video review of J. Haley & M. Richeport-Haley's *Whither Family Therapy? A Jay Haley Version. The Family Journal: Counseling and Therapy for Couples and Families, 9*(2), 227–228.

Hoyt, M. F. (2002). Video review of *Learning and Teaching Therapy With Jay Haley*: A videotape series. *American Journal of Family Therapy, 30*(1), 105–112.

Hoyt, M. F. (2004). *The present is a gift: Mo' better stories from the world of brief therapy*. New York: iUniverse.

Hoyt, M. F. (2009). *Brief psychotherapies: Principles and practices*. Phoenix, AZ: Zeig, Tucker & Theisen.

Klein, R. E. (2001). Foreword. In J. K. Zeig (Ed.), *Changing directives: The strategic therapy of Jay Haley* (pp. xi–xiv). Phoenix, AZ: Milton H. Erickson Foundation Press.

Wylie, M. S. (2007). The accidental therapist. *Psychotherapy Networker, 31*(6), 46–54.

AN ORDEAL FOR PLEASURE: A STORY

Jay Haley

Studying the red face above the clerical collar, Ian Wharf thought to himself that the priest drank more than he should. He wondered whether he should deal with the drinking as well as with the pleasure below the belt.

"You feel this pleasurable sensation every time you take a shower?" Ian asked.

"Not every time," said the priest. "I wouldn't be honest if I said that. But it happens just about every time. Now, Dr. Wharf, it isn't that I'm not supposed to feel the pleasure." In his distress the priest could still look condescending. "The point is I'm not supposed to *give consent* to feeling the pleasure. You not being one of the faith, I should make that clear."

"I think I understand," said Ian, "but sometimes you doubt whether you've given consent and sometimes you don't—is that right?"

"Lately it's happened so often that I rush through a shower as fast as I can. Yet I must give myself a decent wash. I've even considered giving up showers altogether. Never anything but a tub bath. But if I don't take a shower because I fear it, then I'm in sin because I'm fighting against seeking the pleasure." The priest's plump face was determined. "More than that, I won't run from the problem. It's there and I must face it. Yet as soon as that water begins to strike me down there and I feel that sensation, well—I almost go mad."

"I see," said Ian. "How have you tried to solve this problem?"

"Every way there is," said the priest with a gesture of despair. "Prayer mostly. Hours on my knees praying to merciful Mary to release me. I've even tried tranquilizers—a half dozen before a shower. But the doubt is still there—it's still there!" He struck the arm of the deep, comfortable chair.

"Damn it, do I *seek* the pleasure?" Placing his fingers at his temples, he said, "Dr. Wharf, do you think I'm going mad?"

"No," said Ian.

"Well, that's a relief." The priest smirked behind his hands. "I've even thought of taking a knife to the problem. That's a mad thought, to deform oneself, and yet I thought of it." Sighing, he said, "Oh, I wish for old age and the end of such sensations!"

"What if the problem should become worse?" asked Ian.

"Worse! I dread to think about it. I don't understand why I have the problem at all, why it should strike *me*. But I suppose that's why I'm here—to understand it."

"I thought you were here to get over it," said Ian.

"Isn't that the same thing?"

"Not always. Now, I know you'd rather not think about it, but what if the problem should become worse?"

The priest looked at Ian as if seeing him for the first time. "I don't know," he said, "I suppose I'd wonder if I should be a priest."

"Ah," said Ian.

"It's been my life for seventeen years. I have no other."

"Mm-hm."

"Yet a priest must have control of himself. If I'm consenting to the pleasure, I'm sinning. Yet am I consenting? Perhaps I'm quite innocent. That's what drives me to the brink, that doubt. Can you help me, Dr. Wharf?"

"I think so," said Ian, "if you're willing to cooperate."

"You won't find a more cooperative patient. When the bishop said I was to see a psychiatrist, and one not of the faith at all, I doubted his judgment. Yet prayer has not helped, nor penance, nor even a long talk with the bishop."

"If I'm to help you get over this in 30 days," said Ian, "you'll have to do most of the work. It's the first of next month that you leave for your new parish, isn't it?"

"That's right, a promotion which I doubt I deserve. I'll refuse it, if that's necessary for the treatment."

"You're very agreeable," said Ian, with a calculated touch of irony in his voice. "The bishop wants you to accept the promotion; he feels you deserve it. So we'll see if we can't solve this in 30 days."

"It's a relief to hear you sound so hopeful, doctor."

"I can make no promises," said Ian. "But we might have a chance if you'll do exactly what I tell you."

"Yes, sir, anything."

"Fine. First of all, I'd like you to tell me in detail just what time of day you take a shower, how you proceed to wash yourself, and exactly at what point the doubt overcomes you."

Leaning back in his chair as the priest began to talk, Ian Wharf lit a cigar and studied its ash as he listened. Ian was a thin man who looked younger than his thirty-two years, and he liked to tip back in his chair and cross his legs as he listened to a patient. He would study his cigar, at times looking up to watch the eyes of a patient who was talking. He watched the patient's eyes largely with only one of his own because his right eye tended to roll about outside his control. He could see out of it well enough, but as a result of a childhood injury it would drift up and to the side and around while his other eye remained fixed on the person he was talking to. His patients appeared uneasy when they first saw the eye begin to drift, but they became accustomed to it.

As Ian listened to the priest, he wondered what he could do to help the fellow. The obsession was new to Ian, and he was still clarifying in his mind the difference between feeling pleasure below the belt and giving consent to feeling that pleasure. There was the rub—where the obsession could fix itself. Part of his mind listened for the technical details of the shower while another part of his mind drifted to his own problems with pleasure. Ian's doubt was the opposite of the poor cleric's—he wondered whether he gave consent to avoiding pleasure. Why else would I have married her, he wondered? With all the sensuous women in the world, I chose Lucretia of the long blond hair. Yet she had been sensuous. He examined the end of his cigar with his controllable eye as the perspiring priest talked on. The world changes, Ian thought. In the old religion, sexual pleasure could be a sin, and in the new psychiatric religion it could be a sin not to seek sexual pleasure. How determined we are to complicate our lives for no apparent purpose!

When the priest finally paused, Ian said, "I believe I have the picture," and he smiled. "Now, our goal, as I understand it, is to manage the situation so that you can take a shower without worrying about it, just like anyone else."

"That would be wonderful," said the priest.

"Fine. There is an essential first step. To succeed in this, you will have to do exactly what I tell you to do, no matter how silly it might seem to you."

"Yes, sir," said the priest. "What am I to do?"

"Don't be hasty in making this agreement," said Ian. "I want you to think it over for a week before you agree to do whatever I say."

"A week! But we have only thirty days."

"Yes," said Ian. "During this week I want you to take at least two showers and examine yourself carefully while you take them. I want you to have more clearly in mind—to the point of certainty—just when you have this doubt and when you don't. What I tell you to do will depend on your knowing that."

"Well, I suppose I can take two showers before next week." The priest looked carefully at Ian. "Could you tell me what sort of thing you might ask me to do?"

"No," said Ian, "you must agree in advance that you will follow my instructions without knowing what they are. Next week at the same time, then?"

"All right," said the priest.

"One more thing," said Ian as he walked the priest to the door. "I would also like you to think about what consequences there might be when you get over this problem."

"Consequences?" said the priest.

"That's right," said Ian. "Good afternoon." He shut the door, wondering what instructions to give to a priest who feared he was giving consent to pleasure "down there." He had put the man off until next week partly to commit him to doing what he was told and partly to give himself time to think of something to tell him to do. It will come, he said to himself, and he put the priest out of his mind for the week.

That evening in the kitchen, where they were having dinner because the dining-room table was piled with laundry, Lucretia said she wasn't feeling well. She suffered from a vague pain in her chest that she thought might be a cancer. Ian tried to make light of it by saying, "In case it is, perhaps a visit to church this Sunday would ease your mind."

Lucretia stared at him with her pale blue eyes. "Your sarcasm isn't welcome," she said. "I can't help it if I have a pain."

Ian sighed, thinking once again that they were apart as if a plate glass window had stood between them. She knows it's there, he thought to himself, and I know it's there, yet each thing we do to reach out to each other only leaves the glass more solid. Yet she has been analyzed and I have been analyzed and the world has been analyzed, and all of us are in conflict, caught up in it like a web.

The priest came in the following week with a solemn expression for the occasion. "I'm prepared to do anything you say—but with one proviso," he said. "It must not interfere with my obligations as a priest."

"That's fair enough," said Ian, lighting up a cigar. "Tell me about the showers you took this week."

"I took two, and an extra one to be sure," said the priest. "The pleasure was there with all three, but only during two of them was I really in doubt whether I consented or not. The doubt came upon me quite early, before I had soaped myself. As soon as the warm water touched me, I felt the pleasure, and I did not know—I simply did not know—whether I consented to it or not. Each time the doubt ruined my whole day so I could hardly get anything done."

"Very good," said Ian.

"I'm glad you think so," said the priest.

"Ah, I don't mean it's good that you had the doubt, because I know that's distressing to you, but I'm glad you had the doubt so we can both get a clearer perspective about it. Now, you were also going to consider the consequences of getting over this problem."

"I've done that. The only consequence I can see is that I'll be a happier and better man and priest."

"Perhaps you haven't thought about it seriously enough," said Ian, looking doubtful.

"Indeed I have," the priest said.

"Have you considered the consequences with the bishop?" asked Ian.

"I see none there. He'll be delighted when I get over this."

"Of course he will," said Ian, "but he'll undoubtedly have other feelings as well. After all, he spent quite a bit of time trying to help you, didn't he?"

"Yes, he did, God bless him."

"After he did his best, if you come to me and get over the problem in a week or two, how will he feel?"

"I really don't know," said the priest.

"I think he'll feel a little put out at you and at me. He knows you well—he's your superior and your spiritual adviser. Yet you didn't recover when being helped by him, and you did when you went to a stranger."

"I suppose he'll feel that way a little." The priest looked puzzled. "But are you saying I should keep this problem because it might bother the bishop if I get over it, and him the one who sent me to you?"

"I'm not saying you should keep the problem," said Ian, smiling. "I'm merely pointing out there will be consequences to getting over it. As another example, when you don't have the problem, you'll have no reason to decline the promotion in a new parish."

"Well, I want that very much."

"I'm sure you do. Still, you wouldn't have to accept it, would you?"

"I could turn it down if I wished, but I should have advanced years ago. I don't know what my mother would say, she'd be so pleased."

"Ah, there's another consequence, you'd be pleasing your mother."

"Shouldn't I want to? She's been disappointed for years that I haven't advanced."

"Of course you should want to please her," said Ian. He added thoughtfully, "If it was necessary to disappoint her, you could find some other way."

"Disappoint her, indeed," said the priest. "I've devoted my life to pleasing her. I haven't even told her about the offer of a promotion for fear I won't be given it and she'll be unhappy."

"I see," said Ian.

"It was the greatest day in my mother's life when I became a priest."

"I'm sure it was," said Ian. "Well, I can see you haven't really thought about what will happen when you get over this problem."

"I hadn't thought of my mother and the bishop," the priest said, "but what else is there?"

"Oh, there are other consequences. For example, you'll have more confidence and be more sure of yourself."

"Heavens, man, that's no consequence. With this terrible thing on my mind, I haven't had the courage of a mouse. I'm ashamed to look people in the eye."

"Exactly," said Ian.

"I'll be able to hear a confession without feeling guilty about my own sins."

"Yes, that's another matter," said Ian. He leaned thoughtfully toward the priest, staring at him with his left eye while his right eye rolled slowly upward. "You and I are both in the helping business, and we spend our lives dealing with people in difficulty."

"That's true," said the priest. "We may go about our work differently, but surely we try to help people in distress."

"That's right," said Ian, "and I'm sure I don't need to tell *you*, but when we help people who are in misery, sometimes we find ourselves becoming arrogant and superior. We feel we're better than other people."

"That's true, it's the sin of pride."

"Exactly. Sometimes we are saved from that attitude if we have a problem we cannot conquer. A problem gives us humility."

"Are you suggesting I keep this mad thing I have about showers?"

"Not at all. I'm merely suggesting that it is no light problem to give up. Think a moment of the consequences. You'll no longer be a disappointment to your mother, with all the effect that might have on her. You'll have a higher status in the church, you'll be more self-confident, you won't feel guilty when you face the people who come to you for help.

"Really, Dr. Wharf, I think I can stand all that."

"I think you can," said Ian, "or I wouldn't have gone this far with you. However, as you change, you'll find it won't all be sunshine and roses." Ian set his cigar in the ashtray and sat back, folding his arms. "Now, are you ready to do what I tell you?"

"I am," the priest said, his face determined.

"Good. First, I want you to write to your mother and tell her you've been offered this promotion and you look forward to it. I want you to say that you're complimented by the offer and you're sure you can handle the new position. The letter must go off today."

"But what if I must give it up after saying such a thing?"

"Will you be saying what's not true?"

"No—well, yes. It isn't true that I'm sure I can handle it."

"What do you think your mother will reply?"

"She'll be delighted, of course."

"I don't think so. I think she'll write back something that puts you in doubt about your abilities."

"That's not true, doctor."

"I think it is."

"You have your opinion, and I have mine. I might add that I've known my mother somewhat longer than you have."

"If you express confidence about yourself in a letter to her, you'll find out I'm right. But I don't want to ask too much of you. Let me put it this way. You *must* write her that you have this new opportunity and you're pleased with it. Whether you say you're sure you can handle it, I leave up to you, in case you'd rather not risk it. Agreed?"

"Agreed," said the priest coolly.

"Now, then, for the showers." Ian leaned forward and stared intently at the priest, his right eye beginning to roll upward. "Every day this coming week I want you to take three showers—morning, afternoon, and evening."

"Three showers a day?"

"That's right."

"Isn't that excessive?"

"When you take these showers, I want you to examine yourself carefully to see if you're experiencing pleasure down there and to see if you're giving consent to that pleasure."

"I'll be doing that, all right."

"Now if, during a shower, you find you're in doubt about giving consent to the pleasure—even the slightest doubt—then you must do the following: You must step out of that shower immediately and dry yourself completely. When that's done, you must step back into the shower and turn the water a little bit colder. You're to take another shower, and if at any time you're in doubt, even the slightest doubt, you must again get out of the shower immediately and dry yourself completely. Then you're to step back into the shower and turn the water a little bit colder. You're to take another shower, and if you feel any doubt at all, you must do exactly the same thing again until you can complete a shower with no doubt whatever in your mind."

"God bless me," said the priest in consternation, "if I do that three times a day, I might have to spend the whole day in the shower!"

"You might," said Ian.

"This is asking too much, Dr. Wharf."

"Are my instructions clear?"

"Too clear."

"Then repeat them so we can be sure."

After repeating the procedure accurately, the priest said, "I may never get out of the bathroom."

"You must do the best you can," said Ian. "That's enough for today. I want to see you again next week at this same time."

"Now, look, Dr. Wharf," said the priest, "I didn't expect anything like this when I agreed to do what you said. What kind of psychiatry do you call this? I've read Sigmund Freud, I've read Sullivan. You're supposed to have me talk about things—my sex life, or where I learned about pleasure, and things like that."

"We have an agreement," said Ian, getting to his feet. When the priest reluctantly stood up, Ian added, "No one is to know about these instructions except you and me at this time. It's not the business of your bishop."

"I can't tell him why I'm so long in the shower?"

"It's your problem, not his." Ian walked to the door with the priest. "I know this is something you can do successfully. Until next week at this time." He closed the door behind the priest and turned to make his notes so he'd remember what he'd told the man to do.

The day the priest called, Ian had arrived home late in the afternoon. He was just settling down with his paper and a cup of coffee when the telephone rang and his answering service told him there was an emergency call.

"I think I'm going out of my mind," said the priest, his voice sounding far away on the telephone. "I didn't sleep at all last night, and now I have the terrible feeling I'm losing my grip."

"Have you followed my instructions exactly?" Ian asked.

"Exactly," the priest said, "and I don't think I can anymore. It's just too much. Yesterday I spent almost the whole day in the shower."

"You've given me your word," said Ian, "so I expect you to continue."

"Something is happening to me," the priest said. "Can I see you tonight?"

"I'm sure you can wait until our regular appointment," said Ian, estimating whether the priest could or could not. "I suppose we could arrange it, but I don't think it's necessary."

"I'll try to wait if you wish me to," said the priest, his voice trailing off as he spoke.

"Well, I have some time this evening," Ian said casually. "Suppose we meet at my office at nine o'clock and talk it over."

"Thank you, doctor, I'll be there."

Just before nine, Ian called upstairs to Lucretia, who was lying down, and told her he was going to his office.

"Again?" she said.

"This is the first evening I've worked this week. I won't be long."

"Is it really necessary?" called out Lucretia.

"Maybe," said Ian, "or maybe I just want to get the hell out of here," and he left.

The priest's hands were shaking when he sat down in the deep chair and lit a cigarette. "I've begun to doubt whether I should be a priest," he said, "and that's a terrible doubt." His voice had lost the semidramatic quality he had used with Ian. He sounded grimly serious.

"You see this?" The priest held up his quivering hand. "I haven't had a drink in two days, and I have the shakes. Not even a glass of wine."

"Oh?" said Ian.

"It's a mortal sin to kill oneself, and yet I've even considered that," said the priest, his voice assuming the more usual overdramatic style. "Will you release me from this agreement, doctor?"

"No," said Ian.

"Sometimes I think you're the devil. I've put myself in the hands of Satan himself." The priest smirked. "I know it isn't sophisticated anymore to believe in the devil, but I'm not a sophisticated man."

"In my job as the devil," said Ian, "I would wonder why you don't drink to make this difficult period a little easier."

"That's the very point. *I don't want it easier*," said the priest.

"Yet if a drink would make you feel better?" Ian said casually, knowing he'd save time if he blocked the priest off from drinking.

"I don't want to feel better when I have this problem," said the priest. "I didn't become a priest to have an easy life. I did it to sacrifice my life for God." He sighed and rubbed his forehead. "At least that's what I'm supposed to say, but I don't really know why I became a priest. It might've been a mistake. I might not be right for the calling. My father was a drunkard, you know. Oh, yes, and a violent man, too. How he beat my mother and how he'd beat me when he was drunk—if he could catch me! Yet when he was sober, he was the most quiet and pleasant of men. It just didn't happen often that he was sober. How my mother would plead with him! The more she begged him to stop, the more he drank, and the more he drank, the more she pointed at him and told me never to be like him. I believe she really hated him, or perhaps it was the drink she hated, since it gave him pleasure." He looked at Ian from behind his hands and smirked. "If you were a proper psychiatrist, you'd point out to me that I could develop a drinking problem because I identify with my father."

"Oh, you show more initiative than that," said Ian. "I think you could develop a drinking problem on your own."

"You don't mind if I say you're not a proper psychiatrist?"

"I don't mind."

"Do you mind if I say you have the screwiest right eye I ever saw in the head of a man?"

"I don't mind," said Ian.

"I can't tell whether you're looking at me or not. One eye points in my direction, but the other roams the universe. Can you control it at all?"

"Not at all," said Ian.

"How strange. Where was I?"

"You were saying you wanted to be like your father."

"I don't at all. God rest his soul, it doesn't matter now anyhow, for he's long gone. One night he was sitting on the edge of the bed staring at my mother. She was pleading with him to eat something, and suddenly he just lay back and was dead of a heart attack. A bit of vomit and he was gone from this world. I watched him go. When I realized he wasn't just passed out as usual, I was terrified. Bang, so quickly. My mother told everyone at the funeral that she had warned him many times about his heart. She had, too, I grant her that, and she had warned him about his liver and his spleen and every other vital organ. Doctor, will you let me out of this agreement? I simply cannot face that shower again tomorrow."

"No, I won't."

"You're a devil, not a man. You were right about my mother. I wrote to her, as you said. She sent back a letter, which I thought of bringing to show you and did not. She said she was delighted that I was getting my promotion, and the bishop would help me if I should begin to fail in my duties. She said she hoped I wouldn't drink too much and I would keep my health because it would be such a mark against me if the Church placed such a great trust in my hands and I failed. Tomorrow I'll get a box of cookies. Sometimes she treats me like I'm away at Boy Scout camp and not a man at all. When I was nineteen years old, she was telling me I was too young to go out with girls. Sometimes I wonder if she didn't encourage me to go into the priesthood so that she'd never lose me to another woman. That's a silly thought, I know, for she's a terribly devout woman. Well, doctor, this is a terrible thing happening to me, whatever it is. I cannot concentrate on my work. I cannot eat. I cannot sleep, and I simply cannot face that shower again tomorrow. Have you nothing to say to me?"

"I think you're doing fine," Ian said. "This kind of reaction is part of the consequence of going through a change."

"I'm glad you take it so calmly. A little sympathy would help."

"You don't need sympathy."

"Suppose I should go out of my mind?"

"I'll visit you at the mental hospital."

"That's kind of you. Will you cure me, too?"

"I don't think I'd need to. You'd cure yourself after a while, and you'd still have to take a promotion in a new parish."

"It's a heavy responsibility. Oh, I've known some priests who bordered on being idiots who had greater positions, but still it's a burden. My mother might be right, perhaps I'm not up to it. Sometimes I think I became a priest so that never, never again in my life would I have to take orders from a woman. Of course that's not so, but it's one of the merits of this life. Can we make it only two showers tomorrow?"

"No."

"Yesterday I hardly got out of the shower the entire day. I kept getting back in and back in all day. The day before was the same, I almost became waterlogged."

"And today?"

"Oh, today only the first shower was a problem, the others went more easily than I expected." The priest looked at him defiantly. "But that doesn't mean there won't be a doubt there again tomorrow."

"That's true," said Ian, "and you know what you must do if the doubt is there again."

When the bishop sat down to lunch with Ian, he put out his long, thin hand and said, "I'd like to congratulate you."

Ian took the hand, finding it cold. He could see that the bishop was genuinely pleased, yet behind the man's eyes there seemed to be a faint expression of resentment. "He's on his way?" asked Ian.

"Exactly thirty days after he came to see you. He's even confident he can do well in his new position."

"Let's hope so," said Ian.

"I don't believe I've seen a man so quickly transformed. What did you do in those few sessions?"

"He didn't tell you?" asked Ian. "I gave him permission to talk about it if he wished."

"He wouldn't say."

"Well, then, it's his secret," said Ian, wishing he could talk to the bishop about it. "Let's just say he found a way to deal with the problem if it should bother him again."

The bishop smiled. "All he would tell me is that I'd put him in the hands of the devil." Watching Ian sip his wine, he added, "You puzzle me, Dr. Wharf."

"I'm complimented," said Ian. "I'm sure with your experience not many men do."

"I've known a few psychiatrists, and you aren't like them. You seem more like a surgeon than a psychiatrist."

"I'm not sure that's a compliment."

"I'm not, either," said the bishop, smiling. "But I'm grateful to you. This was a difficult problem, and I simply didn't know what to do about it." He watched Ian's right eye drift up toward the ceiling. Then the bishop looked carefully down at his hands. "I've heard rumors that—well, it's not really my business, but I've heard that certain of your colleagues have considered your methods of treatment a bit unorthodox."

"Oh?" said Ian.

"I only mention this because—if an issue should come up and you need some sort of testimonial, I hope you'll feel free to call on me." He looked quickly up at Ian's face. "I hope I haven't offended you by saying this?"

"Not at all," said Ian, surprised at the twist of uneasiness he felt inside himself. "I'm sure nothing like that will be necessary."

"I'm sure it won't," the bishop said, a faint expression of triumph replacing the resentment behind his eyes. "Do you like the wine?" he asked, and from then on the two men could enjoy each other.

4

The Art of Being a Failure as a Therapist

INTRODUCTION

Len Sperry, MD, PhD

Then and Now

Some 40 years have passed since the publication of Jay Haley's (1969a) classic article "The Art of Being a Failure as a Therapist." It is simple and straightforward, but first and foremost it is hilarious. In it, Haley observes, "Too much emphasis has been placed upon how to succeed as a therapist, and too little has been written about how to fail." Haley responds, tongue-in-cheek, by providing a list of 12+ steps or guaranteed ways of failing if consistently applied. This chapter briefly describes these steps and comments on their applicability today. Revisiting this thoughtful and provocative commentary offers contemporary therapists a chance to compare Haley's rather provocative view of the therapeutic landscape 40 years ago with today.

Context of "Failure as a Therapist"

Haley's article is best understood in the context of his book *The Power Tactics of Jesus Christ and Other Essays* (1969b), in which the article is reprinted. "Failure" is best appreciated as an extension of the first essay in the book, "The Art of Being a Psychoanalyst." In the latter, Haley portrayed classical psychoanalysis as a power struggle in which patient and analyst mutually distrust and reciprocally deceive each other. It is a relationship in which the analyst is villainous and the patient skillfully brings out his or her worst. Needless to say, analysts were not amused with Haley's unflattering caricature of psychoanalytic practice (Fraser, 1971).

Haley begins "Failure" by noting that just being on a wait list for psychotherapy resulted in success rates of 50% or better. This phenomenon, called *spontaneous improvement* or *spontaneous remission*, had perplexed psychotherapists and researchers since 1952, when Hans Eysenck gained worldwide attention by proclaiming that the effect of psychotherapy was no greater than that of spontaneous remission. Eysenck insisted that 50% to 70% of clients on waiting lists often improved or recovered from the problems for which they had sought treatment. Based on these findings, he concluded that psychotherapy was not effective. Because a client could get better with or without psychotherapy, Haley rhetorically questioned how any therapist could possibly fail. He "answered" with his now famous 12+ steps for failure.

Unfortunately, a reanalysis of Eysenck's original data does not support his conclusion. Utilizing much more sophisticated statistical tests than were available in the 1950s, researchers found that 50% of psychotherapy patients were estimated to have improved after 8 weeks, whereas only 2% of untreated, wait-listed individuals were estimated to have improved. In short, although spontaneous remission does occur, its effects were found to be considerably smaller than the effects of psychotherapy (McNeilly & Howard, 1991). Spontaneous improvement aside, Haley's article still remains an important historical critique of psychotherapy.

Guidelines to Guarantee Failure as a Therapist

Although classical psychoanalysis was the dominant force on the therapeutic landscape when Haley penned his essays in the late 1960s, it has slowly lost ground to more modern psychoanalytic approaches as well as a wide variety of new forms of psychotherapy, such as cognitive-behavioral therapy (CBT). Nevertheless, classical psychoanalysis was a major target for Haley's arrows. Each of the 12 steps—actually, 14 "arrows"—is first reviewed, reflecting Haley's appraisal of the field (particularly psychoanalysis) in the 1960s, followed by a commentary on what changes, if any, have occurred since then.

Step 1a: Dismiss the presenting problem as unimportant. Haley begins by suggesting that in order to fail as a therapist, one should "insist that the problem which brings the patient into therapy is not important." He suggests that one "dismiss it as merely a symptom and shift the conversation elsewhere." This maneuver allows the therapist to avoid learning the true nature of the patient's distress. In contrast to psychoanalysis, most contemporary psychotherapies today are decidedly problem focused. Largely because of managed care's insistence on accountability and evidence-based practice, therapy is reimbursed based on treatment of presenting problems.

Step 1b: Refuse to directly treat the presenting problem. Haley suggests that the therapist offer some rationale—for example, that the symptoms have "roots"—to avoid treating the patient's presenting problem. As noted above, third-party payment is based on treatment focused on the presenting problem. Implied in Haley's articulation of this step is that the therapeutic relationship or alliance was neither mutual nor respectful, but was basically a power struggle. The implication is that therapists "ran the show," or believed they did, and that the patient's expectations and point of view were unimportant and not incorporated in the treatment process. Probably the most significant research finding in the past 40 years is that the quality of the therapeutic alliance actually predicts the treatment process and outcomes (Horvath & Symonds, 1991). In other words, a successful relationship means a successful therapy outcome.

Step 1c: Insist that there will be symptom substitution if the presenting problem is resolved. If there is some resistance, one can explain to the patient that "if a presenting problem is relieved, something worse will develop. This myth ... will even encourage patients to cooperate by developing a fear of recovery." With regard to the notion of symptom substitution, there is virtually no evidence for this Freudian concept, and it should be abandoned (Tyron, 2008).

Step 2: Confuse diagnosis and therapy. Haley had no use for labels like *passive-aggressive* or *impulse-ridden* because nothing therapeutic could be derived from such language. Instead, Haley objected to diagnosis and decried how the DSM (see, e.g., American Psychological Association, 2000) was influencing the practice of therapy. Rather than identifying their pathology, Haley would highlight patients' strengths, much as positive psychology emphasizes today.

Step 3: Put the emphasis on a single approach, no matter how diverse the problem. Haley states, "Patients who won't behave properly according to the method should be defined as untreatable and abandoned." This reminds me of Abraham Maslow's aphorism that "if your only tool is a hammer, every problem will look like a nail." Today, contemporary therapists of all theoretical orientations have and utilize many therapeutic interventions, even those that might appear alien. That psychoanalytically oriented therapists, like Jeffrey Binder (2004), have admitted to using skill training and related behavioral therapy methods would not have been considered acceptable for a psychoanalyst at the time Haley was penning this step.

Step 4: Have no theory of therapeutic change. Haley says that one should insist "that change be defined as a shift of something in the interior of a patient so that it remains outside the range of observation and so is uninvestigable." This remark about the interiority versus exteriority is classic "tongue-in-cheek" Haley. Clearly, Haley favored observable change, which was central to his own strategic therapy, as it is with many current theories of change.

Step 5: Insist that only long-term treatments work. Another way to fail as a therapist, Haley notes, is to insist that only years of therapy can change the patient: "Fortunately the field of therapy has no theory of over-dosage, and so a skilful therapist can keep a patient from improving for as long as 10 years." Haley insisted that no one should "overdose" on therapy, and now both patients and researchers agree. Today, therapy is primarily short-term treatment, not because therapists want it to be, but because most patients seem to achieve the outcomes they want in relatively few sessions. Researchers are now studying minimum "therapeutic dosage" and find that within eight sessions approximately 50% of patients are measurably improved (Howard, Kopta, Krause, & Orlinsky, 1986). It is particularly noteworthy that in later years, Haley favored "rapid recoveries" and "single-session therapies." In other words, truly effective therapy can be so potent that improvement could come in fewer than eight sessions.

Step 6: Insist that patients will decompensate if they improve. Haley says, "As a further step to restrain patients who might spontaneously improve, it is important to offer dire warnings about the fragile nature of people and insist that they might suffer psychotic breaks or turn to drink if they improve." He adds, "If patients seem to improve even in long-term therapy, they can be distracted by being put into group therapy." The implication is that group therapy is less effective than individual therapy. Although it may not have been considered effective then, today group therapy is considered as effective as, or more effective than, individual therapy (McRoberts, Burlingame, & Hoag, 1998).

Step 7: Focus only on the past. Haley suggests trying to approach patients' behavioral problems in the same unsuccessful way and with the same limited understanding that family members and previous therapists have used. Again, the psychoanalytic method's focus on the early life experiences as a way to deal with behavioral problems is criticized. On the other hand, back then, behavioral therapy and structural family therapy—which Haley helped develop when he worked with Salvador Minuchin—were quite effective in dealing with behavioral problems. It is interesting to note how much things have changed today, in that even some psychoanalytic therapies focus largely on the present and utilize behavior change methods (Binder, 2004).

Step 8: Interpret everything as guilt so patient remains to resolve guilt. Haley does not elaborate on this failure strategy. Today, even though the terms *embarrassment*, *guilt*, *humiliation*, and *shame* are used interchangeably, most researchers and clinicians consider these four terms as separate, distinct experiences. The most commonly made distinction is between guilt and feelings of shame.

Step 9: Attend only to early experiences, inner dynamics, and fantasy. Haley insists on the importance of ignoring "the real world that patients live in," and instead emphasizes the importance of their infancy, inner dynamics, and fantasy life to fail. Whereas more classically oriented analysts may focus primarily on early experiences and inner dynamics, most therapists, including those practicing brief dynamic psychotherapies, focus on interpersonal concerns in the present (Binder, 2004).

Step 10: Avoid the poor and the schizophrenic. Haley advises, "Avoid the poor because they will insist upon results and cannot be distracted with insightful conversations." Another of Haley's "laugh out loud" statements, this one lampoon's insight as being a "poor" substitute for observable clinical change. Similarly, in the 1960s providing only psychoanalysis to those with schizophrenia without medication would all but guarantee therapeutic failure.

Step 11: Refuse to define the goals of therapy. Haley advises, "If a therapist sets goals, someone is likely to raise a question whether they have been achieved." Then, as today, the question of whether goals have been achieved is poignant, although perhaps more poignant today. What is probably quite different is that today, there is unlikely to be an *if.* Today, it is expected that therapists will set goals, particularly if they expect third-party payment because insurance companies and HMOs are insistent upon goals.

Step 12: Avoid evaluating the results of therapy. Haley contends, "Only by keeping results a mystery and avoiding any systematic follow-up of patients can one ensure that therapeutic techniques will not be improved and the writings of the past will not be questioned." Today, the technology to quickly and inexpensively formally assess treatment outcomes and monitor treatment over time is available. The problem today is that not all therapists utilize this formal assessment technology. On the other hand, it is commonplace for therapists to informally review progress made, if only at the time of termination.

Concluding Note

So what might we conclude from this review of Haley's guidelines for therapist failure? First and foremost, we could conclude that the state of psychotherapy in the 1960s was quite different from what it is today. Whereas there were really only four approaches then—classical psychoanalysis, behavior therapy, Adlerian therapy, and Rogerian therapy—today there are 400 or more approaches. It was during the late 1960s and early 1970s that an explosion occurred and many therapy approaches appeared on the scene, including MRI brief therapy, structural family therapy, and strategic therapy, for all of which Jay Haley did, in fact, exert some or much influence in their development. Second, based on my experience as a doctoral student at the time this article was published and having Ken Howard, PhD, the father of psychotherapy outcome research, as one of my mentors, I would agree that Haley's observations were largely accurate, particularly with regard to classical psychoanalysis. Third, the impact of managed care, significant strides in psychotherapy research and funding for it, and the requirement of DSM diagnoses have greatly influenced psychotherapy's shift away from the way it was practiced then, to how it is practiced today. Fourth, it is much harder for a therapist to be a failure today. This may be, in large part, because so many of Haley's ideas about the practice of therapy have become mainstream. Instead, therapist failure today is more likely to be due to impairment or because of alcohol and drug abuse than because of questionable therapeutic technique or method, as Haley portrayed. Fifth, we might conclude that Jay Haley possessed a piercing insight into the therapeutic landscape of that time, and his critique serves as a summary judgment, albeit an irreverent one, of that era.

References

American Psychiatric Association. (2000). *Diagnostic and statistical manual of mental disorders* (4th ed., text rev.). Washington, DC: Author.

Binder, J. (2004). *Key competencies in brief dynamics psychotherapy*. New York: Guilford.

Fraser, A. W. (1971). Book review: The Power Tactics of Jesus Christ and Other Essays. *Psychoanalytic Quarterly*, *40*, 524–527.

Haley, J. (1969a). The art of being a failure as a therapist. *American Journal of Orthopsychiatry*, *39*, 691–695. (Reprinted in Haley, J. [1969]. The art of being a failure as a therapist. In J. Haley, *The power tactics of Jesus Christ and other essays* [pp 71–78]. New York: Avon Books).

Haley, J. (1969b). *The power tactics of Jesus Christ and other essays*. New York: Avon Books.

Horvath, A. O., & Symonds, B. D. (1991). Relation between working alliance and outcome in psychotherapy: a meta-analysis. *Journal of Counseling Psychology*, *38*, 139–149.

Howard, K., Kopta, M., Krause, M., & Orlinsky, D. (1986). The dose-effect relationship in psychotherapy. *American-Psychologist*, *41*(2), 159–164.

McNeilly, C., & Howard, K. (1991). The effects of psychotherapy: A reevaluation based on dosage. *Psychotherapy Research*, *1*(1), 174–178.

McRoberts, C., Burlingame, G. M., & Hoag, M. J. (1998). Comparative efficacy of individual and group psychotherapy: A meta-analytic perspective. *Group Dynamics*, *2*(2), 101–117.

Tyron, W. (2008). Whatever happened to symptom substitution? *Clinical Psychology Review*, *28*(6), 963–968.

THE ART OF BEING A FAILURE AS A THERAPIST

Jay Haley
Director, Family Research, Philadelphia Child Guidance Clinic, Philadelphia, Pennsylvania

Too much emphasis has been placed upon how to be successful as a therapist and too little has been written about how to fail. Twelve steps for failing in psychotherapy are described within the proper ideological framework, and it is argued that any therapist can achieve this end with proper training.

What has been lacking in the field of therapy is a theory of failure. Many clinicians have merely assumed that any psychotherapist could fail if he wished. Recent studies of the outcome of therapy, however, indicate that spontaneous improvement of patients is far more extensive than was previously realized. There is a consistent finding that between 50 and 70% of patients on waiting list control groups not only do not wish treatment after the waiting list period but have really recovered from their emotional problems—despite the previous theories which did not consider this possible. Assuming that these findings hold up in further studies, a therapist who is incompetent and does no more than sit in silence and scratch himself will have at least a 50% success rate with his patients. How then can a therapist be a failure? The problem is not a hopeless one. We might merely accept the fact that a therapist will succeed with half his patients and do what we can to provide a theory which will help him fail consistently with the other half. However, we could also risk being more adventurous. Trends in the field suggest the problem can be approached in a deeper way by devising procedures for keeping those patients from improving who would ordinarily spontaneously do so. Obviously, merely doing nothing will not achieve this end. We must create a program with the proper ideological framework and provide systematic training over a period of years if we expect a therapist to fail consistently.

An outline will be offered here of a series of steps to increase the chance of failure of any therapist. This presentation is not meant to be comprehensive, but it includes the major factors which experience in the field has shown to be essential and which can be put into practice even by therapists who are not specially talented.

1. The central pathway to failure is based upon a nucleus of ideas which, if used in combination, make success as a failure almost inevitable.

   Step A: Insist that the problem which brings the patient into therapy is not important. Dismiss it as merely a "symptom" and shift the conversation elsewhere. In this way a therapist never learns to examine what is really distressing a patient.

   Step B: Refuse to directly treat the presenting problem. Offer some rationale, such as the idea that symptoms have "roots," to avoid treating the problem the patient is paying his money to recover from. In this way the odds increase that the patient will not recover, and future generations of therapists can remain ignorant of the specific skills needed to get people over their problems.

   Step C: Insist that if a presenting problem is relieved, something worse will develop. This myth makes it proper not to know what to do about symptoms and will even encourage patients to cooperate by developing a fear of recovery.

Given these three steps, it seems obvious that any psychotherapist will be incapacitated, whatever his natural talent. He will not take seriously the problem the patient brings, he will not try to change that, and he will fear that successful relief of the problem is disastrous.

One might think that this nucleus of ideas alone would make any therapist a failure, but the wiser heads in the field have recognized that other steps are necessary.

2. It is particularly important to confuse diagnosis and therapy. A therapist can sound expert and be scientific without ever risking a success with treatment if he uses a diagnostic language which makes it impossible for him to think of therapeutic operations. For example, one can say that a patient is passive-aggressive, or that he has deep-seated dependency needs, or that he has a weak ego, or that he is impulse-ridden. No therapeutic interventions can be formulated with this kind of language. For more examples of how to phrase a diagnosis so that a therapist is incapacitated, the reader is referred to *The American Psychiatric Association Diagnostic Manual.*
3. Put the emphasis upon a single method of treatment no matter how diverse the problems which enter the office. Patients who won't behave properly according to the method should be defined as untreatable and abandoned. Once a single method has proven consistently ineffective, it should never be given up. Those people who attempt variations must be sharply condemned as improperly trained and ignorant of the true nature of the human personality and its disorders. If necessary, a person who attempts variations can be called a latent layman.
4. Have no theory, or an ambiguous and untestable one, of what a therapist should do to bring about therapeutic change. However, make it clear that it is untherapeutic to give a patient directives for changing—he might follow them and change. Just imply that change happens spontaneously when therapists and patients behave according to the proper forms. As part of the general confusion that is necessary, it is helpful to

define therapy as a procedure for finding out what is wrong with a person and how he got that way. With that emphasis, ideas about what to do to bring about change will not develop in an unpredictable manner. One should also insist that change be defined as a shift of something in the interior of a patient so that it remains outside the range of observation and is uninvestigable. With the focus upon the "underlying disorder" (which should be sharply distinguished from the "overlying disorder"), questions about the unsavory aspects of the relationship between therapist and patient need not arise, nor is it necessary to include unimportant people, such as the patient's intimates, in the question of change.

Should student therapists who are not yet properly trained insist upon some instruction about how to cause change, and if a frown about their unresolved problems does not quiet them, it might be necessary to offer some sort of ambiguous and general idea which is untestable. One can say, for example, that the therapeutic job is to bring the unconscious into consciousness. In this way the therapy task is defined as transforming a hypothetical entity into another hypothetical entity and so there is no possibility that precision in therapeutic technique might develop. Part of this approach requires helping the patient "see" things about himself, particularly in relation to past traumas, and this involves no risk of change. The fundamental rule is to emphasize "insight" and "affect expression" to student therapists as causes of change so they can feel something is happening in the session without hazarding success. If some of the advanced students insist on more high-class technical knowledge about therapy, a cloudy discussion of "working through the transference" is useful. This not only provides young therapists with an intellectual catharsis but it gives them a chance to make transference interpretations and so have something to do.

5. Insist that only years of therapy will really change a patient.

   This step brings us to more specific things to do about those patients who might spontaneously recover without treatment. If they can be persuaded that they have not really recovered but have merely fled into health, it is possible to help them back to ill health by holding them in long-term treatment. (One can always claim that only long-term treatment can really cure a patient so that he will never ever have a problem the remainder of his life.). Fortunately the field of therapy has no theory of overdosage, and so a skilful therapist can keep a patient from improving for as long as 10 years without protest from his colleagues, no matter how jealous. Those therapists who try for 20 years should be congratulated on their courage but thought of as foolhardy unless they live in New York.
6. As a further step to restrain patients who might spontaneously improve, it is important to offer warnings about the fragile nature of people and insist they might suffer psychotic breaks or turn to drink if they improve. When "underlying pathology" becomes the most common term in every clinic and consulting room, everyone will avoid taking action to help patients recover and patients will even restrain themselves if they begin to make it on their own. Long-term treatment can then crystallize them into therapeutic failures. If patients seem to improve even in long-term therapy, they can be distracted by being put into group therapy.
7. As a further step to restrain patients who might spontaneously improve, the therapist should focus upon the patient's past.
8. As yet another step with that aim, the therapist should interpret what is most unsavory about the patient to

arouse his guilt so that he will remain in treatment to resolve the guilt.

9. Perhaps the most important rule is to ignore the real world that patients live in and publicize the vital importance of their infancy, inner dynamics, and fantasy life. This will effectively prevent either therapists or patients from attempting to make changes in their families, friends, schools, neighborhoods, or treatment milieus. Naturally they cannot recover if their situation does not change, and so one guarantees failure while being paid to listen to interesting fantasies. Talking about dreams is a good way to pass the time, and so is experimenting with responses to different kinds of pills.
10. Avoid the poor because they will insist upon results and cannot be distracted with insightful conversations. Also avoid the schizophrenic unless he is well drugged and securely locked up in a psychiatric penitentiary. If a therapist deals with a schizophrenic at the interface of family and society, both therapist and patient risk recovery.
11. A continuing refusal to define the goals of therapy is essential. If a therapist sets goals, someone is likely to raise a question about whether they have been achieved. At that point the idea of evaluating results arises in its most virulent form. If it becomes necessary to define a goal, the phrasing should be unclear, ambiguous, and so esoteric that anyone who thinks about determining if the goal has been achieved will lose heart and turn to a less confused field of endeavor, like existentialism.
12. Finally, it cannot be emphasized enough that it is absolutely necessary to avoid evaluating the results of therapy. If outcome is examined, there is a natural tendency for people not fully trained to discard approaches which are not effective and to elaborate those which are. Only by keeping results a mystery and avoiding any systematic follow-up of patients can

> one ensure that therapeutic technique will not improve and the writings of the past will not be questioned. To be human is to err, and inevitably a few deviant individuals in the profession will attempt evaluation studies. They should be promptly condemned and their character questioned. Such people should be called superficial in their understanding of what therapy really is, oversimple in their emphasis upon symptoms rather than depth personality problems, and artificial in their approach to human life. Routinely they should be eliminated from respectable institutions and cut off from research funds. As a last resort they can be put in psychoanalytic treatment or shot.

This program of 12 steps to failure—sometimes called the daily dozen of the clinical field—is obviously not beyond the skill of the average well-trained psychotherapists. Nor would putting this program more fully into action require any major changes in the clinical ideology or practice taught in our better universities. The program would be helped if there was a positive term to describe it, and the word "dynamic" is recommended because it has a swinging sound which should appeal to the younger generation. The program could be called the therapy which expresses the basic principles of dynamic, psychiatry, dynamic psychology, and dynamic social work. On the wall of every institute training therapists, there can be a motto known as *The Five B's Which Guarantee Dynamic Failure*:

Be Passive
Be Inactive
Be Reflective
Be Silent
Beware

Endnotes

Amer. J. Orthopsychiat. 39(4), July 1969.
Submitted to the Journal *in February 1969.*
Author's address: Jay Haley, Philadelphia Child Guidance Clinic, 1700 Bainbridge Street, Philadelphia, Pa, 19146.

5

How to Have an Awful Marriage

INTRODUCTION

Michele Weiner-Davis, MSW

When I was asked to write an introduction for *Jay Haley Revisited*, I was honored. I have always greatly admired Jay Haley and his contribution to the field. As I began to think about Haley's work, I couldn't help but take a trip down memory lane and reflect on the profound influence Haley truly had on my thinking and my work. Before I comment on the essay you are about to read, I feel the urge to share a personal experience with you.

It was the late 1970s. I had recently graduated from graduate school. Although I enjoyed being a graduate student, I felt vastly ill prepared for the job ahead of me—working with adolescents and their families. There were all sorts of interesting theories rolling around in my head, but I was clueless as to how to help people change. Unfortunately, my graduate program, although endlessly interesting, didn't offer the concrete clinical skills required of therapists working with challenging families. Sometimes, when I think about my graduate program, I jokingly refer to Robert Fulghum's book *All I Really Need to Know I Learned in Kindergarten*, but with a twist. Everything I need to forget, I learned in graduate school.

So, being the conscientious rookie therapist that I was, I hired a consultant who, after working with me for a while, insisted that I read *Uncommon Therapy*, Haley's wonderful book written in 1973 in which he deciphered Milton Erickson's thinking in simple enough terms that even a fledgling therapist like me could understand. I instantly became hooked. This led me to training and later working with the late Steve de Shazer, whose work inspired the underpinnings of my Divorce Busting approach with couples.

Considerably later in my career, like many other therapists, I read *Leaving Home* (Haley, 1996). This book greatly shaped my understanding of the seemingly uncanny coincidence of adolescents often faltering just as they are about to transition into the real world and leave their parents and families behind. Haley's profound insight into the cultural and familial forces at work when it comes to "individual psychopathology" was enlightening. As tempting as it might have been to blame rebellious or dysfunctional adolescent behavior on the kids or their seemingly incompetent parents, Haley reminded us to broaden our microscopes and learn about the unique stressors that occur as people and families pass through each of life's developmental stages. My strategies for helping parents discover loving yet firm ways to help shepherd their adolescents into adulthood were undoubtedly shaped by this book.

The Developmental Stages of Marriage

Similarly, in the following essay, "How to Have an Awful Marriage," Haley reminds us of the importance of seeing marriage as a living, breathing organism that, like a child or family, goes through predictable developmental stages, and he reminds us that each stage offers new challenges or, in the spirit of this chapter, "opportunities" for relationship breakdown. In essence, Haley is telling us that we might not be as unique as we think. Premarital couples often have (or create) premarital problems. Midlife couples argue about issues revolving around midlife issues. As a veteran married person, it is difficult, if not impossible, to smile with recognition when reading Haley's *War of the Roses*–type (DeVito, 1989) characterizations of couples who quarrel. Haley's insight into the unfolding dance of partnership as it is transformed by betrothal, in-laws, dwindling infatuation, the birth of children, ebbs and flows in sexual desire, the dogged pursuit of careers, aging, illness, and ultimately death is profound.

In the last decade or so, there has been an explosion in the field called *marriage education*. Marriage education is not therapy. Marriage educators believe that people aren't born with relationship skills and that the way people learn about communication and other relationship skills is by observing their own parents, many of whom weren't the best role models. Additionally, due to rapidly changing roles in our society, what worked for one generation doesn't necessarily work for another. Fortunately, we now have a great deal of solid information about the skills couples need to have successful relationships. A great deal of research has been done on what makes marriages succeed and what makes them fail (Gottman, 1995). And now couples wanting to have healthy marriages can take classes and learn skills and strategies stemming from this research. Falling out of love doesn't just happen. A loveless marriage is a skill-less marriage.

Starting Badly

Marriage educators would undoubtedly agree with Haley's take on the stressors experienced by couples as they navigate the different stages of marriage. And because Haley begins his misery formula by suggesting that the best way to have a bad marriage is to start badly—by choosing the wrong mate or marriage for the wrong reasons—he probably would have lauded the many premarital programs offered these days that help dating or cohabitating couples to make conscious decisions about their future mates based on compatibility rather than on lust, infatuation, or some other random reason. (Van Epp, 2008)

Sex and Conflict

Haley writes, "There are two basic areas which can be exploited to the fullest in any marriage: how to make love and how to fight." That's why I feel certain that he would have been pleased with the increased awareness of the importance of a satisfying sexual relationship in marriage and the plethora of books and classes currently available nationwide to assist couples in bringing back passion and intimacy in the bedroom (Love & Robinson, 1995; McCarthy, 2003; Weiner-Davis, 1992, 2002). And because he understood how incessant and ineffective quarreling can destroy any marriage, he would have supported the growing number of marriage seminars that are devoted to helping couples learn how to manage conflict successfully by "fighting fairly" and seeking to understand rather than simply be understood (Hendrix & Hunt, 1990; Markman, 1994).

And Baby Makes Three

Haley also understood several other potential minefields in marriage, including the dangers of couples neglecting their relationship and becoming too child-centric when children are born and as they are being raised. It is now well understood that the best thing a couple can do for their children is to put their marriage first. If they don't, when children leave home, couples will find themselves completely estranged. In fact, the only group of couples whose divorce rate is still on the increase is the "empty nesters." I feel certain that neglecting to invest fully in marriage during child-rearing years with the idea that "we'll have time when the kids are gone" is one of the primary causes for this increase in the divorce rate in this group.

Despite the benefits of marital research at the time of the writing of this book, there are several other prescriptions for creating misery that Haley describes that are dead-on.

Sulking, Silences, and Stonewalling

For example, we now know that one predictable trouble spot in relationships is the tendency in some to withdraw or shut down communication during an argument, a behavior that is referred to as "stonewalling" (Gottman, 1995). So acrimonious is this strategy that, if continued over time, divorce is almost inevitable. That's why Haley is really on to something when he writes that "sulks and silences and withdrawals" will guarantee that nothing ever gets resolved and that quarrels will continue throughout the course of one's marriage. My own work with couples substantiates this prediction completely.

Infidelity

No road map for creating marital misery would be complete without the mention of extramarital affairs. As someone who works with 11th-hour couples day in and day out, I can attest to the fact that one of the best ways to ensure marital distress is for a spouse to be unfaithful. It pretty much works every time. And even with the best of intentions, the impact of betrayal can rear its ugly head for years on end. Haley understood this. Thankfully, both therapists and marriage educators are speaking out publicly about the devastation of infidelity and offering couples concrete tools for healing from it.

Read This Chapter and Call Me in the Morning

When I reflected on this chapter, I couldn't help but think how helpful it might be to have all of the couples in my practice read it in the beginning of our work together. I could insist that people don't really change until they hit rock bottom and if they follow Haley's instructions to a tee, they will bottom out as quickly as possible and we could begin our work in earnest. And in the midst of this musing, I realized that I was dreaming up a "Haley-like" symptom prescription and couldn't help but think that he might have chuckled at the idea.

References

DeVito, D. (Dir.). (1989). *War of the Roses* [motion picture]. Culver City, CA: Gracie Films.

Fulghum, R. (1990). *All I really need to know I learned in kindergarten*. New York: Villard.

Gottman, J. (1995). *Why marriages succeed or fail: And how you can make yours last*. New York: Simon & Schuster.

Haley, J. (1973). *Uncommon therapy: The psychiatric techniques of Milton H. Erickson, M.D.* New York: Norton.

Haley, J. (1996). *Leaving home: The therapy of disturbed young people* (2nd ed.). New York: Brunner-Routledge.

Hendrix, H., & Hunt, H. (1990). *Getting the love you want*. New York: Harper & Row.

Love, P., & Robinson, J. (1995). *Hot monogamy*. New York: Plume.

Markman, H. (1994). *Fighting for your marriage*. San Francisco: Jossey-Bass.

McCarthy, B. (2003). *Rekindling Desire*. New York: Brenner-Routledge.

Van Epp, J. (2008). *How to avoid marrying a jerk*. New York: McGraw-Hill.

Weiner-Davis, M. (1992). *Divorce busting*. New York: Simon & Schuster.

Weiner-Davis, M. (2002). *The sex-starved marriage*. New York: Simon & Schuster.

HOW TO HAVE AN AWFUL MARRIAGE

Jay Haley

Everywhere there are articles, books, and professional therapists offering advice on how to improve and save marriages. What is missing is a guide on how to make a marriage miserable. Granting that some people enjoy marriage, what of the vast numbers of marital couples who seek an unhappy marriage, as they must or they would not quarrel so much and give so little pleasure to each other. Determined to be miserable, these people have nowhere to turn for advice. Often they divorce and marry again and again. Each marriage is a search to find one more awful than the last, when if they had stayed with the first spouse and had a little instruction they could have found sufficient misery there.

Despite all the literature on how to have a happy marriage, only recently has anything been written on how to have one that is unhappy. Fortunately an anonymous author has just completed an in-depth study on how to produce marital misery, whether the marriage is heterosexual, homosexual, or mysterious. Now the primary text in the field, this scientific work is of encyclopedic size and called, *Achieving Misery in Two Group Dyads With Special Emphasis on Married Couples*. Unfortunately it is as tedious to read as it is to suffer the marriage failures it describes. For the interested public, a summary is offered here of the ways to achieve an awful marriage.

We can skip over the history of marriage in that opus and get right to the instructions on how to make marriage miserable. The history only emphasizes that marriage is of such a nature that an outside force has always been necessary to force married couples to stay together. First the church made harsh laws against separation and divorce, and later the state took over the job of making divorce difficult. Now, with the abdication of the church and the freedom given by the state, anyone can divorce at will. The expanding divorce rate is the inevitable result. If one sets out to have a miserable marriage now, there is a risk of separation which did not exist in the past. The ease of divorce has led to a change in the basic marital threat. The spouse who can threaten to leave the other has the most power in a marriage because the other will capitulate in fear of separation. However, now with separation so easily possible, that threat to flee the marriage has become a risky one. Spouses must go after each other with the knowledge that a divorce is easily available. If they miscalculate and escalate quarrels, they risk the possibility that they could separate and the next marriage might be enjoyable.

It is said that anyone can have a happy marriage but people must make their own marital disharmony. That is not quite true. Many people lack the skills to make a marriage awful, and they don't understand the natural development of marriage well enough to take advantage of it. Opportunities for marital misery will be presented here in terms of developmental stages: how to begin a marriage badly, how to make a marriage worse in the early years, what to quarrel about when the children are no longer available, and how to increase marital distress in old age even when strength is failing.

Planning an Unhappy Marriage

One must work at marriage, as every authority agrees. Achieving misery requires conscientious effort. However, the task is surprisingly easy if one can begin badly. There are two general ways to start a marriage so that misery becomes inevitable: one is to marry for the wrong reasons, and the other is to marry the wrong person. Starting a marriage badly is like building a proper foundation for a house: unhappiness is built into the structure from the beginning.

The most popular wrong reason to get married is to flee into matrimony as a way of avoiding something else. A mate for a lifetime is chosen impulsively to get out of a bad situation.

There are many situations to escape from: one can marry to get out of poverty, to avoid going to school, to not have to work for a living, and so on. The most common wrong reason to marry is to escape from one's family. If parents are constantly nagging about keeping a room clean so that pestilence will not become a plague, or about coming home in time to get some sleep, or to give up excessive use of drink and dope, then obviously an escape from that repressive atmosphere is in order. If only one can find a young man, or a woman, to marry and share expenses, then freedom comes with one's own apartment. Fleeing home is estimated to be the reason for 81% of the marriages which are awful when spouses are under 21 years of age. "Free at last, free at last," cry the young people as they rush off to their own domiciles. From that point on they hope never to clean house, to stay out all night, to drink and use drugs until they fall down, and generally to enjoy liberation.

Unfortunately, when the only purpose of marriage is to get away from one's family, the marriage itself has no purpose. There is no basis for enjoying each other as a married couple when the selection was not made for that reason. Even someone limited in intelligence can achieve a miserable marriage in this way. Not having selected a mate for compatibility, in a matter of weeks the couple cannot stand each other. They begin to quarrel over who should keep the house clean, who did or did not come home at a reasonable hour, and the drink and dope bring forth meanness instead of joy. Once this situation is structured, very little effort is required by the young people to achieve marital misery. If particularly determined to enjoy distress, they can add pregnancy as a reason to marry and leave the family. Parents will even encourage marriage when they see a baby enlarging a daughter's figure. The addition of a baby to the young couple's sanctuary is like meringue on the pie: opportunities to be miserable increase. The baby can make a worse mess than the young couple alone, it can keep them up later than parties, and generally the child encourages a suppressed fury at being helplessly tied down by this creature they must care for. Endless quarrels are manufactured over whose turn it is to do what for the baby, who should deal with the community protective service agencies when they are accused of neglect, and whose fault it was they had the baby in the first place. Loud arguments about how great life would be if they had not been trapped will announce to the neighbors that here is a couple skillful at making each other miserable.

Choosing the Wrong Person

Almost equal to the opportunities which arise by marrying for the wrong reasons is choosing the wrong person to marry. How does one know how to choose a mate in order to have an awful marriage? The answer is simple; complex psychological tests for incompatibility are not required. It is also not necessary to make a gross error in choice, such as choosing a person of the wrong race, or wrong religion, or wrong class, although such choices lay the groundwork for inevitable trouble and so have their merits. Basically the selection of a person to marry must be based upon two criteria: he or she must have attractive faults different from one's own, and there must be a determination to reform that person and get rid of those faults. Examples can be found just by glancing in your neighborhood in any direction. The classical pair, which is often used as a model in premarital misery counseling, consists of the overly responsible woman who is attracted to a man whose faults are that he is too irresponsible and carefree. She admires his self-confidence, his willingness to lead the good life, and his entertaining ways. Her faults have always been that she is too shy and responsible and cannot let herself go. The man chooses her on the basis of the same criteria: and he hopes it will correct his tendency to be off the wall, since he wants to settle down. Once married, the couple should proceed at once to reform each other. She must insist he get a better job with longer hours, think about a less pleasant career, not drink so much, stop partying all the time, and save money. He can yell at her to stop counting every penny, enjoy an evening out occasionally, and not be so dreadfully dull. Although this arrangement seems simple, any couple—even one of limited imagination—can use it to make each other miserable for many, many years. Ingenuity is not required, only persistence.

The reverse gender arrangement is also classical in opportunities. The woman who is active and domineering in her career and social life is attracted to a mousy, quiet fellow whose faults are that he is too shy and lacks self-confidence. He, in turn, is attracted to her because she has all the spirit he lacks, and he hopes it will rub off on him. Once married, the two people immediately try to reform each other. It is evident that marital misery is easily achieved with that contract. She need only call him a wimp at regular intervals, while he subtly lets her down to get even with her. By behaving like a wimp, he implies she is an impossibly domineering woman. It is estimated by the eminent Dr. Schiff that at any moment during the day there are 111,200 couples in the offices of marriage counselors with a wife saying she wants the counselor to make her wimp of a husband into a romantic and interesting man to save their marriage.

Variations on this theme are as obvious as pigeons to birdwatchers, but one more common type can be specified. This type of pair is called the Engineer's Syndrome since it is commonly observed among couples where the husband is in the electronics industry. In this arrangement, a wife chooses a husband whose faults are opposite hers. He is logical, precise, rational, and quite unemotional (except in extreme circumstances when his computer breaks down. Then he might become so disconsolate he must be hospitalized). She is affectionate, emotional, capable of immediate crying spells, and she has a tendency to scream and yell during any discussion of a controversial issue, like the way she keeps house. She, of course, is chosen by the man because he seeks someone who can express an emotion to stimulate that tendency in himself. The outcome is inevitable: as the marital disagreements occur, the wife goes wild and yells. He withdraws, saying, "Why can't a woman be rational and reasonable?" With very little effort on the part of either one of them she can spend her life weeping while he is out working on his sports car, constantly improving something that can be improved.

These ways of beginning a marriage—marrying for the wrong reason and choosing the wrong person—are the most simple ways to ensure marital distress. If a couple has a better beginning, more ingenuity is required to make the marriage a misfortune.

Problems of Intimacy and Outimacy

There are two basic areas which can be exploited to the fullest in any marriage: how to make love and how to fight. The best beginning for sexual problems is in the early years of marriage; if well nurtured the problems can continue for many years to come (or years of not coming). The variations on this theme are many, and most couples are capable of all of them. Everyone has heard poor, uneducated people protesting, "Oh, if I only had the education that man has, I could make my wife as miserable as he makes his." That is naive. In the task of creating marital misery, everyone has a fair chance. There is no discrimination on the basis of race, class, or intelligence, as anyone can see simply by strolling about the city and overhearing the action in the houses in different kinds of neighborhoods. The only difference is that one can overhear the misery better in the poor neighborhoods because there are more people and the houses are more flimsy.

The sexual arena offers such opportunity for marital distress that often the marriage hardly begins before the partners decide it is better not to have sexual relations at all, at least with the spouse. The crucial factor for bringing about sexual problems is timing. Sexual arousal and release is a complex physiological and psychological process requiring such timing that interfering with it is not difficult. Generally the rule is to initiate sex at the wrong time, in the wrong place, with the wrong frequency, in the wrong way. The novice chooses one of these wrongs. The expert ensures success by managing to use all of them over the course of a marriage. A husband who is the model for us all will always want sex when his wife is not interested or is occupied with something else, he will want it on the living room rug at noon when the kids are coming home for lunch, he will want it every third hour through the night, and he will want it in a position where they can both watch television at the same time. Protests by the wife meet angry accusations that she is frigid. The wife who is an equal match for such a husband will offer equally powerful techniques. She can be totally indifferent, and she can also arouse him and immediately lose interest. At another time she can yell at him and demand more sex at once, protesting angrily if he has difficulty with immediate compliance. If accused of inconsistency, she can say it is before, after or during her period.

A basic rule for sexual problems used by many couples over the years is to not tell the spouse what one likes or does not like in sex, and then to blame the spouse for not being pleasing. A wife who can only achieve orgasm in a certain way should avoid telling her husband that, and throughout the marriage she can be frustrated and pretend orgasms. The husband who prefers to see his wife nude should politely turn out all the lights so as not to embarrass her. Variations on this simple theme of avoidance are obvious and range from avoiding discussions to avoiding each other. If one mate watches TV late and the other goes to bed early, which is the habitual pattern of most couples, each evening announces sexual avoidance.

Spouses are so vulnerable in relation to sex that bad feelings and quarrels can easily be generated. A combination of sexual frustration and righteous indignation is a winning duo. The righteous indignation is best produced by the couple protecting each other. If the husband is uncertain about his potency, the wife can insist she is unable to enjoy sex and so take the blame for sexual avoidance. Instead of appreciating her sacrifice, the husband will be angry at her for her sexual indifference and feel righteously indignant because he is a deprived husband. The reverse is equally powerful; the husband can protect the wife by approaching her sexually in ways she can rightfully protest. He can also wimpishly emphasize his own inadequacies so the fact that she is cool enough to refrigerate food does not have to be faced. One might think that protecting each other would risk the possibility of kindness and appreciation in return, but that is not the case, as every spouse knows. Like a cancer flourishing in a peach, the protection has a patronizing edge that ripens into successful mutual dissatisfaction.

Every survey shows that most couples achieve the most displeasure in the sexual area, and so techniques for achieving sexual dissatisfactions need not be dwelt on here. Every couple has its own favorite variations and innovations.

Quarrels

Besides problems of intimacy, the opposite problem of difficulties with outimacy is essential if a couple is to have an awful marriage. Fortunately couples have been helped to be experts at quarrels and fights because they were able to observe their parents over the years. However, each new generation likes to make its own contributions, and so much marital time is devoted to developing new innovations in that enterprise. A few standard procedures can be described to help the novice.

Quarrels are nature's way of keeping a marriage alive. Marital misery requires quarreling in such a way that nothing is changed and the quarreling must be repeated again and again. Should an issue be solved, a new issue must be found to quarrel about next time, and most couples do not have the energy or imagination to continually develop new issues. It is better to have a few unresolved problems and belabor those throughout the tedium of the marriage. The two ways to end quarrels so they will occur again and again are at opposite extremes: to withdraw and sulk, or to escalate to violence so the quarrel ends with shock and embarrassment but nothing is resolved.

Outimacy includes quarrels which range from violence through verbal abuse to sulks and silences and withdrawals. The withdrawal is the best way to end an argument so that nothing is changed. If the couple backs off into silence with each quarrel, awful issues can be nurtured and maintained for many years. Ending the withdrawal so that the couple can quarrel again is sometimes a problem. With extreme couples the sulking only ends when they are required to speak because a child breaks a leg, or an earthquake occurs. Many issues can remain unresolved for as long as 42% of their marriage. The record is held by the wife who objected to the way her husband said, "I do," at the wedding ceremony and did not speak to him again throughout the marriage.

Violence is the other extreme way that a couple can keep quarrels going without resolving anything. Sometimes it is thought that only some people can be violent, but that does not seem to be the fact. Even couples who are political pacifists and are kind to animals will hit each other. Of course hitting where it shows can attract attention from the community, so one should use restraint and calculation with violence. It is best to start small, as with a punch on the arm, and steadily increase the blows so that in a matter of months noses are being broken. As with any brutality, proceeding a step at a time is important: each level is explored until the couple is used to it. Then the next level of assault does not seem so large. The couple who has escalated in this way can be surprised when neighbors are shocked by blood and broken bones.

A case may help. Once upon a time there was a Ph.D. Biologist and his M.A. in Mathematics wife who got drunk and fought every Saturday night. Those who think that education might make people less violent should realize that it does not and in fact offers new ways that the proletariat does not have available. For example, such people are experienced as teachers, and this husband would teach boxing to his wife. "Here is a left hook," he would say, and hit her. "Here is a right cross." They could also use their knowledge of anatomy to hit each other where it would hurt most and show least. The wife once hit him in the kidneys with a toaster. Of course in this situation each blames the other for what happens. The wife said her husband was a wimp who turned into a monster with drink. He said she provoked him and was the "out of the blue" type because she claimed he always hit her "out of the blue." Once the husband reported that he decided to give up the addiction to hitting his wife. He vowed he would not be provoked to violence. That Saturday she said something insulting, and he told her he wanted to avoid a quarrel. He went into the other room. She followed him and continued to yell at him, according to his report. He withdrew into the hallway. She pursued him. He went into the bedroom and locked the door. She pounded on the door and yelled. Finally she broke the door down and cursed him. He hit her "out of the blue."

This couple was in therapy, and the therapist insisted that a man should not physically abuse his wife no matter what the provocation. Therefore, if it happened again the wife was to call the police. She did this and it ended the violence, but for an unexpected reason. The wife called the police to complain that her husband was beating her, and a young policeman came to the house. He said, casually, "Well, would you like to file a complaint, lady?" The couple had expected the policeman to be shocked by violence occurring in their expensive neighborhood of educated people. The policeman was so casual, obviously having made a number of visits of this kind in their neighborhood, that the couple was embarrassed because their fighting was not unusual. The snobbish husband was shocked enough to stop hitting his wife, not wanting to be common.

Addiction to drugs, alcohol, and other substances make marriage misery easy, if not inevitable. However, these potions should be used only if the spouses are limited in their range of skills. To get drunk habitually will make a marriage unhappy, but rather than lean on that crutch, greater skill should be expected of the average man, or woman. Every spouse is capable of sober psychological abuse if he, or she, really tries.

An example of how a couple almost solved a drinking problem that made their marriage miserable illustrates the risk of going to therapists. A young psychologist was visited by a middle-aged couple, and the wife devoted the interview to saying that her husband's drinking problem had ruined their marriage. She spoke of herself as a living martyr to his alcoholism. At one point in the interview the husband said that it was difficult to stop drinking, and his wife should know that because she could not stop smoking. She replied that it was not the same thing at all, and his illness was the ruination of their marriage. He said, "I'll stop drinking if you stop smoking." "Don't be silly," she replied. The alert young therapist pointed out that this was her opportunity. Drink had ruined their lives, and now she had only to stop smoking and he would have to stop drinking. The wife provided a 30-minute lecture on how her husband could not stop drinking, and besides she had given up everything in life for him and now she shouldn't be expected to give up her one pleasure, smoking. The skillful therapist, after prolonged negotiations, persuaded the wife to agree that she would stop smoking if her husband would stop drinking. They left the office, and when they came back the following week he was sober and she was not smoking. There was considerable tension between them. They faced the possibility of a more harmonious marriage. The following week the couple came in and the husband collapsed drunkenly into the chair. The wife lit a cigarette. "What happened?" asked the shocked young psychologist. "I'll tell you," said the husband, slurring his words. "Last week I was driving down the street with my wife and she said, go buy me a pack of cigarettes, and she pointed to a liquor store." They had saved their unhappy marriage by good team work, and the therapist gave them up in despair.

Problems of sex, quarrels, violence, and addictions are devices to be used throughout marital life from the teenage marriage to the abuse from wheel chairs in old age. However, different stages of marriage offer different opportunities to magnify bad feelings.

The Early Stages

As authorities have often said, a married couple must work on their marriage. When a marriage does not begin badly, both partners must put in more effort. Generally the early stage of marriage is the time to quarrel about relatives. Children are not yet available and romantic affairs are yet to come. Letting the in-laws intrude into the marriage and then quarreling about them is the primary way to encourage trouble at this time. Whether to go for holidays to the home of her family or his family can be an effective quarrel. Of course if the parents buy them a house or contribute money, the young couple are obligated to stay nearby and maintain the tensions of extended family relationships inside the marriage. A productive quarrel involves in-law employment. The wife, for example, should insist that her husband take that job in father's business. After that, many of the quarrels between them can be about the ways her father intrudes into their marriage. Any complaint of the husband about his job she can take as a criticism of her family and argue that they could not survive financially if it wasn't for her father saving her incompetent husband.

The triangle with mother-in-law can be used in its classic variations and the wise husband will encourage his mother to guide his wife in how to take care of him, because she knows best. An award was recently given at the Awful Marriage Banquet to an elderly couple who were able to quarrel about a mother-in-law for 42 years. Over 60-years-old with their children grown and gone from home, this couple could not live together because the wife's 92-year-old mother had thrown the husband out of the house in an argument 12 years previously. Some couples who fear that the mother-in-law problem might not last and they will have to develop something else to quarrel about should welcome the new longevity of parents and be reassured by this example that a lifetime can be devoted to this quarrel.

Children

It is possible to see the progress of a marriage as a series of tests to see if sufficient misery can be gained from this spouse, or is another choice better and so a divorce is in order. With the arrival of a child, new opportunities arise for couples who are about to separate because there is not sufficient discontent. One can think of it this way; when a couple meet, they feel they can always stop seeing each other. When engaged, they can think that if it doesn't work out they don't need to get married. On the wedding day, they can think, "Divorce is easy, and if this doesn't go the way I like it I'll split, even if all those people came to the wedding." However, with a child arriving, the couple has new responsibilities which force them to stay together and suffer, and it offers wonderful new ways of quarreling. There is a risk, of course, that a child might improve the marriage. However, the odds are that the birth of a child provides a symphony of new opportunities for the couple to make difficulty with each other. Even the question whether to conceive a child, or to keep it when conceived, is an opportunity for intense quarreling.

There are two standard ways to achieve marital distress at birthing time:

a. The wife can ignore her husband and become totally preoccupied with the offspring within her. When the husband comes home from work, saying, "The most important thing in my life happened to me today," the wife can say, "That's nice dear. Wouldn't you like to feel the baby kick?" Conversely, the husband can behave as if there isn't a child on the way. When the wife comes home from work exhausted in her ninth month of pregnancy, the husband can complain that she is simply not keeping up the house like she used to and is neglecting her duties.
b. While the wife is encouraging the husband to resent the baby, the husband can increase marital misery in a way so common it has been given an anthropological name. At this time the wife is vulnerable because she feels ungainly and awkward and unattractive. The husband should choose that moment to take off and pursue life's pleasures. He can disappear with other women, drink to excess, run out of the house at times when she most needs him, and generally share the birth experience by not being there. As she delivers in Philadelphia, he can be on a bat in Schenectady. This way of sharing labor establishes the groundwork for marital bitterness for many years to come. It shows how a baby can be used to promote marital distress before it can itself speak or cause trouble.

The appearance of the baby's head as it comes out to enjoy the parent's company is a sign of opportunity to come.

Obviously the infant who cries constantly and has the croup makes its contribution to marital distress, but is it possible to achieve marital misery even with a happy baby? Thousands of couples can attest to that achievement. Not only does the happy baby give the parents a chance to enjoy it and ignore each other, as well as to quarrel over possession, but the in-laws descend like wolves on the flock and offer a resurgence of opportunity for conflict. The child has miraculously given birth to four grandparents, and the early in-law struggles reactivate. Grandparents can be specially helpful if they raise questions not only about the ways to raise a child but also about its paternity.

There are so many ways of quarreling over children that a special type of therapy, child therapy, has been created for it and it would take a 200-page index here just to list the types of fights. Generally they can be grouped into two kinds of quarrels: those where marital fights are expressed in terms of the children, and those where the children are blamed for marital fights.

Using the children to express marriage conflicts is learned easily by most couples. If a wife is in conflict with her husband over the ways he patronizes her as a woman, she can quarrel with him about the rights of their daughter to be equal to boys. Should the husband despair over the ways the wife messes up the house, he can yell how the daughter never cleans her room. The wife who wishes to call her husband dumb can emphasize that the son, who is just like him, should be tested because he might be retarded.

Obviously the possibility of separation will decrease with more children available to blame for marital difficulties. The childless couple must exercise far more restraint. No matter how awful a marriage, a couple can say it is only because they have this difficult child who makes them nervous. Or they can offer the most common excuse for suffering in marriage; "we must survive these quarrels and stay together miserably for these awful creatures."

Affairs

As the children grow and become preoccupied with school or involved in their own search for difficult mates, a couple must find other resources. At this stage an affair becomes one of the best possibilities for encouraging marital distress. Just as a pyramid is solid because it is constructed as a triangle, so can unhappiness be produced in marriage by triangulating with someone in a romantic affair. First of all, let us set aside the affairs which do not disturb a marriage, because many couples stabilize their marriage by outside involvements. The spouse does not object but is merely relieved to have his, or her, partner diverted elsewhere. The existence of the routine mistress or the quiet affair makes quarreling inappropriate.

The goal of succeeding in arousing bitterness in marriage must involve an affair that really upsets the spouse. The affairs are on a continuum from those that cause the least bad feeling to those that cause the most. Generally, affairs can be classified as mean, puzzling, or mythical.

a. *Mean*. The mean affair is with a best friend (or, at an extreme, with a spouse's parent). A valuable employee is also a good candidate if it risks the loss of the business and shakes the family financially. It is the mean affair that sends indignation highest in a marriage. The Affair Award was recently granted to a wife who managed to have affairs with every single one of her husband's best friends, without exception. This left her husband in splendid isolation from friends and growing bitter about life.

   A variation of the mean affair is to choose a person who is as the spouse was. A husband chooses the moment when his wife is feeling older and despairing over her age and has an affair with a pretty 20-year-old who looks just like she did 20 years previously. Generally, the rule with mean affairs is to think, "Who can I choose that would infuriate my spouse but not to the point of divorce and separation, only to a determination to get even?" When that goal is achieved, the couple is on their way to an awful marriage.

b. *The Puzzling Affair* is one that is most appropriate if one has an overconfident spouse. The plan is to choose to be romantic with something that is so inappropriate it is a mystery choice. For example, a man with a wife who emphasizes fashion and sophistication can have an affair with a fat, tacky, uneducated woman and flaunt her to his wife's friends. A dignified, intellectual wife can choose an affair with an 80-year-old man, or a 16-year-old motorcyclist boyfriend of her daughter. In the extreme case the man can choose a young man to have an affair with. This leaves his wife puzzled over what is wrong with her, or him, that was never noticed in 23 years of marriage.

   The merit of the puzzling affair is that it creates bad feeling but also uncertainty so the spouse hesitates, not knowing whether to recommend a mental hospital or offer savage retribution.

c. *The Mythical Affair* is one which makes a marriage miserable without actually having to go through the trouble of bedding another person. The spouse only needs to believe that an affair is happening to achieve the goal. Such an affair is easy to set up once one grasps the principle: it is merely necessary to use subtle behavior—or gross behavior if one has a dumb spouse—to arouse suspicions. An odd response to a phone call, or a phone number left on the kitchen sink, or an unexplained absence after work, or not being where one is supposed to be—all these ways of attempting to conceal a real affair are done but without the actual affair. When confronted, the denials should be too extreme, of course. Mythical affairs of this kind have been known to carry on for years, eroding a marriage like rust over time.

One of the awards given in this area was to a man who returned from a war, and his wife was delighted to see him. She embraced him as they sat down on the couch together. About to make love after not having seen each other for two years, the man said, "Wait. I have a confession to make. When I was away, I had lunch with a woman." The wife said, "That doesn't matter," and she reached out for him again. Then she paused and said, "If it was only a lunch, why would you confess it to me at a time like this?" A quarrel began, which was still continuing 24 years later. He had arranged that she could never give up trying to find out what had happened at that lunch. Of course it was necessary to regularly reinforce her suspicions, which he did through years of marriage and the raising of four children. When her attention flagged, he would leave a woman's name on a piece of paper in his desk at his office, knowing his wife would check his drawers. In the argument that followed each time, the lunch of many years ago would come up to be quarreled about again. Not everyone can make his marriage miserable and push a spouse's buttons with so little effort. This man sets a standard we can all admire. There are, of course, debates in the field whether a mythical affair is as good as an actual affair. Specially skilled spouses can have both: a real affair is concealed by a mythical affair involving wrong suspicions which lead the partner in the wrong direction. An actual affair has the merit that it can be miserable and so the person can have both a miserable marriage and a miserable romantic affair, achieving two misfortunes at once. A classical case was a man who had a wife and children and also a mistress with whom he had a child and who functioned essentially as a second wife. He had two dinners every night, suffering an argument each evening with both women.

Marital Struggles in Old Age

When the children are grown and one is too old for an affair, how is it possible to continue misery in marriage? Just as young people do not believe that old people have sex, they also don't believe they will be able to continue marital misery in old age. They need look only as far as the nearest leisure community to get their hopes up. Any couple married for many years has developed such a range of weapons and has quarreled so habitually that they need only minimum cues to arouse the most bitter feelings. For example, one can observe a young couple shopping in the early days of marriage. The husband chooses something on the shelf and says, "This would be nice. I read in *Consumer Reports* that it is the best." The wife replies, "I don't think it is a good product, let's not get it and waste our time on something you read about in that silly magazine." The husband says, "It is not a silly magazine, and I will have this, and you won't prevent it, and I'm the one who brings the most money into our house." The wife replies, "I'm sure you think you know best, but I break out in hives if I even have that product in the house, so give it to me and I'll put it back on the shelf." That complex interchange has become rather different by the 42nd year of marriage. The husband says, "This?" and holds up the product. The wife replies, "No!" The man says, "Yes!" The wife takes it from his hand and puts it back on the shelf. Like a telegram with bad news, these few words arouse all the hours of bad feeling that long arguments used to achieve in their youth. When a couple has had the same quarrel 1400 million times, they can follow it without effort like a train follows a railroad track. Many elderly couples sit side by side in wheelchairs, and if they don't have the strength to hit each other they need only say one code word to be able to reminisce and have all previous bad feelings without having to carry out the quarrel. They still have their memories and imagination, even if they hardly have the strength to argue. Therefore, one should not consider old age a desert but look forward to it as a time when one can have an awful marriage even if one has only the strength for minimal moves. People in old age also still have something to look forward to. Many of them believe they will be with their relatives in the afterlife to come. They can glow with the anticipation of continuing unfinished quarrels, and having new ones, in the place beyond time.

6

How to Criticize Your Fellow Therapists

INTRODUCTION

Bill O'Hanlon, MS

Jay Haley was a pioneer in the areas of brief and family therapy, and that adage about pioneers ending up with arrows in their backs is perhaps where this article came from. Haley was describing an approach in which the therapist strived for results and made things both simple and elegant, and he received many objections and much questioning of his results when he reported them in presentations. In later years, he began showing videos to show proof and diminish these dismissive comments. But in these early years (this piece is from 1970, meaning it was likely written in 1969), mainstream therapists were often dismissive and derogatory in regard to Haley's work, family therapy, and brief therapy in general.

I always found the contrast between Jay Haley's in-person style (soft, kind, and gentlemanly) and his written style, which could be quite contrary and caustic. This article has a sarcastic tone that, although ostensibly giving guidance to therapists about how to criticize the approach taken by other therapists reporting about their work at case conferences, actually takes therapists to task for their negative ways of presenting cases and responding to case presentations of colleagues.

Haley once told me that he had ambitions to be a writer before he was a therapist and, in fact, had his first article published in the *New Yorker*. His writing was one of his strong suits and part of what made him such an influential theorist. He could use words well to convey nuances and ideas.

This skill is evident in all the papers and articles in this book, and shows up here in his ironic tone; his use of sample quotations for criticisms, making his points more vivid; and his clever use of an acronym for the nine types of critiques one could offer therapists presenting cases (OPPOSITES) that underlines his main point. He makes sniping comments about Boston and Chicago, which at the time were bastions of analytic thought and practice, without ever mentioning analysis.

What strikes me as sad is that many of these practices still go on quite regularly in our field. It seems to me that most therapists are well-intentioned people trying their best to relieve suffering in others and searching for effective methods of doing so. Yet, therapists often criticize each other and try to convince the field that their approach is the correct one and that others are misguided and/or badly intentioned. Therapy often divides itself into approaches (e.g., cognitive-behavioral therapy [CBT], narrative therapy, solution-focused therapy, and emotionally focused therapy) rather than putting results and alleviation of suffering first. Haley's mission for many years was to challenge that status quo and to bring a new, more practical, results-oriented approach to the field. This article was one of his barbed attempts at poking holes in the unhelpful "delusions of certainties" that we often hold and the undermining need to be right that too often characterizes therapy.

Read on, enjoy, and get cured of "our theory sclerosis."

HOW TO CRITICIZE YOUR FELLOW THERAPISTS

Jay Haley

The fact that many clinicians cannot criticize psychotherapy in a competent manner is because of lack of experience. Until recently, psychologists, social workers, and psychiatrists did not discuss therapy. At case conferences the expected remarks were about what was being overlooked in the patient's nature, not how he was being treated. When a case was presented, one was expected to comment upon overlooked etiological factors, neglected symbolism, unmentioned internalized objects, unsuspected manipulations, or inaccurate measures of ego strength. Even a dullard professional could find something overlooked by the victim presenting his case because any psychological problem is complex.

All things change, even therapists, and now just when everyone is expert in criticizing diagnosis and dynamics, the whole field is shifting to being critical of different kinds of therapy. At any case conference today (outside of Chicago) a clinician is likely to be faced with new therapeutic approaches. For example, he is expected to be critical of Behavior Therapy, Conditioning Therapy, Implosive Therapy, Paradoxical Intention, different varieties of hypnosis, several schools of family therapy, multiple family therapy, network therapy, mini-groups or marathons, and so on. The proper critical views cannot be learned in training because academic institutions still focus on diagnosis while out in the field the talk is all about different approaches to therapy.

This brief review of how to criticize therapy is offered for participants in case conferences who are faced with presentations of a variety of kinds of treatment approaches. It is based upon observation of experts who have learned to follow the fundamental rule of the modern case conference: Whatever therapy method a fellow therapist is offering, it is not quite the right one.

To become a successful critic, one must realize that therapy always consists of polarized approaches. Whichever pole a therapist chooses, he can be hoisted upon the opposite petard. Presented in more detail in an unpublished two-volume manuscript on the true nature of therapy, the main points of this approach can be summarized here.

Crit. 1. Outcome vs. Process[1]: Should a therapist discuss a case of emphasizing the smooth working of the process of therapy, a proper query is not about that process but whether there was a good outcome. For example, a psychoanalyst presented a case of a young man who became anxious while taking his oral examination for his Ph.D. Although he passed his orals successfully, he entered therapy to recover from that anxiety. The analyst reported that there had been a systematic uncovering process and after seven years the patient discovered the subtle way his anxiety during the test was related to an oral fixation on his mother. Although the presentation was effective, a critic dealt with it easily by asking, "Was the patient anxious the next time he obtained a Ph.D.?" This thrust was too subtle for some people in the audience, but it led to a discussion of outcome and the discovery that the patient was still in treatment. The analyst could only lamely assert that the process was still going well.

That type of old-fashioned presentation is now uncommon, except in Boston. More usually the critic faces the problem of a therapist who presents a case with a successful outcome. He describes the miserable presenting problem which challenged him and he ends with the statement that the patient has fully recovered. How can one criticize such a presentation? The skillful professional undermines this type of offering by going to a more general discussion. An appropriate query is, "Are you sure it was your therapy that caused the change? After all, over half the patients on a waiting list get over their problems without treatment, and perhaps the patient would have recovered anyhow." This comment introduces uncertainty about whether it was a therapeutic triumph or a spontaneous recovery. The therapist can only respond by engaging in a statistical debate, which is beyond the range of most clinicians.

Crit. 2. Problem vs. Method: A therapist is likely to present a method of therapy which he says has worked effectively with x percent of patients, it has been taught to vast numbers of students, and it is superior to any other method yet evolved. Such a presentation is typical of a Behavior Therapist. The proper critical approach is to avoid comments on the therapist's method, where he has the advantage, and go to more basic principles. One should object to the narrow idea of a single method. "Granting that your procedure is effective at times, isn't it naive to think that all patients can be fitted into a particular method? You need to change your approach depending upon the problem that comes in the door, not be stuck with one way to deal with all the complexities of life."

If there has been an exceptionally good presentation by someone who describes a range of different therapeutic approaches for different problems, quite the opposite criticism is in order. "The way you present your approach, it is so eclectic that you don't seem to have any method at all. Surely therapy must be systematic enough to be taught; if it's just 'anything goes,' where are we as a profession?"

Crit. 3. Professionalism vs. Benevolence: A therapist will offer a case where he exuded self-sacrifice. Professionals who do not wish to sacrifice their personal lives for their patients must object to his approach, but they find it difficult to be critical because they are supposed to be self-sacrificing helpers. What can one do with the really dedicated? For example, a therapist reports curing a miserable process schizophrenic by maximum effort. He spent many 10-hour days with the patient, he took him home for weekends at difficult times, he accepted calls throughout the night, he sat by his side at a job interview, and he was best man at the wedding. The patient was totally cured and has now been blossoming for twelve years and is an executive with Continental Can. This is not an easy presentation to criticize. One approach is to say that by doing so much the therapist has encouraged dependency, but this has already been anticipated by the therapist showing how temporary dependency led to successful independence. What can one say to avoid sitting all day with a patient and having him home for the weekend? One criticism, although not the most effective one, is to say that the approach is interesting, but given the millions of people who need help, it really isn't practical for the professional therapist to work that way. A better and more daring critical stance is to raise the question whether benevolent help is really good for people. After all, therapy is a business, a contract, which the therapist gets something from—usually a fee—and so does the patient, hopefully a cure. To sacrifice one's personal life for a patient is to be too benevolent and indicates the possibility of unsavory countertransference motives in the therapist. Today this kind of criticism might be shouted down by a group because of the new first commandment: Thou shalt not use psychiatric interpretations against fellow professionals. Rather than sin in that way, it is better to make a broader attack. One can point out that the major crimes in history have been done by self-sacrificing people with benevolent motives. The Christians burned people alive to save their souls, and the Communists shoot and jail people out of a benevolent desire to bring a paradise on earth. This comment will arouse clinicians with a liberal taint to object to anticommunist statements, and the discussion will become so heated and interesting that the therapist will soon be forgotten.

If a therapist goes to the other extreme and emphasizes how he is a practical man solving problems for patients because they pay him a fee to get the job done, the criticism should be about his lack of benevolent feeling. "Aren't professional helpers, after all, in the business for more than money? Is it not also a calling?"

Crit. 4. Overintellect vs. Overemotion? Most properly trained therapists can easily grasp the critical positions necessary in this area. A case will be presented in which the therapist brilliantly brought forth the deepest emotions of a patient, or a whole family, so that a catharsis was achieved and profound relief was felt. The appropriate criticism is about the importance of detachment. Was the patient able to conceptualize what was happening in a sufficiently detached way to make use of the emotions? Conversely, if a therapist has described the way a patient reached insight into the innermost nature of his symptom and character structure by a torturous investigation of historical causes, a criticism about the importance of emotion is in order. "Granting the logic of your ideas, what about the patient's feelings? Aren't you overlooking the need of the patient to express his emotions and integrate his ideas within his affective life?"

Crit. 5. Simplicity vs. Complexity: If a therapist has demonstrated how thoroughly he took into account every complexity of a case before intervening, it is appropriate to comment on the importance of simplicity. "Probably your patient's situation was even more complex than you suggest, but is all that detail really necessary? In therapy we must strike at key points if we are to bring about change, not become lost in complexities."

Should there be an emphasis upon the simplicity of an approach by a therapist choosing only important issues, one can take the opposite tack. "Such an approach is fine for novices, but with experience one gets more understanding of the complex factors which have to be considered in a case."

In this area falls the sub-category of Cautious Treatment vs. Crisis Intervention. When a therapist asserts proudly that he did twenty-three diagnostic interviews before choosing a therapeutic approach, the response should be one about the importance of crisis treatment. People are more malleable when they first enter therapy and quick intervention produces great change. Slow exploration only allows the situation to stabilize and become more difficult to influence.

Should a crisis treatment approach be offered, it is appropriate to raise the question whether a therapist is being responsible when he intervenes before gathering enough information to let him know the consequences of his intervention.

Crit. 6. Inhumanity vs. Humanity: Some therapists emphasize a professional stance and a set of specific operations to achieve a therapeutic goal, while others tend to emphasize joining their patients in common humanity. The two styles obviously offer different opportunities for criticism.

Let us suppose, for example, that a psychodynamic therapist who is uncertain about his results is listening to a case presentation by a conditioning therapist. The therapist describes the precise nature of the problem, the operations designed to eliminate it, the steps in the procedure, and the relief of the symptoms. A weak criticism is to query whether symptom relief is really a change, because the psychodynamicist must then deal with a response about whether *his* therapy even achieves symptom relief. A better approach is to show concern about the humanity of the therapy. "Surely therapy is not so mechanical. After all, we are one human being dealing with another, not robots." Should the conditioner respond by emphasizing the scientific method, he only appears more inhuman. A better criticism is known as the Daniels Device and consists of asking whether anyone would want to spend his professional life putting patients through such a boring ordeal. "Wouldn't training mental retardates as conditioners be appropriate?"

At the other extreme we have the "human" therapist who offers a case where one man encountered the soul of another. It is likely to be a presentation of a four-day group marathon where everyone was nude and jointly experienced the breakthrough of a psychotic episode. One critical approach is to raise a question whether the people were cured of their problems, but the best criticism is to ask, "Can you really feel like a responsible professional with your trousers off?"

The posture of the critic is clear. If a therapist behaves like a human being with his patients, he is open to the accusation of being only a chum. If he emphasizes science and professional detachment, he can be accused of not being sufficiently involved with his patients to touch the important areas of life.

Crit. 7. Telling vs. Implying: Some therapists like to emphasize how they required a patient to make all his life decisions himself. The therapist only reflects back to him his own productions, helps him understand his inner motivations, and he avoids intervening in the patient's life. A critical view of this approach is one which emphasizes its naivete in relation to modern knowledge. "Surely no one still believes that he is not influencing a patient's life decisions just because he doesn't tell him what to do? Experimenter bias studies have shown the enormous influence of occasional comments." If one wants to develop this point, he can ask, "How is it possible not to be directive with a patient? To ask a patient to tell you his problem is to direct him, to ask him to free-associate is a directive, to set an appointment or to inquire about dreams is to direct the patient's behavior." If these ideas are too subtle for the professionals present, one can always say, "Does anyone really believe any longer that a patient changes without directives from a therapist to bring about those changes?"

If a therapist has given up being reflective and has swung to being directive, he might present a case where he skillfully used a therapeutic strategy in which he directed the patient to spontaneously behave differently and so he was transformed. The proper criticism is to shift to a query about the nature of superficial changes. "Does anyone really believe that deep and basic changes in character structure can occur by telling someone how to behave?"

Crit. 8. Ecology vs. Individual: No matter how well presented a case or how successful a therapeutic approach, if the therapist has focused upon an individual, the appropriate criticism is to shift to a larger unit. "Granting the woman changed, have you considered the effect on her husband? Suicides are not unusual among spouses when such changes occur." Or one can say, "Well, seeing a husband alone is one way of intervening into a family, but wouldn't improvement have been more rapid if you dealt with the wife as well in this situation?" If the therapist has taken the wife into account and worked with the marriage, the critical response is to go larger. "You mean you dealt with that couple without doing any therapy with the children?" Similarly, if family treatment of the nuclear family is offered, the proper criticism should shift to the importance of bringing in the extended kin in family therapy. At times one can face a more formidable challenge when a Network Therapist presents a case where he treated the nuclear family, extended kin, and all the other significant people involved. In this situation it is necessary to go to the opposite extreme. "Surely you aren't saying that you can produce deep changes in an individual when you have sixty or seventy people in a treatment session?"

These eight polarities may not seem many, but they are sufficient for the beginner who is not ready yet for deeper mysteries. With this approach even a novice critic can keep the discussion on the nature of therapy and not have to fall back upon dynamics or on personal insinuations as he was taught in professional training.

There may come a time, of course, when a group is faced with a Master presenting a case. Such a therapist will indicate the complexity while emphasizing a simple approach, he will explore but take advantage of immediate opportunities for change, he will be benevolent but draw a firm line about his own sacrifices, he will bring out emotion in an intellectual framework, he will have a method but vary it with the problem, he will reflect but also offer directives, he will include not only the individual but the significant others, and he will be human while having a professional stance. Faced with such a case presentation, the only correct response by the critic is applause.

Endnote

1. The keen reader will note that Criticisms 1 through 8 are written to form an acronym which can be used as a mnemonic device so that notes will not have to be kept on the cuff at case conferences.

7

Fourteen Ways to Fail as a Teacher of Family Therapy

INTRODUCTION

Michael Nichols, PhD

With clear-eyed pragmatism and acerbic wit, "Fourteen Ways to Fail as a Teacher of Family Therapy" rings with all the bravado of a new kid on the block. "Here I am," Haley says, "and the heck with everyone else!" We're a lot less sure of ourselves these days.

Haley's evangelical tone makes "Fourteen Ways" a prime example of what was good and not so good in family therapy's salad days. It's hard to imagine anyone today writing with the condescending glee Haley takes in dismissing psychodynamics, eclecticism, experiential techniques, Bowenian theory, and a number of other things he doesn't appreciate. Maybe you'll enjoy Haley's arch tone, or maybe not; but these digs really have nothing to do with the astute positive recommendations in this paper.

Good therapy, Haley writes, is focused and direct. It is planned and organized, it takes into account the context of not only the family but also the larger community within which the family functions, and it is tailored to the needs of each specific case. Good teachers, Haley says, not only understand these principles but also know how to impart them effectively to the people they supervise.

Just as any therapy worth the name must be more than simply listening sympathetically to clients, so too is effective supervision more than just listening to a recap of what therapists (say they) did, and then telling them how to do it better next time. To treat or teach effectively, you have to know something about what works, and what doesn't work, and you have to know how to get it across.

Haley's first admonition—about dangers of unfocused eclecticism—is even more pertinent today than when this paper was written. Postmodern skepticism has taught us that no one has a corner on the truth; and graduate schools now teach a little of this, that, and the other thing, in the process turning out better critics than clinicians. Although there are many valid ways to do therapy, mixing too many disparate ingredients dilutes the impact of a coherent approach. Intensive instruction and supervision in a particular model provide conceptual focus and the intensity that comes from concentrating on one point of leverage. Postgraduate training programs—like Haley's—once provided an antidote to the superficial surveys of graduate education. Unfortunately, few students these days seem willing to invest the time and expense to seek out advanced training.

Most of the precepts Haley offers in this splendid essay deal with the importance of making therapy a thoughtful, organized problem-solving enterprise. Let me rephrase that: Haley doesn't just characterize what good therapy should be—the way so many writers do—rather, he spells out concretely the specific activities that actually bring about change. The result is a succinct and practical guide to clinical work—just like the kind of therapy Haley developed and taught for so many years.

One caveat: You can get the main points of this deceptively simple paper in one quick read. But read it again later, slowly. There's more than meets the eye here. Reading and rereading this essay after 37 years remind me of so many important lessons about doing and teaching therapy. Reading it is no substitute for finding a great teacher, but it is a start.

I was lucky enough to have three great teachers: Salvador Minuchin, Murray Bowen, and Robert Langs—a structuralist, a, well, Bowenian, and a psychoanalyst. The three of them followed approaches that could hardly be more different from Haley's, or from each other's. However, I think all of them would subscribe to most of the principles so wisely set forth in this little gem of a paper. I hope you enjoy it.

FOURTEEN WAYS TO FAIL AS A TEACHER OF FAMILY THERAPY

Jay Haley

A review of what to avoid when training family therapists can be helpful to teachers planning their programs. This review is based upon observation of training methods that lead logically to poor therapy outcome. Some of the methods can even destroy the natural talent of a therapist and make him more ineffective than he would be with no training at all. Rather than detail all the contraindicated training operations, this summary will examine the major premises of teachers who train their students to do unsuccessful family therapy. Many of the principles also apply to teaching other forms of therapy where the focus is not upon the family. The operational premises that lead to failure will be organized here in terms of the general theoretical approach, specific ways therapists can be taught to mishandle families, and techniques a teacher can use which will incapacitate a student no matter what form of therapy is being taught.

Premise 1: Teaching That Family Therapy Is One Additional Technique for the Clinical Armorentarium

Operating on this premise, a teacher will encourage students to learn family therapy, group therapy, individual therapy, play therapy, behavior modification, primal therapy, use of drugs, sensitivity training, and spiritual advice. The student will be unable to develop a coherent theory or take a clear position when faced with a therapeutic problem, and so he will fail. Observing a therapy session by a student taught in this eclectic way, one finds the results similar to a painting by an art student who paints with a touch of Rembrandt, a bit of Picasso, a dash of collage, a smattering of photography, and a slight fog of marble dust. This way of teaching is most evident in psychiatry training where residents are exposed to everything in the hope they will deserve more money because they will know more than anybody.

Premise 2: Avoid Teaching How to Interview a Family and Avoid "Live" Supervision

If skill in interviewing is taught, therapists become skillful. If supervision is "live" from behind a one-way mirror, the student is guided when he needs guidance and so he can learn to be an effective therapist. To teach a student to fail as a therapist it is necessary to avoid training in interview skills and avoid "live" supervision. Instead, the teacher should focus upon the personal problems of the student. Teachers of individual therapy had the faith that a therapist who had no emotional problems, or who solved the ones he had, would be an expert at therapy. Family therapy can continue this tradition by having students do family sculpturing, encounter exercises, work with simulated families, and other group tasks. It helps if students make public confessions within the group about how they really feel about their mothers. Students can become so excited by these kinds of activities that they forget to ask the teacher how to do therapy with a family. Therefore the teacher doesn't have to know how.

To approach students in this way, the teacher need only establish the idea that student therapists should examine their own souls, contact their extended families, face wife and children in new ways, and discover how it really feels to be a therapist. The student won't learn what to do in therapy, but he will learn to accept his humanity and therefore accept the humanity of ignorance.

Premise 3: Avoid Teaching Students to Define a Goal for Their Therapy

By emphasizing that life is complex, the world uncertain, human nature unreadable, and ways of living infinite in their variety, the student can be persuaded that cure is not definable and therapy should have no destination. Subcategories of this premise are necessary because it entails so many different ways to incapacitate a therapist.

a. Students can be focused upon family diagnosis and taught that process and not outcome is the important matter. Teachers who operate on this premise will encourage students to debate peripheral issues, such as whether structure or process is most important. ("What is the interaction process?" cries one student to another. "That depends upon how you do your structural analysis," is the cutting reply.) When a teacher distracts his students in this way, questions about where the therapy is going and whether it is getting there will never arise (allowing the family in treatment the opportunity for spontaneous change).
b. When the therapy has no goal, the teacher can appear to be imaginative because he can teach the students all kinds of irrelevant but exciting techniques. For example, he can teach them to use group therapy techniques with families, ignoring the thorough dissimilarity between an artificial and natural group. The students can learn to use insightful interpretations, conformations, touching, massage, whooping and screaming, and other stimulating operations so that family therapy will have no more goal than group therapy and so will succeed no more often.
c. Since the therapy has no goal, the teacher can avoid teaching his students how to do follow-up interviews. There is no point in interviewing a family a few months

after terminating treatment if there was no goal for the treatment in the first place. In this way teacher and student can thrash around with the family, hoping for the best, without having to think about ways to find out if the best occurred.

d. By avoiding a focus upon symptoms, the training can leave the goal of therapy unclear and ambiguous. The family might consider the presenting problem important, since that is what they are paying their money to recover from. However, families as well as students can be taught that the problem the family presents is not really the problem. Then teacher and student need not learn how to get people over their presenting problems. If the family continues to insist that their distressing symptoms are important, teacher and student can find togetherness in the idea that they are not as dumb as the family.

Premise 4: Teach That Therapy Can Never Be Done Quickly

When one trains students to believe that change can occur only over a long period of time, if at all, the students will never be able to adapt themselves to the timing of what is happening in the family. Not expecting rapid change, they will neither see nor elicit it; they will even block off that which might occur spontaneously because they will believe it is not really happening.

Premise 5: Let Families Say and Do Anything

The therapist need not know what should happen in a session if he operates on the idea that *everything* should be allowed to happen. If family members express themselves, that is good and cathartic; therefore, anything goes. Children can be allowed to insult parents, wives attack husbands, mother-in-law screams at parents, and family members be permitted to generally make fools of themselves. Having done such shameful things, the families might drop out, but the therapist can continue to believe that encouraging self-expression is a good thing. He need not learn to take charge and see to it that only what *should* happen is what happens.

Premise 6: Interpreting Body Movement Is Fun

When the teacher doesn't know what to teach about how to do therapy, he can make classes interesting by introducing students to kinesics. He can show them how to interpret body movement to families, which is always exciting. The student can learn to point out to father that he has crossed his arms making a barrier, mother that she has crossed her legs away from father, daughter that she is preening herself in a courting way, and son that he is protecting his balls. The family will soon not know how to sit without the therapist taking it personally, and they will begin to say and do things they would rather not. Of course they won't change, but they will develop intense feelings toward the therapist so he will feel that what he is doing is important.

Premise 7: Teach a Method Rather Than a Problem Orientation

A teacher will find his students more cooperative if he accepts the premise that they need not adapt what they do to the kind of problem they face. He can make the students comfortable by teaching them a method of doing therapy into which all families must fit. Examples are: one should always use two therapists, the family should come once a week, the session should be one and one half hours, all family members should be present, no family members should be interviewed alone, and so on. Since no single method will fit every family, the students often will fail, but they will be pleased that they learned well the method of family therapy.

Premise 8: Teaching That Therapeutic Change Is Not the Responsibility of the Therapist

Students will feel better if they are told that if they fail it is the family's fault. This idea frees the therapist of the obligation to produce change, and it frees the teacher of the responsibility for teaching him how to succeed as a therapist. If the family is responsible for change, then student and teacher can comfort each other as failures because so many families were resistant and untreatable.

Premise 9: Apply the Theory of Symptom Substitution in the Form of Family Homeostasis

Teachers of individual therapy were able to instill a fear in student therapists that if they cured a patient's symptom the patient would develop a worse one. This way of encouraging failure can be carried into the family field by teaching the theory of homeostatic balance. A student can be persuaded that if he changes the problem person he will create another problem person, and so the student will find himself curiously apathetic about doing active therapy without knowing why.

Premise 10: Avoid Teaching That the Context of Therapy Is Important

By ignoring the context of the family, such as the neighborhood and the involvement with schools, agencies, and work situation, the family problems can be simplified. More important, the teacher should avoid mentioning the context of the treatment. One can teach that it is irrelevant that a member of the family is in a mental hospital and pretend that the only problem is the family so only the dynamics of the family need be taught. In this way the student won't bother his colleagues who are locking up family members, or drugging them, or have to learn that therapy must be different in different institutional settings. If one ignores the fact that family members are in individual therapy, one need not notice that the family is being pulled simultaneously in different directions, ensuring that change will not take place. The collaboration of many therapists can lead to stable family distress, and all the therapists, including the family therapist, can have a stable income.

Premise 11: If You Don't Know What to Do, Blame the Family

A common objection of clinicians is that family therapists blame the family for a patient's difficulty. This accusation is often based upon the work of family therapists who are well trained in family theory. By various devices the family therapist forces the family to resist change and so supports the theory of family homeostasis. With the help of this view, the therapist can fail and feel he is right even if the therapy goes wrong.

There are several typical procedures used by therapists who operate on this premise:

1. At the beginning of therapy, the family therapist forces the whole family to confront the idea that it is a sick unit. "You are all patients, not just this poor idiot you are pointing to," says the family therapist sympathetically. Faced with this kind of therapist, the family appears to wish it was elsewhere, corroborating the therapist's theory that families benefit from a member's difficulty and is a system that resists change.

Family therapists who take this approach often claim they may be incompetent but at least they are honest with their sick subjects.

2. As the therapy progresses, the student therapist is taught that people will change if they just understand what they are doing to each other. Interpretations are the royal road to failure in this approach. Parents are educated about how they are scapegoating children, wives educated about how they are provoking and castrating husbands, and husbands helpfully shown how they are neglecting their wives and ruining their children. If the family keeps coming in the face of this benevolent onslaught, the therapist brings in the grandparents and gives them insight into what disasters they have been as parents. Termination is a welcome relief to the family approached in this way, so it is pleased with one phase of the therapy at least.
3. If the teacher has not only a family theory but a sophisticated liberal view, he can persuade his students the world is made up of villains and victims. The victim is the person with a problem, and the student is taught to save the victim from the technological world, or at least from his parents. Sometimes this is known as the R. D. Laing approach, and with this view, life becomes a drama. The families approached in this way don't *change*, but sometimes they *react* dramatically. Much of the therapy time is spent showing people how they are mistreating and misunderstanding this poor victim whose creativity and humanity is being stultified. Sometimes the student can have a broader, Marxist view and consider the whole family a victim of welfare agencies, schools, capitalism, and society. It helps if the student does not discover that he too is a victim—of unfortunate training from a teacher who does not know how to teach him to change people.

Premise 12: If You Don't Know What to Teach, Sit In

When a teacher doesn't know what to teach a student to do, he can have the student join him in a family session. Through osmosis the student is supposed to learn what to do. If the student is placed with an experienced person, he learns to sit back and not take the responsibility for what happens in the session—somebody else should do something. These joining operations are based upon the premise that if you don't know what to do, increase the number of therapists. Put in several therapists and surely one of them will be able to think of something.

Premise 13: Avoid Using Strategy in Therapy or Teaching

The teacher doesn't have to know what to teach if he can persuade the student that therapy should be a spontaneous happening. When training is also spontaneous, the teacher doesn't even need to plan a curriculum. This is a great relief to many teachers.

To support this premise, the teacher only need argue that any planning for a therapy session is unnecessary and the use of maneuver to change a family is deceitful and duplicitous. It can be argued that therapists and teachers of therapy never say one thing and do another and they always go directly to their immediate goal, never being devious along the way. This approach ensures that there will be no manipulative therapists or teachers, just poor outcome and an atmosphere of pseudo-honesty.

Premise 14: Avoid Teaching How to Give Directives

Since most teachers never learned how to give directives to families, it is better to argue that to do so is manipulative.

When the student finds that interpretations and confrontations don't change people, he will not know what to tell the family to do. So he will give good advice or a suggestion they don't follow. The teacher can then point out that directives and suggestions are not a good idea, saving himself from needing to know how to give them.

Conclusion

One might expect that improperly trained students would feel unhappy if they continually failed as therapists and they would blame their therapy teachers. Obviously this does not happen, since teachers of individual therapy were never blamed by their students who failed. The techniques of individual and group therapy teachers can be adopted by trainers in the family field, including the following:

1. Do not encourage the therapist to check his or her outcome and then he will not know if he has failed.
2. If he happens to notice he is failing, suggest that his personal problems are interfering and he should seek therapy for himself. In this way he will blame himself and absolve his teacher of blame.
3. The teacher can avoid taking the stance of an expert and instead behave with his student as a peer. By having a warm, human relationship with a student he defines as a colleague, the teacher can present the situation as one where they are two chums facing a difficult if not impossible task together. Caught up in this warmth, the student cannot accuse his teacher of being a failure without feeling like a cad. The student learns to take the same stance with families so they will not blame him when he fails.

In summary, there are a number of basic premises to be adopted if one wishes to fail to train effective family therapists.

A teacher should obscure the fact that family therapy is a new orientation to human dilemmas, restrain the therapist from being active and directive, avoid defining goals, absolve the therapist from responsibility for change, teach that interpretations and confrontations will solve problems, and focus upon the personal problems of the student rather than teaching him skill as a therapist.

Although some teachers might not want to train their student therapists to fail, they should think about expanding the family therapy movement. There is increasing evidence that only methods of therapy that fail become popular and lucrative. Most people seem to prefer not to change, and so they seek out the kinds of therapy which do not threaten any real change, like Psychodynamic or encounter types of therapy. Training family therapists to be effective might prevent family therapy from becoming a popular movement. Fortunately one has only to visit the different family therapy training programs around the country to realize that such a danger is still far in the future.

8

Why a Mental Health Clinic Should Avoid Family Therapy

INTRODUCTION

David R. Grove, LISW

In his article, "Why a Mental Health Clinic Should Avoid Family Therapy," Haley raised several issues regarding family therapy's fit for community mental health. The question is, after four decades, are Haley's concerns still valid? In 2009 can family therapy be easily adapted in community mental health clinics, or do obstacles still abound? I can only wonder about other regions of the country. I cannot really comment on what is happening out west or on the east coast, or down south. But in Ohio, I have a pretty clear answer to this question.

For the past seven years, I have been part of a research and consultation team whose purpose is to develop and implement an in-home family treatment model. We are training mental health clinic staff to provide in-home family therapy for families who are at serious risk to have a child placed outside the home in foster care, juvenile detention, or residential treatment. We are implementing our model, integrative family and systems treatment (I-FAST) (Lee et al., 2009), in community mental health centers and then researching its outcomes. Over the past seven years, I myself have been in 10 different mental health clinics in both rural and urban settings throughout Ohio. Getting our model to work in mental health settings requires much more than simply training staff. For the model to be sustained after our departure, in addition to providing the training itself, numerous clinic-wide changes must be made to ensure the staff can continue to provide family therapy while in a mental health setting.

First, what did Haley mean by *family therapy*? There are many versions, and his is a special brand. Haley believed that problems occur when families get stuck in what he called *sequences of interaction*, particularly those directly related to problems. A person would develop a problem, and family members would always respond to it in the same way. Trouble would then escalate if these sequences interfered with developmental transitions imposed by the family life cycle. Haley believed that for clients to overcome their problems and for families to successfully move through the life cycle, these rigid sequences had to change. His way of changing them was to bring the family together, reach agreements on specific problems they wanted solved, devise a specific plan for that family, and then issue directives aimed at both solving those problems and helping the family get unstuck from the sequences that supported them. Great attention was paid to how families responded to directives. Rather than punish families for not following the directives and then labeling them noncompliant, clinicians observed how clients responded to them and then adapted and adjusted their approach accordingly. This was a collaborative approach stressing a give and take between client and clinician within the larger context that defined the clinician as an expert on how to help people change.

How does this type of approach fit in mental health today? Haley raised several concerns. Looking at his concerns in a broad sense, he noted numerous impediments to its implementation in community mental health. He pointed out that doing his therapy in mental health clinics could cause ideological clashes amongst the staff. He noted that clinic procedures, particularly intake and diagnostic procedures, would impede the implementation of his therapy. He raised concerns about training and supervision of staff. Finally, he posed that implementing family therapy in a mental health setting would disrupt the clinic hierarchy. I will address each of these issues and note how relevant I find them to be in my work in the clinics in which I have offered training. I will then outline how the I-FAST team has attempted to deal with these issues in our attempts to implement I-FAST in these various settings.

First let us take up the issue of ideology. In Haley's article he was most concerned with how family therapy approaches would clash with psychodynamic approaches. Obviously psychodynamic ideology was much more influential 40 years ago. But psychodynamic theory's diminished influence has not saved family therapy from ideological clashes. In 2009, I believe ideological clashes between family therapy and treatment as usual are still a major problem. My observation is that there are two major ideological clashes that are very relevant today. First concerns how to treat parents when the problem is a child. Haley believed that when a child is struggling, the task at hand was to help the parents collaborate with each other, and to empower them to help their own child overcome his or her difficulty. To do this, Haley stressed developing a strong alliance with the parents. Haley's approach was parent friendly. Is the typical child mental health clinic in 2009 parent friendly? My experience is no. Parents are typically worked with nowadays, but the emphasis is still on establishing a therapeutic relationship with the child, not the parents. The family is assessed and problems identified that the parents may or may not want help on. Recommendations are then issued to parents often regarding problems they were not requesting help with. When the parents do not follow the recommendations, they are labeled noncompliant, and a struggle then ensues between parent and clinician. After 25 years of doing this work in mental health settings, I find myself fighting the same battle of the necessity to join with parents rather than blame them. Blaming parents still goes on. I believe it is still very common and not just in Ohio.

The second ideological struggle is over how to view human problems in general. For Haley, human problems were primarily a product of the client's current family interactions. Therapy was to be brief, problem focused, and empowering of the family. In today's world, mental health is dominated by the medical model and the view that problems result from faulty brain chemistry. Medications dominate our field like never before. The pharmaceutical companies have been on a public advertising campaign to promote the use of medications for more than a decade, and they have been very effective at selling their view. Add to this that mental health clinicians are typically young and inadequately trained, and you have a perfect storm for creating a clinic client population that is 99% on medications. When clients, particularly children, are on medications, it is difficult to empower parents when the medication is seen as the solution to the problem. Parents turn to doctors for medications, not to therapists for help at what they might do themselves. Families become dependent on medications they are told will have to be taken for the rest of the client's life, creating a never-ending need for treatment. I am not arguing, and nor did Haley, that there are no clients who need medications. The problem is that in today's world, in mental health clinics, almost all the clients end up on them.

Haley was also correct to point to clinic procedures as an impediment to family therapy. Haley stressed beginning with families correctly. For him that meant defining a clear problem the family wants help on, developing initial hypotheses about what sequences the family may be stuck in, and giving directives aimed at helping solve the problem all in the first interview. Haley believed that it was important to set the precedent right off that therapy was about change, not history taking. In today's clinic, families must endure long initial appointments so the clinic can perform what is called *biopsychosocial evaluation*. This means collecting all information about every aspect of the client's total being. Whose need does this meet, the client's or clinic's? Haley would argue this laborious procedure at the outset of treatment establishes that treatment will be long, be focused on all kinds of problems in addition to what the clients want, and be about history taking, not action. Indeed, when one discovers that many clients have open cases for years at these clinics, one wonders how much of this is due to how the case begins.

Diagnosis is a second procedural problem that Haley took issue with that is still alive and kicking today. Haley's idea of diagnosis was to observe how clients respond to interventions and then adjust one's course accordingly. Of course that is not what diagnosis is in mental health. Ascribing a DSM diagnosis is paramount in our system. The problem is that many of these diagnoses are considered incurable conditions, disempowering rather than empowering families. Second, the diagnosis offers no guidance on how to help other than what drugs the client could be given. Finally, many of these diagnoses stigmatize the client. One question Haley was fond of asking was "How many Social Workers would invite a Borderline Personality Disorder person to their home for dinner?" (Haley, 1994). I ask my master's of social work students this question every quarter, and no one ever raises their hand. If these labels stigmatize clients among fellow professionals, what do they do to the clients amongst the general population?

A third procedural problem involves making sure everyone in the clinic has a job with each family. A family might come in with an out-of-control youth. The parents want help with a teenager who throws terrible fits. Before they know it, the family has seven professionals involved with them. The youth has a therapist, and a psychiatrist to give meds. The mother ends up with her own therapist also, because she turns out to be depressed. The couple has a marital therapist to help with the underlying marital problems. Finally, each sibling also ends up with their own therapist because obviously the out-of-control youth is just being scapegoated and the siblings' problems are being overlooked by the parents. A case manager also must be assigned to do the paperwork for the doctor and make sure no one misses their appointments. Not only is the family being helped on problems they did not come in for, but also there is obviously no priority problem to organize the family around and perhaps get something changed.

Next Haley raised issues about training and supervision in mental health clinics. Regarding supervision, it generally is not offered. What Haley meant by *supervision* is a strategy session about how to help a given family. The therapist is given ideas about what to do. In mental health, supervision seems to be about how to do the paperwork so the clinic will get paid, or how to make sure the therapist is doing enough direct service, or whether or not to call the authorities on the family, or how to proceed on the case to make sure no one gets sued. This supervision is only offered if the clinical supervisor is given the time at all to meet with staff. Supervision costs money. To provide it, not only must the clinic insist it be given, but also the supervisor must not be overloaded with managerial tasks so he or she actually has time to offer clinical supervision.

Finally, there is the issue of whether offering family therapy in mental health clinics still can disrupt the clinic hierarchy. Mental health clinics continue to be governed by the medical model. The hierarchy is psychiatrist, psychologist, social worker or counselor, and case manager. The folks who end up going into the homes are typically the case managers. These are the people who observe families directly, and join with parents who often end up being very appreciative of anyone willing to take the time to come to their home. The case managers are the ones who know the most about the families and the ones who are most likely to win the parents' cooperation. As one can see, though, in the clinic they are at the bottom of the hierarchy. This creates a problem when it becomes apparent that the case managers are preferred by the families over the rest of their clinic colleagues.

It would appear that, broadly speaking, every one of the issues Haley raised about doing family therapy in a mental health clinic is still valid 40 years later. This does not mean it is impossible to do it, but it does mean that clinic-wide changes must occur for it to be sustainably implemented even after staff has been trained. Some suggestions for agencies seriously considering family therapy in their clinic are as follows:

1. Train all staff with an emphasis on training supervisors. If supervisors do not know what to do, staff certainly will not. Also, training the whole staff tends to cut down on ideological debates.
2. Provide time for clinical supervisors to offer clinical supervision. Do not fill their plates with administrative and managerial duties. Spend the money on real supervision. In the end it will be cost-effective, clinicians will be more productive and feel more successful, and the clinic will have less turnover.
3. Create institutional procedures that keep the staff focused on family therapy. State and federal mandates and third-party payees require diagnosis and laborious intake procedures. These will never go away, and they constantly orient staff away from family therapy. To combat this, family therapy–friendly procedures must become institutionalized as well. This means live supervision and/or videotaping of sessions. Institutionalizing these procedures in the clinic will help family therapy training endure long after the training is done.
4. Make therapy fun. Mental health clinic jobs are typically thankless, underpaying jobs that overwork the staff. Morale in these clinics typically sucks. A wise clinic investment is having a weekly family therapy team for a few hours where staff can do interviews

together and/or strategize about their cases. The main purpose of these meetings should be for the staff to have fun. Having fun can give staff something to look forward to and raise their morale. They will enjoy their work more, and their clients will show up for more appointments. The clinic will make more money.

References

Haley, J. (1994). Personal communication.

Lee, M., Greene, G., Hsu, K., Solovey, A., Grove, D., Fraser, S., Washburn, P., Teater, B. (2009), "Utilizing Family Strengths and Resilience: Integrative Family and Systems Treatment with Children and Adolescents with Severe Emotional and Behavioral Problems," *Family Process*, Vol. 48, No. 3, 2009.

WHY A MENTAL HEALTH CLINIC SHOULD AVOID FAMILY THERAPY[1]

Jay Haley[2]

Describing the unsettling effects of adding family therapy procedures to the offerings of a mental health clinic, the author argues that changes in the theory of causation, diagnosis, therapeutic technique, and clinical training are required in order to make such an innovation. Consequences are likely to include disorientation of the staff, radically changed administrative procedures, and others, including service to larger numbers of people and better treatment outcome.

—Editor

It is a fundamental error to assume that family therapy can be added as an additional treatment procedure in a mental health clinic in the same way that one can add group therapy or one of the behavior therapy approaches. A number of clinics have attempted to introduce family therapy and have recoiled as they discovered unexpected consequences. Such agencies returned with relief to the tranquility of traditional individual therapy. This has been particularly so in child treatment facilities, but there are consequences in adult clinics and insane asylums as well. (The problem is illustrated by the fact that the division into child and adult clinics is anachronistic from a family therapist's view.)

The only possible reason for instituting family therapy, except for idle reasons such as joining a popular fad, is to improve the outcome of treatment. Yet there is no solid evidence that family therapy produces better therapeutic results. Even if it does, one can wonder if that is a relevant reason for such an undertaking. Mental health clinics are not primarily concerned with treatment outcome. If they were, every clinic would have a research unit which examines results and changes therapy procedures on the basis of the findings. Mental health clinics have never changed a therapeutic approach or discharged a psychiatrist, psychologist, or social worker on the basis of follow-up results of therapy. More important than therapy results to any clinic is staff harmony. If staff members are to work together in reasonable tranquility, they must be in agreement about what should be done. They must have a stable organization with a clear hierarchy so that each person knows the status of another, they must do what they were taught to do through long years of training, and they must teach students proper procedures and receive the respect of those students. These are obviously the most important aspects of life in an agency and the very factors that are most upset by the introduction of family therapy. Any concern with better therapeutic results must be balanced against the day-to-day needs of the staff.

The arguments against the introduction of family therapy offered here are based on observations of the consequences in clinics in various parts of the country. However, the primary basis is one of logic. Once one grasps the crucial change which is insisted upon by experienced family therapists, logical consequences follow. This crucial change is a shift in the unit of diagnosis and treatment from a unit of one person to a unit of two or more persons. A clinic administrator might think this is a minor change, but he soon finds that consequences follow. It is like assuming that becoming pregnant is a minor alteration without anticipating the shape of things to come. Sometimes an administrator is misled because he introduces a beginning family therapist who does not seem too different from other clinicians. However, as the beginner's approach to family therapy proves not to be effective, this tranquil stage becomes temporary and leads either to the abandonment of family therapy or to a revolutionary shift in ideas about the nature of human dilemmas and what to do about them. The discussion here will center upon the effect on a clinic when the approach of an experienced family therapist is introduced with consequent changes in the theory of motivation, of diagnosis, of therapeutic technique, and of clinical training.

Changes in the Theory of Causation

All therapy is based upon a theory of causation, and any clinician bases his therapeutic approach on his explanation of why a person behaves as he does. When the unit of diagnosis and treatment is one person, the "cause" of behavior must reside within the person. The person did what he did because of an idea, a feeling, an internal conflict, a fear, and so on. When the unit shifts to two or more persons, as it does with a family orientation, the "cause" of behavior no longer resides within the person but in the context of other people. A person does what he does because of what someone else did. Examples could be multiplied to show this different view, but perhaps one or two will suffice. If a woman reports being afraid to go out of the house alone, the clinician using the individual unit will explain her behavior in terms of her fears. With a shift to a unit of two or more persons, the family therapist must describe the function of her staying at home in relation to her husband or one or more other persons in her social network. Similarly, a child who will not go to school will be a school phobia with a unit of one, but the family therapist will be concerned with "cause" in the social network made up of the family and the school.

There are several consequences to this shift in unit and only three of them need to be listed to show the radical nature of the change.

1. The most obvious consequence is the fact that the family therapist must abandon psychodynamic theory as an explanation of behavior. Since that theory is confined to a unit of one person, it is irrelevant by definition. In discarding psychodynamic theory, inevitably the theory of repression is abandoned, along with all explanations built upon an individual's intrapsychic structure. A respectable ideology which has been accepted for 50 years is cast aside.

2. A second consequence is the abandonment of a theory of suppressed emotions as a "cause" of behavior. With a unit of two or more persons, "emotion" must be a type of communicative behavior of one person to another, not a cause of how a person is behaving.
3. Discarding the individual as the unit, the family therapist asks us to believe that a person's history is irrelevant as a way of explaining why he behaves as he does. When "cause" is in the interpersonal context, it cannot be a program built inside the person by his past. With a unit of two or more persons, past traumas or other experiences of an individual become pointless explanations, as does any causal theory based upon previous learning or past conditioning.

These three discards should be enough to persuade any clinician that he should have second thoughts about adopting or encouraging a family orientation. The theory of repression, the importance of history as a causal factor, and the idea of suppressed emotions are the building blocks of established clinical practice. Without them how can the average clinician think or even communicate with his colleagues? It must be emphasized here that it is not a question whether the unit *should be* one person or two or more, the point is that the more experienced family therapists think and describe in terms of the larger social unit, and these consequences follow.

An agency which introduces family therapy will find itself asking its staff to go through a process of disorientation. As an alternative to what he had always been taught, the clinician will find that he is supposed to explore human behavior in terms of dyads and triads and larger networks. He is also expected to explain why people behave as they do in terms of the present context. Inevitably, he is forced to consider the real world and real people as important to psychiatric problems, in contrast to the exploration of fantasy worlds in which he was trained. Is it reasonable to expect the average clinician in any agency to drop his concern with the past, ignore fantasies, take an interest in the real world, and be a part of the effort to innovate new ways of thinking about human behavior?

The logic of interpersonal theory forces yet a more disturbing idea upon the clinician. He must disbelieve the notion that the observer, or therapist, is not part of the system being observed. When he describes a person in terms of a social dilemma, he must logically include himself and his clinic in the description of the problem. With this view there is an argument that there is no outside place to stand to take an objective view. The behavior of family members, and their fantasies for that matter, are partly determined by the person examining the family. So the clinician cannot pretend to be scientific and objective as he could when he saw the individual as a specimen being diagnosed independent of his context and responding only to past ideas and dreams.

A clinic administrator might think the problem is put too strongly here and believe that compromise is possible so that family therapy can be introduced along with individual therapy. Yet the differences in theory cannot be put too strongly when the focus is upon what motivates people and what causes change. The theory of psychodynamic therapy is based upon the sensible and appealing notion that a therapist is a benign influence restoring health to individuals who have suffered noxious influences in the past which are currently determining their behavior. In child treatment, for example, the child is thought to have suffered unfortunate past experiences with his family and he is now responding to noxious parental introjects. By dealing with him permissively and benignly, the therapist substitutes himself, relieves the repressive forces, and transforms the inner nature of the child. He is a benevolent liberator if not savior.

Family therapists have a more unsettling review. They operate on the theory that the child's behavior is adaptive and responsive to his *current* family situation and assume the situation must be changed if the child is to change. Rather than accept the idea of repression, they assume that often the parents are too benign and permissive and that if the therapist behaves in the same way it can be anti-therapeutic. Instead of seeing the parents as a noxious influence, they are said to be caught up in a struggle which includes the child and which is maintained by the social situation. Only reorganizing the current family can lead to change in the child and other family members.

Therapists with these two different views cannot reach agreement about a case. The individually oriented therapist wishes to explore for past causes, discuss Piaget and Bruner, and interpret the productions of an individual. The family therapist wants to explore the current situation, discuss the family's stage of development, and make shifts in the ways family members are behaving. Rather than see the child as responding to an introject or being fixed at a developmental phase, the family therapist sees him as a vehicle in a struggle between other people and expressing behavior adaptive to that struggle.

If a therapist partially adopts a family view and partially an individual view, he is in continual confusion and begins to talk in an odd manner. He tries to describe family quarrels in a language of introjects and internalized objects. Typically he tries to think in terms of two sets of parents—the parents sitting in front of a child and the introjected parents inside the child; the complexities require a computer for sorting. He also points out that a therapist is siding with a person's wife while also saying the person is suffering a transference distortion about the therapist's behavior. A classic example of the typical confusion of inner and outer space occurred in an actual description of a case when a therapist said, "This adolescent has a transference relationship with his father."

Changes in the Diagnostic System

Although diagnostic procedures and discussions take up most of the time in the usual clinic, traditional diagnosis is immediately abandoned when family therapy is introduced. With a unit of two or more persons, the diagnostic classifications become irrelevant. Of the many categories in the American Psychiatric Association Diagnostic Manual, the only ones which might apply are "transient situational disturbance" or "adjustments reaction." If every case is defined that way, what point is there to the classification? One of the first changes observed when family therapy is introduced in a clinic is the impatience of the family therapist during a diagnostic case conference. He is not interested in categorizing one of the individuals in a family into a diagnostic type or examining the symbolic productions of the patient. That has nothing to do with his work and can even handicap his thinking about how to intervene therapeutically. Because the diagnostic system is irrelevant not only to the family view but to any type of therapy, the family therapist avoids case conferences, thereby antagonizing more conservative members of the staff. When the whole staff takes up family therapy, the diagnostic conference disappears and is replaced by a strategy conference to determine what to do therapeutically. Professionals accustomed to spending hours discussing a case without ever dealing with what to do can find themselves in a new and unfamiliar world.

When traditional diagnosis is dropped, intake procedures become radically different and have unexpected consequences. As an example, one can contrast the usual intake procedure in child treatment with a family therapy approach. Traditionally, when a mother calls and reports that her child has a problem, the mother is seen for an interview. After that, the child is seen in a session. Once again the mother is interviewed to discuss what was observed in the child's session. After that the father is interviewed for his views. Information about the child and family behavior is based upon these undoubtedly accurate self reports. The child is then seen again and given a battery of psychological tests. All of these interviews and test results are written up and a diagnostic case conference is held. There is a thorough discussion of the case by all the professionals involved. Treatment is inevitably recommended, and the child is put on a waiting list. Several months later the child is taken on in individual treatment. His parents are simultaneously interviewed by a social worker, or the parents enter individual therapy with different therapists.

If a child clinic takes up a family therapy as the primary orientation, the intake procedure is markedly different. When a mother calls about a problem with her child, the whole family is asked to come in for the initial interview. No matter how this disrupts clinic routine, the family therapist insists on seeing the context within which the child lives and the relation of the child's problem to action in the family. The family therapist combines an examination of the problem with immediate therapeutic interventions, since one of his ideas is that "diagnosis" is the response of the family to the suggestions for change. He also wishes to take advantage of whatever crisis brought the family in at this time because the family is most malleable during the crisis period. The case conference stops concerning itself with proper diagnosis and becomes a supervisory session dealing with the effectiveness of the therapist's first interventions. Psychological tests are, of course, abandoned except in exceptional circumstances since they are only relevant to the individual, and so years of a psychologist's training in testing are simply discarded as wasted time.

One consequence of this approach is that the family therapist and the family often decide treatment is unnecessary. This rarely happens with the traditional child guidance approach since by the time of the diagnostic case conferences there has been so much professional time invested that treatment has to take place. Another consequence is the not uncommon discovery that the child chosen by the mother as a problem really is far less of a problem than one of the other siblings, who would never take the time of the clinic in the traditional diagnostic approach since he would never be seen.

Consider what must happen to the professional if he is asked to accept a family therapist's views. He must give up a diagnostic system in which he was trained, give up hours of diagnostic case conferences where he can debate psychodynamics with other members of the staff, and he must dive at once into a whole family when people are upset. He must also begin his therapeutic interventions promptly instead of having the opportunity to be reflective and waiting weeks or months to think about what might be done.

An inadvertent consequence of the introduction of family therapy is a change in the clinic clientele. Traditional therapy, particularly child therapy, was constructed for the middle-class patient. A family orientation makes it possible to deal with the problems of the poor. A clinic is likely to find itself widening its base to include the low socioeconomic class. The staff soon becomes involved with people who do not keep appointments properly, do not free associate as they should, and who must be dealt with in their homes and on the street. Schedules become disrupted and the staff is asked to give up the tranquility of dealing with the properly behaving patient, who comes regularly and asks little.

If a clinic attempts to compromise and do both individual and family therapy, the diagnostic conference can become an unpleasant debate instead of a cooperative endeavor. The family therapist is asked to categorize an individual, which he considers pointless, and the individual therapist is asked to diagnose the interpersonal action in a family, which he considers secondary. Individual therapists object to the "disappearing" of the individual, insist that the family therapists are ignoring deeper levels of character structure, and mourn the contamination of the transference. Family therapists object to fragmenting the family unit by focusing on the individual, argue that treating an individual is one way of intervening into a family and not the best way, and object to the hostile form the diagnosis always takes. The clinic patients become the field where the battles between staff members take place.

When clinicians work as a team, what one practices affects all the others. The effect is most apparent in child treatment facilities. The child psychiatrist who insists on regular interviews alone with the child is usually forcing someone else to see only the parents whether they like it or not. If a psychiatrist insists on using medication with one person, the therapist dealing with the family must protest how this labels one person as the problem and quiets the crisis. The chief social worker who demands traditional diagnostic procedures is making a psychologist do psychological tests whether he wishes to or not. A supervisor who believes only in individual treatment requires students to interview family members individually and is in conflict with other supervisors who insist on whole family interviews. A clinic which attempts such compromises often appears like a football team in which a few of the members decided to play baseball during the game.

Changes in the Theory of Change

The average clinician in a mental health clinic is trained in the sensible belief that therapeutic change occurs when something inside the patient changes. Change is defined as a person's insight into his unconscious processes, understanding of the past causes of his present behavior, "seeing" how he deals with others, release of repressed emotion, change in perception, and so on. With a shift to a unit of two or more persons, these various ideas of changes are no longer logical. Instead, change must be defined as a different sequence of behavior among intimates. Rather than a therapist attempting to help someone understand, the therapist intervenes to change the ways that someone is dealing with another person. He is a changer of sequences, of relationships, and of social structures.

According to an effective family therapist, a clinician must give up his traditional style of passive interpretations as a way of bringing about change. The family therapist calls that "helpless" therapy since it is dependent upon what the patient does, not what the therapist does. Instead, the family therapist expects a clinician to think strategically and use himself as an active participant in bringing a change about. The average clinician is likely to find that sort of thing a bit too much and he will object that it should not be expected of him. Since the family therapist insists that therapy should be different with different problems, he also asks the staff to give up the security of following a standard method and the tranquility which comes from always knowing the proper therapy routine to follow. In other words, the family therapist often just does not fit in with the group.

Another consequence logically follows when family therapy is introduced. Clinicians become uncertain about the approach, and when there is uncertainty the odds increase that a clinic will begin to examine therapy outcome. In the past when everyone was sure they were doing the proper thing, outcome research was unnecessary. The problem is thereby compounded for the staff member. He must not only work within a new theory of change with new practices, but he is likely for the first time to have someone evaluating the results of his therapy.

Changes in Training Procedures

Most clinics have a trained professional staff, and students from universities are brought to the clinic to learn from them. With the introduction of family therapy, marked changes occur.

1. *Training of staff*: If a clinic risks adopting family therapy, it becomes evident at once that no one on the staff knows how to do it. Universities do not provide such training and so all staff must be trained on the job. To teach experienced clinicians on the staff to do family therapy is often more difficult than training new

young people. The experienced clinician has already been trained in a way that the family therapist considers to be a handicap. He must unlearn one therapeutic approach in order to learn another. Naturally the staff member has investments in what he already knows and he does not like a family therapist telling him his knowledge and experience is to be ignored or called a handicap. Yet when he interviews a whole family he focuses upon one person as the patient, describes the case in terms of that one person and his past, deals with one person at a time, and tries to give insight. His thinking is simply oriented in an individual way and so a teaching session becomes a debate rather than a learning experience.

The professional associations of the staff members make the problem even more difficult. Often they teach in universities, have friends and colleagues still working in a traditional way, and function in organizations where proper methods of thinking and working are frozen. To take up a family therapy view with any enthusiasm can jeopardize their professional relationships.

Because of the difficulty in training the staff of a clinic, it is almost impossible to find a competent family therapist who will do the training. Usually such a therapist has his own place where, with great effort, he has managed a setting in which he can work effectively with families. Why should he go to a non-family oriented clinic and engage in what he considers pointless debates? If a clinic can find a family therapy teacher who will cooperate with a partial introduction of family therapy, it is usually a special type of family therapist. Often it is a young family therapist who wishes to make family therapy acceptable and respectable to a proper institution and so does not insist on a radical change. In such cases the result is a bowdlerized family therapy which fails, and the individual ideology loses what purity it has, so that maltreatment becomes part of the day's work in the clinic.

2. *Student trainees*: In most clinics there are young psychiatrists, psychologists, and social workers who intern in the clinic as part of their training program since students are expected to learn from people who are more experienced. Yet what happens if a clinic takes up family therapy? The staff members are in training themselves and do not know how to do this kind of therapy any better than the students. Sometimes they know less because students have less interest in past procedures and have some acquaintance with family therapy literature. Since students and staff function at the same level of accomplishment, naturally there is an upset in the hierarchy. The staff finds that in a case conference a student is listened to with as much respect as a staff member who has had years of experience. Students also will ignore respected older staff members, who will resign when they feel their contribution is not being appreciated. Typically there is a large turnover of personnel if a clinic attempts family therapy in a serious way.

   Students who intern in a clinic are usually based in universities whose main function is to conserve the best of the past. Therefore only a few of them are including family therapy as a respectable point of view since it is an approach which is only 20 years old. The clinic can find itself in conflict with social work and psychiatric departments because of what it is teaching the students and be cut off as a training institution. If the problem does not become that severe, at least the students become used in an ideological battle between the clinic and the university department, with each defaming the other.

Within the clinic, staff members find themselves faced with a type of self-exposure they have never experienced. In the history of therapy a student rarely ever watched his teacher treat a patient. The student was expected to expose his work while his teacher criticized him, but the teacher saw patients in private. With the introduction of family therapy, a one-way mirror and videotape equipment appears. The staff, and this might include the clinic director, is expected to treat families in front of observers, with students learning the art in an apprenticeship system. During such exposure, incompetent staff members reveal their incompetence. Competent staff become nervous because they must not only demonstrate their skills in a new form of therapy but do so under observation.

Changes in the Professional Hierarchy

The helping professions each have different functions and different backgrounds of training. These differences are constructed on the premise that a person is the problem. When the unit is two or more persons, the differences between the professions begin to blur and wash away. With this change comes unreasonable stress upon staff members.

An example might illustrate the problem. In a small clinic in the Southwest, a case conference was being held and a psychologist said, "If we need to medicate someone we can always bring in a psychiatrist." At this point a psychiatrist sitting at the table, his face red with anger, said, "A psychiatrist has more to offer than medication!" Any observer would know at once that this was a clinic which was using family therapy as a major mode of treatment. The anger of the psychiatrist seemed inappropriate unless one takes into account the shift in the status of the professions which comes about with the introduction of family therapy. Instead of being the accepted authority, the psychiatrist becomes one more professional who might or might not be valuable depending upon his contribution as an individual. With family therapy, all the professions do the same work; the psychiatrist treats the whole family, the social worker treats the whole family, and the psychologist treats the whole family. In fact in a number of places nurses are becoming experts in family therapy, and an even more extreme situation appears when indigenous aides are taught to be family therapists. No profession has any more knowledge or training in family therapy than any other, and so the status hierarchy dissolves without a new one to take its place. The stress on the staff takes different forms. Typically the psychiatrist loses the automatic respect that was once given to his profession, and he must earn respect as a consultant or a therapist according to his individual skills. The psychologist loses his function as an expert on psychological tests and must be able to think in social units and become a skilled clinician. Psychiatric social workers have to give up the birth trauma and their psychoanalytic training and think in terms of families, neighborhoods, schools and other aspects of the real world. They no longer can merely commiserate with parents about a child but must learn something about child development and dealing with children as well as with the parents.

The change brought about by family therapy is most painful to the psychiatrist because he has been highest in status previously and so has the most to lose as the hierarchy changes. The psychiatric profession poses a particularly difficult problem today. If they accept the family orientation, they must abandon the basic ideology of psychiatry and adopt a new treatment approach in which they have no more training and therefore no more status than anyone else. If they oppose family therapy and stay with traditional psychiatry, they risk the possibility that they will not be leaders in the profession but laggards, remaining behind and being ignored while therapy goes in new social directions. The psychiatrist cannot even take refuge in the fact that medical knowledge is important because most psychiatrists have given up medicine and call in a physician if there is a medical examination or problem. Other professions can do that as well, leaving the psychiatrist with uncertain functions in the new social world.

Not only do the helping professions become more alike in their work when they take up family therapy, but in a number of clinics the question is inevitably being raised why there should be a difference in pay for the same work. Why should a psychiatrist, for example, be paid more than a psychologist or a social worker when they are doing the same job as therapists? As differences in function disappear, anger over differences in pay develops among the staff. A clinic can be forced to arrange a salary scale based on merit rather than profession. Such a unique arrangement brings about confusion in the civil service categories and puzzles governmental bureaucracies who have been sold the idea that therapy is medical treatment requiring physicians as primary leaders.

In a clinic which adopts family therapy the social workers and psychologists sometimes seem to gain a certain pleasure in observing the loss of prestige of the psychiatrist (particularly if he is the clinic director). However, on the horizon is a threat which all the professions must consider when family therapy is introduced. Since it is a new approach requiring new ways of thinking, according to many family therapists, and since clinicians trained in individual therapy are the most difficult to teach, it logically follows that there will be more emphasis upon training laymen in family therapy. Right now there are programs for training poor and black people to do family therapy, not as aides but as full-fledged clinicians. They are in training to treat the poor but included in their training is the treatment of middle-class families. If these programs succeed and high school graduates can become competent clinicians with one or two years of intensive training, where will that leave the professionals who are spending years in universities learning peripheral matters? Just as social workers are now hired because they are less expensive than psychiatrists, so it logically follows that trained high school graduates will be hired if they are less expensive than social workers. The community mental health centers in the vast urban slums of this country will undoubtedly select personnel on the basis of economics. Encouraging a family therapy movement might very well lead to a new class of therapists who leave professionals unemployed and protesting.

Ways to Avoid Family Therapy

Adopting family therapy as the major treatment modality can provide severe difficulties for a clinic and possibly the mental health field, while partial use of family therapy causes confusion. How can a clinic exclude family therapy gracefully? If a clinic administrator merely forbids this type of therapy, he will antagonize many of his younger staff and gain a reputation as old fashioned and dogmatic. Every clinic must appear to be eclectic, flexible, and modern in its approach. In a number of clinics a procedure has been developed which appears to be the most effective one if a clinic director wishes to avoid family therapy. The steps can be outlined. When family therapy is suggested by someone on the staff, the clinic administrator should adopt a posture of welcoming all new ideas and approaches. At the same time he should use a strategy of step-by-step resistance. After approving the idea of family therapy, the administrator should delay such a program until the staff has lost interest. If the staff insists that the approach be tried, the individuals involved can be fired for other reasons. If this action is not sufficient, the director can appear to be accepting and liberal by announcing that he is establishing a section on family therapy. However, he should then see to it that no referrals are made to that section. Each case will be found to be inappropriate, so that the clinic can claim to have a family therapy program without the inconvenience. If the staff assigned to that section keep being insistent and force the issue of referrals, it might finally become necessary to actually do family therapy with a case. The wise administrator will see this as an opportunity to finish off the family therapy issues. A very difficult family can be selected, and an appropriate clinician chosen to treat the family. A psychoanalyst or a social worker with a good heart and little experience is usually the best choice. The family therapy will go badly, providing clear evidence that despite the good intentions of the director it just is not wise to take a family approach. After that, the clinic can report that it tried family therapy and found it lacking.

Although this approach for avoiding family therapy is effective, and clinic administrators can develop other appropriate ways, all devices are likely to be temporary ones. A family orientation is developing widely in the field and could ultimately become unavoidable. It is part of the general social change and the wider concern with interacting systems. In every city community mental health problems are forcing a more social orientation, young therapists want more active involvement with people, and the explosion of a whole variety of therapeutic approaches has shaken the field in the last decade. It has even become respectable to say that a method of therapy which consistently fails should be abandoned, no matter how prominent its practitioners or how much has been invested. The times are out of joint and, despite the skill of administrators, change might have to occur even in the institutions devoted to bringing about change.

Summary

If a mental health clinic introduces family therapy as a treatment procedure, the consequences are likely to be disorientation of the staff, radically changed administrative procedures, less harmony among the professions, and confusion in the administrative hierarchy. Staff members will find themselves asked to think in terms of a theory in which they were not trained and to diagnose social rather than individual problems.

The staff will also be expected to intervene actively in human dilemmas, to work with poor people, to do therapy under observation where all errors are visible, and quite possibly to have the results of their therapy evaluated. In exchange for the confusion in clinic administrative procedures and stress on staff members, the clinic receives a relatively small return. There will be service to larger numbers of people, less of a waiting list, more time devoted to therapy and less to other activities, and better treatment outcome. Obviously this is not a sufficient return for a mental health clinic to undertake this adventure irresponsibly.

Endnotes

1. This article was rejected by the *Archives of General Psychiatry*, the *American Journal of Orthopsychiatry*, *Social Casework*, the *American Journal of Psychotherapy*, and *Psychiatry*.
2. Jay Haley was director of Family Therapy Research, Philadelphia Child Guidance Clinic, 2 Children's Center, 34th Street and Civic Center Boulevard, Philadelphia, Pennsylvania 19104.

9

A Quiz for Young Therapists

INTRODUCTION

Kenneth V. Hardy, PhD

I was teaching a graduate-level Family Therapy course at the Virginia Tech–Falls Church campus in the mid-1980s when a student in the class boldly called me a hypocrite for criticizing Jay Haley's strategic therapy model. Jerry, the student, reminded me that my passionate mantra with the students had always been "Try it before you critique it." An ardent follower and self-proclaimed disciple of Haley, Jerry considered it patently unfair for me to unleash what he considered to be an unfounded and harsh criticism of Haley and his work. Although I revered Haley for his stellar contributions to the field, I was often critical of his approach to therapy, which seemed cold, detached, mechanistic, and more tactical than emotional. In many ways, his approach seemed totally antithetical to the more humanistically informed approach in which I had been trained.

As the semester progressed, Jerry continued to speak in godlike terms of Haley and his work. It was obvious that he considered Haley's strategic approach a panacea for all psychotherapy ills.

It was exactly one year following the course I had with Jerry that I decided to enroll at the Family Therapy Institute of Washington, DC, to complete postdoctoral training with Jay Haley. During the course of my career, I completed two postdoctoral training experiences: one with Haley at the Family Therapy Institute of Washington, DC; and one in Palo Alto, California, at the Mental Research Institute (MRI), a place ironically where Jay had spent a significant portion of his illustrious career. Both experiences were life altering for me. These experiences not only changed what and how I thought about therapy but also significantly altered how I thought about the world beyond the private, intimate walls of psychotherapy. The advice of my former student Jerry, who is now an accomplished scholar and academician in his own right, was among the most significant that I have ever received from a trainee.

While at the Family Therapy Institute of Washington, DC, I had the honor and privilege to interact with Jay in small-group didactic sessions and to receive supervision from him behind the one-way mirror. It was these experiences that enabled me to better understand both the nuances of strategic therapy and the man behind it. In the didactic sessions, Haley was insightful, thoughtful, irreverent, and provocative. His ways of thinking about human behavior, the process of therapy, and change were saturated with pearls of common sense, yet they were uncharacteristically uncommon in their complexity and sophistication. Haley had a way of inviting us as trainees to look at that which we customarily gazed at but this time around dare to pay attention to and see what was invariably there all of the time but had gone unseen. His demeanor and approach at times flirted with that thin line that often exists between confidence and arrogance. He was at times pleasantly cynical, as he pointed out the absurdities of a dynamic or interaction with a slither of sarcasm, humor, or wit. As a trainee, I was often intellectually challenged, inspired, and slightly intimidated. Although it was refreshing to be invited to think and "see" differently, it was also intimidating to part ways with many of the irrefutable truths that I held as a therapist.

Behind the one-way mirror, Haley was unexpectedly gentle, supportive, and validating. He had a keen intuitive sense that was often balanced by a well-thought-out conceptual framework that was the reference point for his ideas and interventions. He was always careful to explain why a particular therapeutic strategy was suggested in lieu of one that was not. Perhaps Haley's greatest strength as a supervisor-theoretician was his ability to fully grasp the essence of a client's presenting problem and then design an intervention strategy that was specifically directed toward the amelioration of the problem. His approach was no-frills but effective. Although I had been actively involved in the field of family therapy as a clinician, educator, and professional association executive, it was the time I spent at the Family Therapy Institute with Haley that helped me the most to refine my skill at concisely and precisely designing interventions to help couples and families find solutions to the problems they presented.

As I reread Haley's article "A Quiz for Young Therapists" as part of my preparation for the writing of this manuscript, I was immediately reminded of the time I had spent learning from Jay and his approach to the work. The article, although just a few pages in length, is an insightfully written and provocative essay. In many ways, his ideas are every bit as insightful and provocative when applied to psychotherapy in 2009 as they were considered to be back in 1977, when I first read the article as a doctoral student. It is a brilliant display of Haley's wit, irreverence, and thoughtfulness about the field. The article is part critique, commentary, and prescription. Although many of the questions that Haley posed in his quiz have been partially answered today, many remain critically important questions for clinicians, especially educators like myself, to ponder.

In this article, Haley notes that therapy has reached a level of significance in society such that it has become an integral part of mainstream society. It is a common feature of our daily lexicon, it inundates the literature, it enjoys widespread support throughout private and governmental agencies, and it garners considerable financial support in both treatment and training, according to Haley back in 1977. Haley lamented, and appeared chagrined by, the notion that despite its overall acceptance and popularity, therapy lacked "a proper examination, or quiz, for the aspiring therapist who is turned loose upon the public." After all, Haley wondered. "How does one know that a therapist knows what he, or she, should?" In one sense, the field is at a very different place than it was when Haley first expressed the aforementioned concern. In family therapy at least, there have been a number of developments over the last 30 years that have been enacted to address the concerns expressed by Haley and others regarding the validity, reliability, and accountability of clinical training. The development of a national exam in marriage and family therapy (MFT), the establishment of educational and training standards, and the development of standards for specialized accreditation in MFT educational and training programs were all deliberate, systematic initiatives designed to address the issue of efficacy and clinical education.

Despite these developments and the contributions each has made to the field, I doubt seriously that any of the aforementioned would have satisfied Haley's critique of the field. It is my guess that he would consider licensing exams and accreditation standards as failed attempts to really address the problem. After all, licensing exams are constructed to measure one's knowledge of ideas, rather than what one actually does. I believe that Haley was arguing for the latter. The same argument could be made regarding accreditation standards to some extent. Although program accreditation in MFT requires all trainees to complete hands-on clinical experience and receive supervision based on raw clinical data, in accredited MFT programs, faculty and supervisors can base their appraisal of trainees' development on what they do (with clients), as well as on what they ostensibly know. Unfortunately, this training approach is virtually limited to accredited programs that are relatively small in number, serving small numbers of trainees, and the clinical hours required and upon which the model is based constitute less than a quarter of the requisite clinical-supervisory hours necessary for credentialing. Thus, the majority of the training is based on some combination of academic knowledge, loosely integrated with clinical work that occurs in privacy without guidance or oversight based on raw clinical data.

The nascent trend toward privileging "evidence-based" and "best-practice" models for funding by various private and governmental funding sources is indicative of yet another attempt to address the issue "How does one know that a therapist knows what he, or she, should?" Although the evidence-based models of treatment are based on the types of outcome measures that Haley was alluding to, I believe he would have objected to the orthodoxy, "purity," and fidelity that the very execution of these models espouse.

All of these initiatives point to the fact that Haley's critique of the field in 1977 identified a legitimate void in the field that warranted further and future inquiry. The developments of the past 30 years are also illustrative of the considerable progress that the field has made to address the question(s) regarding what "therapists know," how do we measure or "know what they know," and how do we know that a therapist "knows what he, or she, should?"

Haley constructed a 15-question quiz that highlighted what he considered to be some of the more salient questions for the young therapist to consider. In typical Haley fashion, the questions were at times slightly humorous, pompous, arrogant, and sardonic, but always insightful, strategic, and provocative. Within both the questions queried by Haley as well as the answers provided are pearls of wisdom that he has about the process of therapy and the role that therapists play. If one reads these quiz questions literally and relegates one's reflection to only the issue at hand, a huge part of Haley's genius will undoubtedly be missed. Each one of these questions invites a kind of critical reflection about who we are as therapists, what we believe and stand for, and what our notions—conscious and unconscious—are about the process of change.

A QUIZ FOR YOUNG THERAPISTS

Jay Haley

Therapy is now a major industry with neighborhood clinics subsidized by the government, millions of dollars invested in training, more millions collected by the therapists of many different schools, and a vast literature inundating the nation's libraries. Yet what is still lacking is a proper examination, or quiz, for the aspiring therapist who is turned loose upon the public. How does one know that a therapist knows what he, or she, should? Among the difficulties in developing a proper test is the obvious problem that skill as a therapist can only be determined by examining the result of therapy, not by a written test about ideas. Therefore schools that take the training of student therapists seriously do outcome studies of their therapy. Yet granting that a quiz cannot measure skill, a certain amount of knowledge can be expected from a therapist and measured with a written test. The proper attitude about therapy can also be shown to be present or absent by the results of an examination.

The major problem in developing a test of knowledge and attitude has been the fact that attempts at examinations immediately reveal a dogmatic bias of a particular school of therapy and so the test is not useful to the wider field. What is needed is a quiz based on the big, broad, flexible viewpoint so that it can be given to the therapist of any school to determine if he, or she, knows what should be known. Fortunately a modest beginning has taken place in solving the problem of the unbiased quiz on therapy, and one is offered here. The quiz presents the most important questions in the field, and the correct answers are given for anyone who might not know them.

1. *Should a Therapist Think of Himself, or Herself, as a Skillful Technician or as a Humanist and Philosopher?*

Some authorities argue that a therapist should be a Renaissance man, or woman, who is learned in physiology, psychology, the social sciences, and the arts. When confronted with the problem of a child who wets the bed, the philosopher clinician does not review in his mind 11 ways to cure that problem. Instead, he thinks that the child is wetting the bed as a way of expressing his, or her, conception of the world. Is this child pissing on the universe, asks the philosopher clinician. Yet such a therapist must know the routine ways of curing a child of wetting the bed. If not, what are therapists for?

The proper answer to the question? It is all right to be a philosopher and a humanist if that does not interfere with being a skillful therapist.

2. *In Relation to Being a Successful Therapist, What Are the Differences Between Psychiatrists, Social Workers, and Psychologists?*

Except for ideology, salary, status, and power, the differences are irrelevant.

One should not mention the differences in training of the three professions because of possible embarrassment. If the faculties of departments of psychiatry, departments of psychology, and social work schools really believe that what they teach is necessary for training a therapist, then they should require that all three disciplines have medical psychiatric training, all get Ph.D.s in psychology departments, and then all go to social work school before learning pastoral counseling.

3. Is the Goal of Therapy to Change People to Become Members of Special Elites or to Change Them to Be Normal Like Other People?

Special elites are composed of people who are privileged to have a special knowledge about man or who have had extraordinary experiences shared only by members of the special groups. Therefore elites tend to be created by educational therapies or revivalist therapies. A therapy that solves problems has as its goal people who live normally and are not more special than other people. Take your choice.

4. Should a Therapist Join in the Madness of Others or Remain Outside Their Universe?

Besides a long academic education and excessive self-consciousness, the worst handicap for a therapist is to be unable to accept what is offered by a client. When spoken to, such a therapist interprets, corrects, points out, confronts, argues, debates, patronizes, and so does not join the people who have come to him to be changed. If a therapist is warm and empathic with a patient who is a cold fish, there is something wrong with that therapist and he should be more appropriate and human. If a woman says she gives her child an enema whenever she (the woman) has a stomach ache, the therapist should not say, "My God, you'll never go to heaven behaving like that." The woman will feel that yet another person does not understand her. The therapist must join that woman's universe and from within that universe bring about change.

Yet, if a therapist joins the universe of his clientele, he will be as mad as they are and will thrash about helplessly with them in their failing endeavors. How would a therapist ever change anyone if he only joined them in the ways they are already behaving? He must introduce new ways to them.

The answer: He, or she, must join people in their morass while not allowing that morass to continue.

5. Should the Therapist Work Swiftly or Leisurely?

One of the most important requirements of a therapist is patience. Struggling with human misery, complex social situations and long perduring difficulties, the therapist should not expect quick and magical cures. Life moves slowly and inexorably, as anyone knows who has tried to change people or therapy training institutes. One must have patience and, in a leisurely way, build one small change upon another.

Yet we must recognize that people in distress need immediate relief and often will change only if the action is quick. A therapist must respond promptly with directives to take advantage of the opportunities only available in periods of temporary instability.

The answer: Consider the posture of the diamond cutter. He is patient and yet he swiftly produces his results—and in the therapeutic situation errors are more reversible since opportunities, like merry-go-round horses, are likely to come round again.

6. Will Reflecting Upon Himself, or Herself, Improve the Results of a Therapist?

A therapist should not become so concerned with himself that he cannot see the client. A therapist who is thinking, "Am I responding to this woman before me or to an introjected image of my great Aunt Edna of whom she reminds me," is not responding to the woman who is trying to get his attention. Such a therapist is probably suffering from didactic personal therapy. There is a great deal of propaganda, and no evidence, that personal therapy increases a therapist's skill and improves the outcome of his therapy. Didactic therapy is financially important, perhaps necessary, to the profession, but in fact for some therapists, such a self-reflection incapacitates them. One cannot change another while thinking about oneself. In truth, if one is really doing something he is not there.

Yet the therapist with experience knows that—like the man who turns on the light to see the darkness more clearly—his acts produce the data upon which he acts. The married couple fighting in a therapist's presence are in a fight partly because he, or she, is triangulating with them and spurring on their war.

The answer: A therapist must be unaware of himself and focused upon others while responding to the situation with full awareness of his part in creating it.

7. When One Thinks of Therapy as Poetry, Does a Skillful Therapist Write Sonnets or Free Verse?

A sonnet writer is confined to a set number of lines and rigid meter. Quite the opposite is true of the writer of free verse. Spontaneity is the thing and anything goes. Which approach is most creative? Every therapist must take a position on this issue.

The argument of the sonnet enthusiast is that only under law is there freedom: creative expression comes to an author when he is restricted by rules. Only if a therapist behaves in an orderly manner can he be a professional and practice a disciplined art that is teachable. Being confined within rules forces the artist to new flights of imagination.

The enthusiast for free verse argues that any restriction prevents self-expression: total freedom comes only when there are no rules. A therapist cannot respond appropriately to a new and unique situation if he follows preordained rules, and is not each situation actually new and unique? When faced with the complexity of the multitude of messages happening in any human situation, a therapist does not have time to consciously think through what he should do; he must simply respond. Obviously, a therapist must trust and follow his impulses if he is to adapt quickly to complex situations.

The answer: The therapist must be a spontaneous free verse poet and follow his impulses while observing the rules of professional conduct and having the self-discipline of the composer of sonnets.

8. Will a Therapist Be More Successful if He Is Curious About Life's Complexity or if He Is Single-Minded in His Focus Upon His Goals?

Once a student said to a Zen Master, "Isn't the mountain beautiful?" The master replied, "Yes, but isn't it a pity to say so?" Although that story is not relevant to this question, it is an enlightening story and reminds us all of the narrowness of the world of words. When a woman quietly sighs after her husband speaks, the skillful therapist does not attempt some absurd translation into words of that expressive sigh.

Yet, what of curiosity? Why did that woman sigh and what does it mean? Should not curiosity be one of the most important facets of a therapist? Surely we want explorers with an interest in all the ways of human beings in their infinite variety.

Consider the master Botanist who must grasp the extraordinary complexity of the flower and its growth process while not losing his appreciation of the beauty of a field of poppies. The Botanist who cannot enjoy a flower is as handicapped as the one who has learned nothing about the flower's structure. The therapist must understand and appreciate the extraordinary complexity of a person and his social network. Yet, he must accept the simple process of life and know that children should mind parents and parents respect grandparents.

While appreciating complexity and maintaining an attitude of uncertainty about what is really found in human life, the clinician should be willing to be an expert and say what must be done.

It is evident that the therapist must be a person naturally curious about people while single-minded in his pursuit of goals.

9. Name Two Ideologies That Handicap a Therapist.

(a) The theory of repression that offers a negative and pessimistic view of human beings and confines a therapist to a narrow theory of change.
(b) The theory that therapy is to help people "grow." Such a view excuses a therapist for not knowing how to deal with the real problems of people.

10. Should a Therapist Insist Upon Change?

A therapist must be willing to go to the mat with a client and struggle with the problem until it is solved or the participants are dead. Should a therapist give up too easily he will never win the difficult cases. Some people will never change until they are sure the therapist will not give up! When he, or she, talks of failing, the therapist should do so with anger. Just as the trajectory of a flying ball is determined by the energy with which the player swings the bat, so is the success of therapy determined by the energy and dedication the therapist is willing to put into a case. Let him even pursue the client outside the office and down the street until his goals are achieved.

Yet while being a determined person, the therapist must learn not to care too much. If he is too determined to win, he will be at a disadvantage and lose. More important, what right has he to intrude upon people who have become reluctant to change? The restraint of benevolent helpers is one of the most important tasks for us all. Certainly the therapist should not pursue his client because of pity for him, or her, because a therapist should be a person without pity.

The solution: As every housewife knows, one cannot make a flower grow, or produce an erection, by pulling on it. One can only fertilize the ground. A therapist must be absolutely determined to cure while being casual about his investment in the effort.

11. Is It Unethical to Adopt the Theory That Change Is Slow and Difficult and Every Patient Must Come to Therapy Several Hours a Week for Many Years?

Only if the therapist is paid by the hour.

12. Will a Therapist Be More Successful if He Is Humble?

While self-confidence is important, humility is a virtue that allows one to continue to learn. A therapist should take pride in his ability to be humble. There are practical advantages too: if a therapist is arrogant it becomes a challenge to his clients. They develop a desire to topple him and can easily do so by simply not changing. Therefore, self-confidence in this form can be a handicap. Many therapists have found it wise to retain a symptom themselves so they can reassure themselves they are not superior to the people they cure.

The answer: It is best for the therapist to be humble while full of confidence in his abilities.

13. Should the Therapist Be a Serious Person?

The clientele coming to a therapist are in trouble and in despair. They have gone mad or fear the dark or live in fury at their fellow man, or woman. Failures and incompetents are the daily company of the therapist. In this grim world the therapist must take seriously the human misery upon which he feeds and which he must ease. To treat the lives of miserable folk lightly is the behavior of a cad, or caddess.

Yet, the most important attitude of a therapist is the spirit of play. In his training and in his work the therapist must be able to transcend human suffering and rejoice in a playful and innovative spirit. He cannot allow himself to be as grim and miserable as his clientele for what hope have they in that case? Often it is only the light touch that can turn away wrath and transform despair into grudging optimism.

The answer: A therapist must be serious about the grim situation of his clientele while being free to change the framework of the situation in the spirit of play.

14. What Is Therapy?

The introduction of greater complexity into behavioral systems by changing specific problems. The result must be a change in the complex, repeating sequences of an intimate group and consequently the creation of more alternatives and greater variety in people's lives.

15. Is It True That Therapy in the Past Consisted of Someone Offering an Unformulated Problem to a Therapist Unable to Specify a Goal Who Was Working With an Irrelevant Theory in an Ambiguous Style to Achieve an Immeasurable Outcome?

Well, that certainly is a good sentence.

10

How to Be a Marriage Therapist Without Knowing Practically Anything

INTRODUCTION

Leslie S Greenberg, PhD

Reading this article, "How to Be a Marriage Therapist Without Knowing Practically Anything," my first image was of Jerry Seinfeld delivering many of Haley's pithy lines in one of his stand-up satiric routines that made him so famous, making astute observations about nothing—this time about what marital therapists do. For example, imagine Jerry Seinfeld (if you've seen him) straightening some piece of clothing, saying, "Have you noticed how therapists deal with disappointed customers? They blame them for not noticing what has changed, saying 'more change has taken place than you realize,' or, for not having changed, 'you have gone about as far as you can go right now and need to integrate what we have done.'"

In his paper, Haley chastens us all with his observations on how therapists use their position to conceal their lacks. The master iconoclast and deliverer of prescriptions puts the therapist readers of this paper in a bind by paradoxically prescribing the very things they do. This is done to prompt them to change what they do. Trusting in people's healthy reactance tendencies, he believes that by urging us to continue to conceal our ignorance of how to help couples change by saying such general things as "Tell me more about that," or "Have you wondered why that is so important to you?" or even using more communication theory–inspired statements such as "I want you to talk to each other so I can observe how you communicate," we will stop doing these. By prescribing specific techniques such as active listening, reflecting back to people what they say, getting in touch with feelings, making interpretations, pointing out games, and sculpting positions, all prevalent at the time of the writing of this paper he hoped to prompt therapists to give up these specific tactics for hiding that they didn't know what to do.

Was his "treatment" of the marital field effective? Did Haley's paradoxical prescription work? Well, to some extent yes, in that many of the general factors he prescribed are probably used less, and less randomly, as couples therapy came more under study and couples therapists came to be better trained. Was it first-order or second-order change that was promoted? Probably more first-order change in that couples therapists' behaviors have changed. Haley the archfunctionalist, the systemic behaviorist, would be happy (if it is kosher to prescribe an inner world to him!) that the field has progressed and there is less need to hide ignorance. However, he would, I imagine, be unhappy in that second-order change toward the exclusive use of functional, structural, and communication modes of analysis of interaction did not occur, and many of the processes, like understanding conflict by appealing to motives, intentions, and feelings, the inner world he hoped to expunge in systems therapy, were not dropped.

I was a young therapist at the time of the publication of Haley's paper, trying to learn what to do as a couples therapist, and I can reverberate with his frustration with the dearth of real "know-how" in the field at that time, especially in couple intervention. This lack of knowledge is partly what set me on the path of trying to figure out how couples resolved conflict and to the development of emotionally focused couples therapy (Greenberg & Johnson, 1988). The field, however, has progressed substantially since 1980. In fact, what has occurred is that many of the specific factors like active listening of the 1980s that Haley criticizes have become more general and now are recognized as the generic factors of couples therapy, whereas more evidence-based interventions that specify more clearly what aspects of these methods work when and for what purpose have become the specific factors. We no longer need to hide our ignorance, although we still need to maintain our humility and our humanness, for whatever scientific evidence we have, love, connection, and validation of one human being by another and simply getting along retain some of their mystery.

Evidence-based marital therapy and research on what makes for master marriages and for change in couples therapy have progressed significantly in the years since Haley's paper in 1980. A variety of couples therapy interventions have demonstrated their efficacy in increasing marital satisfaction for distressed couples (Baucom, Shoham, Mueser, Daiuto, & Stickle, 1998; Christensen, Atkins, et al., 2004; Christensen & Jacobson, 2000; Jacobson et al., 1985; Johnson & Greenberg, 1985a, 1985b; Johnson, Hunsley, Greenberg, & Schindler, 1999; Shadish, Ragsdale, Glaser-Renita, & Montgomery, 1995). Couples therapists no longer need to hide their ignorance as they know more about how to promote change.

Behavioral marital therapy, a cognitive-behavioral therapy developed by Robert Weiss and others, is the oldest and most researched of effective couples therapy approaches (Weiss, 1975). It is organized around teaching communication and problem-solving skills, and having couples renegotiate their behavioral exchanges. *Emotion-focused couples therapy*, developed by Greenberg and Johnson (Greenberg, 2002; Greenberg & Johnson, 1988; Johnson, 1994), is a treatment based on a synthesis of experiential (intrapsychic) and systemic (interpersonal) therapeutic interventions that focuses on emotion, attachment, and identity and works by the revealing of feelings underlying interactional positions. It is recognized as an effective approach in resolving relationship distress (Alexander, Holtzworth-Munroe, & Jameson, 1994; Baucom et al., 1998; Goldman & Greenberg, 1992; Johnson & Greenberg, 1985a, 1985b; Johnson et al., 1999). Active listening and getting in touch with feelings, which were rejected by Haley as ways of hiding ignorance, have, by being specified further in terms of when and how to use these approaches, become a key set of interventions that when knowledgeably applied do not hide ignorance, but rather change interactions and emotional bonds. *Insight-oriented couples therapy*, developed by Doug Snyder (Snyder & Wills, 1989), on the other hand, focuses on identifying the origins of relationship themes for each partner and uses this understanding to change current relationship patterns. Again, rather than making connections between "this and that," as Haley recommends to hide ignorance, interpretation can be used to understand current relationships in terms of past ones in ways that lead to change. *Integrative behavioral couples therapy*, developed by Andrew Christenson and Neil Jacobson (Christensen & Jacobson, 2000; Christensen, Sevier, Simpson, & Gattis, 2004), adds an emphasis on acceptance derived from humanistic approaches to the skill-building and contracting foci of behavioral couples therapy. Couples are helped to recognize the polarizing patterns in their relationship, while achieving more realistic attitudes about the possibilities of changing each other and developing their individual capacities for self-care.

Two comprehensive reviews of research on family therapy suggest that the science of couples and family therapy has moved well beyond its originators' footsteps. Both *Effectiveness Research in Marriage and Family Therapy* (Sprenkle, 2002, 2003), edited by Doug Sprenkle, and *The Effectiveness and Efficacy of Marital and Family Therapy* (Pinsof & Wynne, 1995), edited by William Pinsof and Lyman Wynne, consist of state-of-the-art reviews of outcome research assessing the effectiveness of family therapy across a range of clinical problems. There now is clear evidence that treatment does have positive impact leading to differences that make a difference and have an "effect size" comparable to those of both successful medical treatments and individual psychotherapy.

Most of the current approaches integrate individual and couple foci, and see nurturing of the therapeutic alliance as central, whereas confrontation is rare and paradoxical interventions are nowhere in sight. Gone also is the emphasis on single, eventful interventions for which Haley was so famous. In addition, many relationship enhancement programs have been developed. Many of these have their empirical roots in the groundbreaking studies conducted by Gottman (1994, 1998), Markman (Markman, Duncan, Storaasli, & Howes, 1987), Fincham (1997), and others, which have provided an empirical foundation for understanding both what makes marriages work and what factors underlie their dissolution. Both the basic skills associated with satisfying marriages and the skill deficits that typically accompany unhappy relationships have been identified. Although both happy and unhappy couples have arguments, unhappy couples are far more likely to engage in a wide range of destructive fight tactics, including making personal attacks, dredging up the past, losing focus, and name-calling. Satisfied couples are better able to speak clearly with each other and listen empathically. As John Gottman has put it, distressed couples are also far more likely to resort to the "four horsemen of the apocalypse," behaviors highly predictive of later divorce: criticism, defensiveness, withdrawal, and contempt (Gottman, 1999; Gottman & Notarius, 2000). Satisfied couples also have many more positive than negative exchanges and have better problem-solving skills (Weiss & Heyman, 1997). In contrast, dissatisfied couples are much more likely to experience negatively escalating arguments and become stuck in repetitively harmful patterns. There also is some evidence to suggest that, in addition to prevention, these psychoeducational approaches can produce significant improvements in the marital satisfaction of distressed couples (Halford, Sanders, & Behrens, 2001; Kaiser, Hahlweg, Fehm-Wolfsdorf, & Groth, 1998).

Conclusion

Research indicates that couples and family therapy is not a wonder cure, but is a solid set of treatments that help most clients. Ignorance has been overcome—somewhat! However, I feel confident in saying that Haley's paper was successful in that what it has to say is no longer relevant to couples therapy.

References

Alexander, J. F., Holtzworth-Munroe, A., & Jameson, P. (1994). The process and outcome of marital and family therapy: Research review and evaluation. In A. Bergin & S. Garfield (Eds.), *Handbook of psychotherapy and behavior change* (pp. 595–612). New York: John Wiley.

Baucom, D., Shoham, V., Mueser, K., Daiuto, A., & Stickle, T. (1998). Empirically supported couple and family interventions for marital distress and adult mental health problems. *Journal of Consulting and Clinical Psychology*, *66*, 53–88.

Christensen, A., Atkins, D. C., Berns, S., Wheeler, J., Baucom, D., & Simpson, L. E. (2004). Traditional versus integrative behavioral couple therapy for significantly and chronically distressed married couples. *Journal of Consulting and Clinical Psychology*, *72*, 176–191.

Christensen, A., & Jacobson, N. S. (2000). *Reconcilable differences*. New York: Guilford.

Fincham, F. D. (1997). Understanding marriage: From fish scales to milliseconds. *Psychologist, 10*(12), 543–547.

Goldman, A., & Greenberg, L. (1992). Comparison of integrated systemic and emotionally focused approaches to couples therapy. *Journal of Consulting and Clinical Psychology, 60*, 962–969.

Gottman, J. M. (1994). *What predicts divorce? The relationship between marital processes and marital outcomes.* Hillsdale, NJ: Lawrence Erlbaum.

Gottman, J. M. (1998). Psychology and the study of the marital processes. *Annual Review of Psychology, 49*, 169–197.

Gottman, J. M. (1999). *The marriage clinic: A scientifically based marital therapy.* New York: Norton.

Gottman, J. M., & Notarius, C. I. (2000). Decade review: Observing marital interaction. *Journal of Marriage & the Family, 62*(4), 927–947.

Greenberg, L. S. (2002). *Emotion-focused therapy: Coaching clients to work through their feelings.* Washington, DC: American Psychological Association.

Greenberg, L. S., & Johnson, S. M. (1988). *Emotionally focused therapy for couples.* New York: Guilford.

Guerney, B. G., Jr. (Ed.). (1988). *Family relationship enhancement: A skill training approach.*

Hahlweg, K., Markman, H. J., Thurmaier, F., Engl, J., & Eckert, V. (1998). Prevention of marital distress: Results of a German prospective longitudinal study. *Journal of Family Psychology, 12*(4), 543–556.

Halford, W., & Markman, H. J. (Eds.). (1997). *Clinical handbook of marriage and couples interventions.* New York: John Wiley.

Halford, W., Markman, H. J., Kline, G. H., & Stanley, S. M. (2003). Best practice in couple relationship education. *Journal of Marital & Family Therapy, 29*(3), 385–406.

Jacobson, N. S., Follette, V. M., Follette, W. C., Holtzworth-Munroe, A., Katt, J. L., & Schmanling, K. B. (1985). A component analysis of behavioral marital therapy: 1-year follow-up. *Behaviour Research and Therapy, 23*, 549–555.

Johnson, S. M., & Greenberg, L. S. (1985a). Differential effects of experiential and problem-solving interventions in resolving marital conflict. *Journal of Consulting and Clinical Psychology, 53*(2), 175–184.

Johnson, S. M., & Greenberg, L. S. (1985b). Emotionally focused couples therapy: An outcome study. *Journal of Marital and Family Therapy*, *11*, 313–317.

Johnson, S. M., & Greenberg, L. S. (1988). Relating process to outcome in marital therapy. *Journal of Marital and Family Therapy*, *14*, 175–183.

Johnson, S. M., Hunsley, J., Greenberg, G., & Schindler, D. (1999). Emotionally focused couples therapy: Status and challenges. *Clinical Psychology: Science and Practice, 6*(1), 67–79.

Kaiser, A., Hahlweg, K., Fehm-Wolfsdorf, G., & Groth, T. (1998). The efficacy of a compact psychoeducational group training program for married couples. *Journal of Consulting and Clinical Psychology*, *66*(5), 753–760.

Markman, H. J., Renick, M. J., Floyd, F. J., Stanley, S. M., Clements, M. (1993). Preventing marital distress through communication and conflict management training: a 4- and 5-year follow-up. *J. Consulting & Clinical Psychology, 61*, 70–77.

Pinsof, W. M., & Wynne, L. C. (1995). Special issue: Effectiveness research in marital and family therapy. *Journal of Marital & Family Therapy*, *21*(4), 339–618.

Shadish, W. R., Ragsdale, K., Glaser-Renita, R., & Montgomery, L. M. (1995). The efficacy and effectiveness of marital and family therapy: A perspective from meta analysis. *Journal of Marital and Family Therapy*, *21*(4), 345–360.

Snyder, D. K., & Wills, R. M. (1989). Behavioral versus insight-oriented marital therapy: Effects on individual and interspousal functioning. *Journal of Consulting and Clinical Psychology*, *57*(1), 39–46.

Sprenkle, D. H. (Ed.). (2002). *Effectiveness research in marriage and family therapy*. Alexandria, VA: American Association for Marriage and Family Therapy.

Weiss, R. L. (1975). Contracts, cognition, and change: A behavioral approach to marriage therapy. *Counseling Psychologist*, *5*(3), 15–26.

HOW TO BE A MARRIAGE THERAPIST WITHOUT KNOWING PRACTICALLY ANYTHING

Jay Haley

Therapists in training as marriage and family therapists often do not learn techniques for bringing about change. They also do not learn ways to conceal from colleagues and from clients the fact that they do not know how to solve the presenting problems of couples in distress. Both general and specific techniques are reviewed for concealing ignorance as well as ways to make correct excuses for failure. The presentation is designed for therapists who find themselves not knowing what to do with a couple in a particular case and for therapists who do not know what to do with any case.

During their professional training therapists are taught psychodynamic and other theories of abnormal psychology, learning theory, personality development and the science of diagnosis. Some even learn what medications to give troubled people that will cause the least harm. Yet a surprising number of clinicians graduate from departments of psychology, social work and psychiatry without learning how to solve the presenting problem of a client. In addition, a new generation of marriage and family therapists are appearing who do not know how to solve marriage and family problems. Young marriage therapists by the thousands are in graduate schools for members of the "fourth profession" of marriage and family therapists. They not only learn psychological theories but also systems theory, family development, divorce statistics, and what to say to pass the state licensing examinations. Yet a surprising number have not been taught how to change a marital problem. Not knowing ways to change anyone, they have also not been taught how to conceal that fact. This paper is designed for therapists who find themselves not knowing what to do with a couple in a particular case, as happens to all of us. However, it is primarily for a therapist who is ignorant about how to change a marriage relationship in any case and wishes to sound knowledgeable and appear to know what he, or she,[1] is doing.

The many varieties of marital problems brought to a therapist are all dilemmas to the therapist who does not know what to do to cause a change. The problem might be a husband who is insanely jealous of his wife, or a couple might be using a child to carry on a marital quarrel, or a spouse could have a symptom as part of the marriage contract. A symptomatic spouse could be one who drinks, or is depressed, or who has stomach aches, or is anxious, or has some other distressing problem that maintains the marriage and makes it unfortunate.

It does not matter what the marital problem might be when a therapist does not know how to solve *any* problem and can only diagnose, talk about defenses and anxiety, and discuss systems theory. It is incorrect for the therapist to say to a client in distress, "I don't know what on earth to do with a problem like yours." The therapist must pull up his, or her, socks and proceed as if competent enough to be worthy of a fee.

Concealing Ignorance From Colleagues

There are two problems for the therapist who does not know how to change anyone: how to conceal that fact from colleagues, and how to conceal it from the customers. It is most simple to conceal incompetence from colleagues. Methods have been worked out by several generations of clinicians. To review a few common ones:

1. One should routinely insist on the importance of confidentiality in therapy. All doors and walls of offices should be soundproofed so that a colleague casually leaning against a door will not hear a therapist being ineffectual. If it is suggested that videotapes of

interviews be made for training or research purposes, this idea should be banished with a contemptuous comment about unethical practices and a patient's right to privacy.

2. All supervision should be done without recordings or observation. If one takes notes to a supervisor, the notes can emphasize relationship issues. The fact that one floundered ineffectually in the therapy need not be known. Supervisors often prefer to discuss dynamics rather than interventions to cause change since that subject was usually neglected in their supervisory training.
3. Long-term therapy should be done so that colleagues who refer people will forget who they referred. In this way people continue to refer marital problems over the years to a therapist without ever discovering that he never changed anyone.
4. At professional meetings one should emphasize the scientific nature of diagnosis, research, systems theory, and family and child development. Therapy should be referred to as a mere "how to do it" matter. When clinical work is denigrated as practical, in contrast to scientific contributions, therapy is made to seem too unimportant for the revelations of incompetence that might be made by scientific research.
5. When accrediting therapists for licensing, and in academic training, one should emphasize the importance of having the correct degree and not skill in therapy. The accredited therapist is a person who has a Ph.D., an M.S.W., an M.D., an Ed.D., an R.N., or a Master's in Marital Therapy. Basing licensing on degrees protects a therapist who does not know how to do therapy. He, or she, only needs to know how to take classes in a university for a number of years. Should there be a public clamor to base licensing on more than an academic degree because of obvious incompetence, it is

possible to insist that there must also be 102 hours of supervised therapy experience. This is not a problem since the therapist can see customers alone in a room and later disclose to a supervisor only what he wishes to have known (see #2 above). Attempts to accredit therapists by tests of skill or measures of successful outcome should be ridiculed as impractical. One can say, "After all, who can really define a successful marriage in this complex and changing world? Therefore, how can we say that we succeeded in improving a marriage?"

Concealing Ignorance From the Customers

Colleagues need not know what actually happens in a therapy room but clients must. The procedures for concealing from customers the fact that one does not know how to change them can be classed as general and specific.

The general procedure used by most experienced therapists who don't know how to cause change is to encourage the client to talk and talk on the gamble that this will cause improvement. When interviewing a spouse alone, the therapist can use what he learned in academia and from watching television shows and say, "Tell me more about that," and "Have you wondered why that was so important to you?" When seeing the couple together, the therapist can say, "I want you to talk to each other so I can observe your communication." Then he can be quiet and need only encourage them occasionally if their argument sags.

While encouraging clients to talk, a therapist should say as little as possible to conceal the fact that he does not know what to say. This is called "active listening." Silent behavior also introduces an air of mystery, which makes specific skills less necessary, as high priests have known for centuries. Since the client inevitably attributes significant meanings to silence, the therapist is given a reputation for eloquence when the fact of the matter is he just does not know what to say. To further encourage the couple to talk, the therapist can make occasional interpretations, pointing out that the unfortunate things the couple are saying to each other are examples of their poor interpersonal relationship. It is helpful to say, "Isn't that a sexist statement?" at random moments. The couple will begin to prefer the therapist be silent, and then he can be so comfortably without feeling he, or she, should do more.

Discussing past history is always welcomed by clients who would rather avoid present issues. The review of the past might have no relation to change, but it is expected by most people. A phrase to use is, "I see this problem is very distressing to you both. Now tell me what your marriage was like before, and when you first began to notice this problem developing." Unless the clients are mute or retarded, which calls for modifications of the approach, that inquiry will release a deluge of words that can last anywhere from one interview to a whole course of therapy. Married couples enjoy arguing about the past and about who said what and when since they have experience at that. How long the talk will last depends partly upon the loquaciousness of the customers and also on how skillfully the therapist encourages them by saying, "Can you tell me more about that?" Involved in arguing about the past, the customers do not notice that the therapist does not know what to do about their present problem.

An unfortunate happening can occur when the therapist encourages a couple to talk freely, express their feelings, and to argue about who caused what in the past. That type of discussion often leads to such anger and disruption in the marriage that the couple decides to separate. The therapist can feel sad about this. However, he soon finds compensation in the fact that a separation makes it possible to do "divorce therapy." The therapist can help the couple in the difficult task of separating. In the process, the therapist can be pleasantly surprised to discover that one customer has become two customers, each paying a separate fee.

Many therapists who are not able to help couples separate can double their fees by seeing them as a couple in interviews and also placing them in a group with other couples. The therapist does not need skill when doing a couples group because the couples take over the sessions and share and talk and interpret to each other. Everyone feels something important is happening even if they are not changing, and the therapist gains a double fee while needing to know only how to remain silent.

Exploring other problems is something to do either early or late in the therapy. For example, if a couple comes in with a husband who is angry and jealous of his wife who has had an affair, the therapist who does not know what to do should take the focus off the presenting problem as quickly as possible. He can say, "After all, jealousy is just a symptom and we must talk about other matters so we can get at the roots of the symptom in the marriage relationship." Another way to put it is to appear thorough and cautious by saying, "Well now, I would like to put this jealousy problem in perspective. Could you review for me all the different problems about your marriage that have ever distressed you?" Some clients need to be encouraged to bring up other problems, but most of them can think of enough to keep the conversation going. Examples help bring out reminiscences and satisfy the curiosity of the therapist, such as, "After a group sexual orgy do you have special marital conflicts?"

Examining the consequences of the problem will provide clients with the impression that the therapist appreciates how serious it is even if nothing is being accomplished. One can ask how much time is wasted with the problem, what it prevents the couple from doing, how many inconveniences it causes, how embarrassing it is in relation to children or in-laws, and what would be done if the couple did not have the problem. Often the couple will say they had not realized how many consequences there were, and now they are determined to get over the problem. The therapist can say, "Well, you've taken the first step by coming to therapy; that is the important thing."

If the therapist likes to focus upon interpersonal relations, he can make insightful comments about the client-therapist relationship by saying, "Have you noticed that you treat me as if I am an authority figure who is supposed to solve your problem for you?" This kind of comment encourages the clients not to expect the therapist to be an expert and will also bring out reminiscences about bosses and other authorities. The therapist can also have the spouses not only talk about the ways they relate to each other but to all their relatives and friends.

Exploring what has been tried to get over the problem includes discussing previous therapy, if any. One should always explore what advice customers were given in the past. While appearing to explore history, the therapist is actually getting ideas of what he might do with a customer. Therapists communicate about therapy techniques to one another through their clients as they learn what colleagues have done to try to solve a problem.

Before proceeding to more specific tactics, the general ones can be summarized with a case example. Choosing an arbitrary problem, let us suppose that a woman comes to a therapist and says she is failing in her marriage and her career, as well as going out of her mind, because she cannot stop compulsively counting everything she does. When she does housework, walks, plays tennis, has sex, or chairs a board meeting, she must count the numbers of times that everything happens. She reports that a crisis came about when her husband discovered she was counting how many breaths he took when they were having sexual relations. The husband threatened divorce as they entered therapy and said he now looks longingly at women who count less.

What can a therapist do with this problem when he does not know how to change it? In general, he can follow the procedures outlined here. He can keep confidential what happens in the therapy from his colleagues; he can encourage the couple to talk while he actively listens. He can have them explore their past marriage relationship, their past individual histories, and their childhood with their extended families. He can talk about philosophical issues in marriage, including tolerance for weaknesses of mates. Out of the problem he can manage months, perhaps years, of marital therapy without having any idea how to change the couple and without anyone discovering that fact. He might even be able to include the case in a paper or book on the topic of interesting problems in marriage therapy. It should be noted in passing that when a therapist wishes to conceal his, or her, incompetence he should avoid any verbatim transcripts of therapy interviews in a publication. Instead, he should offer summaries of cases. For example, a clinician can say about a woman who has the problem of compulsive counting, "The patient was encouraged to explore the origins of the counting compulsion, and the roots of psychopathology were discovered in childhood experiences." This will sound better than a verbatim transcript which might read, "Therapist: When you were a child, did you refer to different ways of going to the bathroom as number one and number two?"

Specific Tactics

Within the framework of general principles for concealing ignorance, the therapist can use specific procedures learned at workshops or in the literature. Some are passing fads while others remain classic maneuvers because they help give the customer the impression that the therapist is skillful.

Reflecting back to people whatever they say is a classic tactic which has stood the test of time and generations of inadequate therapists. The procedure conceals like a blanket the fact that the therapist does not know what to do to cause change. Most important, it impresses the customer with the idea that the therapist is empathetic and understanding. Reflecting back a person's words gives an illusion of intimacy. A spouse says, "I feel so ashamed of myself because we have this childish marital problem." The therapist replies, "M hmm, you feel so ashamed of yourself because you have this childish marital problem." As far as the couple is concerned, two minds have met and understanding has been achieved. Even a socially withdrawn therapist appears to be warm, empathetic and understanding by just thoughtfully repeating back what people say. The chief merit of the procedure is that it is easy to learn even by people with limited intelligence. Research studies have shown that six-year-old children, both male and female, can master the technique with only one 40-minute training session.

Getting in touch with feelings is another classic procedure which can be done, and always is, by novice therapists. Whatever customers say, the therapist says, "How do you feel about that?" With experience, or with the help of a particularly inspiring professor in social work school, the therapist risks more complex phrases such as, "How do you *really* feel about that," or even "I wonder if you could communicate to your husband the depths of your feelings about that." These statements encourage the expression, or the simulation, of feelings and distract the emotionally aroused customer from noticing that nothing is being done about his problem.

Interpretations which make connections between this and that are, of course, the trusted tactic of a therapist who does not know how to cause change. A customer with even a rudimentary education enjoys interpretations which connect one thing with another, and so they are easily distracted from noticing that nothing is changing. One can find a similarity between a husband and a boss, or a mother and a wife. Since people do not think randomly, there is always a connection between what a person says about something at one time and what is said at another time.

Relationship games and sensitivity procedures are a way to pass the time and give the customers the illusion that change must be happening because they get upset. One can easily learn confronting games from the group therapy literature and popular self-help books. For example, one can confront the couple with the way they are playing the game "help me." The clients are impressed with the self-discovery and do not notice that the therapist does not know how to help. One can point out that the "adult" in one spouse is talking to the "child" in the other, and discuss their games of teasing and rejection, or dependency. Talking about one's own marital difficulties and divorces sometimes helps the therapist and shows that he, or she, is human and that everyone's problem is humanistic.

Another modern technique is "sculpting." One can bring action into the room by having the couple sculpt their problem instead of just talking about it. The husband can lean on his wife to show his dependence on her, and she can hover over him as he leans on her to show how she is burdened with protecting him. The therapist can say things like, "Now we're getting to the basic kinesics and not merely intellectualizing." Couples enjoy this kind of action, and the therapist can learn the technique in an afternoon workshop. Some experience in amateur theatricals helps. With a dramatic type couple one can have them do genograms of everyone in their family networks and then do simulations of their relationships with all their relatives. They might not get over their marital problem, but they benefit from therapy by having lots more to talk about with their relatives and friends.

Excusing Failure

Therapists who do not know what to do will fail, but not in all cases because of the high rate of spontaneous remission. It is spontaneous change which keeps referral sources providing clients and gives the therapist the illusion that perhaps, after all, he really knew what to do even if he did not realize it. Still, failures often occur and the therapist must be able to conceal the fact that failure happened because he did not know what to do.

There are two audiences to be concerned about when failing: fellow professionals, and the customers. Colleagues are the least problem since one can avoid observation and not be involved with outcome studies. There are various ways to avoid outcome studies ranging from the concern with confidentiality through arguments about complexity to the emphasis upon growth as not a measurable issue. One can also use the classic argument originated by Freud where he said that each case is unique and, therefore, cannot be classed with another in any percentage measurement.

Dealing with the disappointed customer is the main problem. Let us suppose that a couple says indignantly that no change has taken place. After months of therapy they are still miserable and their only marital agreement is that the therapist failed with them. There are several standard defenses to follow. (Showing one's state license, or listing one's degrees and naming the famous universities where one trained, might be useful early in therapy but not at this point. The customer will not be impressed, and the *alma mater* is given a poor reputation.) The correct procedures fall into two categories: blaming the customer, and saying that more change has taken place than was realized.

Blaming the client can be done in many ways. When the couple says they are disappointed at the failure by the therapist, they can be asked whether they have noticed that there might be a life pattern here of finding helpers disappointing. This topic becomes a subject to "work on." The therapist has turned an awkward moment into a reason for continuing therapy so they can discuss their past disappointments in people back through their lifetimes.

Another way to blame the customer is more subtle. One can imply that the couple has gone about as far as they can go right now, given the material they are made of. Even with the masterful skills of the therapist nothing more can be done. The implication is that the customers have reached a plateau, not the therapist. Sometimes this can be done by suggesting that a new stage of social development needs to be achieved, like getting older, before the couple can solve the problem. A good word to use is "integrate." One can say that the couple needs to "integrate" their insight into the meaning of the emotional experiences achieved in therapy before it is possible to go further with the problem.

If the customer has not done everything asked, the therapist can imply that more cooperation would have solved the problem, and perhaps the couple isn't quite ready yet to get over it.

An amiable way to end without admitting that one did not know what to do is to say that the customer does not really know how much change has taken place. "The way you talk about your marital problems now, and the way you talked about them when you first came in—well, the change is remarkable." In the case of the woman's counting, the therapist can say, "You might not remember it now, but when you first came in you counted every word I said and every breath your husband took. Now it's only occasional." This kind of statement prepares the way for the classic ending of the incompetent therapist—the customers say they still have the problem but do not mind it so much.

The therapist can also review all the gains made in self-expression, in insight and self-understanding, in resolving problems with distant relatives, and point out that after all these are more important than the trivial presenting problem the customer once thought was so important.

This list of ways to deal with failure is not meant to be all-inclusive, and each therapist has his own favorite way. One way becoming popular recently is to refer to someone in your own group of therapists when you have failed with a couple. That colleague supports whatever you said to the clients and also proceeds just as you did so it appears that all therapists do that and what you did was correct even if it failed. (Some therapy groups of colleagues of this kind are small, and some are quite large.)

In general, dealing gracefully with failure means offering an ending that is pleasing. Termination should leave the customers feeling a bit guilty about not having done all that they should, believing they have gone as far as they are capable of progressing in their marriage at this time and no therapist could have done more, and sorry to have put the therapist to so much trouble when more severe problems are undoubtedly waiting at the door. The customer should also be pleased that the problem, even if it is still there, is really more of an irritation than the misfortune it once was. With these simple techniques a therapist can do therapy for months, even years, with customers who fail to change and they never discover that the therapist knew no more than a plumber about how to get them over the problem they presented when they came in the door.

Endnote

1. The author uses the pronoun *he* for convenience and acknowledges the inequity of the traditional use of the masculine pronoun since ignorance about how to do therapy occurs in both sexes.

11

On the Right to Choose One's Own Grandchildren

INTRODUCTION

Judith Mazza, PhD

We live in a world of strange familiarities. When going to a restaurant these days, the server introduces him or herself by first name, inviting the patron to speak in a personal and somewhat familiar way with them. When placing a carryout order, the vendor prefers that you use your first name to identify yourself, and upon arrival, you may hear them say, "Sally is in the house!" letting the staff know you're there to pick up your order. When calling an 800 number for technical support, the technician wants to know your first name and in turn offers his or her first name. This implies an intimacy that does not truly exist. When did it become acceptable to apply the rules typically used with friends and family to relationships that are casual, professional, or commercial?

Haley does not use words carelessly. He is a wordsmith, communicating complex ideas in what at first glance appears to be a simple way. His sentences are concise, and his words chosen carefully. When it comes to family relationships, Haley likes to call a father a father, and a mother a mother. One story from the double bind project in the 1950s had to do with the "skill" that a hospitalized patient demonstrated when giving his mother a card on Mother's Day. The card said, "You've been like a mother to me." Haley would smile when commenting on this patient. Of course, the card was chosen to give to the patient's biological mother. At the same time, by choosing a card that is typically given to a nonbiological mother, the patient communicated two incompatible ideas simultaneously: that the patient's mother was a mother, and also was not a mother. Haley would say that being able to communicate in this way was so complex that the only hope that a therapist would have in dealing with a patient like that would be for the therapist to be simple, clear, and direct.

So, if it is prized for therapists to be "simple, clear, and direct" when talking about and identifying family relationships, applying a family analogy to describe professional relationships more than muddies the waters. It is to live in a world of fiction.

Consider Haley's basic definition of a family as a social group with a shared history and a shared future. For someone to be a part of a family, the relationships are known by all. By sharing a history and a future, there is an assumption that the parties are, at the very least, known to one another. Thus, one cannot become part of a family by fiat, by just declaring it to be so. In this paper, Haley properly says that if the family analogy was appropriately used, "one must apply it to a group of people associated together over the family life cycle."

When a professional finds him or herself drawn to the ideas of another, or wants to acknowledge the seminal contributions of another, that does not mean that the two have any association in real life whatsoever. The association may be a fiction in the mind of only one party. Can mere declaration of a relationship make the relationship real? Can a belated self-proclaimed "child" adopt a parent?

In this paper, Haley, with his laser-like analysis, sheds light on a practice in which professional colleagues declare themselves to be part of his intellectual life without his knowledge and consent. Haley's contributions to the field of therapy have been so pervasive that many do not understand where the ideas originated. If Haley is, indeed, declared to be the father of many contemporary ideas in psychotherapy, what responsibility does an alleged father have in this situation, other than to ask for a paternity test? Haley does just that.

ON THE RIGHT TO CHOOSE ONE'S OWN GRANDCHILDREN

Jay Haley

The increasing use of the "family" analogy for professional colleagues in the family therapy field is becoming offensive and should be abandoned. To say that a person is the "father" of an idea might be acceptable, but now grandparents, parents and grandchildren are being thrown carelessly into an analogical stew. This problem came to my attention recently in the acknowledgment section of *The Family Life Cycle,* edited by Elizabeth A. Carter and Monica McGoldrick. They say, "Our primary acknowledgement goes to the 'family' of family therapists.[1] We ourselves are 'third generation' family therapists, and as we worked on this book we became more deeply aware of what we owe to the 'grandparents' who founded our family and established our traditions, Murray Bowen and Jay Haley particularly; and to the 'parents' who taught, supervised and sponsored us as we joined the family: Phil Guerin, Tom Fogarty and Don Bloch, among others. Many of our 'siblings' produced the chapters that make up the book..." etc.

To use the family analogy appropriately, one must apply it to a group of people associated together over the family life cycle. In real families there is a continuity of family life over the generations because of long association together. Grandparents associate with their children over the years, and their children produce children who share a common culture with parents and grandparents.

I have not been associated with the editors of this book nor with the people they call 'parents,' and by implication my 'children,' Phil Guerin, Tom Fogarty and Don Bloch. Some of these "parents," "grandchildren," and "siblings" I do not even know, and some of them have ideas so different from mine that if related they must have been put out in foster homes at birth. Calling me a "grandparent" of these people is particularly bizarre when some of them are older than I am.

The implication of the editors is that some people entered the clinical field early, like Murray Bowen and myself, and others were younger and entered later, like the above-mentioned "parents," while others were still younger and so entered much later, like the editors and their siblings who are "third generation." That is not an accurate portrait of what happened. Almost all of these people have been in the clinical field as long as I have, or longer, and some of them spent years opposing the ideas in the family therapy field and my ideas in particular. They came late to family therapy, but not because they were younger and a different generation. Rather, it was because they came to their senses in middle age. When the editors say that I established the traditions of these people, they are curiously unfamiliar with the life cycle of the family therapy field.

If the editors insist on using a family analogy for their acknowledgement page, let me suggest a different version for their second edition, if ever there is one. I think they could continue to call Murray Bowen their grandfather; he seems to be responsible for most of these people and has suffered a lot in his time and so can bear many burdens. However, other grandfathers must be substituted for me. Phil Guerin, whoever he is, should have as a grandfather Michael Solomon, whoever he is. Tom Fogarty is, I believe, a character in the novel *Ulysses* by James Joyce and so should have Joyce as his grandfather. As for Don Bloch, I don't think Murray Bowen wants to be his father despite the identical nature of their theories, because Bloch's hair is too long. As a suggestion for a grandfather for Dr. Bloch, how about Henry Lennard? He has a Blochian fatherly look about him. Or, if Henry should decline the honor, other alternatives might be contributors to the field like Adrian Dreadnaught or Helm Stierlin.

A better plan is to abandon the family analogy in future works. It is really a banal idea. Intellectually it is at the level where the animal behaviorists would be if they anthropomorphized their association and said that the President is the Papa Bear, the President-elect is the Mama Bear, and all the members are teensy weensy little baby bears.

Endnote

1. Actually they should say their primary acknowledgement goes for the idea of the family life cycle to UNCOMMON THERAPY which was published years ago.

12

Sex and Power in Marriage

INTRODUCTION

William J. Doherty, PhD

Jay Haley never failed to deliver subtle and original ideas about any topic, and he was not afraid to weigh into controversial ones like male–female hierarchy in marriage. In this essay, reflecting this career-long focus on power and hierarchy in family relationships, Haley challenges the core feminist idea that greater male power in society (an undisputed point) translates into more power in the family. He argues that this may have been true in the past, when women had limited options outside the home, but that the men-have-the-power truism is misleading in contemporary Western families, and can make for misguided work with families. Haley notes that even when husbands and wives hold to an official hierarchy of male power, the private or operating hierarchy has favored the power of women, particularly in the parenting domain. Support for this dual hierarchy is breaking down now, he argues. Working women have less need for it, and single-parent family and stepfamily forms have thrown traditional gendered power assumptions up for grabs. Although welcome in many ways, the end of the dual hierarchy is causing serious problems because there is more direct competition for authority and leadership among couples. In the days when women called the shots in the home but upheld the notion that the man was the head of the household, there was less threat to the stability of the family system.

After reading this essay, I looked at several articles on gender and power in the March 2009 issue of *Family Process*, a journal that Haley cofounded in 1962. Coming out of a series of qualitative studies by Carmen Knudson-Martin and her colleagues, the articles make the case that the traditional gender hierarchy is alive and well in a wide range of American marriages, including the ethnic minority couples who are the participants in these particular research studies. Although the authors reported that both husbands and wives agree that women direct everyday family activities, the authors still saw male privilege and power as pervasive in heterosexual marriage (Knudson-Martin & Mahoney, 2009).

I'd like to argue that both Haley's perspective and that of feminist therapists like Knudson-Martin are accurate. Haley is correct that in most American homes, wives and mothers are the principal leaders, particularly when it comes to child rearing. There is real power here, not pseudo-power or just additional workload. Mothers direct fathers far more often than vice versa, and even in relatively egalitarian couples the mother tends to function as the greater expert on child rearing. Parent educators assume that the mothers in parenting classes can go home and implement many changes without getting permission from fathers, whereas educators of fathers can make no similar assumption. A therapist with a silent mother in a session is in much more difficulty when it comes to making changes than a therapist with a silent father.

Fathers, of course, are not powerless in child rearing. But much of their power is reactive—resisting or not cooperating with mothers—as opposed to assertive power to initiate changes or make decisions. Some would argue that because this leaves mothers with more child-rearing work, the men are still calling the shots. But parenting is not like housework, where women do more because men won't; doing dishes is a default responsibility more than a source of power. Parenting decisions, on the other hand, are an area of real power because most parents are greatly concerned with how their children are raised. If the mother wants the children in traveling soccer, it's likely to happen whether or not the father approves. Of course, many men are fine with the maternal hierarchy, and it works for their advantage to be less responsible for everyday child rearing. However, men who want more leadership often face their spouse's (and community's) unquestioned assumption that mother knows best.

But feminist therapists like Knudson-Martin are also correct when they focus on inequality in less visible aspects of the marriage, in particular who accommodates to the other's needs and daily behaviors. It seems clear that women in marriage do more monitoring of the preferences, moods, and emotional well-being of their husbands than occurs in the other direction. In both the official and private hierarchies, women are more likely to pay attention to whether men are feeling adequately respected—and adapt their behavior accordingly—than men are apt to attend to whether their wives are feeling subordinated. Women learn from an early age to cater to the ego needs of men. If a woman puts her career interests second because she believes her husband's career is more important to his sense of well-being, is this not a gendered hierarchy at work? Much of men's power in relationships comes from the assumption on both sides that the woman will anticipate and accommodate her man's needs—except when it comes to the well-being of her children. (I'm writing with a broad brush, of course, because there are many exceptions to all of this.)

Feminist critics of Haley's work are also right in saying that he underemphasized the implications of gender hierarchy in the public world for the status of women in today's families. The helpless high-level public official that Haley mentions in his essay had power in his family that stemmed from his status in society, and his wife catered to him in part because of that status. And critics are right in saying that Haley seemed to dismiss the possibility of true power sharing in nonhierarchical couple relationships; it's not obviously true that "someone" must be in charge. But Haley offers his own perceptive critique of the tendency of feminist theory to assume that public male power translates in a straightforward, linear fashion into private power in the home. And he rightly assumes that women, like men, like to hold onto power once they have it. Even if, as some feminists argue, women were forced into being child-rearing leaders when they were denied social and political power, "mother power" is nonetheless real and operative—and many women don't expect to relinquish it when they have additional power in the public sphere. Family relations are riddled with paradoxical loops that Haley was our master at uncovering.

Reference

Knudson-Martin, C., & Mahoney, A. R. (2009). Introduction to the special section—gendered power in cultural contexts: Capturing the lived experience of couples. *Family Process*, *48*, 5–8.

SEX AND POWER IN MARRIAGE

Jay Haley

The fact that men, rather than women, have power in society does not mean that men, rather than women, have power in the home. When we raise the question who is in charge in the family, the answer is not obvious. Scientific studies of power in marriage are difficult to design, and marriage is constantly changing with the high rate of divorce and remarriage. To complicate the situation, we live with ideas about families of the past which can be mythological. For example, it has been assumed that our grandparents' families were patriarchal with father the authority in the family. Mother was secondary and even subservient. These assumptions about the family of the past are increasingly open to question as we learn more about family structures.

The actual observation of family members dealing with each other in one-way mirror rooms and on film in the last 30 years has raised many questions about the reliability of the way people describe their families. What a person says about his or her family often does not match the description made by an observer who sees them in action together. A wife, for example, can say that her husband is a tyrant. An observer of the two of them together could express grave doubts about that. Observers of families note that women are typically dominant in the household. This does not mean they overtly take charge and order people about, although that also happens, but they determine what is to happen in the home. As an example, when I was recruiting families for research on issues of power in the family, I checked a sample of families randomly selected from a high school to see who made the decision for the family to come in and be tested. Examining a sample of 30 families, I found that in 27 of them the mother made a unilateral decision, without consulting her husband or children, to bring the family in. There was one case where a unilateral decision to bring in the family was made by a father. That family did not show up.

How a person behaves inside the home and outside of it can be quite different. A woman can be assertive within her family and quite frightened and shy outside. The reverse also occurs. I recall a father who was a major figure in government. He was known as a decisive man who administered hundreds of people, including many women, and his actions led to important consequences to the country. Yet within his family, consisting of his wife and a daughter defined as schizophrenic, the man was incapable of deciding anything, including where to have dinner. He was helpless in the family and a power outside of it.

The idea that women can be dominant in the family and men dominant outside the family is becoming more accepted and raises issues about the different structures of power.

Hierarchy

In the nature of organizations, including the family, some people are in charge of others, and everyone has a defined status position or is trying to define one. In some cultures one bows differently to people of different status or even talks a different dialect to a superior and an inferior. One person goes first and another second; one tells another what to do and the other does it. Whether in work or family groups of people repeat behavior and so define a structure. One cannot *not* indicate one's position in a hierarchy. Whatever a person says or does not say, verbally and nonverbally, communicates a status position.

In the complex hierarchies of human beings, status positions are based on a variety of factors including physical strength, wealth, custom, costume, intelligence, and all the different ways people differentiate themselves from each other. Within a family organization, a basic aspect of hierarchy is generation lines because the older take care of the younger. Grandparents usually have higher status than parents, particularly in Asian cultures, and parents have higher status than their children. Over time the children become parents, and also take care of the grandparents in old age, and so hierarchical positions change over the life cycle.

Marriage and Hierarchy

One way to view the power situation is to say that when a man and woman first get married they are peers, or equals, because they are at the same hierarchical level. They are equally free to choose each other or not (at least in Western society which is the subject of this discussion). Granting there are economic and other pressures which influence this decision, no longer are women purchased because they have to marry for economic survival.

As peers at the same hierarchical level, neither sex is lower in status because of gender. Either one might be of lower or higher status in the marriage because of the power of their families of origin, but that is not a gender issue. It is also possible that one spouse might be lower in status because of ill health or age, or lack of intelligence or education. Gender is not related to such differences. However, when a couple have a child, the structure of their hierarchy changes. Equality tends to disappear as the existence of the child raises in new ways the question of who is in charge.

Group Leadership of Husband and Wife

With the birth of a child, a married couple become the leaders of a group because they have someone beneath them in the hierarchy. They must agree who is in charge of the offspring to guide it and care for it. As more children arrive, the hierarchical system in a family becomes more complex. The equal relationship of the married couple cannot be maintained because there cannot be two equal leaders in charge of an organization.

Nowhere in human or animal organizations is there a structure with two equal leaders. It is an untenable organizational arrangement. If there were two presidents of a country who were considered equals, there would be obvious difficulties. There are three possible outcomes when two leaders, whether presidents or parents, are defined as equals. One leader either explicitly or implicitly takes charge and the other accepts it, and so there is one leader with a pretense that there are two. Or, the two leaders can continue to struggle for power in endless instability. A third alternative is to divide up the responsibilities so that each person takes charge of a different area. If there were two equal presidents, one would probably take foreign policy and one domestic policy.

Married couples who have a child can begin an ongoing struggle over who is in charge to the point that the marriage dissolves. Or one can take charge and the other accept it while pretending they are both equal leaders. The third alternative is to divide up the territory. One spouse takes charge of the children and the other is in charge of making a living, or one spouse takes the inside of the house and the other the outside. One might take responsibility for school and the other take charge of recreation. Problems and conflict arise when the couple shares an overlapping territory, as in relation to a child or to the budget, where severe marital struggles can occur.

As parents share the responsibility of a child, the issues they struggle over are not necessarily related to gender. Women give birth to the child and nurse it, and so they begin with the greatest responsibility. At some point in today's families a decision is made whether the woman is to continue to do childcare and housework or the husband is to take on, or share, those functions. The issue can be thought of as a practical one, but strong emotions arise over whether there are basic differences between men and women in regard to maternity and paternity. The issues can be taken as related to gender when it is actually an organizational problem of dividing tasks and leadership. Two males raising a child, or two females, have to deal with the same problems. For example, if a wife is a caretaker of the child, usually she knows most about what is happening and so assumes more authority on decisions about it. An observer could make this a gender issue by saying that women are more involved with children than are men. However, if two men, or two women, raise a child and one of them assumes more of the caretaking functions, the same structure can develop. This is evident in families of homosexuals who raise children.

Defining a Hierarchy

Hierarchy, or who has power in a family, is not determined merely by who manifests authority but by who determines what is to happen. An example can illustrate the issue of power. I recall a wife who said that her husband was in charge of everything. He insisted on his own way and the house had to be run the way he wanted it. "He is in charge," said the wife. The husband agreed. However, the wife had a psychological symptom. She was a compulsive handwasher. She had to wash her hands many times a day, particularly if she came near anything she considered to be contaminated. Because of this problem, she could not go grocery shopping; there were poisons and household cleaners in the store that could contaminate her. Her husband had to shop for groceries when he came home from work. The wife could not cook because she had to continually wash her hands while cooking and could not get anything done. She also could not wash the dishes. If she put her hands in water she must keep washing them and could never stop. Therefore the husband did the cooking and washed the dishes. The wife could not do house cleaning, because she could not risk contamination from household cleansers, particularly in the bathrooms. If contaminated, she had to wash hour after hour. Therefore the husband had to clean the house after he did the shopping and the cooking and finished the dishes. By simply having to wash her hands excessively, the wife arranged that her husband do all the work in the household. Yet both of them described a family structure with the husband a tyrant in charge of an oppressed wife.

Clearly the person who is dominating, or has power, in a hierarchy is not necessarily the one who gives direct orders and has them followed. That is only one of many forms of domination. A person can order that something be done or be helpless and require that something be done. Authority is distributed in complex ways in families. Sometimes the person with power takes charge covertly and gives credit to someone else, and the person who is officially in charge may not be actually in charge, whether male or female. I recall a wife who was accused of being managing and dominant in the family, but her husband collapsed and went to bed for mysterious reasons. The wife had to wait on him, essentially like a servant. Taking power by helplessness is not a gender issue but can be determined by who is oppressed. We might expect more psychological symptoms among the oppressed; they will use helpless maneuvers, including psychological symptoms, because that type of tactic is all that is available to them.

Inevitably with a couple sex can also become part of the struggle for power. The withholding of sexual relations, or the imposition of sex, is part of the question who is in charge. Assuming a sex drive that must be satisfied, the object of that drive has power to satisfy or to frustrate. Not only is it a matter of cooperating in the act, but the enjoyment of sex can be an issue of power. There are men, and women, who will concede on other power issues if only the spouse will enjoy an orgasm. Like a symptom, the orgasm is defined as involuntary, and so the spouse cannot help not cooperating. But if the right terms are met it might happen.

The Dual Hierarchy

To accept the idea that one person is officially dominant while another person "actually" is, means accepting at least two hierarchies in an organization. One can assume that hierarchies are always dual in nature. In fact they are multiple, but duality raises enough complex issues. There is an official hierarchy and there is also a second, private hierarchy with covert power. I recall the American radical, Lincoln Steffens, many years ago saying in his autobiography that if one wishes to meet the person in charge in a city one does not seek out the mayor or the city council. Instead, one asks any hotel porter who is in charge and is told the name of the political boss. If we accept the idea that there is always an official hierarchy and a covert one, it is possible to propose that in families there has been a public hierarchy with men in charge and a private hierarchy within the family where the women determine what is to happen.

When a family is described in this way, opposing views are true. Those who say that men are dominant and women are secondary are correct, if one is examining the public hierarchy. Those who say the women are dominant are correct if the private family hierarchy is the focus. The two leaders each have power in his or her own hierarchy and collaborate. In a way they are in coalition together by concealing this arrangement from the world.

One might concede that the woman is more dominant in the contemporary, Western home, but what of the patriarchal societies where women are said to be essentially slaves? One can discuss how much power slaves can have, but it is evident that there has not been research on what actually happens in patriarchal families, particularly those of other cultures. We are left with anecdotes. As an example, I recall being curious about the powerful, castrating fathers described by Sigmund Freud. That type of father seems to have vanished. I asked an elderly woman who was raised in Vienna in Freud's time what her family was like. She said her father was a very powerful man. "We weren't even allowed to sit in Daddy's chair," she said. I asked her how Daddy kept her out of his chair. She said, "Oh, Daddy didn't do that, Mother did. She told us that if we sat in Daddy's chair we would get pimples on our bottoms." It appears that a powerful father can be a creation of mother, which complicates a research description.

As another example, I was informed by a Japanese translator that young Japanese husbands who invite coworkers to their homes will ask their wives to pretend that the husband is in charge at home. The wife agrees to that, often expecting the husband to do something for her in exchange. With a dual hierarchy in the family, women pretend the man is the boss, like the Japanese wife. Sometimes too, the collaboration includes the woman managing the family but using the father as the enforcer of her orders and even building myths about him for the children to live by.

Dissolving the Dual Hierarchy

In recent years the dual hierarchy has broken down and everyone is attempting to adapt to the changes. Women decline to accept a secondary position (and many men do not wish their wives to be secondary). When women insist on a public acknowledgment of their rights and power, and the weakness of the male authority within the family is exposed, the family can be in difficulty. Mothers don't keep children out of Daddy's chair or pretend to his coworkers that he is the boss. Power struggles begin which lead to the breakup of the family if the love which brought the couple together is not sufficient to survive the conflict. It is possible the high divorce rate is a product of the dual hierarchy breaking down.

A dual hierarchy is stable as long as there is agreement about it. Collaboration is essential. It is a division of territory with one person taking charge of one hierarchy and the other in charge of another which overlaps. In the past, with women in charge within the family and men in charge of the external hierarchy, the two authorities worked together, though with various degrees of difficulty. Each spouse accepted the arrangement and supported the other. With the increase in power of women in public life, their financial success in careers, and the encouragement of women's groups, many women have declined to participate in a dual hierarchy. They find it demeaning to pretend that a man is in charge and superior. This discontent leads to an attempt to arrange equal leadership. Inevitably that leads to organizational breakdown as past ways of working together dissolve in disagreements.

One cause of the dual hierarchy breaking down is the need for both spouses to work. With half the workforce composed of women, inevitably the hierarchical issues of men and women come into conflict in the workplace as well as the home. Who is in charge in the work domain is a question added to the issue of who is in charge at home. When only one spouse works, the working spouse is usually in charge of work issues. Questions of hours of work, of bringing work home, of setting aside family recreation when work must be done, are the type of decisions made by the working spouse while the other spouse makes decisions in the home. Conflicts can arise between the home caretaker and the working spouse when the two domains conflict. For example, whether the family should move because it is best for the worker's career can conflict with the distress of the mother and children about changing schools and friends. The family and the work contend for priority. Yet the worker outside the home and the caretaker inside the home can resolve most conflicts with goodwill.

When both spouses work, the conflict goes up geometrically and is less easily resolved. The working wife can object if the husband's work gets priority. She can also object if he does not fairly share the duties at home. The husband can object to the wife wanting priority for her career and expecting him to do more at home when his work is so important. Usually status in a work hierarchy is determined by who makes the most money. Therefore power at home can be influenced by who earns most at work.

The dual hierarchy tends to end with the dual career. When both spouses work, they must decide who is in charge of what in the two domains of family and work. How will housework and parenting be shared? Will the husband take charge of the children so that the wife can travel for her job? The couple must both decide about problems with the children which were once decided by one of them who was in charge at home. When more than one person is making decisions, the opportunity for conflict increases.

In a viable hierarchy a leader needs a second in command to point out to the group that he or she is the leader. That is one reason why military forces have noncommissioned officers to tell the men to listen to the officers. When the couple cannot agree who is primary and who is secondary, neither supports the other by instructing the children who is to be followed. The children get out of control when one parent does not tell them to follow the authority of the other parent. Placing the children within this struggle provides hierarchical confusion and gives children unacceptable power. The child can be unmanageable and irresponsible when the parents are unable to exert joint leadership because of their struggles with each other over who is in charge.

Families seek solutions when a dual hierarchy dissolves and most alternatives are unsatisfactory. When they attempt a single hierarchy with either one in charge, there is dissatisfaction. A woman who takes charge in this way often protests that she does not want a "passive" man, or a wimp. She wants a man who will assert himself, but who will not "boss" her or think himself superior. Often men do not want to dominate a helpless, obedient woman. They protest they want a compliant woman who will manage the family and deal competently with the kids without constantly expecting them to make minor decisions at home.

Since it seems unsatisfactory if either spouse is the only one dominant, they attempt to be equal leaders and find themselves fighting over the most silly and minor issues because every issue raises the question who has power. Sometimes in this struggle spouses become violent. Men, and sometimes women, attempt to establish their authority by battering their spouses.

Therapy

There has been a burgeoning and blossoming of the therapy profession as a popular enterprise. Everywhere one turns therapy is extolled as necessary and fashionable. The mass media show fictional characters in therapy, radio psychologists tell everyone to go to therapy, and anyone who is anyone has had therapy. Now people also go to therapy whether they like it or not since vast numbers of judges require drug, sex abuse, and violent offenders to go into therapy or go to jail. The universities are mass producing experts to provide therapy services, including psychologists, psychiatrists, social workers, educational counselors, substance abuse counselors, marriage and family therapists, and so on.

The recent popularity of therapy might be a result of the conflict and confusion everyone is experiencing as past hierarchical arrangements break down and everyone becomes more unstable. Couples in difficulty with each other, or with their children, seek experts outside the family because everything is changing and they cannot accept advice from family elders who are old-fashioned. More and more therapists are finding themselves dealing with hierarchical conflicts in the form of individual psychological problems.

As the dual hierarchy dissolves and the divorce rate surpasses 50%, family structures do not have a marital bond as their basis. Family therapists who learned to deal with nuclear families find themselves having to learn how to deal with single-parent families and blended families. When we look at past approaches to child problems, the therapy had certain assumptions about family structure based upon both parents being in the home. One popular assumption was that mother was most involved with a child and the father was peripheral. Looking back, we could say this was an implicit acceptance of a dual hierarchy. It was assumed the mother was in charge of the home (even though she was thereby called "dominating") as part of the dual hierarchy and father was focused outside. (Of course at times it was the mother who was peripheral.) There were different therapeutic strategies for dealing with a problem child because of this point of view. Now therapists must learn to deal with single-parent families, blended families of new marriages, and unusual living arrangements where adults, some with children, share a house and are like a family. Even defining a family unit is now more complex.

Many therapists who planned a peaceful private practice find themselves dealing with crises and violence as family power struggles become more physical. Therapists face bizarre and extreme behavior as well as the whole range of psychological and somatic symptoms. With power struggles come threats of suicide and nervous breakdowns. Social control agencies, such as hospitals and jails, are multiplying.

As parents separate and divorce and marry again, therapists, and children, must help them deal with quarrels over money, child custody, and all the issues that come with dissolving a family. When the couple marry again, therapists must deal with complex blended families where there are several parents and several children and grandparents. One issue that comes up with blended families is sex abuse which therapists find to be increasing. Whatever taboo there is on incest between blood relatives, there seems less of it with people not related biologically, such as stepparents and stepbrothers and sisters. Sex abuse tends to create sex abuse since an abuser often repeats on others the abuse he or she experienced in the past. Therapists not only face the problems of working with the courts to stop the problem, but they must also relieve the suffering of the adult person who has after effects of such trauma.

Part of the problem of families today is affluence. As the economy improves, families no longer need to hold together for economic reasons. Work is available, and government welfare provides support for single parents and children. One might think that affluence would be a blessing, but it can make it possible for wives and husbands to leave each other and young people to avoid the authority of their families by having an income at an early age.

One cannot look back on the past with nostalgia, because there were many injustices in the patriarchal system. Some men might think of the past family structure as a period when they were more dominant and more protected. Some women might think of it as a period when they had more protection at too great a cost. As a result of the many changes being initiated, new forms of family organization are being created. We cannot anticipate the kinds of changes in the future except to know they will be unpredictable. One prediction is possible: as families change, therapists, social controllers, mediators, and negotiators of all kinds will find employment in increasing numbers in the years to come.

13

How Should a Gentleman Talk to a Feminist Family Therapist?

INTRODUCTION

Judith Mazza, PhD

Although feminism as a defined political movement probably reached a crescendo in the 1970s,[1] gender "consciousness" remains an important force today. In the 2008 presidential election, many women became extraordinarily involved in the campaign run by Hillary Clinton and explained their involvement because they wanted a "woman in the White House." The Republican Party, not to be left behind, chose a woman for the vice presidential spot, hoping to capture some of the energy and excitement of gender-based politics. Many of these women, who appeared in huge numbers at campaign rallies, supported their chosen candidate largely due to the candidate's gender. These women came of age in the 1960s and 1970s, and their renewed activism harkened back to that era of social change.

The radical feminism of the past, in vogue when Haley wrote his paper, was one in which activists demanded egalitarian relationships. Radical feminists, who were extraordinarily sensitive to perceived power imbalances, demanded that men and women be seen and treated as equal in every respect. A woman could substitute for a man and no distinction was to be made between genders; they were interchangeable modules. Brassieres were burned in public as a symbol of liberation. Large rallies and marches were held, with much attention from the press. The social justice movement of radical feminism was, to a large extent, successful. To crack one glass ceiling after another, women assumed aggressive postures at home and in the workplace in an effort to prove their worth; and were vigilant and outspoken when they perceived that they were being thought of or treated unfairly. In fact, the "unwritten contract" that had heretofore existed between men and women appeared to be breaking. That contract, in existence for hundreds of years, was one in which the man said to the woman, "If you cherish me, I will die for you." As the radical feminists expressed unwillingness to cherish gentlemen, the gentlemen no longer knew how to behave; their willingness to be the protector was being rejected.

It is against this backdrop of radical feminism that Haley, with his keen sense of satire and paradox, develops rules that "gentlemen" should follow when dealing with radicalized feminist family therapists. It may be difficult for those who have watched radical feminism morph into a more liberal gender equality movement to understand the abrupt change that appeared to dominate relationships between men and women during the early years of radical feminism. Old rules were thrown out, new rules were rapidly evolving, and no one had the manual. Simply having a cup of coffee with a feminist could be a minefield for a gentleman. Who should pay for the coffee? Should they share equally in the cost? Is it putting the woman down to treat her to coffee? How should the man respond if the woman insists on paying for both coffees herself?

Just by the title of the article alone, in which the man is described as a "gentleman" and the therapist as a "feminist," Haley begins to set the stage to demonstrate once again the power of taking a "down position," where the locus of control is disguised, and overt aggression is dealt with in a Gandhi-esque fashion. Early feminists were aggressive and self-righteous, and many men were confused and taken aback by their apparent anger.

What is the definition of a gentleman? A gentleman, as described by Haley in this paper, should always be gracious, shy, and self-effacing. A gentleman should be noncontroversial, firm, yet protective, and be ready to agree that men can also be feminists.

What does it mean to be a feminist family therapist? According to one study (Whipple, 2000) based on in-depth interviews of women who identified themselves as feminist family therapists, there were five components to this self-identification:

1. Encourage a nonhierarchical client–therapist relationship.
2. Include gender as a topic in therapy.
3. Encourage egalitarian relationships.
4. Affirm women.
5. Empower clients to change and support social change.

When a therapist follows these principles as a part of her therapy, she is making a value judgment that these principles "trump" the microculture of the family, and that it is the duty of the therapist not only to create change in the areas where the family is requesting change but also to act as an unsolicited social change agent. When the feminist family therapist has a personal agenda, independent of the needs of the clients, she misses out on certain therapeutic opportunities, such as utilizing the culture of the family to accelerate change, and maintaining a flexible therapeutic posture to solve problems.

However, as Haley discusses in this paper, a gentleman should always be gracious. Haley used to say that for a therapist to tell people things they already know is discourteous; and he was interested in therapists being courteous to their clients, and supervisors being courteous to their trainees. So, is it being discourteous to the feminist family therapist to tell her that to be true to her principles, she should reveal her agenda to her clients prior to the start of therapy? Especially knowing that doing so may very well have a negative economic impact on her caseload, especially in this day and age, as families "vote with their feet" and choose who they wish to be in therapy with.[2]

In interests of full disclosure, just as clients are expected to read and sign confidentiality and treatment agreements, should not a feminist family therapist reveal to the client something about her feminist agenda, so the family can agree or decline to participate? I would think that doing so would fulfill all five of the aforementioned components of being a feminist family therapist. That seems only fair.

I believe that we are in a postmodern era in which there is a new paradigm evolving, where men and women are no longer seen as being interchangeable modules, and the aggressive stance taken by early feminists is no longer necessary or appropriate. We are entering an era in which each gender respects the other, as well as their different competencies and aptitudes; and where universal human rights will ultimately prevail. In this new paradigm, both men and women have the flexibility to choose their role in the family. They can be stay-at-home parents or breadwinners and can shift these roles according to their own interests and the needs of the family. In this next era, the "gentleman" will be able to speak his mind as clearly and unabashedly as the feminist, without fear of retribution for not being politically correct. Likewise, the feminist might allow the gentleman to occasionally hold a door open for her. In so doing, both will ultimately find that they may have something to learn from one another.

Endnotes

1. In 1972, Congress approved the Equal Right Amendment (ERA), and by the end of the year, 22 of the needed 35 states ratified it. In addition, Title IX of the Higher Education Act was passed at that time, enabling equal participation, on the part of both sexes, in federally funded educational programs.
2. Many times, clients seek a therapist with a particular point of view, whether that is a "Christian family therapist," a "short-term problem-solving family therapist," or even a "psychodynamic family therapist." It would not be surprising that some clients would choose to avoid a therapist who disclosed that she has a feminist agenda.

Reference

Whipple, V. (2000, March 20–25). What does it mean to be a feminist family therapist? Poster presented at the annual conference of the American Counseling Association, Washington, DC.

HOW SHOULD A GENTLEMAN TALK TO A FEMINIST FAMILY THERAPIST?

Jay Haley

Women are becoming increasingly organized in the family therapy field. They are winning office in the various local and national family therapy organizations as women vote for women, and their articles on the persecution of women in the family are increasing in numbers. With this feminist movement enlarging and perhaps ultimately dominating the field, male therapists must consider how to engage with these women. A few suggestions are offered here which were developed in male caucuses during breaks at poker games, in pool halls, and at half time at football games. Whether a sample of non-poker playing or pool-shooting males would agree with the ideas here is unknown because their gatherings are difficult to find, those kind of men being what they are.

One should emphasize, of course, that few women therapists are feminists, just as are few men. Gender is not yet the criteria for the existence of empathy for the status of women. However, conflicts in gender-to-gender social intercourse are escalating. The question is how should a gentleman discuss therapy during such intercourse?

The fundamental rule agreed upon by the majority of males is that a man should always be a gentleman. No matter how difficult the interaction with a feminist on a panel or in a conversation, the man must be gracious. This rule not only expresses the essence of men, but it is based on the premise that women's power continues to increase, and direct confrontation with them could be unwise.

Rule #1 A Gentleman Should Be Shy and Self-Effacing

It is best to pretend compliance to the other sex even if one is resisting in his heart. For example, suppose three feminist therapists (they tend to be more aggressive in triads) corner a man at a meeting and one of them says, "The only effective therapy is feminist family therapy, isn't that true?" It would be incorrect, neither gentlemanly nor grammatical, for the man to respond, "Nobody seems to know what feminist family therapy is nohow." Instead, the gentlemanly family therapist should respond, "Certainly the feminist view has contributed greatly to our understanding of families, and particularly to our awareness of gender differences, but I have been doing my best to understand what feminist family therapy actually is and with my instrumental thinking and masculine emotional deficits I lack the ability to get in touch with my feelings and find myself needing your guidance."

In the same way, when discussing family interviews, the male therapist must bow to women colleagues by agreeing that women are powerless. At the same time he must be watchful that the women do not overpower him. For example, when observing a family from behind a one-way mirror, the male therapist in a training group might note that the mother in the family is constantly talking and organizing what everyone is saying, including the therapist. The man should not cry out, "That is a dominating woman if ever I saw one!" Such a remark will result in the remainder of the day being devoted to feminist therapists helping the gentleman understand gender differences while accusing him of being a chauvinist constructivist. Occupied with this feminist discussion, nothing will be learned about therapy that day. To avoid such tedious days, men must innovate more subservient responses. Observing a mother obviously dominating a session, a gentleman can say, "I wonder what is driving that woman to make herself the target of opposition by talking so much?" The feminists will be glad to produce a genogram and educate him on how it is the woman's parents in the past and her husband in the present who are driving her to act in such an irrationally dominating way. That takes less than an hour and a half, and so the remainder of the training day can focus on what to do about the family to change it (an issue which seems curiously absent from the literature of feminist family therapy).

Since therapy is the art of coalitions, a therapist must join or oppose factions in the family. For example, the better therapists will be on the side of an adolescent and also on the side of the parents even when the two sides are in conflict. Similarly, the skillful therapist will side with both a wife and a husband even when they are opposing each other's position. What should a male therapist, or supervisor, say when he observes a feminist therapist side with a wife who is attacking her husband and exploring all his flaws as a husband, father and male? He should not say, "That woman is an idiot who will drive that man and the family out of therapy." That would be rude, and the fundamental rule is to be a gentleman at all times. Instead the therapist, or supervisor, might innocently say, "How cleverly that therapist is overtly siding with the wife while covertly joining the husband in such a way that one cannot see how she is doing it." In the case discussion the therapist will be forced to take credit for her skill at secret coalitions or admit she is siding against the husband.

It is when we turn to feminist theory that men can be most amazed. The feminist therapy theorists have borrowed their basic ideas from the society's feminists of the last 30 years. When one searches for how these theories create new approaches in therapy, it is difficult to find. A therapist philosopher, known as The Macho Man, put the matter this way: "Feminist therapy theory is as important as Einstein's theory, but it has similar problems in that it is difficult to understand how it relates to therapy." Of course men should compliment feminist therapy theory whenever they can find any. As a guideline, it seems to consist primarily of the discovery that families are composed of two genders and this is anti-systems. One curious happening is that Gregory Bateson, the systems theorist, is being credited by feminists as the source of many of their ideas in feminist family therapy. As one feminist fundamentalist put it, "At last we have a neutral therapist as Bateson wished and so a Bateson family therapy." The gentleman family therapist should not point out that Bateson was not a family therapist, nor was he neutral, nor was he a feminist (although at times he was known to show an appreciation of differences in gender).

Rule #2 How to Deal With Feminist Theory

There are supervisors who say that helping a woman therapist recover from a feminist ideology is part of basic training in therapy. They compare it with helping therapists recover from psychodynamic ideology. That is not the correct approach. Although the psychodynamic ideology is a handicap in doing therapy, it is a view which leads to interesting discussions, and that is important in the tedious therapy day. For example, if a client steals women's panties and has closets full of them, of what appeal is a systems explanation, which might only say that this behavior repeats every spring when the man's grandmother visits. The psychodynamicist will be more entertaining with a discussion of sexual identity and confusion of body parts and things going in and out, and all that. Of course if one wishes to save women from having their panties stolen in this way, psychodynamic theory will not help change the villain and can even be a handicap.

The psychodynamic and feminist orientations offer new and interesting explanations of many of life's mysteries and the history of man and womankind. The task of a gentleman therapist is not to change the ideology of the feminists but to prevent those ideas from doing harm in therapy. Just as psychodynamic theory induces a terribly negative life view in a therapist, the feminist view can organize a therapist to think the only important issue in life is differences in genital equipment and the battle between the sexes. To prevent that harm, male therapists must plan a strategic way to save clients, and feminist therapists from misfortune.

Rule #3 Be Firm and Protective as a Gentleman Should Be

Although it has been recommended that men should not openly oppose feminists because of the risks, this is not a unanimous opinion among the various male groups surveyed. One evening, after a game of snooker, which he lost, a gentleman known as Fast Eddy protested such compliant behavior. "After all," he said, "if a baseball catcher can crouch with his legs spread apart and receive baseballs traveling 90 miles an hour between those legs year after year, surely men can risk what a feminist might do to them." When asked what more bold step should be taken, several of the fellows in the hall volunteered ideas which can be touched upon here with the language cleaned up.

Suppose, for example, a feminist says that only women can understand women and therefore only women should do therapy with women. What can a gentleman say in response to such a statement? The compliant way to respond (Rule #1) is to say, "I hope that some day I will understand women better, and perhaps you can help me achieve, at least partially, that goal." A more bold reply is to say, "It takes a man to know what women are all about. I don't think women understand women at all." If even more daring, a Macho man can say, "Most women don't like other women and would demand a male therapist, especially if they are told they cannot have one." In the ensuing discussion, the man can wish that he was equipped with protective garments like the baseball catcher. Yet such courage is necessary. Otherwise we might see a one-gender therapy where a woman supervisor works with a female therapist dealing with, and giving workshops on, mothers and daughters. There is a school of therapy called MAW therapy which recommends that. Should such therapy become popular, male therapists will be seen quietly leaving the buildings which surely women do not want. In fact, one task of males is to prevent their gender from leaving the family therapy field. The oldest living family therapist, who does not go to meetings since he already knows everything, recalls a time when only women were counselors with families. Men dealt with important tasks, like research and individual therapy. He reports going to a Family Service agency in the 1950's to recruit some families for research. The staff was made up of 31 women and no men. They spent their time interviewing wives and talking to them about their unhappy marriages. The husbands were not included. The oldest living family therapist, who admittedly is prejudiced, claims that it was when men joined the family field that family therapy became an activity of high status. If feminists are now successful and women take over the field, they will be regressing backwards 50 years. Men will begin to withdraw and let them have the field of family therapy. Some men seem to be doing that now when they talk about how family therapy is really only individual therapy in a group and family systems are psychological perceptions and physiological problems. Apparently they are seeking to go back into a style of therapy, and to professions, where men are dominant.

Rule #4 Be Noncontroversial at All Times

In the practice of therapy, argumentative interchanges behind the mirror should be avoided; there are enough of those in front of the mirror, as at home. A gentleman should say that the subject of gender is so complex it cannot be dealt with by yelling back and forth and there should be theoretical discussions instead. A gentleman's wisest theoretical position is to emphasize biology. In response to the idea that life would be better if only females existed, a gentleman can point out that throughout nature it takes both the male and female to produce another. Perhaps in time women will be able to reproduce without a man participating, except to have intercourse with a test tube in a laboratory, but is that the way to *raise* a child? One might recall Milton Erickson's gentlemanly response to the question of how to persuade a dominating mother to allow her husband some say in the raising of the children. One should emphasize biology, he said, and persuade her that it is her maternal duty to see to it that her husband imposes male influence on her children. A perfect child requires the biological influence of both male and female. He added that if one has her "see to it" that her husband is involved, she will dominate the situation so that she becomes less dominant.

Biology is the basic bedrock on which to build agreements when one is discussing child-raising issues with feminists. It is the only irrefutable argument that men are necessary. The ovum needs the sperm, as the yin needs the yang, and on the basis of that argument the idea is unavoidable that men are necessary in the lives of children. However, the gentleman must be prepared for difficulties. Suppose, for example, that one proposes that a father is necessary to teach a daughter how to flirt, negotiate with, and understand men. One will meet the argument that when fathers are not sexually abusing daughters they are patronizing them and treating them like little girls, never allowing them to be independent, assertive women. "All men treat females like morons," a feminist is likely to cry out in a case discussion.

What can a gentleman reply to such a comment? Discussing the importance of morons to the world would not be appropriate at that moment. Stout denial would also not help since examples of patronizing men could be found and enjoyed by the feminist contenders. It is best to say something nonconflictual like, "My gracious sakes, I had not realized that happens with some men in some families. How distressing. What can we teach men who behave in that way?" The feminist must reply with some constructive suggestion, since merely saying that men should not be allowed near daughters would be clearly inappropriate in a discussion with such a reasonable man. In general, when under attack, the man should lean upon the woman who is attacking, taking advantage of her natural maternal and protective instincts. He should turn to her with the attitude of needing care and solace. If that can be combined with some sex appeal, promising pleasure to come, the man is sure to survive.

Rule #5 Emphasize How Men Can Be Feminists

Sometimes we forget that the most adamant feminists have fewer maternal instincts because they are men and have different equipment. A special section of the *Feminist Catalogue* is devoted to male feminists, and so they need not be discussed here. Often one finds them at feminist meetings, eager to obtain the certificates given out as proof a person is a woman feminist. Pityman O'Rourke is, of course, the classic example of the male feminist. At any meeting, if the speaker suggests anything that is a slight to women, it is Pityman, a southern gentleman, who is first on his feet and protesting. Many of these men volunteer at battered women's refuge houses. They make themselves available for women to vent their anger upon, sacrificing themselves for all the beatings malekind have given femalekind in history.

The Case Example

Let us examine the classical case example and expose the gender and non-gender approaches. Suppose a feminist therapist is interviewing a family with a problem daughter, and the mother in the family says, "I would like to go to work, but my husband won't let me." Her husband smiles in agreement. Although it could be taken as a mild remark, to a vigilant feminist therapist such a statement is like tossing a steak in front of a hungry lion.

What can a gentleman, who might be a supervisor, behind the mirror comment? He cannot say, "Now there is a husband who knows what he wants." Any compliment of the husband at this point would be inappropriate. He might say, "I wonder what Kimberly (the therapist) will do with that?" Such a remark might placate the women behind the mirror, but it would not help Kimberly in the room. If alert enough, he could grab the telephone and call Kimberly, saying, "Would you step out a moment?" That would give her time to recover her senses and deal rationally with the situation. However, some feminists would reply, "No thanks," and would defy the supervisor, staying in the room to attack the mother's statement, i.e., the husband.

There are different feminist responses to this situation which are determined by the class of feminists involved. These categories of feminists, according to the men surveyed, are as follows:

1. *FF. The Fundamentalist Feminist.* She, or he, is sometimes called the reflex feminist. Any mention of gender, or any comment that could be remotely connected with gender, will immediately become a feminist issue. When offered the opportunity to discuss men not letting women work, the feminist in this category would refuse to leave the room for consultation. She will say to the wife, "What do you mean he won't let you work, who the hell is he to say whether you can work or not?" This kind of comment, which offers the therapist moral satisfaction, has been known to encourage a lack of enthusiasm for therapy in the husband.
2. *SF. The Suffragette Feminist.* This type is almost as adamant as the Fundamentalist Feminist, being willing to sacrifice her life for her standards, but she is also more strategic. She will plan a campaign to advance

women and put down men. If the wife said her husband would not let her work, this type would snort like a horse on the parade ground enjoying the opportunity to display her glory, but she would say, "Tell me more about that, since it is such an extraordinary statement." She might even say to the husband, "I'm sure your wife must have misunderstood you." Observing his reply, she would plan how to dismount him from his appallingly high position.

3. *AF. The Academic Feminist.* This type is more circumspect and would think to herself, I have this man trapped in therapy because he wants his daughter helped. Therefore since he is a captive audience I can give him a speech about how women should be the ones to decide whether they have careers or not. She might decide to use her Women Studies #301 lecture which was so effective with undergraduates trapped in her class and needing a good grade. She would begin politely by saying, "I would like to offer you all some contemporary ideas to counter your old fashioned ways of thinking." Then she would talk the remainder of the hour about the history of women, helping the family understand that therapy is quite an intellectual exercise in propaganda, and they don't have to solve the presenting problem.
4. *FF. The Flexible Feminist.* Having all the characteristics of the other feminists, this type would also be aware of her context. She would be as indignant as the Fundamentalist feminist, as strategic as the Suffragette feminist, as knowledgeable as the Academic feminist, but she would be concerned about achieving the goals of her work. She would feel a responsibility to the daughter who is the presenting problem. Therefore she would not want to antagonize the father. If he is powerful enough to prevent his wife working he would also be powerful enough to take the family

> out of therapy. However, could such a feminist actually overcome the basic bias of the feminist coalition with women? If she says to the wife, "How interesting that you would make your decision about work in that way," her tone and body movement are likely to indicate that she thinks the woman is an idiot for putting up with a husband who is a tyrant. She would also be aware of her obligation to teach the daughter, the new generation, not to allow men to make decisions like that. Try as she might to be cool, she might have too many feminist groups looking over her shoulder to be able to avoid joining the women in the room against the men. She will hitch up her mini-skirt and reveal her feminist position.

One can, of course, list many other more subtle categories of feminists. However, let us consider how this case example would be dealt with by a non-gender oriented therapist, either of the male or female gender, who has the big, broad, flexible, tolerant and wise viewpoint.

If a mother should say, "My husband won't let me go to work," the sensible therapist would assume the wife is fostering an illusion since men do not have such power in the American family. Women might be secondary in the world at large, but anyone with any experience in family therapy knows that in families the woman is in charge. Even a family therapist with a learning disability could not avoid the vast literature accepting women being in charge in the home by describing the family as made up of dominating mothers and passive fathers. That has been reported since the birth of family therapy 30 years ago. It was first reported with families of schizophrenics, then families of delinquents, then families with children with psychosomatic symptoms, then families with school problems, and families with normal children, and so on, and on. Therefore the therapist must assume the wife does not want to go to work and she avoids life in the factory by saying her husband will not allow it. The husband cannot pressure her to get out and work, so he can buy the boat he wants, because she has trapped him in the Macho position of "taking care of her." The daughter, who lives in the family, knows perfectly well that mother pretends that father is in charge to get her own way. Therefore the daughter does not need education on this issue. She just needs to slip out to practice her femininity on her weak-willed boyfriend.

Feminists who are family therapists have seen inside the structure of families and know that women are in charge in the family. Yet, curiously, many of them talk about women being powerless and dominated by men in the home. By now everyone in the family field knows that there is a dual hierarchy and so women can lack power out in the world and yet be in charge at home. It might be argued that in non-Western, patriarchal societies women are helpless and men dominant, but there is no family research by feminists to support that view. For example, I recall asking a woman who was raised in Vienna at the time of Freud what her family was like. She said, "Oh, my father was a very powerful man. We could not even sit in Daddy's chair." Impressed with this corroboration of Freud's view of the powerful, castrating father, I asked her how father kept his children out of his chair. "Oh, he didn't do that," the woman said. "Mother did. She told us if we sat in Daddy's chair we would get pimples on our bottoms."

A similar indication of the need for research came up in a discussion of another patriarchal culture. While supervising a therapist with a Japanese family, I talked to the Japanese woman translator about families in Japan. She said that when a young husband is bringing his coworkers to his home, he will ask his wife to pretend that he is the boss in the family while they are there. The wife agrees to pretend her husband is in charge in exchange for some favor from him. These are incidents in places supposedly made up of patriarchal men who are dominating women. Where are the feminist research teams investigating the power of women in such families? There might be as many discoveries there as were made when we first began to discover that mothers are dominant in American families. One might add that if the reports of the awful subjugation of women in third-world families are true, feminist family therapists should be picketing the Saudi Arabian embassy instead of picking on a frightened male family therapist in Schenectady. One other curious fact is that in marriage therapy the vast majority of couples contain a wife complaining that her husband is not equal to her. The husband is lower in education, or financial status, or the power of his family, or in some way that requires the therapist to devote much of the time trying to raise the status of the male. Yet feminists therapist can struggle with this problem in therapy and then in public print complain that men are Macho and dominating women in marriage. Obviously the task of feminist therapists should be to uplift men and they are shirking that way of helping women.

In relation to power, some feminist therapists seem to think power is only when he or she tells someone what to do and gives orders. They ignore all the other ways they have learned to gain power. Although some women dominate families directly, and some men occasionally do, that is obviously not the only way to achieve power. What of the husband who becomes helpless with a mysterious ailment and requires his wife to wait upon him like a servant. Is he not in charge? Of all people, feminist clinicians should know that symptoms are powerful in human relationships. The wife who has a psychological headache or a stomach ache and cannot do what her husband is insisting that she do has taken charge and has power. Certainly it should be assumed now that one can dominate with weakness as well as strength. The alcoholic who says to the bartender, "If you want me out of here, throw me out," has arranged what is to happen and so has power. The non-gender oriented therapist has the flexibility to consider all these possible power situations in the statements of wife and husband.

To return to the question of how a gentleman should deal with these issues in the day-to-day situations of therapy, clearly confrontation whether spoken or written is not wise. This means there is a definite risk in publishing articles with any criticism of the feminist position. Yet some men like to write articles, and are reluctant to give up that pastime. So what can they do? One choice is to write under a pseudonym, preferably one beginning with Ms. Some of the odd names of the feminist therapists might have their origin in this concealment. A more interesting and safer technique was developed by a compulsive writer. He drafted a paper on the biased nature of feminist family therapy which reflected some of the ideas expressed here. Wisely, he did not publish it. He also did not put his name on it which meant he could later deny authorship. He sent it to a feminist therapist woman friend, asking for her opinions in confidence. The woman friend was too indignant to keep the article to herself. She faxed it to all her feminist colleagues. In that way the gentleman got a critical paper, which he could deny was by him, distributed to key feminists at no cost, either financially or to his equipment. Techniques such as this become necessary when dealing with powerful opponents, and feminist family therapists should be warned that gentlemen are sharing notes on devious ways to pursue critical ends and yet survive.

One obligation of a gentleman is to keep people, including feminist therapists, from coming to harm. One way to help feminists is to lighten the burden they have taken on in trying to save all the women in the world. The task of helping feminists be less burdened is complicated by their lack of a sense of humor. One cannot make their struggle less grim by joking about the issues. For example, suppose a man is discussing rape and he wishes to lighten the topic. He tries to join women in a joking way by saying, "The length of that miniskirt, obviously the woman was inviting rape, ho, ho, ho." Only when he picks himself up will he realize that humor is not welcomed by feminists. Even milder jokes are not welcome. For example, a male therapist who said, "I hope you feminists have other men for the wives whose marriages you break up," has mysteriously disappeared and is thought to have gone to Lake Titicaca. A serious example of humor occurred with Pityman O'Rourke. Defending women as usual, he said that feminists do indeed have a sense of humor if the joke is a sophisticated one and not a dumb one like the rape joke. On a bet he told such a joke at a woman's meeting. He said, "How do men and women respond differently when they win the Nobel Prize? The man thinks, 'What will I say at the presentation?' The woman thinks, 'What will I wear at the presentation.' Ho, ho, ho." Unfortunately Pityman was Ho Ho'd right out of the building and lost his bet.

To review how a gentleman should behave with feminist family therapists, the guidelines are now clear. A gentleman should be pleasant, smiling, and shy in all case discussions with feminists. He should not confront issues head on, but exert his power behind the scenes. His sexual attraction, if it exists, should be used to gain an advantage, and he should lean upon the nearest feminist therapist for support. He should manipulate the other gender by pretending they are competent and he should compliment them at every opportunity. When necessary he should use a symptom to gain power and to avoid situations when they become stressful: developing a headache when certain types of cases are to be discussed at meetings is appropriate. Finally, what should he say when three feminist therapists corner him and ask him why he has not joined a feminist organization or gone to a meeting? He should honestly reply, "My wife won't let me."

14

How to Be a Therapy Supervisor Without Knowing How to Change Anyone

INTRODUCTION

Michael D. Yapko, PhD

Many years ago, when I was a novice clinician, I remember asking Jay for some advice about how to help a particular client I was seeing. I asked him directly what he thought I should do in treating her. Not really knowing Jay at the time and being blissfully oblivious as to how far off I was in my approach to him, I tried to impress him with my clinical acumen and mastery of diagnostic jargon. I asked him what he would do with this woman who I was sure had a dependent personality disorder with compulsive features, and who was anxious and dysthymic and engaged in avoidant coping behavior. Boy, was I barking up the wrong tree! He paused for what seemed a very long time before he kindly said, "Well, I wouldn't let her have those problems!"

I was deeply perplexed by his answer, and he was content in that moment to simply watch me squirm. I must confess it took a long time before I really understood how profound his reply to me was. Once I finally did, aided by the ongoing support of our discussions, it revolutionized my understanding of how to do therapy. The importance of defining problems in solvable, rather than unsolvable, terms was and continues to be a foundation of good therapy in general and Jay's brand of strategic therapy in particular. This core teaching is evident throughout Jay's writings, and is especially prominent in this particular piece.

In this article, Jay's views of what constitutes the essentials of competent supervision are on open display. Also on display are his wit, insight, judicious use of sarcasm, and considerable impatience with some of the orthodoxy of the therapy field. In this brief introduction and commentary, I'd like to draw the reader's attention to several of Jay's points that I think are especially relevant to the contemporary practice of psychotherapy. In the nearly two decades since a variation of this article first appeared in the *Journal of Systemic Therapies*, the field has collectively faced a number of issues that have significantly altered how therapy and supervision are conducted. Jay was clearly prescient of these changes because some of them were alluded to in this very article. Jay could not have predicted, though, how powerful these forces would eventually become.

Ambiguity, Action, and the Nature of Therapy

In this article, Jay is deeply critical of Freud and the psychodynamic model of psychotherapy. He is also critical of solution-focused approaches, cognitive approaches, behavioral approaches, and even some family therapy approaches that he sees as more theoretically convoluted than a good, practical therapy need be. Jay is a pragmatist: He is convinced that *any* one-dimensional approach will work against developing the unique solution he believes every differing problem requires.

Jay describes the confusion of both supervisor and supervisee when faced with the direct challenge to actually do something to help someone. The confusion is understandable, though; we are dealing with the inherent ambiguities of the problems we are asked to treat. For example, when someone presents a problem—say, depression—the problem is complex and has many different facets; each can give rise to a plausible intervention with a plausible underlying rationale. Someone can identify the biological symptoms and reasonably suggest the use of antidepressant medications, someone else can identify the cognitive distortions evident in the person's thinking and plausibly suggest cognitive therapy, and someone else can recognize social deficits and family dysfunction and sensibly suggest some form of interpersonal therapy.

When there is empirical evidence for virtually contradictory viewpoints, how is the novice, the experienced therapist, or the seasoned supervisor to make decisions in the face of such ambiguity? Jay is not advocating that there is a single "right" way to do therapy. On the contrary, he advocates for flexibility in doing therapy, but with at least some minimal standards, which he identifies clearly: taking responsibility for the therapy by being directive, and striving to resolve the symptoms the person presented.

What has changed in the field since this article first appeared is that many therapists can no longer simply do what occurs to them to do in a burst of strategic creativity. The ambiguous nature of therapy, the poor judgment of many clinicians, and the earnest desire to prove the merits of psychotherapy have given rise to a new standard in the field, namely, the imperative to use methods that have attained empirical support. Therapies are even being standardized and manualized and thus actively *discourage* the development of novel solutions as Jay suggests. Even a most basic requirement for conducting therapy, the provision of an informed consent to treatment, legally requires therapists to be able to cite the empirical basis for their specific treatment recommendations.

Ambiguity creates uncertainty, and uncertainty creates indecision. Jay is absolutely correct, though, and the scientific data regarding therapeutic efficacy unequivocally affirm, that ultimately what matters in therapy is *action*. The term *behavioral activation* is used across treatment models, highlighting the importance of action in producing change as opposed to mere reflection. Jay's observation, "Generations of therapy supervisors were taught that therapy and supervision are leisurely inquiries featuring reflection rather than action," has proven more relevant today than when this piece was written.

The Rise of Biological Treatments as a Substitute for Therapy

Jay wrote, "When supervisors train psychiatric residents today, diagnosing and choosing a drug, or even three or four, are the only activities." When Jay wrote this, a new generation of antidepressant medications (ADMs) had just been launched with the release of Prozac just a few years earlier. Currently, ADMs are the most widely prescribed class of drugs in the United States. Too many therapists have taken a self-deprecating secondary position of importance in treatment, having absorbed the message from psychiatrists, psychopharmacologists, and biological psychologists that medications are the primary form of treatment.

Jay's view that medicating people is, in essence, a whole new rationale for *still doing nothing* as a problem-solving therapist is easy to appreciate. The evidence is unambiguous that the use of medications as a sole form of intervention in the treatment of depression, for example, has the highest rate of relapse of *any* form of treatment. There are too many aspects of people's problems, especially the interpersonal ones Jay was so immersed in, that medications alone simply cannot address (Yapko, 2009).

In the same way that Jay critiques Freud's methods when he writes, "He devised a form of therapy in which the therapist, and therefore the supervisor, didn't take responsibility for changing anyone," that same criticism can now be applied to the use of medications that "just didn't work." The psychiatrist's views regarding the "biochemical imbalance" are not challenged (although recent contradictory evidence indicates they *should be*). Rather, the medication is blamed as being rendered ineffective simply because the person was deemed a "nonresponder." Jay is a powerful advocate of doing *something*, from defining problems in solvable terms to taking deliberate and effective action to disrupt the problem's hold on the client. Jay's disappointment with problems being defined in biological terms is evident in this exchange I had with him in 1999 (see Yapko, 2001):

YAPKO: What about the view that says it's not only the individual that we should study, but, even more reductionistically, the individual's biochemistry? People seem enthralled with biological explanations of behavior.

HALEY: I'm not an enthusiast for attributing so much to an individual's biochemistry. I think that it is important for certain problems, but I think that the overselling of medications is one of the worst problems in the field, and it is getting worse all the time. Some psychiatrists now don't even seem able to talk to people—they only listen to decide which medications to prescribe. It's a shame. (p. 202)

Therapists and Collective Delusions

Jay criticizes Freud (and his followers) on yet another count when he writes, "He proposed that therapy should never deal with the real, only the fantasy, world." He goes on to write, "What should a therapist do about an incestuous father? According to Freud, one should say nothing happened.... When talking about a fantasy instead of facts, who can say the supervisor is right or wrong?" This is a harsh criticism, but there is good reason to consider its merits given what happened in the field not long after Jay wrote this.

As I documented in my book *Suggestions of Abuse: True and False Memories of Childhood Sexual Trauma* (Yapko, 1994), up until the mid-1970s, if a woman claimed she had been sexually abused by her father (or someone else, for that matter), there was a good chance the therapist would dismiss the claim as merely fantasy material rather than truth, believing it indicated some psychologically based pathology to be identified and treated. The claim was discounted and transformed into an "issue" needing "resolution."

Then, in the 1970s, researchers finally began to ask the question as to how prevalent the sexual abuse of children might actually be. The evidence became unambiguous that not only was sexual abuse common, but also it was more common than anyone could have ever imagined. Tragically, therapists missed the boat: The entire field had *for decades* trivialized and otherwise distorted claims of abuse simply on the basis of their inconsistency with the prevailing theories. Therapists' mass delusion prevented victims from getting the help they so desperately needed. When they realized their error, many therapists overcompensated by seeing abuse nearly *everywhere*, even as the hidden cause of common symptoms (e.g., being overweight, or smoking) that were presumed to have their origins in childhood episodes of sexual abuse that had been "repressed." The splintering of the field over the legitimacy of repressed memories is powerful affirmation of Jay's criticisms of those who can't distinguish theory from reality.

In another example, until the most recent incarnations of the *Diagnostic and Statistical Manual* (DSM; see, e.g., American Psychiatric Association, 2000), there was no category included for childhood depression. It was simply assumed that children did not have the necessary level of personality development to experience "true" depression. Besides, "expert" therapists said, "What do kids have to get depressed about? It's not as if they have mortgages or financial pressures!" So, with the rates of childhood depression rising rapidly, therapists know far less about childhood depression than they need to in order to help simply because their theory didn't allow for acknowledging and learning about it.

The dangers Jay warned of in this article continue to be relevant concerns to this day. The ease with which we define problems in vague biological terms in order to justify (over)medicating people, and the ease with which we evade the responsibility to do something to help because the theory says that "conversation and not action is what therapists should do," are *still* a part of the mental health culture.

Summary

Jay's enthusiasm for the merits and intricacies of therapy never waned, even when his keen insights were channeled in the direction of being a sharp-tongued critic of some of therapy's silly foibles, such as those he pokes at in this article on ineffective supervision. Jay's ability to see the innate contradictions and incongruities within the field and articulate them with a dry wit and mischievous style endeared him to clinicians literally all over the world. In 1969, Jay published an enormously popular paper in the *American Journal of Orthopsychiatry* called "The Art of Being a Failure as a Therapist." He described ways to fail, including advice on dismissing the presenting problem as unimportant, refusing to treat the presenting problem, and using labels that don't translate into good therapy. These patterns obviously persisted over time, and thus became the theme for this later article on ineffective supervision. He described insightfully and articulately what he saw too many therapists and their supervisors doing, prodding us to reexamine our ideas and methods in ways that time and good research have subsequently shown us he was right to do. Jay was a man ahead of his time, a powerful catalyst for the development of modern, outcome-oriented therapies.

References

American Psychiatric Association. (2000). *Diagnostic and statistical manual of mental disorders* (4th ed., text rev.). Washington, DC: Author.

Haley, J. (1969). The art of being a failure as a therapist. *American Journal of Orthopsychiatry*, *39*, 691–695.

Yapko, M. (1994). *Suggestions of abuse: True and false memories of childhood sexual trauma*. New York: Simon & Schuster.

Yapko, M. (2001). Jay Haley on Jay Haley. In J. Zeig (Ed.), *Changing directives: The strategic therapy of Jay Haley* (pp. 183–202). Phoenix, AZ: Milton H. Erickson Foundation Press.

Yapko, M. (2009). *Depression is contagious*. New York: The Free Press.

HOW TO BE A THERAPY SUPERVISOR WITHOUT KNOWING HOW TO CHANGE ANYONE

Jay Haley

Therapy trainees, like flocks of doves, flutter in increasing numbers from universities and private training institutes. All of these therapists must be trained by supervisors. Where can competent supervisors be found who know how to change people? Without enough trained supervisors, particularly in a brief and family-oriented therapy, there is a crisis. Young therapists in the field must change clients who won't eat, are on drugs, won't stop crying, are acting crazy, are abusing children, are attempting suicide, are afraid, or can't stop behaving in foolish ways. The desperate trainee turns to a supervisor and says, "What should I do to cure these people?" Supervisors who were never taught what to do with such problems experience difficulty. Vast numbers of trainees are being taught by supervisors who know how to reflect on life's problems but do not know what to do to solve those problems. In the last few years therapy has changed to an active, directive style partly because the insurance industry and the courts require that therapy be brief and that a successful outcome be evident. Those who manage care expect supervisors to teach a short-term therapy, telling trainees what to do to solve therapy problems and how to do it quickly. Generations of therapy supervisors were taught that therapy and supervision are leisurely inquiries featuring reflection rather than action. They were not trained to solve a client's problem but to discuss other matters, like why people are the way they are and how they got that way. As Al Titicaca, Ph.D. (not his real name), said, "I can establish a good relationship with a trainee, and we can have a productive talk about personal problems, how to make process notes, and the dynamics and childhood origins of a case. Then the trainee asks me what to do with a client who won't ever take a bath. I talk about the deeper meanings of bathing, but I don't really have any idea what to do." A female supervisor, Virginia (her real name), said, "I was supervising a therapist with a client who compulsively sang, 'The Star-Spangled Banner' every time she had an orgasm. I simply didn't know what to do to help her over that embarrassing problem despite my years of training as a supervisor. I can join therapists in a feminist perspective, and I can discuss systems theory at length, but when they want to know what to do to change someone, I'm just lost and have to call upon my experience at faking it."

Most supervisors are like Al and Virginia, in need of help to conceal the fact that they don't know how to change people. Guidelines are offered here for making use of basic supervision techniques that have helped teachers conceal ignorance for generations. These include arranging the proper context, offering the correct presentation of self, and recognizing that the different clinical theories were designed not so much to guide therapists as to help supervisors who don't know what to do.

The Importance of Proper Context

The supervisor can take comfort in the fact that the social context frames all statements. Just being in a supervisory job means that one is assumed to be knowledgeable. If a supervisor can find employment in a well-known institution, even banal comments are thought profound. A dumb statement in a wise context, such as Harvard University, will be admired, as many dumb teachers there have found. It helps if the supervisor explains that he or she is descended from a distinguished line of supervisors. Attending weekend workshops featuring famous, even legendary, supervisors means one can identify them as former teachers and refer to them by their first names. It is also important to be properly licensed and to display these awards prominently in one's office. Certification as an approved supervisor is not difficult to obtain: It only requires paying a fee, attending classes, writing papers, and talking about dynamics. Evidence that the supervisor has successfully taught trainees any therapy techniques, such as skill in the use of various interventions, is not required.

The Presentation of Self

How should supervisors present themselves when facing a class of beginning trainees? It is best to present one's self as having a flavor of both wisdom and wit. If only half of either quality is present, the condition can be concealed by a thoughtful manner. A contemplative personal style—as if one is always considering all aspects of every situation—should be cultivated. Supervisors must appear to have what the title implies, namely, "super vision." Two vision mannerisms are helpful: (1) a faraway look that implies one is considering all aspects of the larger situation, and (2) a keen incisive look that shows the student that one is alert and quickly grasping the essentials. When a nervous student is worried about the fate of the client in his or her hands, the supervisor can win respect and even adulation just by being there, remaining calm, and looking wise. The faraway look and thoughtful silence can, at times, cause the trainee to become impatient enough to come up with an idea of something to do. The supervisor can accept the trainee's idea, perhaps implying that he or she had that very thing in mind and merely wanted the trainee to think of it spontaneously. If a student already has a plan and is seeking approval for it, a sharp, knowing look by the supervisor is correct even if he or she doesn't understand the plan.

The proper manner alone cannot prevent students from being critical. One must develop a personal relationship with trainees so that they will have such loyalty that they minimize, or even overlook, one's deficiencies. Generally, it helps if the supervisor can remember a student's name.

Occasional personal comments are also important, for example, "I understand your wife had triplets this morning. Well done." It is personal involvement that encourages students to be uncritical, even protective, of the incompetent supervisor.

With the correct manner in an impressive context, a supervisor can win the respect of trainees even without knowing how to induce therapeutic change. However, what if the supervisor is specifically asked what to do to change a client with a serious problem? There are accepted ways to deal with this crisis. The most popular way is to behave like a cognitive therapist and obscure issues by rationally discussing theory. It's no longer a secret that the basic ideologies of therapy were designed to protect supervisors who don't know what to do to bring about change.

The Ideal Theory

Let us examine the criteria of a clinical theory that would be ideal for supervisors who don't know how to bring about change. Such a theory would need to address the following issues:

First, is it possible to arrange that a supervisor cannot fail? That sounds difficult, but wise heads have applied themselves for the last century and provided solutions. What if, after completing training, a student hasn't changed a single client and lacks all skill except the ability to say, "Tell me more about that"? Can a supervisor avoid being blamed as a failure?

Second, how can a supervisor avoid having to innovate different therapy techniques for each case? If one could devise a single method simple enough for any teacher to understand and explain to trainees, no one would expect teachers to devise unique interventions.

Third, if a supervisor is ignorant of how to bring about change, what can he or she talk about that would distract trainees from therapy issues? It should be something interesting and intriguing to fascinate young intellectual types so that they won't notice that they are not being taught how to change real problems.

Fourth, can a supervisor not have anything expected of him or her for years and so avoid criticism until the issues, and the case, no longer matter?

Fifth, can one arrange that a supervisor is never proven wrong? In the ideal teaching situation this is the most important task. A trainee might say bitterly, "After years of therapy under your supervision I haven't accomplished anything in the way of change in this client, and you have never given me any help." The teacher needs to respond so that the trainee slinks away, chastened and ashamed for having been critical and for making foolish demands on the supervisor.

In summary, the ideal situation for a supervisor would be one with no responsibility for change, no risk of being wrong, and no risk of criticism. Is it too much to expect this ideal to be found anywhere in the real world? We must turn to the classic schools of therapy to discover how this ideal has been achieved. We will find that the primary purpose of the powerful procedures and ideologies of the therapy field is to help supervisors who don't know how to bring about change.

Past and Present Theories

Examining classical theories isn't of merely historical interest but can actually be a discussion of contemporary psychotherapy. Generations of therapists were trained in those ideas, and supervisors today practice as their teachers did. Therapy techniques may change out in the field, but supervision procedures to protect incompetent teachers never change.

It is well known that the therapies with the least practical value and poorest outcome are based on psychodynamic theory. Yet those ideas are still a popular set in the field today. Why is that? Obviously, it's not coincidence that (1) the theory is perpetuated by supervisors and that (2) it is the theory that is more protective of incompetent teachers than any theory yet devised. Contemporary contributions offer only modifications.

Before the turn of the last century, in that great period of hypnotic therapy, Freud went about visiting the hypnotherapists of his day. What he observed was live supervision of therapy. A supervisor would demonstrate hypnotic therapy with a patient, focusing on the symptom the person wished to recover from. The trainee would watch the hypnotic expert solve the problem. After observing the teacher, the trainee would work with a patient and solve a problem while the teacher watched. This live supervision was based on the assumption that training in how to do therapy involves the teaching of a skill.

After watching these hypnotherapists at work and trying it himself, Freud decided to give up hypnosis and take a very different approach. The only explanation for this change is that he must have said to himself, "The fellows I work with could never teach therapy this way. They couldn't invent a strategy for each case. They could never demonstrate such skill in curing new symptoms and so couldn't teach that to trainees. Therefore, I must develop another form of therapy, one that allows teachers to have prestige and be admired even when they don't know how to bring about change. Can I build an organization based on this principle?"

After long hours of meditation, perhaps sitting nose to nose with his friend and consultant Wilhelm Fliess, Freud came up with the classic approach that is still in daily use 100 years later. It's a tribute to Freud that he achieved every requirement in our fantasy about how to save incompetent teachers. So great is his influence that his supervisory ideas are used today even by teachers of different therapies with new and more fashionable names.

Homage to Freud

Freud went to the heart of the matter at once by proposing a two-pronged approach to save the teacher. He devised a form of therapy in which the therapist, and therefore the supervisor, didn't take responsibility for changing anyone. He added the idea that any failure of the trainee is the fault of the trainee's emotional problems, not the failure of his or her teacher. With these two basic assumptions, any incompetent supervisor could divert the slings and arrows of outraged trainees who might notice that they are failing to change anyone.

If a patient says, "Isn't it your job to change me?" the traditional therapist is taught to reply, "No, my job is to help you understand yourself. Whether or not you change is up to you." This has been acknowledged as a way to arrange that therapists need not know what to do. Overlooked is the fact that this instruction contains a covert agenda for the supervisor. If trainees say the same thing to their supervisor—for example, "Isn't it your job to tell me how to get this client over his misery?"—the supervisor can respond, "It's not my job to help you change people but to help you understand why you have problems in dealing with this patient." The supervisor can even give a smile of derision and inquire about the trainee's unresolved emotional problems. "Have you examined your omnipotent fantasies of saving patients?" the supervisor can ask, and the embarrassed trainees will drag themselves away to deal with their emotional problems, not noticing that their teacher didn't know how to solve the client's problem. The blame of the trainee's own problems also persuades the trainee to be a person who distrusts his or her judgments rather than one who criticizes the teacher.

As part of Freud's schema, he did away with live supervision and insisted that therapy be confidential. It should be done in private offices with double doors so that no one can watch or hear anyone say or do anything, even when leaning against the door. In this way teachers need not demonstrate their skill to trainees or observe techniques of interviewing by trainees. Trainees who lack skill cannot be held responsible if no one ever sees them do an interview.

Freud's second step was to insist on a single method. The supervisor teaches that the patient should do all the talking while the therapist only asks an occasional question (this is called "making an interpretation"). The insightful interpretation is the invariant prescription that distracts the client into wondering why he or she has the problem rather than what to do about it.

Great emphasis was put on being nondirective. The argument was offered that telling people to do anything—except lie down and talk to the ceiling—was demeaning to them and would interfere with the goals of neutrality. It was argued that only a one-way monologue caused change. In this way supervisors could avoid having to learn how to give directives and how to determine which ones to use for particular problems.

A third step to save teachers from knowing how to cure symptoms was to say that symptoms are unimportant and that what should be discussed is what's behind, or around the corner from, them. Since this innovation created a therapy without goals, no supervisor can be faulted if the trainee doesn't achieve a goal.

Supervisors were especially helped because therapy was designed to be long term. Years passed and generations passed away before a therapy was over. How could anyone know whether the case, and therefore the supervisor, had failed?

With two more prongs Freud, who was fond of a prong, solved the question of (1) what interesting topic could be talked about and (2) how a supervisor could never be proven wrong. He proposed that therapy should never deal with the real, only the fantasy, world. There is a current controversy over why Freud gave up the issue of sexual abuse of his young female patient in the real world and turned it into a wish, or fantasy, that lurked in the dark recesses of their minds. What should a therapist do about an incestuous father? According to Freud, one should say nothing happened. Apparently, he wished to save his teachers from having to deal with reality, where they could be proven wrong and would have to know what to do about real people, like horny relatives. When talking about a fantasy instead of facts, who can say the supervisor is right or wrong?

What about the major challenge, namely how to distract the trainee from the issue of how to change people by having the supervisor talk about something else really interesting? Look what Freud, in his genius, provided: He not only presented an intriguing explanation of human motivation and new ways of seeing human kind but focused his training on all the most exciting issues in life. He recommended that the teacher talk about sex, power, conflict, the envy of different types of genitalia, and the stark human dramas of fantasies of murder and incest. Does the boy have a secret passion for his mother? Does the daughter get electrified with desire for her father? All else seems idle talk in the face of such dramatic issues. Choosing to talk about what normal people would censor as unmentionable, Freud ensured that supervisory sessions were endlessly titillating. Each consultation with a supervisor was an adventure in awfulness. How to change people could be overlooked as a side issue.

Freud managed to achieve every single one of the ideal ways to protect incompetent teachers. In addition, he persuaded everyone that conversation and not action is what therapists should do. Therapy supervisors have been benefactors of his ideas for a century. Even new therapies with different ideologies continue to base the training of therapists on Freud's principles for saving supervisors.

Up With Diagnosis

Of course we need not give all credit to Freud. Other schools of therapy have added ways to save supervisors. We need not dwell on how supervisors are protected with the approach of Carl Rogers. They only teach the therapist to reflect back what the client says. Most supervisors can manage that.

The value of diagnosis for the supervisor who doesn't know what to do is well known. Rather than talk about therapy, it was discovered that hours of supervision time can be used up discussing the proper diagnosis. Dwelling on the DSM-IV, the supervisor who discovers that a client fits into a category, or even three or four of them, will arouse an excited feeling of accomplishment in the trainee. "Clearly a borderline personality and not a schizoid state," says the supervisor. "Gosh!" says the trainee in admiration. It takes time doing therapy in the real world before the therapist notices that the diagnostic system is irrelevant and even a handicap to changing people.

When supervisors train psychiatric residents today, diagnosing and choosing a drug, or even three or four, are the only activities. A record for talking about medication was established by a group in the University of Iowa Department of Psychiatry. They are reported to have talked for 2 hours and 38 minutes about which medication should be used to defeat the unfortunate side effects of Haldol, which had been given to a woman when she complained of anxiety while bungee-jumping off the Tallahatchie Bridge.

New Times

As times change, something new for supervisors is becoming necessary. Let us outline the challenge: Many protective procedures of supervisors are being abandoned just when more supervisors are being trained. Confidentiality, the key protection for supervisors, is being threatened with the development of the one-way mirror and the audio and video recording of interviews. The supervisor's lack of knowledge is put on public display instead of being shown only to one supervisee in confidence. Live supervision requires that a teacher know how to guide a trainee during an actual therapy interview, not later when the discussion can only be about what might have been. Because of the popularity of live supervision, it is the lucky supervisor who can avoid the one-way mirror.

Therapists are also under great pressure to know what to do about presenting problems. A reliance on the past and on fantasies is being given up as the real world of clients is discovered to be a pain. At the same time, social changes are occurring and the poor and new ethnic groups are descending upon therapists. Traditionally, therapists were impatient with the poor and refused to treat them since they wouldn't come on time or pay their bills regularly. Supervisors needed only to have keen insight into the middle classes; now they must deal with poor people as well as with members of 180 ethnic groups, many of whom do not even speak English. Therapy is also being applied to more difficult problems, such as violence, suicide, rape, drug abuse, incest, criminal activities, and other troubling behaviors. To deal with these unfortunate people, therapists have to know what they're doing. Supervisors who don't know how to teach what to do are under attack. The latest complication for supervisors is the discovery that therapists and clients come in two genders. Feminist therapists protest past and present biases and blame supervisors. How can supervisors conceal incompetence and sexism when all is visible and the focus is on actual people in the real world? Can that challenge be met? Let us discuss how theory can be helpful, as always.

Modern Theory

One way to salvage the supervisor with theory is to provide a theory so complex that no one can understand it, not even, a supervisor. This is what happened with the theory of family therapy. Alternatively, one can provide a theory so simple that any supervisor, no matter how dumb, can understand it. This is what happened with the theory of behavior therapy. Pavlov discovered that if a creature is rewarded for doing something, it will do more of that something. If it's punished for doing something, it will do less of that something. To this remarkable finding was added the idea that if people are holding their noses when they are punished, they will get uneasy whenever they touch their noses. (This has been one explanation of the concern with noses of Freud's friend Fliess.) Skinner leaped upon this theory and expanded the ideas slightly. On that rock was built the church of behavior therapy, a system most teachers could grasp.

Family therapists took quite the opposite approach, seeking more complexity. They created theories so complicated that no teacher could be expected to understand them. Fortunately, there was a giant brain in the field whose ability to be ambiguous was legendary: Gregory Bateson, who became the theoretician of family therapy. Although not particularly interested in therapy, he, along with Don Jackson, introduced the idea of homeostasis into the field and applied that view to whole families he began to interview on his research project. This cybernetic view allows teachers to confound trainees with a complex set of ideas about governed systems, feedback processes, step functions, and negative entropy, all wrapped up in the second law of thermodynamics. Trainees try to conceal the fact that they don't understand the theory and so don't notice that their teachers don't understand it either. It's not necessary for the teachers to teach how to change anyone because the theory is about how systems correct themselves and do not change. European intellectuals like this theory because they believe that changing is actually not changing because it is all constructivist. Americans tend to be more pragmatic and practical, and so they are just confused. A new discovery was recently made that has resulted in a change in the cybernetics of family therapy: third-order change. First-order cybernetics was the discovery that family members respond to each other. Second-order cybernetics was Harry Stack Sullivan's discovery that there is a therapist involved in the observation and that he or she influences the data. Third-order cybernetics is the discovery that supervisors need cybernetic theory to conceal the fact that they don't know how to change anyone.

When Bateson died, systems theory was in danger of becoming more understandable. However, sophisticated theoreticians, faced with the threat of having to know how to do therapy, leaped in to offer complex theories of aesthetic epistemologies with dissociated states with narratives based on constructivist principles. Teachers could continue to avoid teaching how to bring about change and be wise and impenetrable. The post of Chief of Ambiguity is still open and eagerly sought by many contenders. There are two main schools in the competition: One is the "tom-tom" school, whose theme song is a tale of Hoffman and which prides itself on following a different, soundless drum; the hope of leaders of this school is to find a foreign philosopher somewhere who will make them wise. Another school is called the "gray is not white no matter what anybody says" school. It is difficult to find since it is becoming more and more obscure. When a trainee asks what to do to change someone in therapy, a supervisor of this school may respond with the following quote.

> The constitutionalist perspective that I am arguing for refutes foundationalist assumptions of objectivity, essentialism and representationalism. It proposes that an objective knowledge of the world is not possible, that knowledges are actually generated in particular discursive fields. It proposes that all essentialist notions, including those about human nature, are ruses that disguise what is really taking place, that essentialist notions are paradoxical in that they provide descriptions that are specifying of life; that these notions obscure the operations of power. And the constitutionalist perspective proposes that the descriptions that we have of life are not representations or reflections of life as lived, but are directly constitutive of life; that these descriptions do not correspond with the world, but have real effect in the shaping of life. [The reader is challenged to find the source of this quote. It is on page 125 of a book that is better avoided.]

We can only admire this example since it shows that therapy can always produce major theoreticians to obscure the issues and save supervisors.

Still, what is to be done with trainees who persist in saying, "Bosh to theory. What do I do to stop a man from beating his wife and molesting his five children?" Family therapy forces attention on the real world, and trainees expect supervisors to tell them something practical to do. The family emphasis risks clarity, but fortunately it also touches on sensitive issues for trainees who are still disengaging from their own families and wondering if they are dysfunctional. Discussing parents and children and in-laws is always highly charged with personal biases and memories of mistreatment. By dwelling on the personal experience of the trainees, supervisors can distract them from concerns about how one causes change.

The most popular approach with families continues to be the emphasis on the individual. Each year the individual is said to be rediscovered, especially by supervisors who never lost him. An alternate objection that comes up each year is that it's improper to plan what the therapist is to do because advance planning is power oriented. If the therapist just goes to the interview without preconceptions and hopes to find out what might be relevant to something, this approach is more spontaneous and not coercive. A new objection is to say that the one-way mirror is undemocratic and that all the therapists should be pals with the family and join them in the interview room. This is a way for the supervisor to avoid needing to be an expert who knows what to do. Of course, it is hoped that the disagreements among the professionals will not escalate and will somehow transform the clients.

Avoiding the Need to Teach Skills

When we look objectively at family therapy training, we notice that there has not been a new contribution to save teachers. Even though doing a new form of therapy, most family therapy training programs simply make use of past ideas of training. The primary way trainees are taught in family therapy is to focus on themselves in personal therapy or with the use of family histories in the form of genograms. However, the language is more contemporary. For example, one enthusiast put it this way: "Training in systems awareness calls the attention of trainees to the resonances from level to level of continuous systems. The resonances with one's most intimate person produce the sharpest learning curve." (This quote can be found hidden in an advertisement for family therapy training, published in an appropriate place.)

Some supervisors know how to interview a family and explore problems but don't know how to change them. When such interviews are objected to as being irrelevant to changing people, one solution for a supervisor is to prove that such interviews are important by bringing in guest interviewers for public demonstrations to the trainees. These national teachers are sometimes called "master therapists" by the people organizing the workshops. Apparently, the organizers call anyone who ever spoke in public a master therapist. To distinguish teachers from therapists, a way must be found to differentiate a master therapist from a "legendary supervisor" (defined as someone who has spoken in public more than once). On the national scene these legendary supervisors demonstrate the interviewing of families in front of crowds. Thousands of young people have learned to interview families before a large crowd, if they can only find one.

Stealing Ideas

Is it possible for contemporary supervisors to provide the trainee with solutions to problems without themselves having to think of any? Does that seem too much to ask? Fortunately, supervisors have found a way.

If one cannot think of a solution to the client's problem, an obvious thing to do is to ask the client for a solution and use that. This is called "solution-stealing therapy." It is easier to teach this procedure to therapists than to teach them to innovate solutions of their own. There are two opposite approaches: One is to ask clients what they have tried to do to solve their problem and then to tell them to go ahead and do more of that. The other is to ask clients what solutions they have tried and then tell them that what they tried didn't work but that a slight modification of their solution will solve their problem. This is called the "client must be wrong or he or she wouldn't have a problem but still I can borrow that solution" approach. In this way the supervisor need not think of any new solution but only swipes the one the client offers.

Is there any other possibility to save supervisors who cannot come up with a solution or a therapeutic plan? If supervisors could just tell people to stay the way they are, they wouldn't need to think of anything new for them to do. This innovation has been introduced by contemporary supervisors. It is called "paradox" and is commonly used in therapy, but usually its value to the supervisor is not discussed.

A paradoxical intervention is one where therapists direct clients to continue as they have been in situations where they are asking for a change. They are told to continue with their symptom, as couples are told to maintain the marital quarrel, and families are encouraged to do whatever they've been doing that results in distress. It seems apparent at once that this technique must have been developed for teachers who could not think of what to teach a trainee to do. A supervisor need only teach trainees to tell the client families to stay as they are. It is evident that supervisors on the lower scales of intelligence can grasp that intervention.

Conclusion

As we look back over the past 20 years, it would seem evident that therapy training in its many forms has largely borrowed from the past and has not introduced new ways to save the therapy teacher who doesn't know what to do. After all, there have always been obscure theories, paradox, personal therapy, and demonstration interviews.

Someone, perhaps a naive trainee, might ask, "Why save the incompetent supervisor?" Why protect the teacher who doesn't know how to change people? Shouldn't we encourage trainees to rebel against the incompetent? When considering such a reckless plan, let us examine one aspect of training that has been forced upon us with the advent of family therapy and systems theory. It has become apparent that what happens in the training program happens in the therapy. That is, what happens behind the one-way mirror duplicates what happens in front of the mirror (even if there is no mirror). If incompetent trainees are excused by saying that they have emotional problems, the same idea will be fostered in client families, whose members will excuse each other in the same way. If insight is imposed upon trainees in the observation room, it is also imposed by trainees upon the families in the therapy room. If trainees accuse each other with interpretations about their awful psychopathology, as found in the DSM-IV, family members, in street language, can accuse each other of curious categories of abnormal psychology. When supervisor and trainees are pals and humanistic together with democratic teams mirroring each other, the family in therapy will lose its structure and its hierarchy will become disorganized. Hierarchies mirror hierarchies in the therapy field, as the neoconstructivists insist.

How is this relevant to saving supervisors? If training programs don't protect incompetent supervisors but encourage trainees to disrespect them and even laugh at them because they don't know how to change people, what happens to the families in therapy? On the family side of the mirror all authority will be ridiculed, causing confusion everywhere as helpless parents become more so. If respect is to be maintained for, and among clients, every training project must respect and protect the many inadequate teachers.

At the moment, there are increasing numbers of dissatisfied therapy trainees who protest that they aren't learning how to do therapy and who even seek to avoid their supervisors. What can be done? An ideal solution would be to make it illegal for trainees not to listen to supervisors. As a matter of fact, that is now being arranged. The powerful lobbyists who represent professional organizations have persuaded legislators that a therapist must be licensed by them to earn an income. Anyone who does therapy without a license is breaking the law. To gain the license, the therapist must listen to a supervisor and pay for the privilege. So now the law requires therapists to listen to supervisors if they are ever going to make a living. The supervisor, too, must be certified, but fortunately that does not require much. Showing success in teaching therapists how to induce change is not required; all that is needed is many hours of therapist and supervisor sitting and talking together. Any supervisor with a comfortable chair and healthy vocal chords can manage that.

Fortunately, the number of supervisors who know how to change people is increasing, and we can hope that this fortunate trend will continue. Those who don't know what to do will continue to surmount that obstacle in ways that previous generations have used. Large numbers of supervisors of therapy are respected and revered and even have establish new schools of therapy, although they are not teaching anyone how to change anyone no how, in no way, with no problem, of no kind.

Endnote

A variation of this article was previously published in the *Journal of Systemic Therapies* (1993, Fall), 4–52.

15

The Brief, Brief Therapy of Milton H. Erickson

INTRODUCTION

Jeffrey K. Zeig, PhD

I first met Jay Haley when he keynoted the first International Congress on Ericksonian Approaches to Hypnosis and Psychotherapy, held December 5–8, 1980. The Congress was a tribute to Milton Erickson, who had been my mentor from 1973 until his death in 1980. Jay was one of the most important members of the faculty for the first Congress because he had spent so much time studying Erickson's work in the 1950s and 1960s, when Erickson was physically stronger. Subsequently, Jay keynoted many Congresses that I organized through the Erickson Foundation. He was one of our most popular lecturers. The essay to follow was presented as a keynote at the 1996 Brief Therapy Conference, but is previously unpublished.

Jay was one of Erickson's many intellectual heirs, and one of the most important. Jay also was a formidable force in 20th-century psychotherapy, having developed strategic therapy, which was Jay's school, and one of a number of schools of psychotherapy that were heavily influenced by Erickson.

Jay defined *strategic* in the opening pages of *Uncommon Therapy* (Haley, 1973): A therapy is strategic when the therapist has a goal in mind and works to establish that goal. In 1973, when that book was published, that was a radical pronouncement. Therapy at the time was heavily influenced by psychoanalysis and Rogerian methods, which were anything but strategic. Jay's strategic school was one of the most important branches of Erickson-influenced methods. It incorporated systemic thinking and family therapy. Jay's work helped define the field of family therapy. Jay's training center in Washington, DC, was one of the most important in the world.

In *Uncommon Therapy*, Jay introduced the family life cycle, a concept for which he has never been adequately credited. Problems group at transition points in the life cycle of a family: when a child is born, when a child leaves home, and so on. In *Uncommon Therapy*, which took Jay 5 years to write, he grouped Erickson's cases according to family life cycle transitions. In the process, he brought Erickson into the mainstream of psychotherapy.

Previous to *Uncommon Therapy*, Erickson was renown in hypnosis circles. *Uncommon Therapy* cast Erickson as the father of brief strategic approaches. Haley emphasized how Erickson used directives to facilitate change. Directives were congruent and incongruent (paradoxical or symbolic) tasks that would help clients realize inherent strengths that would catalyze change.

Jay was not a "hypnosis" person. His approach deemphasized formal hypnosis. Methods derived from hypnosis were applied without the necessity of formal trance. Jay's approach was systemic, based on using directives. In "The

Brief Brief Therapy of Milton Erickson," Jay presents fundamental ideas about how directives facilitate enduring change.

Readers will encounter Jay's wit and wisdom. He was a phenomenal writer and speaker. Jay was as meticulous in his writing as a poet would be in using words and verbal images. And Jay had the acerbic wit of a social critic.

The essay to follow is Jay at his best: thoughtful, wise, and piercing. Jay outlines essential principles of using directives to catalyze change. He fearlessly challenges the excesses of traditional practice, seeing through dogma to uncover fundamental truths about the change process.

Reference

Haley, J. (1973). *Uncommon therapy: The psychiatric techniques of Milton H. Erickson, M.D.* New York: Norton.

THE BRIEF, BRIEF THERAPY OF MILTON H. ERICKSON

Jay Haley

Once again I find myself presenting my version of the work of Milton H. Erickson. My excuse is that as fashions change in therapy and new issues appear, Erickson's ideas continue to be relevant. Today brief therapy is in fashion, and Erickson's approach was short term with his own special style. I will discuss some of the premises on which his brief therapy is based, and his influence on me, with some cases for illustration.

The most popular term in clinical literature today, at least temporarily, is "brief therapy." Some of us who are older find that to be astonishing. We lived through times when short-term therapy was condemned and its practitioners criticized rather rudely, if not slandered. Clinicians who worked briefly and gave directives were often described as being manipulative and having personal delusions about power.

Clinicians now attach "brief" to titles or workshop presentations. Often only the terminology changes, not the approach to therapy. As an example, "deep" and "insightful" therapists looked down on the term "behavior." It was used only by therapists oriented to learning theory. As behaviorism became more successful and popular, the name was added to other therapies. Cognitive therapy became "Cognitive Behavior Therapy." Rational Therapy became "Rational Behavior Therapy" and now the term "brief therapy" has been adopted. Cognitive therapy has become "Brief Cognitive Behavior Therapy" and there is now the "Brief Therapy of Family Object Relations Behavior Therapy."

Brief therapy is not a school of therapy. One can use a variety of therapy approaches and do them briefly or extend them over time. For many clinicians brief therapy is doing less of what they do in long-term therapy, such as giving less insight. I think it is better to take the position that a revolution has been taking place in therapy for the last 40 years. The banquet of workshops offered illustrates that. We are not dealing with merely new terminology or changing techniques. Basic premises are changing which lead to a variety of approaches. Since this is a discontinuous change, the therapy world is being divided between those who seek to save past traditions, by changing names but continuing as before, and those who change the basic way of thinking about therapy. Erickson was marginal in the 1950's and has become mainstream today, partly because his approach led to short-term therapy. He was at the threshold of the basic change now taking place in the field. Before him therapists prided themselves on being non-directive. After him the problem is where to learn the skills of directive therapy. He did not sometimes use brief therapy and sometimes long-term therapy. His therapy was short term because it was based on a set of beliefs which he thought led to the most effective way to change people.

I could present Erickson's brief therapy by contrasting it with the long-term therapy we are now hopefully abandoning. That framework would be easy to compose since each of Erickson's ideas and techniques can be presented as simply the opposite of orthodox ways. I will try the more difficult task of summarizing some of the premises and techniques on which he based his therapy and illustrate them with cases. Some of the cases you might have heard before. If so, hearing them again will make you doubly wise.

What is required to do Ericksonian brief therapy? It is necessary first to have courage, second to have energy, third to have ingenuity, fourth to give directives, fifth to have a positive view and expectation of change, sixth to plan a strategy for a case, and seventh to be trusted by clients.

Perhaps the most difficult requirement for brief clinicians is thinking in terms of the real world and common sense. As an example, back in the 1950's I was doing therapy with schizophrenics by helping them work through the stages of infancy from the oral period to the genital period and so on.

I had a patient who complained his stomach was filled with cement. Obviously this was a metaphor about his oral period with his mother and was so interpreted to him without much in the way of results. I asked Erickson what he would do with such a case. He replied, "I would go to the hospital dining hall and check out the food. Then I would talk to the patient about digestion."

A case of Salvador Minuchin illustrates the same "back to reality" point. He was treating a 9-year-old girl who was starving to death. He saw the family, and later showed the videotape to the staff. Two psychiatric fellows said that they wished they had known about this case because they were collecting cases of anorexia nervosa. Dr. Minuchin said, "This is not a case of anorexia nervosa. This is a little girl who won't eat." That is a diagnosis Erickson might make, and one does not find it in the DSM-IV.

Courage Required for Brief Therapy

Of course there was a social context from which brief therapy emerged. In the 1950's psychodynamic long-term therapy had been around for decades and was established in the practices and training programs of almost all clinicians. The ideas were interesting and the organization Freud founded was powerful. The psychoanalytic movement had won a struggle against traditional biological psychiatry and against other ways of doing therapy and so dominated the field. However in the 1950's everything became more social. Animals were studied in their natural environments, and individuals were seen and studied in families. We discovered that we cannot not communicate. A therapist was a real person influencing clients, not a neutral blank screen to project upon. The issue was not between long-term therapy and brief therapy but rather between an orthodox individual therapy and those therapists who dealt with the social context. As Gregory Bateson once said, deriving it from Zen through Alan Watts, "The mind is outside the person."

In a political age, careers can advance or fail depending on one's loyalty to orthodoxy.

It required courage to propose an ideological deviation, far less propose short-term therapy. A psychiatrist who went against orthodoxy, like Milton H. Erickson or Don Jackson or Thomas Szasz, or Murray Bowen, took severe criticism. I should acknowledge that it was easier for some of us to be courageous and try out new ideas. An outsider, improperly trained, like myself, was outside the group.

When outlining the premises of Erickson's brief therapy it seems obvious that the first requirement was to be courageous enough to take a deviant position. This is still true, particularly in the large cities where there are serious investments in training programs with long term therapy traditions.

Erickson apparently examined psychodynamic theory and practice and decided to work a different way. He also practiced hypnosis when that was forbidden in psychiatry training because Freud had recommended against it. Erickson thought hypnosis was valuable as a human phenomenon relevant to changing people. He used it extensively in research and for rapid changes in therapy. Erickson's willingness to work as he thought best, ignoring opposition from higher authorities in his profession was characteristic. In a time of discontinuous change, which means that what is coming will not be like what is past, therapists must have the courage to take new approaches.

Erickson not only did not base his therapy on psychodynamic theory, he also did not use the developing reinforcement language of Behavior Therapy. He didn't say, "You did that well," or "I like the way you did that." Many brief therapists consider positive reinforcements and encouragements necessary. For example when coaching a client to enter a phobic area, "You can do it," they say, or "You did well for a start." They use as a model "The Little Engine That Could."

Since he was the most persuasive of therapists, it is important that Erickson did not typically use positive reinforcements but other ways.

An Erickson Conference on Brief Therapy

I interviewed Erickson on the topic of brief therapy in 1957. That was more than 40 years ago when ideas about therapy were changing. Let me say a little about that encounter. I had taken a hypnotic seminar from Erickson in 1953 and, with John Weakland, I began to do research on hypnosis. We interviewed Erickson at length. Our interest was in the similarities between schizophrenic behavior and hypnotic phenomena. Since schizophrenic symptoms could be induced in normal people by hypnosis, we wished to examine whether the interaction of a hypnotist inducing a trance was similar to the type of interaction of parents with a schizophrenic offspring. To study this phenomena, it was necessary to think of hypnosis as interpersonal and schizophrenia as a social phenomena.

In 1957 I had gone into private practice as a hypnotherapist and a family therapist, which the Bateson project was beginning at that time. My referrals were for brief therapy, not long term. The medical doctors referring clients were dissatisfied with long-term therapy and they wanted a symptom solved quickly. They didn't think a headache or a phobia should take years to change. If I could briefly resolve symptoms with hypnosis I could have all the referrals I needed. My problem was that I knew a lot about inducing hypnosis and had been teaching it, but I did not know how to use hypnosis to change anyone. I also found that some clients were not good subjects and I needed non-hypnotic brief therapy techniques.

Another problem came up when I found my therapy was successful. I did not know how I did it. A woman with twenty years experience with serious headaches stopped them in the first interview and never had one again, despite my insistence that she have one so I could work on it with hypnosis. I searched for an explanation of that change. There was also a man who had insomnia to the point where he was exhausted all day and was failing in his career. He was not a good hypnotic subject. I suggested that when he went to bed he was to lie there and if he could not sleep he should think of all the most awful things he could bring to mind. As he went out the door he said, "You mean like putting my wife in a whorehouse?" I said, "That's a good one."

He slept that night and with that simple procedure he slept every night. I did not understand this case.

In my experience interviewing Erickson about hypnosis I discovered he had a special style of therapy, which was brief, and which often did not involve inducing a trance, directly at least. On the Bateson project we had investigated a number of therapists, and none of them seemed to work as effectively and briefly as Erickson. So I made an appointment with him to spend a week in Phoenix consulting about my brief therapy cases.

When I arrived in his office Erickson said, "What is it you *really* want from me?" and we began. The consultation proved very helpful, and I repeated such a visit over the years. I recorded those sessions and considered publishing them under the title *Brief Therapy*. However, in those days publishers had no enthusiasm for a book on brief therapy, I ended up weaving this work into a three-volume text on various topics which I called *Conversations with Erickson*.

I found that Erickson often dealt with insomniacs the way I had done. He would require a task of them if they could not sleep. For example, he directed a man to read books all night when he could not sleep. Since he might fall asleep sitting in a chair or lying down, he was to stand at the mantle and read all night long. I learned that Erickson used ordeals for a variety of problems. When it works, the ordeal works quickly.

Intermittent Interviewing

There are different ways to measure brief therapy. The measure can be the number of interviews, or the number of hours or the length of time of the contact of therapist and client. Erickson rarely saw a client for regular sessions week after week. He would often start something in the first interview and follow it up with intermittent interviews. Let me quote Erickson when he made a comment on brief therapy. He said, "I have a reputation for using short-term therapy. I like to see patients and I like to get rid of them. When I accomplish something with a patient, I get the patient's referrals. My therapy has no rules or regulations except that I conduct the therapy for the benefit of the patient, not for my benefit, and I do it in as painless a way as possible."

One possible explanation of Erickson's brief therapy is that he would get bored listening to a patient day after day or even week after week. One could not imagine him listening to a few patients 5 days a week for years as was the orthodox procedure.

Varieties of Interventions and Energy Needed

One requirement for doing Erickson brief therapy is that you need far more energy than you need for interpretive therapy. Actually long-term therapy was so easy. One could simply learn to say, "Tell me more about that," or "How do you feel about that?" One did not need to make anything happen except to reflect about life with the client and the fantasies he structured his life upon. In Ericksonian brief therapy you see clients intermittently on the basis of what is happening, not on an interview schedule. One result is that you need twice as many referrals as you do when seeing people week after week for months or years. If successful you have a large turnover, and you are not sure whether your hours will be filled next week. Clients are on a variety of schedules to fit different directives. Your problem becomes an ethical one. You can decide the client will continue to improve without an interview next week, but if you don't see him you have an empty hour and the rent must be paid. I remember envying the long term therapists who contracted with clients to come for months, even years.

Erickson preferred to see clients intermittently and would typically start something in the first interview and recess the client for a time to let the change develop. Then he would see the person again and continue some development that could carry on without him. At times he saw clients regularly, but more typically he did not. He assumed that some people change more after therapy than during it. He would also deal with problems by mail or by telephone, and somehow find the time for a busy correspondence.

Erickson's brief therapy caused him to work at all hours of the day or night, which required energy. He was always available. He not only interviewed clients in his office, which was in his home, but he would meet with them in their homes. In fact he would see them in airports on the way somewhere, or in his hotel room when giving a seminar in that city. I recall a friend of mine having an interview with him when he came to San Francisco. Later when I visited her home there was a can of beans on her bathroom shelf. I asked her why the beans were there. She said Erickson made her put them there. If she picked at her face in front of the bathroom mirror, which was her problem, she had to eat the beans, and she hated beans.

Erickson's willingness to do therapy at all hours is part of the territory. Because of the demands upon a brief therapist, it must be not only a job but a calling, since sacrifices will be made. I once had a contract to train all the mental health workers in a state, and I met for the first time people who thought of therapy as a job. They protested doing an interview at 5 o'clock since that was quitting time.

Specialty

In the past a therapist could choose a type of client and a therapy approach and do only that. One could do therapy only with children or middle class adolescents, or eating disorders, or depression, or young people locked up in residences. If one is doing brief therapy and so needing many clients, it is obvious that a therapist must learn to use a variety of therapy techniques on a variety of people. It is necessary to know how to do therapy with children, as well as adolescents as well as the aged. One must have skill in resolving the variety of problems that are offered. Being a specialist is going out of style. When dealing with a child one can no longer overlook the parents and must be able to influence adults as well as play with children. Supervisors are having more demands put upon them to teach therapy with different psychopathologies and different ages of men or women.

Erickson, more than any other therapist I've known, was able to do therapy with the full range of life's problems. He could sit on the floor and play with children or resolve the pains of old age. Every type of psychopathology was welcome.

Therapists today must also be able to do therapy with the variety of new ethnic groups who are flooding the country. Not only must the therapist have some understanding of a variety of cultures but must learn how to deal with ethnic cases quickly. Erickson had a surprising range of anthropological knowledge. He felt a therapist should understand a variety of cultures and work within their framework. I recall he once had an East Indian couple who believed they were possessed by an evil spirit. They communicated with the spirit by table rapping. Erickson knew more about table rapping than the couple did, and so he arranged that the table produce some good spirits. When there were enough of them to counteract the evil spirit, the problem was solved.

Brief therapy Erickson style requires a maximum flexibility of the therapist. I am reminded of the woman who had psychotic episodes, and he had her mail them to him in manila envelopes so she would not have to experience them. One of the techniques we used with schizophrenics in those days was to take their metaphors literally, as Erickson did with this woman's hallucinations. He seemed to prefer that approach to involving the family, though he also brought in whole families often enough to be counted an early family therapist.

Often clients traveled a long distance to see him, and Erickson would see them for many hours on a weekend. I recall once asking him if it wasn't a lot of pressure on him to have to change a client briefly who flew to see him all the way from New York or Mexico City. He said it was actually an advantage. The person was more likely to accept a change if he or she had invested so much in getting there. I recall a concert pianist who visited Erickson from New York one weekend with the problem that he could not perform because of panic attacks. He had an important concert coming up and wished help. Erickson explained that he himself was tone deaf and so could not play the piano. The weekend of therapy was largely Erickson teaching the concert pianist how he should play the piano. For example, he must strike the key a little harder with the little finger than with the forefinger because the little finger didn't have the strength of the forefinger. After traveling across the country to spend a weekend being lectured on how to play the piano by a tone-deaf therapist this concert pianist was so angry that he went back and performed his concert. As Erickson put it, after that weekend the man had to let him know he was successful on his own.

The Need for Ingenuity

It seems apparent that brief therapy Erickson style requires adapting what one does to the needs of a particular person. Each client receives an appropriate directive which might or might not be correct for someone else. There is no method but rather ingenuity is required, and also a flexible way of thinking. For example, when the focus is on the problem, and not what is behind it, what directive to give becomes more obvious. If one starts by taking a history, or doing a genogram, the therapy is quite different and more lengthy than when starting with a problem. Erickson took the minimum information in a first interview and sometimes started with action.

One premise of Erickson is that people will change. It is a hopeful therapy. That is communicated in everything he did as well as the idea that therapy can be brief, which was difficult to accept by many clients who were only familiar with long-term therapy. One factor which helped Erickson be hopeful was his view of the unconscious. It would seem that among hypnotists the unconscious divided about the turn of the century. One view of the unconscious was that it was a place with unfortunate and awful ideas carried over from the past which must be brought out despite resistance. Every inquiry of a therapist with that view is to discover what guilt and anxieties and buried hostilities the person has. A first interview is devoted to bringing out what is negative. The other school argued that the unconscious is a positive force. If one gets out of the way of one's unconscious, it will achieve positive ends. Erickson represented that view. He searched through the client's statements to find out what were the capabilities, and he would build on those. For example, a boy envied and resented his brother because he was so big and strong. Erickson did not explore his jealousy and its unconscious negative meanings. He helped the boy realize that a smaller person can be quick and agile compared with a guy who has a big clumsy body. What a person had that was positive, whether a view or a talent or an idea to be developed, was what Erickson emphasized.

How serious Erickson was about the positive unconscious was impressed upon me when he said that if he misplaced something he did not spend time hunting for it. He assumed that his unconscious had put it somewhere and would reveal it to him at the correct time.

Amnesia

One hypothesis which every brief therapist must take a position on is how to think about amnesia. The traditional therapy view was that amnesia should be eliminated. The therapist should help the client remember everything, including every awful thing that had happened in their lives. The focus was upon bringing into consciousness any unconscious ideas whether expressed in associations or dreams or actions. Amnesia was the main preoccupation and took time to lift. If a therapist did not focus on lifting amnesia, he or she was not doing deep therapy. The theory of repression, the basic idea of psychodynamic theory, was an idea difficult to drop, but many of the purist behavior and family therapists managed to do it.

Erickson had the idea that amnesia has important functions and should not be eliminated. He considered it an essential aspect of life. We forget what is painful and should do so. Therefore he did not mind terminating a client who did not remember everything that had happened in his life or even what had happened in the therapy. He was an expert at dealing with amnesia. If he wished to lift amnesia, Erickson did it with great care so the client would not unexpectedly remember something painful.

In this age of a concern with false memories, when we cannot trust reports about the past, we find Erickson has been there. He would build in false memories with clients, as in the case of the February Man, where he changed memories and so the past.

I recall once visiting Erickson and he brought in an elderly man who was in therapy with him for pain. I talked to the man about what Erickson had done in his therapy, and the man described it to me. Mostly he said that Erickson gave him advice which seemed to me rather banal. After he left, I asked

Erickson if what the patient described was what happened. Erickson said not at all. The therapy had been quite different and the man had amnesia for what actually happened. I was impressed by the way the man had not described his therapy accurately, which raised questions about outcome studies. I was also impressed with the way Erickson did not correct the man at all. What the man reported about the therapy did not seem to Erickson relevant to the outcome.

Today many rational and cognitive therapists would be unhappy if the client did not describe what happened correctly or present the proper theories he had been taught. Brief therapists Erickson style must simply accept a positive outcome and not insist that clients have special training in the ideology of the therapy. Erickson did not mind keeping the machinery of therapy private as far as clients were concerned.

One of the curiosities of brief therapy is the way clients forget the encounter the briefer it is. Sometimes they forget the severity of the problem. They can arrive in distress about how bad the symptom is and after they are over it they look back and say, "Oh yes, I did sort of have a problem with that." Sometimes they seem to even forget the therapy happened. I think therapists who solve a problem in a few sessions sometimes have a problem remembering the client.

I once had a woman come to me who had a severe itch all over her body. She was referred for hypnosis by a medical clinic where they had tried what they could and she had not improved. She was in distress with this problem. I was about to go out of town for three weeks, and I would have to postpone the therapy until I got back. Since her itch was serious, I decided to try to do what I could in one session, Erickson style. I asked about her family situation, and she said her husband was distressed about his job, but other than that everything was all right. I asked her to describe the itching to me, and she did, mentioning that the itch had been worse on her upper body, but now it seemed worse in her lower body. I said I thought it quite possible that this itch was leaving her.

Sometimes an itch like that descended from the upper body, went down to the lower, and left the body out of the soles of the feet. Perhaps that was happening with her. She said she had noticed it was worse in her feet lately and she gave other evidence so I could support the idea that the itch was leaving her. At the end of the session I said I wanted her to call me in three weeks when I returned, and if she still had the problem we would deal with it. However, I thought it quite possible she would not have it.

Three weeks later she called me and said the itch was gone. I checked with her doctor a few weeks later and she had continued to be without the itch. Several months later I was doing research on families by bringing them together in an experiment. I was comparing families with a problem member with a normal sample. A family came in to be tested, and I thought the mother in the family looked familiar. I gave them their experimental instructions and started them in the test. I checked their name and recognized the mother as the woman I had treated. She apparently did not remember me, and I almost did not remember her. I have found that the briefer the therapy the more people forget it.

Stages of Therapy

It is obvious that most therapists who committed themselves to brief therapy know the stages. There is the formulation of a problem, an intervention to change it, a response to the intervention, and a disengagement. Different brief therapists handle these stages differently, but all of them are being required to think of therapeutic change as discontinuous. It is not a continual change where people change bit by bit over time. There is a shift in the problem as the brief therapy goes through stages.

Milton Erickson designed a therapy for each case, but he also appeared to follow stages in his therapy. I will cite a case which was the first one that I could characterize as an ordeal therapy. A client came to Erickson who was having more and more panic attacks just before he went on television as a news man. He would choke and gasp for 15 minutes before he was to go on the air, and then when he broadcasted he would be calm. He was afraid this choking and gasping would get worse and he would not be able to perform and would lose his job. Erickson defined the problem for the man as panic attacks caused by an excess of energy. It was characteristic of Erickson to define a problem in such a way that something could be done about it.

The task was to do something about the excess energy. He directed the man to do deep squats every day to get rid of the excess energy. He should start with 25, but it would probably take 100. Erickson said, "His lame, sore legs all day long convinced him that he had used up plenty of energy." He had no need for the energy used in choking and gasping. This was a typical ordeal directive by Erickson. He would have someone do something that was harder on them than the symptom and they would stop the symptom. The therapist wins both ways: the ordeal is good for him, and giving up the symptom is good for him. The man found he liked that use of energy and he began to go to the gym to exercise. It should be noted here that in that non-directive age Erickson was one of the few leading therapists who seemed to assume that a directive is necessary to bring about a change. Conversation and interpretations will not do it unless there is an implicit directive in the conversation.

Relapse

The man came back to Erickson and said his trouble was recurring as he got in better shape. He had lost weight and gained muscle and had a lot more energy but he had noticed he was taking deep breaths before he went on the air.

Brief therapy typically includes a relapse. Sometimes this is misunderstood. A therapist makes a brief intervention and the client improves and then relapses and the therapist considers the therapy a failure. It is best to consider a relapse to be a part of the stages of brief therapy. If a client has struggled with a problem for a long time and a therapist intervenes briefly and solves the problem, the therapist has become too powerful. The client will correct the power balance. One way to do that is to relapse and demonstrate that the therapist has done no better than he could. There are ways to handle this as part of the routine of therapy. One way is to encourage the client to relapse. The client rebels by not relapsing and both client and therapist win.

Another way to deal with a relapse is to avoid taking credit for the change. The therapist can say that it is a mystery what happened. If it is a mystery the therapist must not have done it. Another way is to give the credit to the client for having solved the problem.

Another way to deal with a relapse is the one Erickson used in this case. If it is an ordeal intervention, and there is a relapse, one can increase the ordeal. With this man Erickson defined the relapse as a psychological reaction. Now the man needed to do something about his psychological energy. The way to do that was to get up in the middle of the night to do his 100 deep squats. Erickson knew the man really liked his sleep. The man followed the directive and was over the problem. Then he came back again, still over the problem but worried about it recurring. Erickson asked him what was his lifelong ambition. He said it was to buy a home, and he was planning to do that. Erickson said it would really make him sweat and get rid of his excess energy to buy a home and do all that yard work. After that the man had no recurrence of the problem.

This way of ending a case is a typical stage of Ericksonian therapy. He goes from an unusual therapy solution to a situation where the problem is resolved by normal activity. Choking and gasping was an abnormal way of dealing with the panic. Exercising before broadcasting was a more normal way, and yard work was a yet more normal activity. The cure is an integration of the therapy task into normal living.

In Erickson's brief therapy, arranging normal living and social life is often part of the stages of therapy. He seemed to assume that if someone's living situation is normal they will be normal. He had a variety of brief techniques for introducing lonely and withdrawn clients into normal living. Part of what made his therapy brief was that he did not wait for a person to spontaneously get involved with other people. He would arrange that clients meet each other, often not knowing that Erickson was behind this happening. He knew the community well and made use of it. An example is the lonely young man who avoided people. Erickson required him to go to the library where he could be lonely and avoid people. Erickson assumed someone would speak to him there in time. The young man was spoken to by an enthusiast for exploring caves and began a social life.

A classic case example was the young woman who came to him so depressed and lonely she was considering suicide. She also had a gap between her front teeth which made her talk with her hand over her mouth. She had no social contact with anyone, although she mentioned in passing that a young man, who was a fellow worker, would show up at the water cooler when she did. He apparently was too shy to speak to her. That was sufficient information for Erickson to design a directive. He taught the young woman to spray water through the gap in her front teeth. He had her practice this ridiculous task until she achieved accuracy at several feet. She did this without knowing why. Then Erickson persuaded her to go to the water cooler and when that young man showed up she was to squirt water at him through the gap in her teeth. After considerable persuasion, and feeling that life was hopeless anyhow, she agreed to do that. When she sprayed the young man, he grabbed her and kissed her. This took her quite by surprise. She began to reevaluate her life as well as the value of the gap between her teeth.

Erickson's emphasis upon the real world rather than fantasies of the person proved to be helpful to others who learned from him. I recall a miracle cure with hypnosis that was done by John Weakland which was his version of an Erickson approach. A woman was referred to him for hypnosis because she had a facial pain which had resisted a variety of treatments at the medical clinic. She had even had the nerves cut in her cheek which failed to help the pain and made her angry about the paralysis of her cheek muscles. She was also angry at being referred to a hypnotist as if the problem was all in her head. Weakland interviewed her and said she offered him a problem. He said he might be able to help her pain with hypnosis, but if he did it would cause difficulties for him. He had to keep on good terms with the medical clinic because they referred clients to him. If he cured her pain quickly, after the long struggle of a variety of doctors at the clinic had failed, he would upset them since they did not know how to use hypnosis. They might stop his referrals. Would the woman keep the cure a secret? She said she really did not care what problems he might have with the clinic, she wanted to get over this pain and he should promptly hypnotize her. Weakland did so, and in one or two sessions her pain was gone. The woman went to every doctor she had been to at the clinic and showed them that she was cured of pain. She asked them each why did they not use hypnosis with her long ago?

Why Not Brief Therapy?

One can wonder why there was so much resistance for so long to the adoption of brief therapy, particularly Erickson's style. The question involves a larger issue. It would seem that therapists don't change their approach on the basis of outcome. Nor do they seem to continue with an approach because it is successful. There is something else involved, such as fashion or politics. Erickson was teaching successful techniques 40 years ago, and yet the less successful techniques continued to be the primary popular therapy. Let me speculate on why brief therapy has been so slow to develop.

A major factor has been the lack of training. Once long-term therapy ideology was established in the universities, there were several generations of teachers who taught the ideology and to change an approach required offending one's teacher. Brief therapists were pocketed off as deviants, outside the mainstream. Trainees were not taught such techniques as paradox, or the use of metaphor or ordeals, or any of the other directive techniques. Directives were against the rules. The ideology that was popular was one where there was no problem formulated and so no goal to be achieved, nor could the therapist fail since he or she was not responsible for change. The primary training was therapy for the therapist, with the idea that a training analysis would teach the therapist how to understand human problems. Whether therapists who had therapy had a better outcome than those who did not was never measured. There was no observation of the trainee at work, even when one-way mirrors and videotape became available and so the teacher could only guess what happened in the trainee's interviews. There was a gap between the training program in the university and the problems faced in the field. Students had to go to private institutes or workshops to learn what to do in therapy. The technique taught was conversation, not how to solve a problem.

Financing

Someone in the 19th century had the idea that therapy should be paid for by the hour. Everyone liked that. We don't need to dwell on the temptation to do long term therapy with that method of payment. It is obvious the deeper the therapy the more financial gain. Many therapists neglected the opportunity to use the fee as part of the therapy, as Erickson typically did. Erickson would, for example, ask people to pay him what they thought he was worth, which was an interesting problem for an obsessive client. Or he would charge a fee only if the person got over the problem. Or he would charge a fee if someone did not get over the problem. Or, as one of his clients said, "He would charge me a fee only if I didn't cooperate in doing what he said." All that flexibility is lost with set fees and a set number of interviews.

Metaphors

Part of the prejudice against brief therapy was caused by the metaphors developed in long-term therapy ideology. It was said, for example, that long-term therapy was "deep" and the past was "buried." Brief therapy was said to be "shallow." Clearly, once the long-term therapists imposed such vertical metaphors, they would win a popularity contest. Who would want to do a therapy that was shallow and dealt with only the surface and couldn't deal with buried complexes. Behavior therapy and family therapy were condemned as not deep.

What came with systems theory to oppose these ideas was the theory that metaphors should be horizontal and go round and round. The sequences in a self corrective system were the problem to change.

It seems evident that if one wishes to do brief therapy the vertical psychodynamic theory must be abandoned.

Another reason why long-term therapy continued to be popular is the fact that the outcome was not a complete failure. Cases were successful, even perhaps half the time. A therapist who could succeed with half his clients could feel his or her therapy approach was not too bad. Then came a dark cloud when outcome began to be measured. There was research which compared therapy outcome by a therapist against a control group of clients on a waiting list. The result was that 40 to 60% of the clients on the waiting list got over their problems and did not need therapy. That could mean that if a therapist did nothing, half the cases would be successful. This research finding was distressing. Fortunately for the long-term therapists the situation was solved. Research with that control group was stopped.

Often long-term therapy was a comfort to a person who just needed someone to listen. It was also helpful to people who felt guilty about their lives, like advertising executives, and could do penance by going to pay money and talk about a miserable past. It was also fashionable in many intellectual circles to be in long term therapy. So there were, and still are, many reasons why brief therapy is resisted and long-term therapy continued.

An Alternate Theory

If we seek a short-term therapy theory it seems evident we must give up vertical theories and focus on horizontal ones. This new theory must abandon the idea of the influence of the past and focus on the causes in the present and how to change them. Obviously the theory must specify a goal and have a clear outcome as a destination. It also needs to leave the interior of the client and deal with the organization that both therapists and clients respond to in real life. The organizational hypothesis should be one that leads to a positive view of therapy.

You can undoubtedly think of a half dozen theories which meet these criteria. Let me offer one that I contributed to and published about. Of course it is derived from the short-term therapy of Erickson.

When I was writing *Uncommon Therapy*, a book on Erickson's therapy, I was trying to think of a framework that explained the unique ways he dealt with symptoms. Over time I began to realize that many of his cases ended in a certain way. He would say, "And then she got married," or "Then the child started school," or "Then she went off to college." That is, he seemed to describe problems as part of the stages of family life. I worked out the hypothesis that symptoms don't occur randomly in the family life cycle. They cluster at certain points. Implicit in that description is the idea that a brief therapist can help a family past one problem stage and into the next one. The stages are obvious: there are problems right after marriage, there are serious problems with childbirth and infancy, there is the time of starting school and partly leaving the family. There is adolescence which seems to be primarily a stage preparing for leaving home. The leaving home stage when parents are only faced with each other can be a difficult time. Then there is retirement and old age with the problems that nowadays people are living forever. I recall a couple who had been married 64 years. They came in with a marital problem.

A Final Case

I will cite a famous case of Erickson in closing. It illustrates the stages of his brief therapy. A half century ago, during the Second World War, Erickson was a psychiatrist on the Draft Board in Detroit. He not only had to judge whether a young person should be drafted, but he also tried to help young men who wished to be drafted but were held back by a symptom. A young man came to him who could only urinate through a 24-inch wooden tube. It would be difficult for him to be in the army if he had to carry that tube around. He wanted to be drafted. Erickson focused upon that presenting problem and offered directives. He directed the young man to pee through a 26-inch bamboo tube. Therefore the young man accepted the idea that the tube could be different in material and in length. Then Erickson had him discover that, since length and material could be changed, his cupped hand was a tube he could pee through. Finally Erickson had him discover that his penis was a tube and he could pee through that. The young man succeeded in urinating normally, without equipment, and went off to war, getting past the stage of leaving home.

That was brief therapy done a half century ago, so we can appreciate that brief therapy techniques have been available to us a long time. Examining Erickson's therapy, we can use him as a model and a challenge. Erickson's brief therapy was not only brief, it was elegant.

16

Zen and the Art of Therapy

INTRODUCTION

George W. Burns, B.A. (Hons)

There is a simple Zen story that reminds me of Jay Haley whenever I hear it. It is not a story that I am aware he ever told, but, nonetheless, it speaks to me of his work and of him as a person.

The philosophy, tales, and pragmatic approaches of Zen Buddhism had a big impact on Haley and his developing attitudes to, and applications of, therapy, as he describes in the following paper. I feel privileged to have been sitting in the audience, hearing him present this paper, and am now humbled by the invitation to comment on it and track some of the developments since Haley conceived these ideas more than half a century ago.

The Paradox of Haley

Before beginning, let me note not only that Haley researched, wrote about, and spoke of paradox in communication and therapy but also that he was a paradox. My first introduction to his work was a well-worn photocopy of his 1969 paradoxical article, "The Art of Being a Failure as a Therapist." In it Haley assured me and other readers that "the problem (of being a failure as a therapist) is not a hopeless one" (1969, p. 691) and went ahead to offer 12 practical steps on how to fail. This was the first challenge to the orthodoxy of therapy that I had been taught at university. His humorous, but very poignant, use of paradox was one of the influential factors to launch me on a career-long search for effective therapeutic interventions. This search, in turn, now gives me the opportunity to update how the seeds that he planted in the 1950s have blossomed into several crucial fields of current therapeutic practice.

Other aspects of the paradox that was Haley are evident in the fact that he was a man of the West but one who was open to look to the East for inspiration and ideas (as we see in this paper on Zen and the art of therapy). He was a man whose logic and reason were astute and incisive but one who proposed the values of anti-intellectualism in therapeutic practice. He was a man who was a product of his time, who questioned the thinking of his time, but was, as I hope we will see in this discussion, also a man who was way ahead of his time.

Looking to the East

When Haley's approach to, and research on, therapy was being influenced by the ideas of Zen in the 1950s, the field of therapy was still rather myopic, ethnocentric, and perhaps one might even say xenophobic. The orthodoxy was in psychodynamic theory and therapy with very few deviations. To look to other cultures, religions, or philosophies for ideas about the mind and the practice of therapy was tantamount to heresy. Yet, as Haley said in an interview with Michael Yapko, "I have been in opposition for so many years" (quoted in Yapko, 2001, p. 197). And he certainly did oppose the orthodoxy of the time by looking outside the confines of the therapeutic box.

Although therapy in general continued its unidirectional, blinkered approach, Haley was exploring the relationship between Zen practices and the therapeutic practices of Milton H. Erickson. Now the field has broadened significantly, and there is a general acceptance that the West alone does not hold all the answers to the mind. Sufi stories from the Islamic tradition have found their way into therapy (McNeilly, 2007). Buddhist practices of mindfulness have not only been the subject of scientific investigation but also become a commonplace therapeutic intervention (see the following section). And, in a previously uncontemplated step, Eastern and Western scholars of the mind have come together to discuss their principles and practices for understanding human psychology and promoting greater wellbeing (Goleman & Thurman, 1991).

Meditation and Mindfulness

Perhaps one of the most important therapeutic adaptations to come out of the East is the use of meditation and mindfulness practice in therapy. Although Haley acknowledged the core role of meditation in Zen, he also described it as one of the differences between Zen and strategic approaches to therapy, perhaps omitting to see at that time how it would develop as a significant therapeutic tool. His omission may, in part, have been due to the association he refers to of proctors beating trainees with sticks to prevent them going to sleep or into trance. Nonetheless, mindfulness and meditation practice have, in recent decades, been incorporated into a variety of therapeutic approaches for effectively dealing with a diverse range of therapeutic problems such as depression, anxiety, pain, trauma, and health (Hassed, 2010; Kabat-Zinn, 1990). What had previously been seen as a spiritual practice that had little or nothing to do with modern psychology has now been recognized for its qualities of cognitive control, being in the moment, acceptance, relaxation, and well-being.

Acceptance

An important concept of Eastern, Buddhist thinking to be incorporated into the context of Western therapy in recent years is that of acceptance. Haley highlighted this in the following paper when he pointed out the paradox of change: A person who wishes to stop being constantly preoccupied with a particular thought tries not to think about it but the very act of trying not to think about something means that a person has to think about what they are trying not to think about. Haley described it as "like trying not to think of an elephant." This effort sets up a struggle or conflict that tends to exacerbate rather than ease the problem. Zen held a solution: Give up the fight and accept the thought. Let it come and let it go, as thoughts do, without investing in it or the struggle.

There is now a whole school of thought about therapy that emphasizes acceptance—which, paradoxically, is a change. It involves the client in taking a different tack, or engaging in a different process. The concept of acceptance is perhaps summed up in a statement I once heard the Dalai Lama say: "If you have a problem that you can change, you don't have a problem. And if you have a problem that you can't change, you don't have a problem." This acceptance of feelings, emotions, and experiences as a way for people to give up the battle or struggle with their problems has become one of the core components of acceptance and commitment therapy (ACT; Hayes & Stroshal, 2004; Wasler & Chartier, 2010).

Psychopathology

Another point Haley makes in this article is that in Zen, there is no concept of psychopathology. This puts it in stark contrast to most orthodox Western approaches to the mind that have developed comprehensive manuals and extensive classifications for the problems of the human psyche.

For me, one of the key contributions of Milton Erickson was that he pioneered the reorientation of therapeutic focus from the problems to the positive. Rather than asking what was wrong with a client, he looked at what was right with a person, what resources the client held, and how those resources might be utilized toward reaching a positive outcome (Erickson, 2010). Whereas Erickson may well be seen as the father of applied positive therapy, and whereas others, such as Haley, directed therapeutic attention to solutions and outcomes, it is Martin Seligman who coined the term *positive psychology* and formed a movement that directed scientific study toward flourishing and fulfillment, as opposed to mental illness (Seligman & Csikszentmihalyi, 2000). To counterbalance the strong psychopathological orientation such as in the *Diagnostic and Statistic Manual of Mental Disorders* (American Psychiatric Association, 1994), Peterson and Seligman (2004) developed the Values in Action (VIA) assessment that focused more on a person's signature strengths. This shift of therapeutic focus to look for strengths instead of symptoms has become one of the cornerstones of positive psychotherapy (Linley & Burns, 2010).

Metaphors

A final point I would like to make in regard to Haley's comparison of Zen and Ericksonian therapy relates to how they both use stories, analogies, and metaphors. Stories have a special power to communicate, and communicate effectively. From the time that we humans first developed language, we have used stories. All the great teaching traditions throughout our human history have employed them to share information, teach values, invoke emotions, discipline, and provide pathways to change (Burns, 2001, 2007). Clients come into therapy and tell us the story of their lives. They use as many as three metaphors per 100 words in a single hour of therapy, according to Ferrara (1994). They tell us that they are feeling *at rock bottom*, that their life *is falling apart*, that a partner or boss *is driving them around the bend*, or that life *sucks*. If our clients are using such frequent figurative language in story and metaphor, then it would seem both logical and effective to join them in their style of communication. The question is not so much as to whether you use stories or not but rather how to craft them, like a Zen master, to meet the desired needs and goals of your client.

And the Zen Story?

When Haley was formulating thoughts on the relationship between Zen and psychotherapy more than half a century ago, orthodox therapy was racing down a freeway that allowed few pathways on which to deviate. Haley didn't allow himself to get caught in this mainstream of traffic but instead began to look for alternate routes. His vision had him exploring Eastern approaches to change, the relevance of meditation, the concept of acceptance, the alternatives to psychopathology, the processes of cognition, and the value of therapeutic stories. Slowly the world of therapy has caught up with Haley. Now we virtually need a GPS to navigate us through the numerous routes for doing therapy—something I am sure that Haley would have welcomed but also something that he seemed to lament. In typical Haley style, he said toward the latter stages of his career, "One of the problems is that there is no longer any orthodoxy in the field. When there is no orthodoxy, you can't be a deviant" (quoted in Yapko, 2001, p. 201).

And what is the Zen story I mentioned at the beginning that always reminds me of Jay Haley? In answer to that question, I was going to respond by describing the ways it speaks to me of Haley, his style of thinking, and his approach to therapy ... but that is not what a Zen practitioner would do. So in true Zen style, let me simply offer the story and leave any interpretations to you. I think Haley would have liked it that way.

The Zen master, who had been away teaching, returned to find the tiny hut he called home had burnt to the ground, destroying what few worldly things he possessed. Standing, looking at the charred remains, the master thought to himself, "At last I have an uninterrupted view of the sky at night."

References

American Psychiatric Association. (1994). *Diagnostic and statistic manual of mental disorders* (4th ed.). Washington DC: Author.

Burns, G. W. (2001). *101 healing stories: Using metaphors in therapy*. New York: John Wiley.

Burns, G. W. (2007). (Ed.). *Healing with stories: Your casebook collection for using therapeutic metaphors*. Hoboken, NJ: John Wiley.

Erickson, B. A. (2010). What's right with him? Ericksonian positive psychotherapy in a case of sexual abuse. In G. W. Burns (Ed.), *Happiness, healing enhancement: Your casebook collection for applying positive therapy*. Hoboken, NJ: John Wiley.

Ferrara, K. W. (1994). *Ways with words*. New York: Oxford University Press.

Goleman, D., & Thurman, R. A. F. (1991). (Eds.). *MindScience: An east-west dialogue*. Boston: Wisdom Publications.

Haley, J. (1969). The art of being a failure as a therapist. *American Journal of Orthopsychiatry*, *39*, 691–695.

Hassed, C. (2010). Doing nothing, changing profoundly: The paradox of mindfulness in a case of anxiety. In G. W. Burns (Ed.), *Happiness, healing enhancement: Your casebook collection for applying positive therapy*. Hoboken, NJ: John Wiley.

Hayes, C., & Stroshal, C. (2004). *A practical guide to acceptance and commitment therapy*. New York: Springer.

Kabat-Zinn, J. (1990). *Full catastrophe living; Using the wisdom of your body and mind to face stress, pain and illness*. New York: Delacorte.

Linley, P. A., & Burns, G. W. (2010). Strengthspotting: Finding and developing client resources in the management of intense anger. In G. W. Burns (Ed.), *Happiness, healing enhancement: Your casebook collection for applying positive therapy*. Hoboken, NJ: John Wiley.

McNeilly, R. (2007). Night, night, sleep tight, don't let the sharks bite: "What's missing?" in metaphors. In G. W. Burns (Ed.), *Healing with stories: Your casebook collection for using therapeutic metaphors*. Hoboken. NJ: John Wiley.

Peterson, C., & Seligman, M. E. P. (2004). *Character strengths and virtues: A handbook and classification*. Washington, DC: American Psychological Association.

Seligman, M., & Csikszentmihalyi, M. (2000). Positive psychology: An introduction. *American Psychologist*, *55*, 5–14.

Wasler, R., & Chartier, M. (2010). Laying out in anxiety: Acceptance and commitment therapy for values-based living. In G. W. Burns (Ed.), *Happiness, healing enhancement: Your casebook collection for applying positive therapy*. Hoboken, NJ: John Wiley.

Yapko, M. D. (2001). Jay Haley on Jay Haley. In J. K. Zeig (Ed.), *Changing directives; The strategic therapy of Jay Haley*. Phoenix, AZ: Milton H. Erickson Foundation Press.

ZEN AND THE ART OF THERAPY

Jay Haley

Haley describes how he was introduced to Zen Buddhism by Alan Watts and then used Zen as a model to understand the paradoxical therapy of Milton H. Erickson, M.D. Haley compares Zen parables with Erickson's cases to illuminate the process of change.

Zen Buddhism is apparently the oldest continuing procedure in which one person sets out to change another. For at least 700 years, Zen masters have responded in a one-to-one relationship with someone who wishes to change. I will attempt to clarify the nature and influence of Zen on the ways of changing people in Western therapy, particularly in relation to the strategic, or directive, approach best represented by Milton Erickson.

For those pursuing the spiritual aspects of therapy, I should emphasize that here the focus is not on the spiritual side of Zen, but on the practical side of the art of changing people. That is, there is an interpersonal setting for spiritual development, which does not "just happen," just as therapeutic change does not "just happen." To achieve satori in Zen, one is not struck by enlightenment while sitting under the bo tree. A special relationship with a master is required, and a set of procedures, some of them bizarre, make up the interpersonal setting for spiritual growth. What I am emphasizing here is the materialist situation that frees an individual to develop spiritually. The actions to achieve enlightenment in Zen can be seen as similar to the actions that lead to change in strategic therapy.

The ideas of Zen influenced me in the 1950s when I was developing a therapy approach and doing research on the nature of therapy. For 10 years, I was a member of Gregory Bateson's research project on communication where we investigated the paradoxes that occur because of the nature of classification systems. In 1953, the year I joined the project, I attended, with my colleague John Weakland, a series of lectures by Alan Watts on "Eastern Philosophy and Western Psychology." Watts was the Director of the American Academy of Asian Studies at that time. An authority on Zen, he became an informal consultant on our project since we shared the enthusiasm for paradox. Watts became interested in therapy as it related to Zen and later published a book on this topic (Watts, 1961). At that time, little was known about Zen, even in California where many philosophies flourished. Watts described himself as "backdoor Zen," since he had not officially trained with a Zen master in Japan. His interests were both personal and intellectual and his fascination with Zen was contagious.

In 1953, the same year we discovered Zen, I took a seminar on hypnosis from Milton Erickson and began to study his therapy. I found the premises of Zen to be just about the only way of explaining Erickson's directive therapy, which at that time was quite deviant in the field. As an apprentice of Erickson, I used ideas from Zen to understand his supervision.

I should make it clear that I am not an authority on Zen and that what I have to say about it is largely confined to its relevance to the field of therapy. There are also many different views, and schools, of Zen, ranging from ritualistic rites and bureaucratic procedures to sheer spontaneity. I am offering a view largely based on the ideas of Watts, which were in some ways deviant (just as Erickson was a deviant in the field of therapy and Gregory Bateson a deviant in the field of anthropology). For example, some authorities on Zen consider extensive meditation to be essential to enlightenment. Therefore, the path to satori can become a life of painful sitting while proctors hit the trainees with sticks if they go to sleep or into trance. Watts considered meditation personally important, but he saw these ritualistic procedures as ordeals imposed on trainees to help them discover that enlightenment occurs in other ways.

Perspectives on Zen

Zen Buddhism had its origins in India and traveled through China before being introduced into Japan in about 1200 when Zen monasteries were established there. A body of literature has grown up on this topic, even though it is the premise of Zen that one cannot achieve enlightenment by reading about it, but only by experiencing it personally. In Zen stories, there is an antiliterature, if not an antiintellectual view. As an example, a woman who was a student of Zen died and left her son a letter in which she said: "There are 80,000 books on Buddhism and if you should read all of them and still not see your own nature you will not understand even this letter. This is my will and testament." Signed, "Your Mother, Not born, Not dead" (Reps, undated, p. 49).

A more typical example is the following Zen story (Reps, undated, p. 59).

> The Zen master Mu-nan had only one successor. His name was Shoju. After Shoju had completed his study of Zen, Mu-nan called him into his room. "I am getting old," he said, "and as far as I know, Shoju, you are the only one who will carry on this teaching. Here is a book. It has been passed down from master to master for seven generations. I also have added many points according to my understanding. The book is very valuable, and I am giving it to you to represent your successorship."
>
> "If the book is such an important thing, you had better keep it," Shoju replied. "I received your Zen without writing and am satisfied with it as it is."
>
> "I know that," said Mu-nan. "Even so, this work has been carried from master to master for seven generations, so you may keep it as a symbol of having received the teaching. Here."
>
> The two happened to be talking before a brazier. The instant Shoju felt the book in his hands, he thrust it into the

> flaming coals. He had no lust for possessions. Mu-nan, who never had been angry before, yelled: "What are you doing?"
> Shoju shouted back: "What are you saying?"

This antiliterature view contrasts sharply with the intellectual tradition of Western therapy where something is said to be true only if a reference can be made to a previous authority, or prophet, who had written it. Yet it is reminiscent of the teachings of Milton Erickson. He rarely quoted past authorities and never as evidence that something was true. He did not say that something was so because a previous authority had said it was so. In a pragmatic American way, he said, "It is so, and if you try it, you will find that out." Although this kind of pragmatism was often misunderstood by clinicians who came from the European tradition of scholarship, it is typical of Zen.

The goal of Zen is satori, or enlightenment, which is assumed to come about in relation to a teacher who, when successful, frees the student from a preoccupation with the past or the future (or with trying to become enlightened). The relevance of Zen to therapy becomes apparent when one observes that Western ideas of psychopathology are extreme versions of the problems of the average person dealt with in Zen. The client in distress is typically said to be preoccupied with the past, with guilts, obsessions, or desires for revenge. Or the client can be overpreoccupied with the future, as with anxieties and phobias about what might happen. He or she struggles to control his or her thinking, wanting to be rid of certain thoughts. Sometimes the client fears death and sometimes the client seeks it, being so depressed about living. Interpersonally, the client is often so attached to a person, either in anger or love, that it is like an addiction. Sometimes the person is fixed on material possessions or compulsively works and never enjoys a nice day. By definition, a symptomatic person keeps repeating behavior that causes distress while protesting that he or she would rather not be doing so and cannot help it. These kinds of foci and fixations are assumed in Zen to be preventing a person from fully experiencing the present moment, which is one way to view enlightenment.

Zen and Erickson's Therapy

In the 1950s when Zen ideas began to enter the clinical field, there could not be a comparison with therapy. The psychodynamic ideology, which was what was available, contained premises so opposite from Zen that the two approaches could not be related. The focus on insight was in sharp contrast to the Zen focus on action. However, one therapist was establishing a therapy with a different set of ideas. Milton Erickson was known as the leading medical hypnotist of that time, and he was practicing a therapeutic approach that was new and was based on an ideology different from that of psychodynamic theory.

When I began to practice therapy in the mid-1950s and sought supervision from him, Erickson was the only therapist I knew about who had a new set of premises relevant to brief therapy. I also realized that one way to understand his directive therapy, which was incomprehensible in the nondirective psychodynamic framework, was to view it within the framework of some of the ideas of Zen. I talked to Erickson about the similarities between his work and the approach of Zen. His response was typical: He gave me case examples. These stories illustrated some of his views on the attempt to live in the present moment. For example, he described a case in which he hypnotized a golfer. The golfer was instructed to live only in the present moment and so focus total attention on one shot at a time. When the man next played golf, he was aware only of each shot. On the 16th hole, he was shooting his best game, but he did not know what his score was or what hole he was on. He was aware of only the present moment and not of the context.

Psychopathology in Terms of Classification Systems

A basic characteristic of human beings is that we are classifying animals. In fact, it appears that we cannot not classify. We must hypothesize about and categorize whatever is, or is not, happening. Past social psychology experiments and current brain research (Gazzanaga, 1985) suggest that we constantly make hypotheses; perhaps there is a nodule of the brain devoted to that. Since we must classify, we are vulnerable to the nature of classification systems. There are several important factors about classification related to the therapy field.

When we create a class, we automatically create other classes. If we create the classification "good," we also produce the class of "bad," as well as those of "not so bad" and "not so good." If something is "high," something must be "low." It is in the nature of classification that one cannot have the figure without the ground to contrast it—in fact, multiple grounds or other classes. Therefore, a person pursuing a class creates the opposite class, even when not wishing to do so, as when pursuing happiness, one creates unhappiness. Lao-tse put it this way, "When everyone recognizes goodness to be good, there is already evil. Thus to be and not to be arise mutually."

Another consequence of a classification system is that paradoxes inevitably are generated. This happens when the class of items conflicts with the item in the class. If a person says, "Disobey me," the responder cannot classify that in a way that allows either obedience or disobedience. The person who disobeys is obeying as instructed. To obey requires disobeying. Paradoxes of this kind are generated by the nature of classification systems (Whitehead & Russell, 1910) and human beings must deal with them. The classification problem has been recognized since Epimenodes said, "If a man says he is lying, is he telling the truth?" Another aspect was emphasized by Korzybski and the general semanticists. Once something is classified, we tend to respond to all the items within the class as identical when they are not. The phobic responds to each phobic situation as identical to every other. As Korzybski (1941) liked to point out, "Cow 1 is not Cow 2."

Changing a person means changing the person's classification system. Individuals have difficulty changing on their own because they think within that system. The task is given to therapists and to Zen masters to induce change. For example, a person who wishes to stop being constantly preoccupied with particular thoughts or actions tries not to think of them. It is the act of trying not to think of them that creates the class whose items one must think about in order not to think of them. It is like trying not to think of an elephant. A person wishing to be liberated and to behave more freely can try to achieve that by deliberately attempting to be spontaneous. Yet a person who *tries* to be spontaneous must fail, since spontaneous behavior is a class that does not include the item "trying." It is like trying to free-associate when the fact that one is directed to do so means it is not "free," but "purposeful." Similarly, if a person tries to be tranquil, it is like trying to try, since tranquility is a class of behavior that requires not trying. The more one tries to be tranquil, the less tranquil one becomes. As another aspect of the problem, if one tries to change oneself when the way one classifies is what must be changed, each attempt to change activates the classification framework, which prevents change. Like the self-corrective system of systems theory, the attempt to change is what activates the governors that respond to prevent change.

An inevitable problem in therapy and Zen is how to change a person when to do so means changing how the person classifies the helper who is trying to change that system. By asking for help, the client classifies the relationship between himself or herself and the therapist in a certain way, as being unequal. The goal of therapy is to achieve the point where the client is defined as equal to the therapist in that the client does not need help. The client is to become a peer, rather than a supplicant who asks for help. Yet how can the therapist change the helping relationship to one of equality when every act of help, guidance, giving interpretations, or giving a directive defines the relationship as unequal and the client as being helped by a helper? The acts of helping a person to change mean defining the relationship as not changed. The therapist, or Zen master, must influence the person to change "spontaneously" and so escape the helping relationship. This is the essential paradox of Zen and of therapy. One solution is the example of a student who attempted again and again to answer a Zen master's koan, only to be informed each time that he was wrong. Finally, he simply sat down beside the teacher. That was the answer, since he was behaving as an equal.

Many Zen anecdotes illustrate the problem of changing classification. Reps (undated, p. 11) provides a subtle example.

> Just before Ninakawa passed away, the Zen master Ikkyu visited him. "Shall I lead you on?" Ikkyu asked.
>
> Ninakawa replied, "I came here alone and I go alone. What help could you be to me?"
>
> Ikkyu answered: "If you think you really come and go, that is your delusion. Let me show you the path on which there is no coming and no going."
>
> With his words, Ikkyu had revealed the path so clearly that Ninakawa smiled and passed away.

Systems Theory and Zen

In the 1950s, the cybernetic revolution was influencing the field of therapy by introducing the ideas of self-corrective systems. Erickson had been a participant in the first Macy Conference in the late 1940s and he was familiar with systems theory. The relevance of this to Zen appears with the basic premise of Zen that human beings are trapped on the wheel of life and keep repeating distressing behavior. The more a person attempts to escape from this destiny, the more he or she is caught up in it because the attempts to change cause the system to continue. One goal of Zen is to free the person from the repeating system so that new, spontaneous behavior can occur. Obviously, that is also the goal of therapy. It is the assumption of Zen that the attempt to change, or help, causes the reaction that prevents change or help. Obviously, that is the assumption of a cybernetic, self-corrective system. As any element moves toward changes in the parameters of the system, a reaction occurs that prevents the change. How to change without activating the forces that prevent change is the paradox of both Zen and therapy. It requires an almost trickster approach to free the person from preventing change. As an example, how can one obey a teacher who is instructing one to think independently and not to obey teachers?

As part of the trickster aspect of enlightenment, both Zen masters and Erickson have been accused of being too concerned with interpersonal power and manipulation. In both situations, the need of a teacher to have power and skill in influencing people is simply assumed. As an example, Erickson liked to describe how someone in an audience called out that he could not be hypnotized and he defied Erickson to try. Erickson shifted the issue to whether the person was able to refuse to do what he was told. When the person insisted he could refuse, Erickson told him to come up the right aisle and sit beside him on his left. In defiance, the person came up the left aisle and sat beside him on his right. Erickson continued to induce a trance, assuming that is what the man wanted (Haley, personal communication).

There is a Zen story one cannot read without thinking of Erickson (Reps, undated, p. 8).

> The Master Bankei's talks were attended not only by Zen students, but by persons of all ranks and sects.... His large audiences angered a priest of the Nichiren sect because the adherents had left to hear about Zen. The self-centered

> Nichiren priest came to the temple, determined to debate with Bankei.
>
> "Hey, Zen teacher," he called out. "Wait a minute. Whoever respects you will obey what you say, but a man like myself does not respect you. Can you make me obey you?"
>
> "Come up beside me and I will show you," said Bankei.
>
> Proudly, the priest pushed his way through the crowd to the teacher.
>
> Bankei smiled. "Come over to my left side."
>
> The priest obeyed.
>
> "No," said Bankei, "we may talk better if you are on the right side. Step over here."
>
> The priest proudly stepped over to the right.
>
> "You see," observed Bankei, "you are obeying me and I think you are a very gentle person. Now sit down and listen."

One problem in helping a person who seeks help, or a person who seeks enlightenment, is that to help that person one must change his or her way of life of constantly seeking help. I recall Watts telling a story of a Zen master who wished to inform his students that he could not enlighten them by teaching them something new. All the knowledge they needed to become enlightened was within them, so he could only help the students discover what they already knew. He said to a student, "You already know anything I could teach you." The student assumed that this was a wise master withholding, for some educational reason, important truths. The student could not escape from the classification of himself as a student yet that was the goal of the relationship.

Zen, Erickson, and Self-Monitoring

In the 1950s, I began to find similarities among Zen, systems theory, and the therapy of Erickson. There was a way to describe human problems and an ideology for therapy that was an alternative to psychodynamic theory and practice.

It was also different from the learning theory therapies that developed later. One dissatisfaction with psychodynamic therapy was the growing realization that people were being created who spent their lives monitoring themselves and hypothesizing why they did what they did. The constant preoccupation with exploring one's past and watching out for unconscious conflicts led to an extreme self-consciousness. In the attempt to use self-exploration and awareness as a way to avoid distress, people became preoccupied with their distress and its origins. Supposedly the self-preoccupation was to free people from the past, but such a change was not occurring. After years of therapy, people were habitually monitoring themselves. Even while having sexual relations, they would be wondering why they were enjoying the experience.

In contrast, Milton Erickson came from the tradition of the unconscious as a positive force. One should give up trying to monitor one's unconscious consciously and allow it to direct one's actions. The centipede should not attempt consciously to coordinate its 100 legs. Erickson's goal was to have people respond to their impulses in the present without being concerned about whether or how they were doing so. In the same way, the primary goal in Zen is simply to live rather than to be preoccupied with how one is living. The goal is to recover from self-monitoring. In fact, it is said, "When you are really doing something, you are not there." As an example (Reps, undated, p. 18):

> Tanzan and Ekido were once traveling together down a muddy road. A heavy rain was still falling. Coming around a bend, they met a lovely girl in a silk kimono and sash, unable to cross the intersection, "Come on, girl," said Tanzan at once. Lifting her in his arms, he carried her over the mud.
>
> Ekido did not speak again until that night when they reached a lodging temple. Then he no longer could restrain himself. "We monks don't go near females," he told Tanzan,

"especially not young and lovely ones. It is dangerous. Why did you do that?"

"I left the girl there," said Tanzan. "Are you still carrying her?"

The goal of therapy is to change someone's actions or to change the ways the person classifies actions and thoughts as bad or good, painful or pleasant, useful or not useful, and so on. Rational advice does not usually solve such a problem. The change must occur in action, according to Zen. One way is for the master to direct the person in some action and resolve the problem as part of that activity. As a result, Zen is often structured as a joint activity between master and student in some type of art. Often, it is taught through archery, swordsmanship, or the tea ceremony. There is a task, and the student associates with the master as part of the task. In that process, the master is directing what happens, rather than merely reflecting with the student.

As an example, one way to practice Zen is to apprentice to a master swordsman. A student who did that was given the task of cleaning the floors of the master's house. As he swept the floor, the student was surprised by the master's suddenly hitting him with a broom from around a corner. This happened again and again. No matter how the student anticipated where the blow of the broom would come from next, and got set to defend himself, he was hit with the master's broom. At a certain point, the student learned that he was best prepared to defend himself from some surprising direction by being unprepared in any direction. Then he was ready to receive a sword. He had begun the move toward enlightenment in the context of action between teacher and student. Zen masters pride themselves on being responsive in any direction. Watts told me of one who asked another, "What do you know of Zen?" The other immediately threw his fan at the man's face, and the man tilted his head just enough for the fan to fly by, and he laughed. (Once when Watts was visiting my home, my wife asked him, "What is Zen?" Watts happened to be holding a box of matches and he threw it at her. I don't know if she became enlightened, but she became angry.)

This active involvement of master and student in a task contrasts sharply with traditional psychodynamic, nondirective therapy. When I searched for a therapy relevant to Zen, I found that the directive therapy of Erickson included activities he set up between himself and the client, just as Zen master and student related around an activity.

As an example, a mother brought her 50-year-old son to Erickson, saying that he would do nothing and that he constantly bothered her, not even leaving her alone to read a book. Erickson said that the son could use exercise, and he suggested that the mother drive the son out into the desert and push him out of the car. Then she was to drive one mile and sit and read her book in the air-conditioned car while the son walked in the hot sun to catch up with her. The son would have no alternative except to walk. The mother was pleased with this task, but the son was not. After some time walking his mile in the desert, the son asked Erickson if he could not do some other exercise while his mother read her book. When he suggested that he would rather go bowling, Erickson agreed. Erickson pointed out to me that his use of classification in this way was calculated; the son would reject walking in the desert, but when he protested and wanted something else, he would remain within the classification of exercise and choose another exercise (Haley, personal communication). This example is typical of Erickson's way of getting into a relationship of action with a problem client, as is done in Zen.

Traditional therapy was based on a theory of psychopathology. Symptoms, thoughts, and character were classified according to a diagnostic system that was shared by clinicians and differentiated them from other people. A little girl who would not eat was classified as a case of anorexia nervosa, not as a little girl who would not eat. The language of psychopathology set clinicians apart from those who thought of human problems as dilemmas that arise in life. In contrast, a directive therapist prefers to think of problems as temporary, as a fluctuation in normal living that must be corrected. For example, when I was testing families of different kinds, it was necessary to select a normal sample. I found that I could not use clinicians to select normal families because they never found one. They always discovered some psychopathology in a family. It was characteristic of Erickson that he emphasized problems of living rather than pathological states. Instead of describing a child as having a school phobia, he would emphasize the problem as one of avoiding school and he would have a way of dealing with that. He did not call a woman an agoraphobic, but a person who could leave the house only under special circumstances.

One problem in finding similarities between Zen and therapy is that in Zen there is no psychopathology. There are simply problems on the road to enlightenment. It is particularly significant that in Zen there is a way of classifying and dismissing human dilemmas that clinicians might consider serious psychopathology. In Zen, hallucinations, fantasies, and illusory sensations are called "makyo." It is said (Kapleau, 1989, p. 41), "Makyo are the phenomena—visions, hallucinations, fantasies, revelations, illusory sensations—which one practicing zazen is apt to experience at a particular stage in his sitting... These phenomena are not inherently bad. They become a serious obstacle to practice only if one is ignorant of their true nature and is ensnared by them." Describing the phenomena further, hallucinations are said to be common, whether verbal or auditory, as are other sensations. "One may experience the sensation of sinking or floating, or may alternately feel hazy and sharply alert... Penetrating insights may come—suddenly come... All these abnormal visions and sensations are merely the symptoms of an impairment arising from a maladjustment of the mind with the breath." The author adds,

> Other religions and sects place great store by the experiences which involve visions of God or deities or hearing heavenly voices, performing miracles, receiving divine messages or becoming purified through various rites and drugs. ... From the Zen point of view all are abnormal states devoid of true religious significance and therefore only makyo... To have a beautiful vision of a Buddha does not mean that you are any nearer becoming one yourself, any more than a dream of being a millionaire means that you are any richer when you awake.

The phenomena that could lead to a diagnosis of psychopathology are assumed, in this view of Zen, to be a product of the special situation of the person and will change as that situation changes. That is also the view of a strategic approach to therapy: such phenomena are a response to a situation and not a character defect or a permanent malady.

Change in Zen

A strategic approach to therapy has no single method that is applied to all problems. Each case is considered unique and requires a special intervention for that person. Similarly, in Zen there is no method that is used to enlighten everyone who comes. There are standardized procedures, such as meditation, but it is assumed that a unique intervention must be made for enlightenment to be achieved. In a similar way, in a strategic approach to therapy, there might be standardized interviewing, but the directive must fit the unique situation. In Zen, learning and cognition are not considered the path to enlightenment. One is not taught how to live or instructed how to relate to others. In addition, neither strategic therapy nor Zen is based on the theory of repression. Therefore, insight into unconscious dynamics is not considered necessary to change nor is the expressing of emotions a goal. It is assumed that expressing emotions, like expressing anger, leads to more expressions of emotions and so to more anger.

In Zen, change is described as sudden and discontinuous, not as cumulative and step-by-step, as when learning or being educated. Similarly, in strategic therapy, the client is not educated by being taught to behave in a certain way or taught how to be a spouse or a parent. Nor is the Zen student taught how to become enlightened, and, in fact, one discovers that one must give up theories about it to achieve it. The assumption is that when the situation is changed by an intervention, the behavior will be appropriate to that new organization without ritual learning.

One of the characteristics of Erickson's therapy was the use of imagery. Often he would have a client image a scene in the past or in the present and use it to induce change. Such imaging might seem unrelated to Zen practice, where the focus is on reality, but a Zen story describes a wrestler named Great Waves who was of champion caliber in private training, but was so bashful that he lost all public bouts. He went to a Zen master for help (Reps, undated, p. 11).

> "Great Waves is your name," the teacher advised, "so stay in this temple tonight. Imagine that you are those billows. You are no longer a wrestler who is afraid. You are those huge waves sweeping everything before them, swallowing all in their path. Do this and you will be the greatest wrestler in the land." The young man did that to the point where, "Before dawn the temple was nothing but the ebb and flow of an immense sea." The next morning, the master said to him, "You are those waves. You will sweep everything before you." And he did.

There is another similarity to Erickson's therapy that could be emphasized. In Zen, there are stories, or analogies, told over the centuries to illustrate the path to enlightenment. Erickson also told stories to illustrate his view of changing people. In both cases, education is accomplished with analogies and metaphors. As an example, Erickson liked to tell of an experience he had when he was 17 years old. He was totally paralyzed by polio and his doctor said he would not live until morning. Erickson asked his mother to arrange a mirror so that he could see the sky outside the window. He wished to enjoy his last sunset.

How similar that is to a parable Buddha told in a sutra (Reps, undated, p. 22).

> A man traveling across a field encountered a tiger. He fled, the tiger after him. Coming to a precipice, he caught hold of the root of a wild vine and swung himself down over the edge. The tiger sniffed at him from above. Trembling, the man looked down to where, far below, another tiger was waiting to eat him. Only the vine sustained him.
>
> Two mice, one white and one black, little by little started to gnaw away the vine. The man saw a luscious strawberry near him. Grasping the vine with one hand, he plucked the strawberry with the other. How sweet it tasted!

When we compare Zen with other therapies, we can think of examples where it is difficult to find parallels. We can turn to the Zen metaphor of Gutei's finger (Reps, undated, p. 92).

> Gutei raised his finger whenever he was asked a question about Zen. A boy attendant began to imitate him in this way. When anyone asked the boy what his master had preached about, the boy would raise his finger.
>
> Gutei heard about the boy's mischief. He seized him and cut off his finger. The boy cried and ran away. Gutei called and stopped him. When the boy turned his head to Gutei, Gutei raised up his own finger. In that instant the boy was enlightened.

When one examines different schools of therapy to find a case similar to this painful removal of a finger, it is difficult to do so, particularly in this age of litigation. If one existed, it would be a case of Erickson. One of his classic cases comes to mind (Haley, 1986, p. 197).

A mother came to Erickson saying that her adolescent daughter had stopped going out of the house. She would not go to school or see her friends because she had decided that her feet were too big. The girl would not visit the office and so Erickson visited the home on the pretext that mother was unwell and that he needed to examine her as a physician. When he arrived at the house, he observed that the girl's feet were of normal size. He examined the mother, asking the girl to help him by holding a towel, and he maneuvered the girl so that she was standing beside him. Suddenly, he stepped back and trod on her foot as hard as he could. She yelped in pain. Erickson turned angrily to her and said, "If you would grow those things big enough for a man to see, I wouldn't be in this difficulty." That afternoon, the girl told her mother that she was going out and she went to visit friends and returned to school. Apparently, she was enlightened.

In this case and the Zen example, it is assumed that a sudden intervention causes change, that inducing path can be a necessary part of an intervention in some cases, and that no education or cognitive and rational discussion is needed.

Related to this example is the use of ordeals, which are commonly part of both Zen and Erickson's work. The path to enlightenment is often painful, with an ordeal sometimes arranged by the master and sometimes voluntarily by the student, such as suffering hunger and colds.

With all the similarities between a strategic approach to therapy and Zen, one might wonder if there are differences. There are many, of course. For one, there is often a long-term involvement of years in Zen. Strategic therapy is briefer. Also, a primary difference is the remuneration to the therapist. One does not find therapists in yellow robes with begging bowls. They have reconciled financial success and therapy as a calling. There is also no emphasis on meditation in therapy; the activity is conversation and directives. One other difference is that strategic therapy has its origins in hypnosis and practitioners often use trance to achieve their ends. In Zen, if one is meditating and goes into a trance, one is hit with a stick, since trance is not a goal of the interaction with a teacher. However, one might note that Erickson did not encourage meditating trances, but active responses.

There is also no family approach in Zen. Monks typically live with each other, not in families. Interventions by masters do not change families to change the individual. Once enlightened, the Zen monk might marry and live in a family, but the task of Zen is not to change a family constellation.

One important similarity is the use of humor in Zen and in therapy. There are many Zen stories that are amusing, and a characteristic of Erickson's therapy was his humor and practical jokes. Related to humor is the Zen use of koans and Erickson's use of riddles. Both techniques seem designed to help a trainee change perspective and to recover from being rigid and intellectual. When dealing with a client who believed that change was not possible, Erickson would pose a riddle that seemed impossible to solve. Then he would show the obvious solution. One riddle he liked was that of diagramming how to plant ten trees in five straight rows, four trees in each row, without lifting the pen off the paper. When the client tried and failed to do it, Erickson would show how simple the answer was if one can escape from rigid and stereotyped ways of classifying.

In the same way, and apparently for the same purpose, Zen masters build much of their work around koans and such impossible riddles. "What is the sound of one hand clapping?" is an example. One that provokes action rather than tranquil reflection is the koan where the master holds a stick over the trainee's head and says, "If you say this stick is real, I will hit you. If you say it is not real, I will hit you. If you don't say anything, I will hit you." The student must solve that koan or be hit. Such examples make one wonder whether much of Zen might not have been created to cure young Japanese intellectuals of being so self-conscious and rational.

Perhaps the most basic similarity between strategic therapy and Zen is the willingness to make use of the absurd to change logical classification systems. Not only are absurd riddles and koans used, but absurd actions are demanded. With particularly rational and logical clients, Erickson would give them absurd tasks (Haley, personal communication). He would tell an overrational, intellectual person, for example, to go exactly 7.3 miles out into the desert, and there to park the car carefully, get out of it, and find a reason for being there. I have replicated this technique with overly logical scientists by sending them a certain distance up a mountain road to find a reason for being there. When they come back, they are different. Erickson's directive to climb Squaw Peak might have had similar purposes. It should be noted that when Erickson sent clients into the desert, they always went, and always found a reason for being there. When they came back, they were different—less rational and less logical, and perhaps more spiritual.

Summary

In summary, what are the procedures of Zen that are relevant to therapy? In Zen, enlightenment is sought through a relationship with a master who believes that change can be sudden and discontinuous; who becomes personally involved with the student; who joins the student in a task that involves directing him or her; who attempts to escape from intellectualizing about life or monitoring personal behavior; who poses impossible riddles and insists on solutions; who approaches each student as a unique situation; who has a wide range of behavior and many techniques, including a willingness to be absurd; who focuses on the present and not the past; who solves the systemic problem that attempting to change prevents change; and who, within a kindly framework, uses ordeals to force a change. These are also the characteristics of a strategic approach to therapy.

If we take a broad view of the task of changing people, Zen practitioners and therapists have much to offer each other. Clearly, Zen came first, by a few hundred years. However, even though a latecomer, therapy has developed many innovations in recent years. When we take a broader view of enlightenment we see that Erickson was not simply a unique therapist. He was working in a centuries-old tradition of masters sending people out into the desert to discover new ways of spiritual being.

References

Gazzanaga, M. S. (1985). *The social brain*. New York: Basic Books.
Haley, J. (1986). *Uncommon therapy*. New York: Norton.
Kapleau, P. (1989). *The three pillars of Zen*. New York: Doubleday.
Korzybski, A. (1941). *Science and sanity* (2nd ed.). New York: The Science Press.
Reps, P. S. (Undated). *Zen flesh, Zen bones*. New York: Doubleday.
Watts, A. (1961). *Psychotherapy East and West*. New York: Random House.
Whitehead, A. N., & Russell, B. (1910–1913). *Principia mathematica* (Vol. 3). Cambridge: Cambridge University Press.

17

Ideas That Have Handicapped Therapists

INTRODUCTION

Jay L. Lebow, PhD

Jay Haley was one of the brilliant minds of the 20th century. In the idiom of the 21st century, he thought "outside the box," bringing a lens to widely held thinking that challenged the orthodoxy of approaches and viewpoints in his time. Furthermore, he brought great passion, wit, and conviction to his challenges. Few writers in the world of psychotherapy could command the same degree of interest and attention. I, personally, was deeply affected by his writing, which opened for me new vistas of understanding in illuminating systemic processes within and beyond the family and which, with *Techniques of Family Therapy* (Haley, 1967), opened a window of curiosity for me to a wide range of approaches to family therapy.

Papers such as the one that follows, "Ideas That Have Handicapped Therapists," point to the degree to which Haley took strong and provocative positions toward the practice of family therapy and, more generally, toward the practice of psychotherapy. Haley's writings served in part as the foundation for the then newly launched family therapy movement, sounding a call to questioning other methods and winning over many to the movement. We should not underestimate what was accomplished. Haley, with a small group of others, challenged the academy of the world of therapy of their time and in a short period of time boosted family therapy into a major form of practice of psychotherapy and the systemic perspective into a major orientation in treatment.

Nonetheless, in reading "Ideas That Have Handicapped Therapists" in the 21st century, we must also ask how much of what Haley argues has been supported over time and how much, albeit convincing in its day, fails to survive the test of time. Today, from the perspective of the 21st century, we can see both Haley's prescient wisdom in this article and limits to his arguments. In some sense, he was well ahead of his time; in others, he could not even see the wisdom that was present in his own time, let alone what would be revealed in the future.

At the core of "Ideas That Have Handicapped Therapists" lies Haley's greatest contribution in being one of a half dozen innovative thinkers who brought systems theory into juxtaposition with the world of psychotherapy. Before systems therapy, psychotherapy was exclusively the province of the examination of individuals and to a great extent with one dominant (psychodynamic) ideology. Systems theory brought a paradigm change to see the behavior of individuals in the context of the systems in which they lived. Although this paradigm shift at the end of the first decade of the 21st century is far from complete (Haley remains ahead of even these times in this way), seeing behavior in context now has become far more commonplace among psychotherapists, and systems therapies and the systems viewpoint have become well-established methods of psychotherapy. Such uniquely effective approaches as functional family therapy (Alexander & Sexton, 2002), multisystemic therapy (Henggeler & Borduin, 1995), and multidimensional family therapy (Liddle et al., 2001) derive in substantial part from Haley's view.

The second great shift that Haley spoke to was to a focus on results. This too is apparent in this paper. The context in which Haley's work emerged was one in which psychoanalysis could go on for interminable lengths of time in which the focus was almost exclusively on therapy process and not on outcome. In fact, problems in progress were typically explained as based in problems in the clients, not the treatment. Haley cut through this tautology by asking pragmatic questions about whether treatments in fact result in people changing. He was one of the first therapists and theorists in the family field to focus on outcomes achieved, laying the groundwork for today's progress research (Pinsof & Wynne, 2000). Moreover, as in this paper, he does not limit such questioning to the work of analysts but also brings this lens to the work of his fellow family therapists. For Haley, the question is not whether we are able to come up with an elegant systemic explanation for what is occurring but whether the therapist can do something to bring about change. This focus on progress and results has become much more common in the 21st century; it is situated primarily in the evidence-based movement.[1]

Third, in part because of the sorts of questions that Haley raised in papers such as this one, therapies that have been weak in producing cost-effective change, such as psychoanalysis, have become much less popular as treatments. The ironic tone that Haley brought to explicating the unusual nature of this particular method of practice and its less than logical or testable assumptions became part of the underpinning of what emerged as a broad questioning of these methods. Although not quite yet extinct, we today find far fewer practitioners of the sorts of methods of psychotherapy that Haley most questioned such as psychoanalysis than in Haley's time.

Fourth, Haley in this paper challenges the medical model of mental health. Although the extent to which Haley stated this challenge even about the most grave problems has some difficulties associated with it (see below), Haley was able to cut through and challenge the assumptions made by many that mental health problems are basically biological or genetic and best treated with medication. He pointed us, along with Laing (Laing & Esterson, 1965) and Goffman (1969), to the dangers in such assumptions and where they might take us. Those fully invested in a biology-only explanation for severe mental illness and as a crucial ingredient in more typical psychological distress would do well to read such critiques today. Paying greater attention to such arguments might also temper the assumption made more and more today to organize treatments around DSM disorders rather than other aspects of life.

Haley also anticipated in this paper the negative feeling that families in groups such as the National Alliance for Mental Illness would later bring to family therapy based on the then prevalent view among many family therapists that families were to blame for problems. Haley, anticipating the therapy practices of our time, sees the therapist as the ally of the family rather than invoking blame. It is also interesting that in this paper, Haley, having been part of the original group that formulated the double bind theory of schizophrenia (Bateson, Jackson, Haley, & Weakland, 1956), points to the difficulty among experts in agreeing about what is a double bind, showing he had moved from this formulation. The problem he notes in agreement about whether a double bind was present is perhaps the crucial reason why this theory now has passed into a historically interesting document, a theory for which no proof has emerged.

Yet, from a balanced view today, given Haley's willingness to make widely generalized statements, he also can be seen to be in many ways handicapped by ideas, albeit a different set than those that handicapped most other therapists of his time. Those ideas caused him to see the world through a particular lens, and at times to do precisely what he argued against: to ignore the data in front of him and to fail to anticipate other data that later would emerge.

This is probably at no place clearer in this paper than in Haley's view of biology and major mental illness. Haley simply did not see a role for biology in mental health. Even in his time, his statements about the lack of evidence finding a link between biology and schizophrenia in this paper ignored findings available (Reiss, 1974). From the perspective of 30 years later, the evidence is now in on this question, and that evidence clearly indicates Haley was wrong (Anderson, Hogarty, & Reiss, 1980; Plomin & McClearn, 1993; Tienari et al., 1994; Wynne, 1989). Although Haley was right to question the simplistic "drug as the treatment" concept in treating severe mental illness, he missed the possibility of any potential role for medications. Today's treatment of choice mixes medication, skills training, and family therapy in the treatment of these individuals and finds results far better for this mix than with any single method (Anderson, 1977; McGill, Falloon, Boyd, & Wood-Siverio, 1983). Although he was one of the inventors of family therapy, Haley was uncomfortable with these evidence-based family therapy approaches for severe mental illness, which include an assumption that biology is involved and that medications are helpful when properly utilized, and which have proven to be very effective.

The second way Haley shows he was handicapped by his own ideas lies in this paper ignoring the psychological. Haley was able by virtue of his training in a field other than a mental health profession and his own brilliance to see things that others mired in the discipline could not see. However, he could not see what others trained in the discipline could see. The notion of possibility of client progress through insight escaped him. That some might actually learn from looking into their inner experience seems lost on him when he describes these as ideas that handicap therapists. Furthermore, Haley fully ignores, or identifies with ideas that handicap therapists, the common factors that are the center of most effective therapy (Norcross, 2002).

The third limitation evident in this paper lies in viewing things through the lens of his own preferred methods and conceptual frame. By the time this paper was written, Haley had moved from witty critic, a Tom Wolfe of the world of psychotherapy, to someone who felt he knew the best ways to effectively help people change. My personal favorite papers of Haley are the early ones where he is open, listening, and bringing a fresh viewpoint to the enterprise of psychotherapy as in *The Power Tactics of Jesus Christ* (Haley, 1969) or the superb view of the early world of family therapy in *Techniques of Family Therapy* (Haley, 1967).

By the time Haley describes a method of treatment in *Leaving Home* (1996), he presents his own school of treatment. Although this method still has advocates, it is a method that today has far fewer practitioners than during Haley's lifetime. Further, the gestalts of today's dominant methods of practice have moved in quite different directions, most prominently away from paradoxical directives. Treatments of those with severe disturbances have moved in very different directions from those described by Haley in this paper and book. Sometimes "staying home" may be the best solution for a person with schizophrenia, particularly in a world of poorly funded mental health and social service programs. Other directions for developing consumer-oriented treatments that are effective have led to evidence-based treatments for treating schizophrenia described already, treatments much different from his own (Anderson et al., 1980). Good ways of achieving change through learning of various kinds (be they behavior, cognitive, or emotional) seem to have become the sorts of treatments that Haley, an outcome-oriented metalevel critic of the world of psychotherapy, might find effective. Ironically, these treatments are largely based in old ideas that have been refined and adapted over time (such as helping the person with the disorder build new skills) and that Haley might have included as antidotes for ideas that handicap therapists. Although Haley did work with clients on skill development, this vital aspect of almost all effective treatments today for working with severely disturbed clients receives little prominence in writing such as this essay.

Nonetheless, to dwell on the limitations would be to miss the brilliance of this paper. Papers such as this one argue for a systemic viewpoint still much needed among clinicians and invoke us to get outside of our own worldview and look at psychotherapy from a new perspective. Perhaps most importantly, papers such as this one prompt our thinking about what we do and questioning whether and how our assumptions apply, a message and spirit from Haley I hope we can all work to preserve even as we look at our own work and his work. Haley remains a great influence on the field of family therapy today, nowhere more clearly than in having instilled the tradition of examining our work through multiple lenses, and learning from the conversation that ensues.

Endnote

1. An irony that Haley would appreciate is that the evidence-based movement has to date recognized only a few family therapies precisely because those in charge of that movement who control funding of research only reluctantly support research on family therapies, leaving the biological and individual cognitive-behavioral therapies studied at least 25 times as much as family therapies despite the evidence for family therapy in every existent study of family therapy. Systemic understandings continue to help us understand even the knowledge we come to possess.

References

Alexander, J. F., & Sexton, T. L. (2002). Functional family therapy: A model for treating high-risk, acting-out youth. In F. W. Kaslow (Ed.), *Comprehensive handbook of psychotherapy: Integrative/eclectic* (Vol. 4, pp. 111–132). New York: John Wiley.

Anderson, C. M. (1977). Family intervention with severely disturbed inpatients. *Archives of General Psychiatry, 34*(6), 697–702.

Anderson, C. M., Hogarty, G. E., & Reiss, D. J. (1980). Family treatment of adult schizophrenic patients: A psycho-educational approach. *Schizophrenia Bulletin*, *6*(3), 490–505.

Bateson, G., Jackson, D. D., Haley, J., & Weakland, J. (1956). Toward a theory of schizophrenia. *Behavioral Science*, *1*, 251–264.

Goffman, E. (1969). The insanity of place. *Psychiatry: Journal for the Study of Interpersonal Processes*, *32*(4), 357–388.

Haley, J. (1969). *The power tactics of Jesus Christ and other essays*. Oxford: Grossman.

Haley, J. (1996). *Leaving home: The therapy of disturbed young people* (2nd ed.). New York: Brunner-Routledge.

Haley, J., with Hoffman, L. (1967). *Techniques of family therapy*. New York: Basic Books.

Henggeler, S. W., & Borduin, C. M. (1995). Multisystemic treatment of serious juvenile offenders and their families. In I. M. Schwartz & P. AuClaire (Eds.), *Home-based services for troubled children* (Child, Youth, and Family Services Series, pp. 113–130). Lincoln: University of Nebraska Press.

Laing, R. D., & Esterson, A. (1965). *Sanity, madness, and the family: Vol. 1. Families of schizophrenics*. Oxford: Basic Books.

Liddle, H. A., Dakof, G. A., Parker, K., Diamond, G. S., Barrett, K., & Tejeda, M. (2001). Multidimensional family therapy for adolescent drug abuse: Results of a randomized clinical trial. *American Journal of Drug & Alcohol Abuse*, *27*(4), 651–688.

McGill, C. W., Falloon, I. R., Boyd, J. L., & Wood-Siverio, C. (1983). Family educational intervention in the treatment of schizophrenia. *Hospital & Community Psychiatry*, *34*(10), 934–938.

Norcross, J. C. (2002). Empirically supported therapy relationships. In J. C. Norcross (Ed.), *Psychotherapy relationships that work: Therapist contributions and responsiveness to patients* (pp. 3–16). London: Oxford University Press.

Pinsof, W. M., & Wynne, L. C. (2000). Toward progress research: Closing the gap between family therapy practice and research. *Journal of Marital & Family Therapy*, *26*(1), 1–8.

Plomin, R., & McClearn, G. E. (Eds.). (1993). *Nature, nurture and psychology*. Washington, DC: American Psychological Association.

Reiss, D. (1974). Competing hypotheses and warring factions: Applying knowledge of schizophrenia. *Schizophrenia Bulletin*, *8*, 7–11.

Tienari, P., Wynne, L. C., Moring, J., Lahti, I., Naarala, M., Sorri, A., et al. (1994). The Finnish adoptive family study of schizophrenia: Implications for family research. *British Journal of Psychiatry*, *164*(Suppl. 23), 20–26.

Wynne, L. C. (1989). Family systems and schizophrenia: Implications for family medicine. In C. N. Ramsey, Jr. (Ed.), *Family systems in medicine* (pp. 503–511). New York: Guilford.

IDEAS THAT HAVE HANDICAPPED THERAPISTS

Jay Haley

Therapy techniques for problem young people have been improving over the years. Many ideas that caused consistent failure have been discarded, and new strategies have led to more success. Discarding ideas and theories that one has learned in training from respected teachers is never easy. It would seem that only when the social milieu of a therapist changes is it possible for him or her to change ideology and behavior.[1] The illusion that the individual freely chooses his ideas and theories, no matter what his social network, is in itself a difficult idea to abandon. A review will be offered here of the ideas that handicapped therapists of young people, particularly those defined as schizophrenic, and which have been abandoned over the last 20 years, at least by therapists who learn from experience.

Whether an idea is useful for a theory of therapy can be determined on the basis of certain criteria. The most obvious criteria are the following:

1. The ideas should be relevant to a theory which leads to successful outcome. Not only should the theory lead to better results than some other theory, and to results superior to no therapy at all, but it should not lead a therapist to acts which cause people harm.
2. The theory should be simple enough for the average therapist to understand. When important issues are clearly understood, the therapist is not distracted by clients who are experts in complexity and obfuscation.
3. The theory should be reasonably comprehensive. It need not explain all possible eventualities, but it should prepare a therapist for most of them.

4. The theory should guide a therapist to *action* rather than to reflection. It should suggest what to do.
5. The theory should generate hope in the therapist, client, and family, so that everyone anticipates recovery and normality.
6. The theory should define failure and explain why a failure occurred when it did.

Given these criteria as the most obvious ones for a theory of therapy, their opposites are what a sensible therapist should avoid. A therapist should not accept a theory that prevents a definition of a goal, leads to poor therapy outcome, or does harm. He or she should avoid any theory so complex it is incapacitating, one that attempts to explain everything, one that leads to philosophical speculation rather than action, one that does not generate hope, or one that causes everyone to be uncertain about whether they have succeeded or failed.

Unfortunate Ideas

A few of the ideas which most handicap therapists who work with problem young people can be summarized.

Organic Theory

There is a tradition from 19th-century European psychiatry that there is something organically or genetically wrong with deviant young people, particularly those who have been diagnosed as schizophrenic. Although there are those in psychiatry, especially among clinicians doing therapy, who do not take this idea seriously, still it remains a major assumption in the field. The impression given in the literature and in the teaching of psychiatric residents is that there is solid evidence for a genetic or physiological cause of psychosis. That is simply not true. In fact, the literature contains statements that there are "indications," "leads," "expectable trends," "possible pathways for research," and "hopeful possibilities" in that direction. There is no physical test that shows that a person diagnosed as schizophrenic is different from any normal person, nor is there any solid genetic finding. The clinician who doubts this should ask that his patient be physically examined to determine whether he or she is schizophrenic or not. The response will be a discussion of vague hopes for the future.

Millions of dollars went down the drains of research laboratories to find evidence of organicity, and that research was necessary and important. Unfortunately, the public-relations job to raise money for the effort persuaded many professionals and the lay public that something must be physically wrong with people diagnosed as psychotic. Probably no class of people was ever so stigmatized on so little evidence. Monthly announcements continue to appear, saying that the breakthrough promised for a hundred years is about to occur; the biological and biochemical discussions have become more complex and mystifying; and the results remain negligible. (There is more evidence that being a psychiatrist, or certainly being a doctor, is genetic than there is that being a schizophrenic is genetic.)

Today the argument between the organic and social views is not a minor one. The consequences for adopting the idea that there is a physiological cause for madness have been significant.

1. The assumption of a physical cause for psychosis has determined the custody settings for many problem young people. They were called "sick" and placed in hospitals under the care of doctors and nurses, even though nothing was found to be physically wrong with them.
2. Because of a supposed physical problem, massive doses of medications have been used in ways which civil libertarians would not have allowed with any other deviant population, such as criminals. These

medications have proved to be not only incapacitating in many ways, because of their side effects, but actually dangerous. Irreversible neurological damage, such as tardive dyskinesia, is being caused in thousands of people by both the irresponsible and responsible use of these drugs. Many medical people continue to drug people even when they would rather not because the focus on medication in their training has left them not knowing anything else to do. Nonmedical people are unable to prevent the use of these drugs because of the power of medical people in the field and because of their own doubts about whether the organic theory is a myth.

3. The organic theory required a family-oriented therapist to believe that a schizophrenic behaved in strange ways because of a mysterious disease and also in response to his family. That is, the disease theory held that the patient was responding inappropriately and maladaptively because he suffered from an internal defect. The family view held that the strange behavior was adaptive and appropriate to the person's social situation. Attempting to combine these views led to a therapy of mystification and confusion, not only for the therapist but for the clientele. While taught that psychotics had an underlying biological defect which was incurable, the therapist was also taught that he should do therapy to cure them. This meant the client faced someone who was trying to cure him with a theory that he was incurable, which was a rather classic double bind and provoked strange and bizarre behavior.
4. The therapist with an organic theory would think of the schizophrenic as a defective person who was limited in intelligence or ability. Since such young people were typically failures, the organic theory seemed reasonable to young professionals, who thought there

> must be something wrong with someone who was not striving to succeed. If, however, one recognizes that the social function of young psychotics is to fail, in spite of having nothing wrong with them to give them the excuse to fail, their abilities deserve more respect. Such young people are more skillful interpersonally than the average therapist, and so they are able to fail more successfully than the therapist can cause them to succeed. A theory that they were defective caused the therapist to underestimate their interpersonal skill and so to lose in the struggle with them. To assume a crazy young person is defective, and then try to win in a contest with him or her, is like entering a chess championship match with the idea that your opponents are retarded.

These objections to findings that remain mythical does not in any way imply that a mad young person should not have a careful physical examination. There should also be the most sophisticated neurological investigations whenever they are indicated. One of the objections to psychiatry departments today is that they are so quick to assume a chemical imbalance as a causal factor that they do not carry out the obvious neurological investigations.

A final argument is that the medical theories and the medications that have followed from them have not solved the problem, and hundreds of thousands of young people continue to fail in life and behave in strange and bizarre ways. The wisest strategy for a therapist is to assume that there is no organic basis for mad behavior and to proceed as if the problem is a social one. His success will increase.

According to the criteria of a theory of therapy, the organic theory was obviously a disaster and has become a heavy burden to psychiatry. Since the approach confused social control and therapy, it did not lead to success and even prevented spontaneous remission in clients who would have changed if they could have gotten away from the professional. Treatment by custody, medication, and pessimism because of a supposed physical defect reinforced the need for custody, medication, and pessimism. The biological theories were not simple, and even medical researchers did not seem to understand them. No hope was encouraged in client or family, and the theory could not define success. If a person called schizophrenic became normal, he or she was said to be either temporarily in remission or to have been misdiagnosed.

Psychodynamic Theory

Another theory that proved unfortunate was an ideology which, like organic theory, was based on the notion that the individual had something wrong with him independent of his social situation. That was the psychodynamic theory of repression and the therapy that followed from it. Although it is difficult to describe that theory simply, without seeming to parody it, the relevant points for the therapy of young people can be mentioned. According to that theory, a person behaved as he did primarily because of past ideas and experiences that were repressed outside awareness. He was secondarily influenced by his current social situation, although the emphasis was largely on how he viewed that situation through the conceptions built into him by the past. The merit of the theory was that it offered researchers interesting explanations for different varieties of strange behavior. When the ideas were brought into the therapy situation, however, the theory was a handicap. With the theory of repression, it was difficult for a therapist to view the family members as interrelated in their responsive behavior. The unit was a single individual, not a dyad or triad. Each person was viewed as a repressed individual responding to projections and misperceptions. The symptoms of a person were not seen as responsive and appropriate to his social milieu, but as maladaptive, irrational, and a response to past experiences more than present circumstances. Therefore the present, which is all that can be changed, was not focused on as the area to be changed. How extreme this view can be is illustrated by therapists I knew who worked in hospitals and did therapy with individuals, and who were so focused on the past that they did not know if the patient was married.

It is difficult to take a positive approach in therapy with a psychodynamic theory, because the orientation is toward the negative side of people. It is the darker side that is repressed, including fear, hostility, hatred, incestuous passion, and all that. When the primary therapy technique available is to make interpretations to bring this repressed material into awareness, it forces a focus on hostile and unpleasant aspects of people. (I recall a family therapy team presenting a case with a schizophrenic. They reported proudly that after three years of therapy the mother finally admitted that she hated her mother. This seemed to me to be irrelevant to getting the son and family back to normal, but to them it was a triumph, because they operated from the theory of repression.)

Psychodynamic theory tends to encourage a therapist to be an exploring consultant to the family rather than someone involved in giving directives and getting changes to happen. The tendency of the therapist to explore the past leads to the parents being blamed, since the past was their responsibility. When past actions are the issue, the parents are implicitly accused of causing the young person's problem. The therapist with a theory of historical causes often sees himself as a savior of the patient from parents who were a noxious influence, and so his exploratory interpretations tend to antagonize parents and make it difficult to win their cooperation. When the therapist observes their lack of cooperation, it confirms his idea that the past behavior of difficult parents caused the problem, and he feels he must save the young person from them.

Another therapy procedure following logically from the theory of repression was the idea that people would change if they expressed their emotions. It was thought that if people expressed their bad feelings to each other and got their anger out, even by screaming, everyone would be cleared of their repressed feelings, and the schizophrenic would go off whistling down the street.

The free expression of feeling might have merit in some situations, like religious revival meetings, but in family therapy interviews it was a misfortune which could prevent changes in organization. The experiential therapist trained to bring out emotions in artificial groups had no theory of organization and so did not know how to reorganize a family. A family member could avoid an issue or disrupt an interview at any time by getting emotional, with the encouragement of the therapist. Everyone had a catharsis and did not have to follow a therapeutic plan or achieve any goal. The young person, whose job it was to prevent conflict from developing between the parents, could become self-expressive and upset whenever necessary, and so prevent the resolution of any parental conflicts. Sessions based on making behavior conscious and bringing out feelings tended to be incoherent, disorganized, concerned with defense and proof of innocence, abrasive, and interminable. They also encouraged a "communication theory" of the families of schizophrenics, because such interviews generated peculiar communication.

The theory of repression did not lead to good outcome, was not simple, did not guide the therapist to action (but rather to reflection), and did not generate hope, because the causes were rooted in unchangeable childhood experience. It did not define failure or explain it when it occurred.

Systems Theory

The organic and psychodynamic theories were carried over from the past, while the social theories developed at midcentury. The idea of family systems was based upon cybernetic theory, which was developed in the late 1940s.[2] With this theory it was possible for the first time to conceive of human beings not as separate individuals but as an ongoing group responding to one another in homeostatic ways, and so behavior had *present* causes. The family system was said to be stabilized by self-corrective governing processes which were activated in response to an attempted change. The idea that a family, or any other ongoing group, was a system maintained by feedback processes brought a whole new dimension into the explanations of why human beings behave as they do. There was the awesome realization that people seemed to do what they did because of what other people did; the issue of free will came up in a new form. Family members were seen to be helplessly caught up in sequences which repeated and repeated, despite the wishes and attempts of the members to do differently. Therapists too were caught up in these repeating sequences, both in endless therapy and in endless conflicts with fellow staff members in agencies and hospitals.

The chief merit of a systems theory is that it makes certain happenings predictable. The chief demerit of the theory for therapeutic purposes is that it is not a theory of change but a theory of stability. Family therapy, the attempt to change families, developed within a theory of how a family remains the same. As interesting as this theory might be for explaining animal and human behavior, it was not a simple guide to what to do in therapy. It even handicapped the therapist by leading him to believe that an attempt to intervene activated resistance, because of governing processes to keep the family unchanged. This led to the kind of pessimism that ideas of resistance in psychodynamic theory had led to. This theory also suggested that if you caused a change in one part of a family, there was a response in another part. For some therapists, this activated the old myth about symptom substitution and caused them to hesitate to take action to bring about change.

Systems theory, as it was applied to families, tended to describe participants as equals, which made the theory difficult to use when planning the restructuring and reorganization of the family hierarchy. To consider the power of a grandmother, or to support parents as authorities over a child, was difficult within a theory which tended to equalize everyone as responsive units.

A primary problem for a therapist is the way systems theory takes away individual responsibility from the participants in a system. Each person is driven to do what he does because of what someone else does. Interesting as that theory may be for a philosopher concerned with free will, family therapists seem, in practice, to need to emphasize individual initiative. So within a theory that people cannot help doing what they are doing, the therapist is suggesting that family members act differently.

Family systems theory did not seem to lead to good outcome. It also was not a simple theory, as one found when attending theoretical discussions. Often one did not understand what the speaker had said, though it sounded profound. The theory, because of the emphasis on high levels of abstraction, was even used to obscure the issue of whether anyone had really changed during therapy.

The Double Bind

Finally, there was the double-bind theory, published in 1956, which was not a theory of family therapy but became part of the enterprise. That theory included the idea of describing communication in terms of levels, with the possibility that those levels could conflict and generate a paradox, or bind, where no acceptable response was possible. The theory was an attempt to describe some of the processes in the learning situation of the schizophrenic. At first it was described as a bind imposed on a child by parents, and later as a reciprocal bind that people impose on each other. There was also a suggestion that a person could impose a "therapeutic bind" by so binding a person that he was forced to behave normally.[3]

As interesting as that theory was, and as valuable as the concept of levels was in describing behavior, I don't think the theory was helpful to therapists of families of schizophrenics. Not only was it a hypothesis about what happened, rather than a suggestion for how to change what was happening now, but it encouraged a description of a family in terms of a victim; helpful therapists found themselves siding with the victim against the parents. Since therapy is an art of coalitions, it is difficult to plan carefully how to be involved in factional family conflicts if one's theory biases one toward rescuing someone in the family. Just as the idea of a "scapegoat" was a misfortune for therapy, so was the idea of a "victim" of a double bind. From what we know today about the nature and importance of hierarchy, for an expert to side with a "victim" low in the hierarchy against someone higher can cause family distress rather than relieve it.[4]

The view of the family implicit in a theory of victims was the negative view that people do bad things to each other. This orientation made it difficult for a therapist to organize his thinking in a positive way and gain the cooperation of the family to bring about change.

Whatever the problems of using the "double bind" in a family description, they were compounded when combined with the idea that change is caused by making interpretations to help people understand what they are doing. Family members were forced to listen to helpful therapists point out what dreadful double binds they imposed on each other. The response was defensive and angry behavior by the family members at being misunderstood. This was interpreted as resistance to the therapists, and so the therapists condemned the behavior they were evoking, which is rather like a double bind.

With the theory of the double bind and the concept of levels, the communication processes in the family became more interesting from a research viewpoint. Body movements, vocal intonations, and words with multiple meanings showed an astonishing intricacy. There were metaphors about metaphors about metaphors. A therapist who explored these meanings in interviews found himself unknowingly obscuring more basic issues. There were fascinating and endless discussions with a mother about how she wanted her child to do what she said spontaneously. It was pointed out to a father how he condemned his son for thinking as he himself did. The family seemed to prefer such discussions to taking any action toward change.

Researchers and Clinicians

I have summarized a few of the theoretical and research ideas of the past, but there was another assumption that seems strange today. It was taken for granted that a therapist and a researcher were of the same species (although the therapist had a more second-class status). It was even thought that research training was a way to train a therapist, and many young people spent years in graduate school doing research as a way of getting a degree to do therapy. Today, it seems more apparent that the research stance and the posture of the therapist are quite the opposite of each other. The researcher must keep distant from his data, be objective, and not intrude on or influence what he is studying. He must also explore and explain all the complex variables of every issue, since he is a seeker after truth. The therapist's stance is quite different. He must be personally involved and human, not distant and objective. He must intrude actively on the data to influence people, so that what has been going on will change. He must also use simple ideas that will accomplish his goals and not be distracted by explorations into interesting aspects of life and the human mind.

It seems evident that the creation of a researcher and the creation of a therapist are different enterprises. Yet in the past these enterprises were confused. When looking at an interview, one could not tell whether a person was doing research on a family or setting out to change them.

Family Therapy From These Ideologies

Given these theories, what therapy with the family of a schizophrenic logically followed? A family would be brought in, and the parents would expect to be blamed for driving their offspring crazy. Otherwise, the therapist would only have done therapy with the offspring. The parents would typically behave in distant and defensive ways because of the accusatory context. Sometimes they would ask, "Do you think it is our fault our son is crazy?" The therapist was likely to reply that the cause was complex. If the parents said, "We did not drive our child crazy," the therapist would say, "Oh?" with just enough of an inflection to let them know they were at fault. The scene was like a Kafka trial, where parents began to defend themselves against charges which had not been made. Since the approach was psychodynamic and nondirective, the therapist did not take charge and organize what was to happen. He did nothing and waited for the family to initiate action. The family did not know what they were supposed to do and so waited for the expert to do something. There were long, significant silences. Sometimes the therapist would say, "Isn't it interesting what a silent family this is?" or, "How does it feel to be so silent?" To fill the silences without revealing signs of guilt, a father would try to talk about other things, like the cold in Antarctica. The therapist would point out to him that he was being tangential and avoiding the real issues. If the father asked the expert, "What are the real issues?" the therapist would reply, "What do you feel they are?" When the family began to be upset or angry, the therapist would ask, "Have you noticed that you are upset and angry?" This would make the family angrier, which pleased the therapist, since he had the idea that being emotional would help them unrepress their emotions. If the parents got too upset, the schizophrenic child would do his job by being rude or acting delusional, to make it clear that he was the problem, not the parents. With relief, parents and therapist would talk about the patient's irrational ideas. Sometimes, if the therapist could not think of anything else to do, he would interpret the family members' body movement to them and point out its real significance. Soon the family members did not know how to sit to avoid the therapist's making comments about their underlying negative impulses.

The task of the therapist was to keep the family coming to the interviews and getting them to talk, in the hope that something would change. The task of the family was to find out what they were supposed to say and do in the interviews and why they were there. The therapist could not tell the family to do anything because that would be manipulative, which was against the rules of therapy in the 1950s. He could not ask the parents to take charge of the child and make him or her behave, thereby structuring a hierarchy, because the therapist operated from a theory that the parents were a noxious influence; they had harmed the child in the past and should not be in charge in the present. Another reason the therapist could not put anyone in charge was that he could not take charge himself. He could only respond as a consultant to the family, with the idea that they somehow should help themselves; his task was only to make them aware and hope for the best. His only therapy technique was an interpretation; a comment on the meaning of something, no matter how trivial. If the family gave up trying to find out what to do and merely sat, the therapist helped them understand how resistant they were to facing their resistance to dealing with their family system.

Typically, the therapist communicated an underlying apathy, despite a forced cheerfulness, because his theory said that the patient was really a biological and genetic problem, or fragile from infantile traumas caused by the parents, from which he would never recover.

If the patient turned normal and the family began to reorganize, the therapist was often surprised by a colleague stoning the patient with medication or hospitalizing him because he had become troublesome. Then the therapist had to start over, waiting for the family to initiate something so he could respond with an interpretation, and hoping that somehow everyone would get "better," whatever that was.

New Developments

How did therapists recover from these theories? One could not merely put aside past theories and adopt a new one, because there was not a new one that was satisfactory. Every therapist faced the difficult task of choosing which ideas to discard and which to retain.

I have experienced a transition in my own thinking which parallels the change apparent in the work of many therapists. Dealing with mad young people over the decades, it has become more evident that madness is an expression of a malfunctioning organization. What became clearer to me was that all learning animals organize and cannot avoid doing so. The organizations are hierarchical in form, some members having more authority and status than others. This obvious fact was slow to be appreciated in the family field. Families were described as groups of individuals, as a coalition system, or as a communication system, but only slowly was it acknowledged that they were organizations with a hierarchy deserving of respect. A therapist who ignored a powerful grandmother or joined a child against parents was simply naïve. His theory did not include the fact that levels of power in an organization must be recognized by an outsider entering the organization. Sometimes therapists were quite concerned about status and power in their clinics and hospitals but ignored such issues when dealing with patients and their family organizations. In an interview, a child would be encouraged to bring out his hostility by attacking his parents, without concern for the effect on an organization when an expert called in by parents encourages a problem child to attack them.

Over the years, as more families were observed, it became increasingly evident that, both in the hospital and at home, a mad young person was responding to a particular kind of organization. The hierarchy was not the usual one of parents in charge, with executive authority over their children, and with the grandparents advising the parents. Cross-generational coalitions were occurring, in that one parent sided with a child against the other parent, or a grandmother was joining a child against parents, or the expert joined one faction of a family against another. There was confusion in these families and also in mental hospitals, where it was not clear whether the doctor had authority over the whole ward, or the nurse, or an aide. Similarly, the powers of a hospital social worker or psychologist over other staff members or a patient remained undefined.

When it became clearer that psychopathology was the result of a malfunctioning organization, it became self-evident that the task of a therapist was to change the organization. It was also evident that some past theories made that task difficult if not impossible. For example, to encourage free association in an interview among all family members was a way of introducing randomness rather than a way of restructuring an organization.

The steps in my own thinking and in the thinking of many other therapists were as follows: In the 1940s it was believed that a mad individual suffered from confused thought processes which *caused* him to communicate strangely and to establish deviant relationships. The therapy task was to correct the person's disordered thoughts and misperceptions of reality on the assumption that, as his thoughts were corrected, he would communicate differently and organize different relationships. In the 1950s the families of mad young people were observed, and it was noticed that the intimate relatives communicated in deviant ways. It began to be assumed that a young person had deviant and disordered thoughts because he lived in a communication system where such thoughts were appropriate. If a mother communicated to a child that he should spontaneously obey her, that multilevel paradoxical communication was thought to be causal in the child's disordered thinking. The therapy task was to focus on changing the communication system by educative and other interventions, and then the young person's mad thoughts would change.

Finally, in the 1960s, came the realization that people communicated in deviant ways if they were organized in a way that required such communication. The disordered thought process was therefore a product of disordered communication produced by a malfunctioning organization. For example, if a mother communicated to a child that he should spontaneously obey her, the mother was in an organization where she did not have sufficient executive authority over the child to *require* him to obey her. Some other adult at her level, such as the father, was joining the child against her and giving the child more power than she had. Or an authority at another level, such as a grandmother or an expert professional, was in coalition with the child against her. Therefore the mother did not take charge of the offspring because the organization was of such a nature that the child had more power than she did, and there would be organizational consequences if she exerted authority. When an organization was thus confused, the therapeutic task was to reorganize its structure so that the adults, particularly the mother and father jointly, had executive authority in the family. When the family was reorganized, the communication system would change, and so would the thought processes of the mad offspring.

As this way of thinking spread, it became evident that other theories made the therapeutic task difficult and would certainly fail to change the mad young person. For example, if the therapist viewed the offspring as a victim of parents who had been a noxious influence, the therapist would attempt to save this "scapegoat." That approach would mean joining the child against the parents, increasing the malfunctioning nature of the organization and thus further confusing the hierarchy rather than restructuring it.

From this view, past theories can be examined in terms of how they handicap the therapist.

Organic Theory

The trouble with the biological or genetic theory of schizophrenia is not only that there is no evidence to support it but that the mad young person's problem is defined as being in the medical rather than the parental domain, and so the therapist has no leverage to restructure the family hierarchy. He can only commiserate with the parents for having an incurable child. The problems became so severe that I largely discarded the term "schizophrenia." A therapist becomes incapacitated by that term and cannot approach the problem with hope, particularly if he or she is a psychiatric resident. I was reluctant to give up the term, but it proved impossible to keep the focus on therapy when "schizophrenia" was used. The focus could never be shifted from diagnostic issues, and from endless discussions about which medication to use, to therapy technique. If the Food & Drug Administration bans psychiatric medications because they have dangerous side effects and cause irreversible neurological damage, this generation of psychiatrists is likely to be mute in case discussions.

The main reason I dropped the term "schizophrenia" was that it so handicapped the teaching of therapy. I found it almost impossible to persuade psychiatric residents—or social workers, since they follow the lead of psychiatrists—to expect a "schizophrenic" to become normal. They would hesitate when they should have pushed for normal behavior, and the family would hesitate because the expert did so. Soon everyone was treating the "patient" like a defective person, and therapy failed.

I have never understood why some therapists escaped from the biological view and others could not. I was greatly influenced by Don D. Jackson in my therapy with these families. He believed that there was nothing wrong with a person diagnosed as schizophrenic. It was inspiring to watch him work with a family with a mad offspring who was an expert at failing. I recall one who would not speak. She would sit pulling at her hair like an idiot. Yet Jackson treated her as if she were perfectly capable of normality, given a change in her family and treatment situation. The family was forced to accept her normality, partly because of Jackson's certainty.

When teaching therapy, I tried different ways of dealing with this problem. With some students, I found it effective to say that the person was misdiagnosed as schizophrenic, despite the hallucinations and delusions. The therapist could then treat the person like a human being, because he was not really schizophrenic.

In desperation, I also created a new diagnostic category to solve the problem. I said the person was a "pseudo-schizophrenic"; that is, a person who has all the symptoms of schizophrenia but is not really schizophrenic. That effort was defeated too, and finally I simply dropped the category "schizophrenia." I tried to avoid calling anyone that and searched for other terms: "mad," "crazy," "eccentric," and "problem people."

Some psychiatrists can escape this problem by staying within the politics of medicine while using more of the advances of modern medicine. The idea that schizophrenia is genetic or irreversibly biological is 19th century medical ideology. In this century, medicine is more flexible in diagnosis, more concerned with stages of an illness, more doubtful about the irreversibility of any ailment, and more innovative in the temporary use of drugs.

Psychodynamic Theory

Psychodynamic theory is based on the idea that the psyche of the individual is the problem, not the situation in which he lives. It is therefore difficult, if not impossible, to use that theory effectively to change an organization. The psychodynamic therapist focuses on the person's misperception of the organization. Essentially, that theory guides a therapist to encourage a mad young person to express himself and guides authorities to be permissive and allow that expression. From that posture, it is almost impossible for a therapist to require parents to assume executive authority and to expect respect from the offspring. To restructure an organization, conversation must be directed and organized by a therapist rather than being free-flowing and expressive. The permissive, passive therapist and the correction of hierarchy are not compatible.

Often clinicians with a psychodynamic view criticize more active therapy and object to the use of any force. This view is hypocritical in that such clinicians often avoid treating crazy people, and so they criticize without offering an alternative. More important, they tend to hire other people to use the force. I can recall permissive and benevolent therapists doing psychodynamic therapy in mental hospitals, particularly private ones. They would say the therapist should only be kind and encourage self-expression, and they would object to any therapist asking parents to restrain their offspring physically if he or she got violent. Yet these same therapists worked in a setting where hired employees handled the violence, while therapists pretended they did not. Muscular aides taught patients how to behave on the wards with force and violence, while the psychodynamic therapist chatted with the patient in his office and called the aide if there was trouble. The institution also used shock treatment, medications, tubs, packs, and isolation rooms, so that the psychodynamic therapist would have a compliant patient to be kind and permissive with. Ignoring the social situation and focusing on the psyche allowed a therapist to avoid thinking about the social system of which he was part.

A final important aspect of psychodynamic theory is its assumption that what people do is based on aggression, hostility, and self-defense. Such a view is the opposite of that offered in this work. It is best for a therapist to assume that what people do, no matter how seemingly destructive, is basically protective. It is the benevolence of people that poses problems. If a wife has a sudden onset of anxiety attacks that make great demands on her husband, it is best to assume that she is protecting him by that problem. Whether anxious or angry, a spouse should be assumed to be motivated by a benevolent concern for the other spouse. Similarly, it is best to assume that a mad young person is not defending himself or being hostile to his family by his troubled and violent behavior. The question is, what would happen to his family if he did not behave that way? For therapeutic purposes it should be assumed that mad young people are sacrificing themselves to stabilize their families. Stability in a system is the motivating force that drives the members. If he has that view, a therapist tends to be more positive in his approach to everyone involved in misfortune.

If one wishes to do effective therapy with mad people, it is best simply to abandon psychodynamic theory. The therapist who attempts to be broad minded, trying to bring together psychodynamic theory and an approach based on restructuring a family, will be the most handicapped.

Systems Theory

Systems theory is a more difficult problem because it has many merits as well as demerits. I found it necessary to deemphasize the issues of homeostasis and stability and to focus more on the aspects of change. Thinking in terms of systems, one can plan a therapy in which a crisis is induced in a family, and the family must reorganize to deal with it. Alternatively, one can begin a small change and persistently amplify it until the system adapting to it must reorganize.[5]

The chief merit of systems theory is that it allows the therapist to recognize repeating sequences and so make predictions. He can then plan his therapy in anticipation of what will happen. There remain the problems of how to simplify the sequences so they become recognizable and useful, and how to use the concepts of hierarchy and sequences in a system. The past tendency to equalize the elements in a system makes all family members equally powerful, and conceptualizing differing statuses and powers in a hierarchy is correspondingly difficult.

The Double Bind

I largely discarded the term "double bind" and returned to Gregory Bateson's original term "paradox." I found I did not know what a double bind was anymore, because so many people used it in so many different ways. Paradox is a clearer and more precise term for describing conflicting levels of communication. The term "paradoxical intervention" also has a less negative connotation than "double binding" a client.

The communication ideas which came out of the Bateson project are a valuable way of describing human beings dealing with one another. The idea that a message at one level conflicts paradoxically with a message at another can be carried into a description of organizations. After all, an organization is merely a system of repeating sequences of communication. As people communicate with each other in systematic ways, that communication becomes the organization. When one person tells another what to do, and the other does it, a hierarchy is being defined by that process. When one person tells another to "disobey me," the communication is paradoxical, and the organization is likely to be a malfunctioning one.

Out of the struggles with difficult young people and their families have come a number of ideas. Something valuable has been developed from systems and communication theories, while at the same time a new view of organizational power has been developing. Out of failure, as well as out of success, has come the view that youthful madness is best understood as a product of a family life-stage where reorganization is taking place, and that the youth's behavior is adaptive to that social context. Only with a change in the social context can normal behavior become appropriate. Changing a social organization to which they belong is the task of family therapists, and theories that guide them to induce that change are necessary for effective therapy.

Notes

This chapter, in a somewhat different form, was originally a paper given at the 1977 conference called "Beyond the Double Bind." It was published as part of the proceedings of that meeting in M. M. Berger (ed.), *Beyond the Double Bind*, Brunner/Mazel, New York. 1978.

1. It is not appropriate to use only the pronoun *he* in referring to a therapist or a client, since they come in both sexes. The author uses *he* routinely for reasons of convenience and acknowledges the inequity of the traditional use of the masculine pronoun.
2. See N. Wiener, *Cybernetics*, Wiley, New York, 1948. The systems idea was circulated from a variety of sources, one of the more important ones being the conferences supported by the Josiah Macy Jr. Foundation in the late 1940s and early 1950s.
3. G. Bateson, D. D. Jackson, J. Haley, and J. H. Weakland, "Toward a Theory of Schizophrenia," *Behav. Sci*, 1:251–264, 1956. For a history of the ideas of that project see J. Haley, "Development of a Theory: A History of a Research Project," in C. E. Sluzki and D. C. Ransom (eds.), *Double Bind*, Grune & Stratton, New York, 1976. The reader interested in the communication ideas of the Bateson project should read the writings of the project members, who were Gregory Bateson, Jay Haley, John Weakland, and part-time consultants Don D. Jackson and William F. Fry. They published extensively from 1956, when they wrote the article on the double bind, to the end of the project in 1962. Their 70 papers and books are listed in "A Note on the Double Bind, 1962," in *Family Process*, 2: 154–161, 1963. Bateson's basic ideas are presented in *Steps to an Ecology of the Mind*, Ballantine, New York, 1972, and *Mind and Nature*, Dutton, New York, 1979.

4. For a description of hierarchy in these terms see J. Haley, *Problem Solving Therapy*, Jossey-Bass, San Francisco, 1976.
5. M. Maruyama "The Second Cybernetics: Deviation-Amplifying Mutual Causal Processes," in W. Buckley (ed.), *Modern Systems Research for the Behavioral Scientist*, Aldine, Chicago, 1968.

18

Development of a Theory: The History of a Research Project

INTRODUCTION

Carlos E. Sluzki, MD

A Fond Reminiscence

A few months after Don D. Jackson's untimely death in 1968—it took place while I happened to be in Palo Alto, California, doing an internship at the Mental Research Institute, but still living in Buenos Aires—I read in a bulletin of the MRI a note informing that *Family Process*, of which Jay Haley was editor-in-chief, was in the process of organizing a Don D. Jackson Memorial Conference. I reacted with elation: An homage to Jackson—a prime contributor to the birth of the field of family therapy—was in my view long overdue, as Jackson's demise had been followed by a disconcerting and chilling institutional silence.[1] I immediately mailed an enthusiastic letter to Jay—with whom I had had many exchanges during the months I spent in Palo Alto—congratulating him for the initiative, commenting on how strongly I sensed the need for such an homage to be made, and asking for details about the meeting so I could be registered on time and all that. Jay, with his habitual terse style, replied with a three-liner informing me that that conference was being organized as a closed meeting of advisory editors of *Family Process*. Mounting on my paranoid Pegasus, I responded in turn with a furious letter, accusing him of carrying out some kind of personal vendetta, convinced that he was upset with me because of a heated discussion we had a few months earlier at his home during dinner (he had mounted a frontal attack on psychoanalysis, whereas I—by then with one foot timidly standing on the new arena of family therapy but the other still responding to my parallel persona as a psychoanalyst-in-training—had argued with equal vehemence that intra- and interpersonal constructs were reasonably discontinuous, object relations theory excepted; that each model had its own internal consistency; and that it wasn't necessary or useful to demonize one in order to gain validation of the other … or something like that.) I remember that it was a page-and-a-half single-spaced letter, written in the best "Spanglish" that my wounded pride allowed, the text full of those quirks and printing overlaps that a portable Olivetti would produce in that preelectronic era. And, lo and behold, a couple of weeks later I received another equally terse, equally three-line letter from Jay informing me that I had been appointed advisory editor of *Family Process*. My inclusion in that conference was clear but left implicit. A better portrait of Jay's style I cannot find: His "Yup," "Nope," Midwestern cowboy social style permeated much of his interpersonal contacts as well as his work, never boasting his intellectual power but never avoiding an "OK Corral" fight, at the same time tough and gentle, and exuding dry humor (I can imagine his laughter while reading my, and while writing his, second letter, and do remember his chuckling, "Well, well, look who's here!" when a few months later I joined that conference in Asilomar!).

More comfortable in the intellectual open field than sequestered by the four walls of a tight creed (a style that he shared with his mentor, Gregory Bateson), Haley's trajectory led him to both become a major figure in the field of family therapy, a field that in fact he contributed to create, while retaining marginality in the academic establishment, a choice that gave him freedom and took away a stable venue for his work. The Bateson team was, for one of the most productive periods of his life, his intellectual home, and his debt to it is patent in this essay. Schizophrenia was, in turn, as Jay himself comments, a serendipitous area of inquiry to start with, as the Bateson team was more interested in logical types and their paradoxes as expressed in different human (and other mammals') scenarios than in specifically exploring the interactional roots of schizophrenia, or even in family processes. And, what is equally interesting, he did with himself what he later did with Milton Erickson's work, namely, rather than assuming that the clinical practice he developed a few years later derived from preexisting models, he undertook a serious attempt at going from practice to theory, that is, deducting the models that guided him by analyzing the presuppositions of his own practice (exploring what Donald Schon [1983] called a "theory of practice"). This reflexive stance allowed him to forge his own original and influential model for change, *strategic therapy*.

Haley in History

History is but a punctuation of the sequence of relevant events and contexts, and constitutes an account of the historian's selection of components and interpretation of circumstances. Haley, of course, knew that well—please notice the "A" (instead of a "The") in the title of this chapter.[2] Jay's "History" constitutes, regardless of punctuation, an invaluable document of the process and products of one of the most influential teams in the dawn of the field of family therapy, one that generated foundational papers in the field of interpersonal processes. Some of the articles he discusses in this paper may be dated—we are, as usual, able to look farther and perhaps to correct the acuity of vision when standing on the shoulders of giants. Others are extraordinary pearls of wisdom and revolutionary proposals. Many portray in their sequence the complex process of cracking a hard-to-pin-down concept, and provide a paradigmatic example of how hypotheses lead to new hypotheses, how intuitions are transformed into researchable formulations, and how to ask wise questions and tolerate incertitude.

The richness of the conceptual basis of the Bateson team, and the key contributions by Haley to that endeavor, as detailed in this chapter, allows us to grasp, if there was any doubt, the profound impact that it had in the development of the fields of family therapy and of brief therapy, original ways of thinking about human relations and human dilemmas. And, to belabor the obvious, that doesn't even take into consideration the major influence exerted in the field of therapy by the many other books and articles that Jay Haley wrote since those early days as a maverick member of an equally maverick, if not revolutionary, team until his recent death. In fact, we may keep on recognizing his ideas here and there, but, as with true founders, many of his core contributions have become amalgamated into the conceptual common ground where our professional field nourishes and flowers.

Endnotes

1. A partial explanation for that freeze may be inferred from a commentary Haley made on Jackson's death in his tender prologue to a recent volume of selected papers by Don D. Jackson (Ray, 2005).
2. When this article was first published by Dr. Sluzki in 1976, it was titled "A History." In 1982, when Dr. Haley republished the article in his book *Reflections on Therapy*, he retitled it "The History."

References

Ray, W. A. (Ed.). (2005). *Don D. Jackson: Selected essays at the dawn of an era*. Phoenix, AZ: Zeig, Tucker & Theisen.

Schon, D. A. (1983). *The reflective practitioner: How professionals think in action*. New York: Basic Books.

DEVELOPMENT OF A THEORY: A HISTORY OF A RESEARCH PROJECT

Jay Haley

This history of Gregory Bateson's research project on communication (1952–1962) was written in 1961 as the project was ending. It is presented here without change except for some minor editorial corrections since it was written at a particular time for a particular purpose and belongs to that period. At the end of the article are some brief contemporary comments by the project members.

Since the publication of the "double bind" theory in 1956, quite a number of papers have appeared in the literature commenting upon the theoretical approach of the Bateson project. These papers acknowledge the relevance of the theory to problems in psychiatry and human relations in general, but they also demonstrate many misunderstandings of the ideas proposed. It would seem worthwhile to provide a history of the theoretical developments in the research over the period of the ten years of the project's existence.

This review will largely emphasize the published papers of the project members, and the reader is referred to these papers for a detailed presentation of the ideas which were developed. Of course only a small part of the project work was ultimately published and a vast amount of material was presented in lectures, seminars, and professional meetings. Emphasizing published statements is a way of partially dealing with the problem of credit, although individuals who have published least are not adequately represented. When a team is in intimate association for 10 years, with hundreds of hours of conferences and discussions, the origin of ideas must inevitably be seen as a product of the group. Often an individual will have an idea which is stoutly opposed, and some time later the colleague in opposition will "discover" the same idea as if it were new. At other times a passing phrase may crystalize an idea so that credit is inextricably wound up in a conversation. However, when an individual goes through the labor of systematizing ideas sufficiently for publication, the presentation is a formulation of his point of view as well as his responsibility. In this research, the director permitted project members to investigate and publish whatever interested them.

The project officially began in the Fall of 1952 when Bateson received a grant from the Rockefeller Foundation. Prior to that time he had been interested in the problems of classification in the natural sciences, particularly those classification systems relevant to evolutionary change. In his field of anthropology, he had also applied to the study of culture various general ideas about self-reinforcing systems, particularly in his book, *Naven* (5), and papers on such problems as armaments races. His interest in the way a culture perpetuates itself was carried into the study of the individual with his idea that the perpetuation of learning situations in a person's life provides the ongoing framework within which he learns. He argued that learning is not a single-level phenomenon, but a person also learns to learn. For example, the dog in the Pavlovian experiment not only learns to salivate when the bell rings, but at another level he learns to see the world as a place where he passively waits for reward and does not actively seek it.

His interest in levels of learning and levels of classification systems led Bateson to request a grant from the Rockefeller Foundation to investigate the general nature of communication in terms of levels. His point of departure was the Logical Types of Russell and Whitehead in *Principia Mathematica* (71), where they emphasize that a class of things is of a different level, or Logical Type, than the members of that class. What interested Bateson was the idea that there is a discontinuity between classes and their members: each is of a different level of abstraction, or Logical Type. Because of this discontinuity, it is possible for paradox to occur in classification:

the classic one being the "class of classes" paradox. A more apparent one is the Epimenides paradox: if a man says, "I am lying," is he telling the truth? If he is telling the truth, he is lying. This paradox can occur because a negative statement classifying another negative statement occurs in a single message so that the class and its members are self-referent and the discontinuity between the two classes is breached.

It is possible that Bateson was the first person to apply the theory of Logical Types to communication. For Russell and Whitehead, Logical Types were an aspect of the mathematical approach to classification systems, not a method of analyzing communication. Bateson saw not only science as a classification problem but man as a classifying animal who must label the messages he emits and receives. He was particularly interested in those moments when man classifies messages in such a way that insoluble paradox is generated.

With a two-year grant from the Rockefeller Foundation to investigate paradoxes in communication, Bateson began to collect a staff. He was joined by Jay Haley and John Weakland in the beginning of 1953. Haley's previous interest centered in the social and psychological analysis of fantasy, particularly in popular films. He was working on problems similar to those Bateson had met with his analysis of the German film, *Hitlerjunge Quex* (1943). Weakland, who had earlier been a chemical engineer, came from the field of cultural anthropology with a special interest in China. Later in the year the group was joined by Dr. William Fry, a psychiatrist, who was just finishing his residency. Dr. Fry continued as a part-time consultant with the project except for a one and one-half year absence in the Navy in 1955–1956. His major interest was the study of humor from the point of view of Logical Types.

The first year of work primarily involved an attempt by the research team to come together on a common approach. Since the field of investigation was communication in general, any data was relevant. But the approach to communication in terms of levels was unique and difficult to assimilate. The first difficulty within the group centered on whether the paradoxes of abstraction were relevant to anything important in human life. Were these paradoxes merely the toys of object linguists and logicians? At that time there were several paradoxes as examples. Besides the "class of classes" and the "I am lying" paradoxes, there was another derived in the following form from Hayakawa:

All statements within this frame are untrue.

Naturally, if the statement is true it is untrue.

These examples appeared artificial and not evident in the stream of human and other animal communication. People do not say to each other, "I am lying," in so many words, and less often do they draw a frame and write within it such a statement as the one above. A particular center of controversy was whether the question of truth and untruth, so dear to the logician's heart, was relevant to the analysis of human communication. In an artificial language the truth or untruth of a statement is important, but in language as it is used in everyday life the meaning and response to a statement rather than its truth value seemed important.

Part of the problem centered in developing some common language within the research project to describe levels of communication. At this time there were at least the following terms which tended to be used as synonyms: Logical Types, Levels of Abstraction, Levels of Communication, Message and Metamessage, and Metacommunicative Level. All of them referred to the relationship between a message and the message which qualified it. A beginning development in terminology occurred with the idea that one message "frames" another message, and so the "framing message" became an additional term. With this term, it became possible to see a relevance between a paradox such as, "All statements within this frame are untrue," and a piece of human communication where one person indicates with a framing message how his subsequent message is to be received.

The data that first year were diverse and included the following: a study of otters playing, a study of training of guide dogs for the blind, an analysis of a popular moving picture, a filming of Mongoloid children in a group, analysis of humor and a ventriloquist and puppet, and the utterance of a schizophrenic patient when a project member began to interview him early that year. This particular patient demonstrated so much confusion in the way he "framed" his messages and classified himself that it was uncertain even who he was or where he was from; the authorities doubted his statement that he was born on Mars and that his name was Margaret Stalin. Another patient interviewed also demonstrated a difficulty with classification. He would rarely speak, and when he did he would repetitively say, "I think my thinking is not good."

The early emphasis upon animals in the research was related to a desire to begin with as simple natural history data as possible, as well as to a general interest in the subject of ethology. The work of Lorenz and Tinbergen became part of the stream of project thinking. It was of particular interest at the time to inquire whether animals qualified their messages, or seemed to have an awareness of signaling, and before the Rockefeller grant in 1952 Bateson was filming otters at the zoo to determine this.

Out of the miscellaneous types of data and the beginning formulations of a theoretical point of view within the group, there came sufficient progress to present two papers early in 1954 to a meeting of the regional research section of the American Psychiatric Association in Mexico City. Since Bateson could not attend, Haley presented an evening's discussion of the research which was summarized in "Paradoxes in Play, Fantasy, and Psychotherapy" (30), and he delivered to the group copies of Bateson's paper, "A Theory of Play and Fantasy" (1).

The general points made in these papers can be summarized. Bateson presented a series of generalizations to describe the hypothesis under investigation. He suggested that human verbal communication operates at many contrasting levels of abstraction and the majority of metacommunicative messages remain implicit. In the evolution of communication, an important stage occurs when an organism gradually ceases to respond "automatically" to the "mood signs" of others and becomes able to recognize the sign as a signal which can be trusted, distrusted, falsified, denied, and so on. He reports that when he went to film animals at the zoo to discover whether they evidenced any awareness that signals were signals, he noted that the animals were playing. This play was "an interactive sequence of which the unit actions or signals were similar to but not the same as those of combat." Play can only occur if the participant organisms are capable of exchanging metacommunicative messages—signals which would carry the message "this is play." Bateson argued that the message "this is play" contains the elements of a paradox of the Russellian or Epimenides type—a negative statement containing an implicit negative meta-statement. The playful nip of the animal denotes a bite, but it does not denote what would be denoted by the bite. The two senses of the word "denote" in this sentence are logically inadmissible because they are of different Logical Types and when treated as synonymous produce paradox; but in the course of animal and human interchange this confusion of types occurs. Bateson also mentions other contexts where a metacommunicative signal is crucial to the "framing" of a situation—fantasy, ritual, threat, and so on. He concludes with a discussion of psychological frames and set theory and draws parallels between play and psychotherapy, which is defined as an attempt to change the patient's metacommunicative habits. Before therapy, the patient thinks and operates in terms of a certain set of rules for making and understanding messages, and after successful therapy he operates in terms of a different set of rules. Paradox is a framed interaction between two persons, in which the rules are implicit but subject to change."

At this meeting Haley showed Bateson's film, *The River Otters, Part I*, as data for discussing play. He pointed out that the animals playing must indicate that the bite of play is not the bite of combat or courtship. Therefore a framing statement such as "this is play" must qualify the bite. Conceivably this statement could be implicit in the bite itself, and thereby a message would qualify itself and paradox could be generated—as in the "I am lying" paradox. A pathological animal might misinterpret the "this is play" message and respond with combat rather than play. This difficulty in interpreting the metacommunicative messages of otters was compared with the difficulty the schizophrenic has in dealing with others. When someone said something to such a patient, he responded as if he did not know, or labeled wrongly, what sort of statement it was. A friendly gesture might be responded to as if it were a threat, and a joke might be taken dead seriously. The emphasis in the research at the time was on the "as if" nature of schizophrenia. The patient would behave as if a metaphor were a literal statement and vice versa. He would indicate he got so mad he hit the ceiling, and he would point to the top of his head to show the bump. Or he would say, "I have butterflies in my stomach," and then add, "I don't mean real butterflies." Schizophrenic utterance seemed a clear example of confusion of Logical Types, particularly when the patient was talking "word salad."

The importance of the "framing" message was also illustrated with a discussion of fictional films. The audience attends a movie and it is clearly labeled as fictional by the theater setting, custom, and so on. Yet if the audience is to respond emotionally to what occurs on the film, it must be in some sense "real" to them. A person can become frightened at a film, and he can light a cigarette or talk to a companion, thereby reaffirming the fictional frame, just as a child says to another, "It's only a picture." The peculiar nature of popular films seems to center in the confusion over what sort of message the film is: it is fantasy, and so one need not take it seriously, and yet it is real and therefore one can be deeply moved.

At that time the project interest in psychotherapy was in the extensive playing with labels which occurred. The psychotherapy situation is labeled as unreal, in the sense that it is not an ordinary relationship, and yet within that framework the patient responds as if it is a very real situation. The therapist is both father and not father, just a guy and not just a guy. The framing of the sequence of messages is the focus of therapy. Haley gave examples of the way John Rosen would say to the patient, "I am your mother," and at another moment, "I am not your mother." In passing, it was pointed out that in the work of John Rosen there seemed to be a benevolent framework for therapy and within that framework the therapist would behave in a severe or depriving way, sometimes oscillating between the two types of behavior.

In general at this time, the project was analyzing many complex activities in human and animal life in terms of levels, with emphasis upon the possible conflict which can occur between a message and a qualifying message so that paradox occurs. In play, a bite might be a message of affection; in films the story is real but not real at the same time; in psychotherapy the therapist is a real person in an unreal or transference frame; and in schizophrenia the real world is talked about in an unreal way.

The Emphasis on Schizophrenia

In 1954 the Rockefeller grant terminated and was not renewed. Support for an investigation so unique in approach and general in theory did not appear forthcoming. Partly for practical reasons, and partly from a developing tendency in that direction, it was decided to apply for a grant to investigate schizophrenic communication. The obvious confusion of Logical Types in schizophrenic utterance seemed to indicate a fruitful area of research for this point of view. A two-year grant was obtained from the Macy Foundation to make such an investigation.

The approach developed at this period can be illustrated with a description taken from a grant application. "The proposed research will focus upon an entirely different aspect of schizophrenic communication (from an approach in terms of symbols, delusional content, condensation, displacement, projection, etc.). It is generally agreed that schizophrenics have difficulty in discriminating between 'reality' and fantasy and also that they have difficulty in the use of nonverbal and implicit signals. They may be oversensitive to such signals; they may ignore them; they may misinterpret them. The research, starting from these two generalizations, will study the schizophrenic's use of that particular category of nonverbal and implicit signals which indicates whether a given utterance is literal or metaphoric, jocular or serious, sincere or histrionic, etc. This class of signals we call *'reality qualifiers.'*" (The term "reality qualifier" would seem to have been used to describe the metamessage which indicates, or frames, what sort of message another message is. These were also called "mode identifying signals" in this period.)

By this time it was clear that not only does one verbal message "frame" another verbal message to indicate what sort it is, (i.e., playful, sincere, ironical, etc.), but that verbal messages are framed by gesture, vocal intonation, and the physical context in which the message is emitted. Further, it was becoming clear that this was not an hierarchical order with something primary, such as the verbal gesture. Both the verbal message and the gesture qualify each other and both qualify and are qualified by the other "channels" of communication: vocal intonation and context. Therefore there was no "message" but only metamessages qualifying one another. At this time, after considerable debate, it was decided to use the term "contradiction" for messages which qualified each other in a conflicting way at the *same* level and the term "incongruence" for messages which conflicted at *different* levels. The central interest was the conflict between levels: the discontinuity between a class and its members or between two metamessages which qualified each other, because it was in this conflict that paradox was generated.

The complexity of communication, when analyzed in terms of levels of classification, or Logical Types, was becoming more apparent. There were now at least four "channels" of communication (words, voice, body movement, context) each emitting messages which qualified each other and so were of different Logical Type, and within each channel any message which qualified another was of another Logical Type. The number of metalevels began to appear infinite. The general tendency of the project was to simplify toward two levels of message and a third level qualifying those two.

Conflict in Learning

While attempting to develop some descriptive terminology for levels of message, the project at this time was putting considerable emphasis upon the perception, or interpretation of messages. Thus there was an emphasis upon ways of communicating and an emphasis upon learning to interpret the communication of others. These two points of view were brought together in terms of a conflict between levels by Bateson in a letter to Norbert Wiener in 1954, which is worth quoting at some length since the term "double bind" came to be applied to this conflict.

> As I understand, the minimum constellation necessary for (Logical) Type confusion is a language plus a metalanguage. Now thinking over our conversation, it appears that in play there are two such minimum constellations. We have most concerned ourselves with the paradoxes potentially present in the message "this is play." We observe that this message can be exchanged nonverbally between mammals and

that when it occurs it is usually implicit in those meaningful actions which are qualified by the statement "this is play." The message "this is play" thus seems to qualify itself and something like an Epimenides paradox arises.

The second constellation is that to which you referred the other day and on which I once published a paper called "Deutero Learning," i.e., learning to learn.

A question which I cannot clearly resolve is whether these two sets of two-typed communication are really identical or are both independently operating in such phenomena as play.

As I understand it, type contusion leads to paradox when both message and metamessage contain negatives. On this principle we can imagine the generation of paradox in the deutero-learning system when an organism experiences punishment following some failure and learns that it must not learn that punishment follows failure. This would be approximately the picture of a man who, having been punished for failure, later is punished for showing his expectation of punishment after failure, e.g., is punished for cringing.

Many of the organized physical games and other types of less organized play which simulate combat have exactly this characteristic—teaching the boy to be a man by penalizing his expectation of punishment. It thus seems to me that the Epimenides paradox latent in the message "this is play" becomes almost the same as the paradox generated by unlearning to unlearn. But of this last step I am unsure.

By the end of 1954 the idea was described in a grant application:

The theory is derived in part deductively from what has already been said about the capabilities, and in part inductively from experiences with schizophrenics and the literature describing their communication.

1. *Aetiology.* It is suggested that the base for later psychosis may be laid in infancy by the experience of dealing with a mother who both punishes the child for certain

> actions and punishes the child for learning that punishment will follow those certain actions, i.e., she generates paradox in the child by combining negative learning with negative deutero-learning. That such an experience would be traumatic for the child is easy to imagine. But we are not concerned here with the mere matter of pain. Our hypothesis concentrates upon the formal structure of the pain producing context. We are also not concerned at this point with identifying the act which is punished or the nature of the punishment. In passing, however, we suggest that the child is punished with an apparent withdrawal of love both for these gestures and for that whining which expresses the child's demand for love and his expectation that such demands will be punished. Such a picture of childhood trauma fits remarkably well with Rosen's description of the "perverse" mother; and it is worth noting that the mother's conduct is especially likely to take this form when it is necessary for her to be hypocritical about her lack of, or inhibition of, love for the child. With such hypocrisy she is driven not only to punish the child's demand for love, but also to punish any indication which the child may give that he knows he is not loved, since such an indication threatens the base of her hypocrisy.

In another section of the same application it is pointed out that paradox will occur when there is a combination of negatives in message and metamessage, and

> paradox will...be generated when both learning and deutero-learning are, in some sense, negative. Such seems to be the case when an organism is both punished for some action and punished when he shows by avoiding this action that he has learned that it would be punished. To make this abstract example more vivid, we refer to the very unpleasant experience of receiving punishment for cringing.

Paradox Leaves and Double Bind Enters

With the shift to an investigation of schizophrenia, and the emphasis upon a conflict in levels of learning, the project began to discard the term "paradox" and substitute the term "double bind." At this time there was no example of a double bind drawn from natural-history data; it was a hypothesis about what sort of thing "must" have happened in the life history of the schizophrenic given his confusion of Logical Types. Within the project there was controversy over the specific nature of the double bind. When the Macy grant was received, Bateson, Haley and Weakland spent two days in seclusion in the mountains outlining the research to be done. During those two days Bateson insisted that the mother of the schizophrenic punished the child for expecting punishment, and his colleagues raised the question of what evidence there was of this fact. When they discovered that Bateson meant the child must have been caught in "this sort of" bind rather than this particular one, agreement on the investigation was achieved. From that point on the term "double bind" was applied to "that sort of" situation, and for a considerable time there was no verification of the hypothesis from actual data.

In 1954 Dr. Don D. Jackson had joined the group as a clinical consultant on problems of doing therapy with schizophrenics. Although at first his contact was largely one of clinical supervision, he soon became a participant in the theoretical investigations of the research team. He was particularly suited to the needs of the project because of his concentration upon the interpersonal involvements of the schizophrenic. Investigation of the way a schizophrenic deals with other people and analysis of his communication in terms of levels were common interests.

The interest in cybernetics of the project also appealed to Jackson. He had previously written on family homeostasis (47), where he pointed out the repercussive effects among family members when a patient improves. He mentions, "Another way of considering the topic of 'family homeostasis' would be in terms of communication theory; that is, depicting family interaction as a closed information system in which variations in output or behavior are fed back in order to correct the system's responses" (p. 79). The idea of levels of communication appealed to both his interests in homeostatic processes and his interests in describing the complicated interactions of family members. The idea of schizophrenics caught in double binds particularly appealed to him from his previous experience with such patients.

Through 1955 the Double Bind was increasingly defined as a conflict between levels of message as well as between levels of learning. What had been an artificial example of a paradox composed of two negative statements qualifying each other became, after considerable debate, a description of the behavior of one person in relation to another. The fuller description included the idea that when one person communicates two levels of message to another when these levels both qualify and conflict with each other, the other person is faced with an impossible situation. He cannot respond to either level without violating a prohibition at the other level, and so he is wrong whatever he does. The bind becomes complete when the "victim" cannot leave the field or comment upon his impossible situation.

Toward a Theory

In 1956 the project published its first joint paper, "Towards a Theory of Schizophrenia," (3) which was also the first publication of the "double bind" theory and surveyed the general interests of the research team. This paper suggested the importance of investigating the field of psychiatry, and related fields of human life, from the point of view of levels of communication.

The paper was defined as a preliminary report which summarized the common agreement of the research team on the broad outlines of a communication theory of the origin and nature of schizophrenia. The central thesis of the theory was that there is a discontinuity between a class and its members; the class cannot be a member of itself nor can one of the members be the class, because the term used for the class is of a different Logical Type from terms used for members. However, in the psychology of real communication this discontinuity is continually and inevitably breached and we must expect, *a priori*, pathology to occur in the human organism when certain formal patterns of this breaching occur in the communication between mother and child. Further, this pathology at its extreme will have symptoms whose formal characteristics would lead to the pathology being classified as schizophrenia.

The framing, or labeling, of messages becomes exceedingly complex in the communication of human beings. The framing message may become the message itself, or it may be falsified. The ability to discriminate among the different classes of messages is a learned skill and so multiple levels of learning and the Logical Typing of signals are inseparable phenomena. Since a learning context is a frame for the messages within it, it should follow that the individual who exhibits a confusion of Logical Types in his discourse must have suffered sequential patterns in his learning context which helped him acquire the mental habits which would produce that confusion in his discourse. The schizophrenic "must live in a universe where the sequences of events are such that his unconventional communication habits will be in some sense appropriate." Further, "The hypothesis which we offer is that sequences of this kind in the external experience of the patient are responsible for the inner conflicts of Logical Typing. For such unresolvable sequences of experiences, we use the term 'double binds.'"

The paper points out that these experiential sequences will not be specific traumas in the infantile etiology but characteristic sequential patterns. The necessary ingredients are two or more persons, repeated experience, a primary negative injunction, a secondary injunction conflicting with the first at a more abstract level and enforced by punishments or signals which threaten survival, and a third negative injunction prohibiting the victim from escaping the field. It was further suggested that once the individual has learned to expect this pattern, almost any part of a double bind sequence may then be sufficient to precipitate panic or rage.

The paper went on to provide illustrations of the effect of the double bind in terms of the inability of a schizophrenic to discriminate between literal and metaphoric statements. Given this inability, he might defend himself in ways which would be classified as paranoid, hebephrenic, or catatonic. With his inability to metacommunicate about the messages of others he could not correct himself.

The learning context of the schizophrenic was largely described in terms of his relationship with his mother; her hostile behavior which is aroused when the child approaches her, and her simulated loving behavior aroused when the child responds to her hostile behavior by withdrawing. The mother's sensitivity to blame prevents the child commenting on, or discriminating accurately, what she is communicating. Father enters the picture largely as a negative factor; he is unable to support the child in his relationship with mother.

The therapeutic aspects of the double bind were also first suggested in this paper. It was pointed out that hospital structures may include a repetition of the double bind found in the patient's family, but it was also suggested that there is a therapeutic bind. An example is given of Dr. Fromm-Reichmann treating the delusion of a patient as real while indicating it isn't, and so forcing a patient to respond to her. If the patient insists that her personal God is real, she must do as Dr. Fromm-Reichmann has told her and tell the God he is not as powerful as the therapist (and therefore not God). If the patient does not tell the God as instructed, she is admitting her doubt about the reality of the God and so admitting her attachment to the therapist.

The paper emphasized schizophrenia, but it was also an argument for analyzing and describing many fields of human activity in terms of levels of communication. Mentioned in passing were play, humor, ritual, poetry, fiction, and hypnosis as well as schizophrenia and psychotherapy. An example was also drawn from Zen Buddhism. Alan Watts, an authority on Zen, had been a consultant to the project because of his interest in the nature of paradox.

There are several general objections which might be made to that first attempt to introduce the concept of levels into psychiatry. First of all, the impression was given that the "double bind" was a clearly definable, countable sequence which occurred in human relations. Although it was qualified as a pattern and described in general terms, the concept was concrete enough for the project later to consider counting double binds in tape-recorded interviews. We would, today, not consider the double bind as so clearly distinguishable in the complicated network of multiple levels of message in human discourse.

Another objection which might be made would be the ambiguity in the paper on the limitation of double bind sequence to schizophrenic learning contexts. The statement that double bind sequences were a part of the etiology of schizophrenia did not imply that they were not a part of the etiology of other pathologies or even of normal discourse. The fact is that human beings will be caught in conflicts of levels as they communicate with each other; we now assume and assumed then that with schizophrenia a special case of systematic patterns of that conflict occurs.

A further objection might be made that the double bind was largely limited to two-person interaction. It was said, "We do not assume that the double bind is inflicted by the mother alone, but that it may be done either by mother alone or by some combination of mother, father, and/or siblings." But the emphasis in the paper was largely upon one individual, the victim, facing conflicting levels of message imposed by another. Within this description, it was a strain to include other family members in double bind patterns.

The response to this paper has revealed several sorts of misunderstanding of the ideas proposed. The idea of a schizophrenic being caught in an impossible situation apparently seemed to fit the experience of many clinicians who had worked with such patients and their families. However, such readers often attempted to place the double bind in the framework of other theoretical formulations without grasping the difference in approach in this point of view. Typically readers assumed that when faced with a double bind the "victim" is faced with a "damned if he does and damned if he doesn't" situation. They assumed that the person was faced with two contradictory messages rather than two messages which conflict because they are at different levels.

If faced with a "damned if he does and damned if he doesn't" situation, a person may choose the lesser of two evils. But when faced with two conflicting levels of message, he cannot choose one without the other. If I say to someone, "I will be angry if you obey me and I will be angry if you disobey me," he can choose one or the other. However, if I say to someone, "I want you to disobey me," he has no alternatives nor is he faced with a contradiction. He cannot choose the least bad of two possibilities. His bind is this: if he obeys, he is disobeying, and if he disobeys, he is obeying.

Related to the difficulty in grasping the double bind as a conflict of levels, or logical types, was the attempt by some readers to equate the double bind with the typical conflict-learning situation which is again a problem of distinct choices. Such learning situations can be seen in terms of levels, but only if translated from the usual psychological terms. Similarly, there was an inevitable suggestion by some clinicians that the double bind was synonymous with ambivalence. The term "ambivalence" usually refers to the state of an individual when faced with choices of equal or near equal value to him. It is a statement about mixed feelings. However, the double bind is a term describing a context within which a person is trying to function. For example, if *A* tells *B* to do something spontaneously, *B* is not in an ambivalent situation—he is in an impossible one. If he does what is asked, it is not occurring spontaneously, and if it occurs spontaneously, *he* is not doing what was asked. The request involves an order to do some activity—one level of message, but this activity is to occur without being a response to the order—another level of message. Since the class and the item within it conflict, no choice is possible, any more than one can choose between a "fried egg" and "truth" since they are different orders of statement.

A possible reason for some of the confusion among readers could be an ambiguity in the paper which was related to differences in view developing within the project. The paper defined the double bind not only as a context but also as a statement about the subjective state of the "victim." Although the paper emphasized communication and behavior, the definition of the double bind, and certainly the response to it, emphasized the experience of the individual caught in it. He suffered feelings of "helplessness, exasperation, and rage," and he "learned" to expect such sequences. His behavioral response to the double bind was not described.

Up to this point in the research, statements about the etiology of schizophrenia had been largely deductive: given the pathology of the patient, what learning situation would create it? Occasional examples of double-bind-like situations were suggested by Jackson from his practice, but there was no systematic recording of parents and schizophrenic patient interacting with each other. Although for years Bateson had been filming disturbed children in their families, the investigation had not yet included films of schizophrenic patients with their families.

Early in 1956 a project member brought in the parents of a patient to discuss with them why the patient panicked whenever he saw them for even a few minutes. The parents were seen once a week jointly with the patient, although the treatment was not family therapy as such. The previous hypotheses about the development of schizophrenia in childhood began to be confirmed by the study of the recorded interaction of an adult patient still involved with his parents. The mother would, for example, encourage her son to criticize her and then condemn him when he did. The son similarly imposed paradoxical situations upon his parents; for example, he sent his mother a commercial Mother's Day card which said, "You've always been like a mother to me." The father began to be emphasized as more important to the family system than had previously been thought. From this point on, the project began to focus upon the study of actual behavior of family members with each other with the use of recordings and films. Previously films had been made of disturbed children with their families; now films were made of adult schizophrenics and their families.

With this shift to more emphasis upon actual family behavior, the problem of developing a descriptive language became more important. To propose that a patient was punished for expecting punishment was one sort of approach; to analyze an actual interview and determine what sequences indicated punishment and what sequences indicated an expectation of punishment was quite another.

At this time a more intensive study of individual communication was conducted which included the analysis of body movement as well as vocal patterns. Ray Birdwhistell functioned as a consultant on body movement, and an attempt was made to find a compromise between description of gross gesture and minute description of each movement of a person in conversation. In the area of vocal intonation, the project had previously used Dr. Paul Moses as a consultant on the study of speech. In this period, the study shifted to the more detailed examination of linguistics. Yet this kinesic and linguistic study does not seem to have added much to the theory of the project. Except for the increased perceptive abilities of members of the research team, kinesic and linguistic patterns proved too difficult to bring within the theoretical framework, perhaps because they were devised for the study of the individual rather than patterns of relationship.

In this period it became more evident that there was a large gap between the idea of levels of message, and specifically the double bind, and the raw data which appeared on a film or tape recording. Some kind of theoretical model was necessary to describe a family in conversation and the particular sorts of behavior of the family which contained a schizophrenic member. In agreement that the theoretical models and terminology of psychoanalysis and other psychological approaches were inadequate for the problem, the group began to disagree upon what approach to take. A difference in view in the project which had been inherent in the work from the beginning became more evident. There had always existed in the project a controversy over what aspect of communication to focus upon and what terminology and theoretical models to use. A schism developed between (a) a strictly-communication approach dealing with the description of observable messages in terms of Logical Types, and (b) an approach which emphasized the codification of messages, or the internal processes of the receiver, and centered on perception and learning.

The internal processes wing of the project argued that it was not an internal processes wing but that the distinction between a message and the codification of a message by a receiver was fallacious. Later this wing argued that the terminology should be established at a higher level of generalization than merely the description of messages. Typically, this wing used such concepts as learning, perception, awareness, expectation and the language of emotions. The sort of questions asked were whether the receiver was aware, whether he was misperceiving or misinterpreting, and what his state was—was he suffering trauma, was he experiencing grief, was the experience hurtful, and so on. This "higher generalization" wing objected to confining the double bind to specific interpersonal situations and preferred to use the term in the broadest sense possible. From this point of view the double bind was applicable to evolutionary processes and telencephalization of the brain, while it was also a specific entity in family relations which induced severe trauma.

The argument of project members who emphasized the study of strictly observable messages, to be called here the behavioral wing, was based upon the idea that age-old problems of psychology could be avoided if the emphasis was upon what could be observed and verified. The concept of levels of communication made it appear possible for the first time to develop a systematic description of human behavior. The movement in the social sciences from the study of the individual to the study of two or more persons had been attempted with models drawn from individual psychology. To continue to deal with metaphoric statements about the internal processes of the individual, even if conceived in a different way, would lead to the study of the individual rather than the interactive system. It was further argued that the more focus upon the interchange of messages the more complete the description. If it is said that a schizophrenic faced with certain messages misinterprets or misperceives them, the description must end there. If his response is also described in terms of messages, the descriptive system becomes more complete. The more highly generalized the definition of terms, such as the double bind, the more difficult it would be to develop a systematic description which could be applied to the data.

The behavioral wing further argued that a communication description could ultimately lead to describing human beings in terms of a theory of systems, which was also the desire of the higher generalization wing. If one says that certain learning situations cause an individual to "see" the world in a certain way, that is as far as the description can go. The next step would be to say that the individual "expects" the world to be a certain way, which would still be a statement of internal process. The following step would be to say that he "prepares" for the world to be a certain way. At this point, the participation of the learner begins to enter the situation. Finally, one might say the individual "invites" the world to respond to him in a certain way. At this point it is possible to see a circular system; not only does the learning situation affect the individual, but he affects the learning situation. Only with a description of communicative behavior, argued this wing, could the circularity of a system become apparent.

The higher generalization wing argued that the behavior wing was too narrow in approach and the behavioral wing argued that the other was too diffuse and ambiguous to have useful application to the data. Interestingly enough, both approaches might be said to have been present in the letter to Wiener: the emphasis upon messages in the indication "this is play" and the emphasis upon learning and deutero-learning. In that letter Bateson includes both approaches under the one heading of communication, but he also differentiates between them when he says, "A question which I cannot clearly resolve is whether these two sets of two-typed communication are really identical or whether they are both independently operating in such phenomena as play." Inevitably, of course, the behavior wing argued that the term "learning" was not a communication term for descriptive purposes, and the higher generalization wing argued that it certainly was and should be used in a description of the data. The differences in approach did not begin to appear in publications until 1958, the next year that project members published papers.

Exploration in All Directions

After 1956 there were several possible directions for the research to take: (a) The specific conflict called the double bind, as defined, could be pointed out in verbatim data involving schizophrenic etiology and broadened in scope to include phenomena outside the field of schizophrenia. (b) The double bind, as one instance of a conflict of levels, could be placed within some interpersonal theoretical context. (c) An organizational description of a family could be made in terms of a conflict of levels, in contrast to the two-person double bind description. (d) The double bind, as well as the approach in terms of levels, could be documented as a part of schizophrenic etiology in some objective way. (e) There could be an investigation of psychotherapeutic change in individuals and families from the point of view of conflicting levels of communication.

Instead of choosing one of these possible alternatives, the research project set out upon all of them simultaneously. The resulting activity had an appearance of galloping off in all directions, although a homogeneous theme ran through the various endeavors and this theme will be emphasized and clarified in this review.

In 1958 several publications appeared which were the culmination of work which had been proceeding for some time.

The Double Bind Illustrated With Verbatim Data

In "Patient and Therapist Observations on the Circumstances of a Schizophrenic Episode," Weakland and Jackson (65) analyzed a therapeutic interview with a psychotic patient to describe the context of his breakdown in terms of the double bind. With the argument that stress is an individual matter, the authors published the interview with the patient and analyzed his description of his breakdown in terms of the double bind nature of his stressful situation. The double-level communication posed the patient by his wife is analyzed, as well as the trap in which the patient found himself in a setting which included his mother and his wife's father. Within the framework of talking to the therapist about his hospital situation, the patient describes the home situation at the time of his break. Parallels are drawn between the two settings, and the psychotic state is described as a result of the double bind conflicts at home as well as a creator of formidable problems because of his hospitalization. An emphasis is put upon the patient being faced with conflicting levels of message which give an appearance of being alternatives but which actually are not. This "illusion of alternatives" encourages the patient to attempt to resolve an irresolvable problem until finally he manifests hallucinatory solutions.

In 1959, Erickson, Haley and Weakland published "A Transcript of a Trance Induction with Commentary" (23). A recording was made of Dr. Milton H. Erickson hypnotizing a subject, and then Haley and Weakland questioned him while listening to the tape, and this conversation was recorded. The paper presents the two conversations and is a detailed analysis of a hypnotic induction with an emphasis upon the double bind nature of the induction. For example, Erickson gives the patient the post-hypnotic suggestion to say that she *wasn't* in a trance. If she then says this, she is acknowledging that she is following a post-hypnotic suggestion and so *was* in trance. This detailed presentation of an induction was perhaps the first presentation of what actually happens in trance induction with comments by an articulate hypnotist upon why he did what he did.

In 1959 Fry extended the discussion of the double bind to include an explanation of a violent episode on a hospital ward in "Destructive Behavior on Hospital Wards" (25). He suggests that a riot which occurred could be described as a product of a double bind situation because of a conflict of levels in staff communication with a group of patients.

An Interpersonal Context for the Double Bind

The double bind, as first proposed, was not described in terms of its function in a relationship. People communicated messages which conflicted at different levels and "victims" had to respond. A child was punished and then punished for expecting punishment, but the function of the double bind in a mother–child relationship remained unstated. It was something that just happened. However, implicit in the description of the double bind was a characterization of the mother as an individual; she was a mother who punished but did not want to be labeled a punishing mother. In other examples it was implied that the person imposing the bind could not tolerate closeness but also could not tolerate being labeled as one who could not tolerate closeness. In this sense the double bind was presented as having a function for the individual but not a function in a relationship. It was presented as a *product* of individual motivations which were only implied.

Not only was the double bind presented as a product of the individual's motivational conflicts, but it was largely presented as a unidirectional transaction. That is, the parent imposed conflicting injunctions which precipitated subjective distress in the child, such as panic or rage. The child might *also* impose double binds upon the parents, but these then would be unidirectional—from child to parent.

When it became necessary to describe the actual interchange between two people and to describe the contribution of each person to the pattern of sequences which occurred, it was not sufficient to discuss a sequence in terms of its function for the individual or in terms of a unidirectional transaction. For example, it became important to note that the mother was imposing conflicting injunctions, but also to note that these conflicting injunctions were *responsive* to what the child was doing. If a continuing interchange between two people was to be described, it was necessary to postulate a function for the double bind which involved both people rather than merely the motivation of one of them. A mother might communicate the injunction, "Do as I say or I will punish you," and qualify it with the secondary injunction, "Don't see me as a punishing agent." But to describe mother and child in these terms is to describe individual rather than interactive behavior since the "function" of the double bind when described in this way involves only the characteristics of the mother.

The research was shifting its focus of description from the individual to a system of two or more people, and the premises about motivation which had developed in the psychology of the individual appeared inadequate. To say that two people talking together do what they do to relieve anxiety, to avoid pain, to attempt to achieve a logical universe, to avoid closeness, or to satisfy instinctual drives did not seem satisfactory if one was attempting to explain the persistence of patterns of behavior in ongoing relationships.

Assuming that a relationship between two people was homeostatic in the sense that it was a governed, self-corrective system, the idea began to develop in the project that the "governors" of this system were the people involved in the relationship. Just as the governor in a cybernetic system controls the range of the elements in that system, so it began to be suggested that people in a relationship control the range of each other's behavior. This idea provided a function for the double bind which included both participants rather than merely the individual; the double bind could be seen as a tactic in the interchange between two people as they each attempted to gain control of the range of the system.[1] By imposing a double bind, a person can effectively prevent another from governing what sort of relationship they will have.

This control idea was first presented in a memorandum by Haley in 1956 in an attempt to explain the peculiar behavior of the mothers of schizophrenics. This memorandum suggested that ordinarily two people work out areas of their life together where each, to the satisfaction of both, is in control of what sort of relationship they will have. "This could be called successful setting of the limits of the relationship. However, they may come into conflict and settle the matter by termination of the relationship. Or they may become involved in a constant struggle over *who* is to determine what type of relationship they will have, as in the schizophrenogenic situation." The peculiar mixture of domination and helplessness evident in the mother of the schizophrenic has its origin, according to the memorandum, in the fact that "The mother of the schizophrenic is not concerned with who is boss, but who is to decide who is boss, and she cannot discriminate between the two. Such a woman cannot stand anyone saying to her, 'You're the boss,' just as she cannot stand an intimate saying to her, 'I'm the boss.' It isn't that she can't stand being in charge; she can't stand someone else deciding who is in charge," or governing what sort of relationship there will be. As a result, if her child wants to tie his own shoes, she cannot permit this autonomy because she interprets his message as a signal that he is deciding what sort of relationship they will have, rather than deciding that shoe tying is in his domain within a type of relationship determined by his mother. "If the child of such a mother indicates that she is (or isn't) the boss, the mother must reject this message because it means the child is deciding who is the boss." Thus whatever the child does is classified as not the sort of thing that should be done. When a mother is peculiarly sensitive to having her behavior governed by others, she will even interpret compliant behavior by the child as demanding further direction from her and so governing her behavior. The only solution for the child is to qualify whatever he does as not done in relation to mother and therefore he will not be governing her behavior. However, he will then be accused of not being responsive to mother, and so he must again respond to her only to find that his response is rejected.

The control idea was first published by Haley in 1958 in "An Interactional Explanation of Hypnosis." (32) The project had been investigating hypnosis since 1953, with regular visits to Phoenix to consult with Milton H. Erickson about the nature of hypnosis and the process of hypnotic induction. Of particular interest to the research was the observation that schizophrenics and hypnotized subjects often behave in similar ways. This observation raised the question whether there could be a similarity between the ways a hypnotist induces trance in a subject and the ways a mother induces schizophrenia in a child (which was thought to be a possible way of looking at schizophrenia at the time). However, the investigation of the similarities between these two types of relationships required some way of comparing relationships—a more formidable problem than comparing differences between individuals.

The concept of double bind, as originally proposed, was not helpful as a method of classifying and comparing relationships. Although double binds occurred in the relationship between mother and schizophrenic child and also in the relationship of hypnotist and subject, such an observation was insufficient since double binds also occurred in other relationships. Additionally, when the double bind was applied to hypnosis it became evident that the concept was meaningless unless some motive was assumed for imposing the bind. Any postulated motive would be useful only if it was defined at the relationship level. With the idea that the hypnotist–subject relationship is one which centers upon the question of who is to govern whose behavior, it became immediately apparent that the hypnotic relationship could be seen as formally similar to the relationship between mother and schizophrenic child. In both cases there is a struggle over who is to govern what sort of relationship there will be, and in both cases one of the participants deals with this struggle by defining what he does as not done in relation to the other person.

Hypnosis and schizophrenia have always been two of the most peculiar phenomena in human life and both have been inadequately explained by psychological theories centering on the individual. As long as hypnosis was defined as the state of an individual, there was confusion about the nature of the state, the depth of the trance, the question whether such a state even existed, and so on. However, when hypnosis is described as responsive behavior rather than a subjective state, the problem looks rather different. The concept of levels is particularly appropriate for making such a description if it is assumed that there is a struggle for control in hypnotic induction.

In his attempt to describe and differentiate the hypnotic relationship from other types, Haley suggested that all behavior exchanged between two people can be said to define what type of relationship they will have together. Drawing upon terminology used by Bateson in *Naven* (5), he suggested that all types of relationship can be roughly classified into two types, either symmetrical or complementary. A symmetrical relationship is one where the two people exchange the same sort of behavior. For example, one gives something and the other gives something. A complementary relationship is one where they exchange different behavior. For example, one gives something and the other receives it. A third type of relationship was proposed, the metacomplementary, where one person encourages the other to define the relationship as symmetrical or complementary and so at a higher level is defining the relationship as complementary.

The process of trance induction can be described as a struggle over which of the two people will control the type of relationship they will have. The hypnotist defines it as a complementary relationship by offering suggestions to be followed. If the subject resists, he is defining the relationship as symmetrical. The hypnotist then counters this resistance by encouraging resistant behavior and so redefining it as occurring at his suggestion and so defining the relationship as complementary. If the subject does not resist but cooperatively follows suggestions, the hypnotist "challenges" him to resist. The "challenge" is a double level request for symmetrical behavior—"try to open your eyes but they will remain closed." This is the "disobey me" paradox. The subject cannot disobey without obeying. When the challenge is successful, the subject finds that he must concede that the hypnotist is defining the type of relationship. When the subject responds but indicates *he* is not responding, then he is behaving like a hypnotized subject;

he is indicating that *he* is not defining the type of relationship. Therefore ultimately the hypnotist is labeled as the one who controls the kind of relationship hypnotist and subject will have together.

The double bind as a tactic effectively prevents a person from being the one who defines a type of relationship. A person is governing his relationship if he does what he is told or if he does not, but he is not governing his relationship if he indicates that *he* is not responding or he is not responding in this place and time.

The peculiar responsive behavior of the hypnotic subject is a result of the double-level requests typically posed by the hypnotist in the hypnotic induction. For example, the hypnotist tells the subject to hold his hand still, and then he tells the subject the hand will lift by itself. Similarly, a hypnotist will ask a subject to keep his eyes open and look at a point, and then he will tell him that his eyes will involuntarily close. When it is seen that the hypnotist asks the subject not to do something and qualifies this statement with a request that he do it, the double bind is apparent. In fact whenever one requests involuntary behavior from another person, he is posing conflicting levels of message: he is saying do it but don't do it. If the subject does it, it is not happening involuntarily. Faced with this double level request, the subject can only respond appropriately if he both responds and indicates *he* isn't responding. The peculiar behavior of the subject in trance is the result of the incongruent messages he is offering—he is doing what he is told, but he is qualifying his actions with an indication that he is not doing them or not doing them in this place at this time.

Both the subject in a trance and the schizophrenic qualify what they do as not done in relation to the other person. However, when the hypnotic subject behaves in this way, the hypnotist accepts his responses and encourages the subject to continue behaving on his terms. When the schizophrenic behaves in this way, his mother condemns him for not responding to her and indicates she would rather not be the governor of the relationship.

From the control point of view a variety of phenomena could be described, including the peculiar responsive behavior of the schizophrenic. In his paper "An interactional Description of Schizophrenia" (34) Haley analyzed a conversation between two schizophrenics with the suggestion that each could be described as a person struggling *not* to define his relationship with another. The schizophrenic communicates the message "I am communicating with you in this situation" by classifying each element in it incongruently on *every level.* For example, he indicates that *he* isn't speaking by using an alias, but he will disqualify that alias by making it so fantastic that it is unbelievable, e.g., the male patient's statement that he is Margaret Stalin. As a result, the schizophrenic exhibits a style of communication where each qualification is incongruent with every other qualification, in contrast to the hypnotic subject who manifests a single incongruence. From this point of view, the schizophrenic has dedicated himself to negating any comment he makes about his relationship with another person. Since inevitably whatever response he makes to another person will be a comment on that relationship, he must negate whatever he says.

In 1958 Haley also published "The Art of Psychoanalysis," (31) a somewhat facetious presentation of the idea that analyst and patient are struggling to control their relationship with each other. Therapeutic tactics were described as ways of preventing patients from using symptomatic behavior to gain an advantage in a relationship.

Also in 1958, Jackson published "Guilt and the Control of Pleasure in Schizoid Personalities," (50) a paper dealing with the conflict between mother and schizophrenic child over who was to control their relationship. The pleasure of the child in onanism provoked an extreme reaction in the mother because she received his action as a statement of autonomy and so a statement defining what sort of relationship they had together.

With an approach in terms of control, it seemed possible to provide a relationship context for the double bind and so differentiate different behavioral responses to it. The response might take the form of hypnotic behavior, schizophrenic behavior, the development of symptoms, or a shift from symptomatic to nonsymptomatic behavior with the binds of psychotherapy.

An Organizational Description of the Family

By 1959 the members of the research project had been able to conceptualize the problem of family organization sufficiently to publish upon it and these publications will be described in the order in which individual project members presented them.

Whereas the shift to the double bind had been a shift from the study of the individual to the study of the relationship between two people, the move toward the organization of the family required a description of three or more people interacting with one another. There were several goals in the family study: the need to (a) provide a descriptive model for a single family system; (b) provide a way of differentiating the family with a schizophrenic from other types of family; and (c) describe schizophrenia in such a way that it could be shown as adaptive to a particular kind of family system.

The data for the research were largely a group of families with a schizophrenic member in family therapy, with occasional observation of families with a delinquent member. In addition, a number of families, both schizophrenic and "normal," were placed in a structured interview situation and filmed.

While interested in the double bind as a specific entity, Bateson also envisioned this concept as an explanatory principle for a variety of phenomena in the world. Searching for a model to describe the family of the schizophrenic, he carried the double bind into other fields in "The New Conceptual Frames for Behavioral Research" (11). Presenting a discussion of Game Theory as such a model, he extended the discussion into a parallel between individual patterns and evolutionary patterns. Essentially he argued that two sorts of processes are apparent in a variety of phenomena: the phenomenon of habit, in the largest sense, and the changing context of the environment. The individual, whether plant, animal, or man, develops characteristics for adapting to a certain sort of environment and then that environment undergoes change. This is the recurrent condition for evolutionary creativity. "We know, for example, that any characteristic be it anatomical, physiological, or behavioral will, if it continues to be adaptive over considerable periods of time, be sunk deeper in the organizational structure of the system. That is, the constellation of causes which bring about the adaptive characteristics will gradually change in such a way that, when this process reaches its later stages, a gross disruption of the total system may be necessary to prevent the production of the previously adaptive characteristic. Moreover, the dilemma in which the system then finds itself will be formally comparable with what we call the double bind. It will appear to the system (again personifying) as if it can only achieve external adaptation at the price of internal disruption" (p. 67). The individuals in the family of the schizophrenic feel that external adaptation could only be achieved at the price of internal disruption and, to this view of the family environment, the patient adapts by forms of communicational behavior in which either the internal world, or the external, or both, is implicitly or even explicitly denied. He suggests that this type of family is narrowly homeostatic. Characteristically the family members are unable to reach decisions because each will not take responsibility for settling any matter in a decisive manner. However, rather than having a system which is flexible and free to undergo profound changes because of this indecisiveness, it becomes a system which is rigidly indecisive. If a system does not achieve economy by "sinking" its adaptive processes to deeper parts of its organization, it must be continually occupied in solving and resolving the old problems. The types of behavior of one individual which prevent habit formation in another are patterns of double binding. At the family level, the inability to establish parameters produces a system of group indecision which is essentially similar to Von Neumann's coalition patterns where the total group of players, if more than three in number, will be unable to reach any stable pattern of coalition. Group indecision becomes synonymous with a statement about the instability of coalitions; if one member of the family proposes something and the suggestion can neither be followed nor discarded by the others, this characteristic group behavior can always be described in terms of coalitions.

After presenting the decision-making process in Game Theory where three robots will tend to form coalitions and reach stable decisions the more information they have about each other's choices, Bateson points out that this procedure is not true of the family of the schizophrenic. The more information each family member has about the preferences of the others, the more unable the family is to form a coalition or reach a group decision. Although he implicitly suggests thereby that Game Theory is not an appropriate model for such a family system, he uses that model for illustrative purposes.

Bateson again returns to Game Theory in a discussion of the organization of the family in "The Group Dynamics of Schizophrenia" published in 1960 (13). His emphasis is upon whether the peculiarities of the identified patient can be seen as appropriate in terms of the characteristics of other members of the family group. Presumably the patient cannot learn at random, but can learn only to be like or unlike those around him, and therefore it is necessary to look at his experiential setting.

Examining the schizophrenic, Bateson points out that he eliminates from his messages everything that refers explicitly or implicitly to the relationship between himself and the person he is addressing. He commonly avoids the first- and second-person pronoun, he avoids indicating whether his messages are literal or metaphoric, and he has difficulty with all messages which imply intimate contact between the self and some other. "What remains is likely to be a metaphoric statement unlabeled as to context. Or, in extreme cases, there may be nothing left but a stolid acting out of the message, 'There is no relationship between us'" (p. 97). Bateson adds, "This much is observable and may be summarized by saying the schizophrenic communicates *as if* he expected to be punished every time he indicates that he is right in his view of the context of his own message" (p. 97). The double bind is then "summarized by saying that it is an experience of being punished precisely for being right in one's own view of the context" (p. 97), and repeated experience of punishment will lead the individual to behave habitually as if he expected it.

Bateson describes the experiential setting of the patient as a family situation where disqualification and metacommunicative incongruencies are common, and "the identified patient sacrifices himself to maintain the sacred illusion that what the parent says makes sense" (p. 98). The systematic distortions of communication in the family are precisely "those which would seem appropriate when the victims are faced with a trap to avoid which would be to destroy the very nature of self" (p. 99).

The problem posed by Bateson is to offer a hypothesis about why these double bind sequences are specially frequent or specially destructive in the families which contain schizophrenics. "The problem is to construct a model which will necessarily *cycle* to recreate those patterned sequences over and over again" (p. 100). Once again Bateson returns to the Theory of Games with a discussion of the way a five-person game cannot settle to a stable set of coalitions and so "the robots (owing to their total intelligence) will be unable to decide upon a single 'play' of the game" (p. 101). He adds, "I offer this model as being reminiscent of what happens in schizophrenic families" (p. 101). In a Von Neumannian game, five hypothetical entities are required, but *three* human beings seem to be enough to achieve a similar instability of coalition. "Perhaps they are not totally intelligent, or perhaps they are systematically inconsistent regarding the sort of 'gain' in terms of which they are motivated" (p. 102).

Bateson suggests further that to use a Game Theory model it is necessary to discard the assumptions about Game Theory robots and depend upon certain psychological assumptions about the human individual as a learning organism. To be prone to schizophrenia, the individual must both adapt to demands of the personal environment and become committed to the adaptations discovered. Since the Von Neumannian robot is not a learning organism and cannot experience the pain which human beings feel if continually proven wrong, it is not comparable to human beings who have a commitment to the solutions they discover, and "it is this psychological commitment that makes it possible for them to be hurt in the way members of a schizophrenic family are hurt" (p. 102). He concludes, "this type of family is an organization with great ongoing stability whose dynamics and inner workings are such that each member is continually undergoing the experience of negation of self" (p. 104).

A paper only peripherally related to family organization was "Minimal Requirements for a Theory of Schizophrenia," published by Bateson in 1960 (12). The paper surveyed the field of behavioral science, evolutionary theory, and biological epistemology, and it dealt only in passing with the family system. Bateson defines the schizophrenic individual as someone who confuses logical types in an overt way, and the parents of the schizophrenic as "covert schizophrenics" who respond to the messages of others as though these were of a different logical type than the speaker intended. "So long as the covert schizophrenic can succeed in putting the other in the wrong, his or her pathology is obscured and the blame falls elsewhere" (p. 487). Assuming that both patient and parents must be included in the description of schizophrenia, Bateson raises the question of what sort of genetic factors could be involved and "how these two degrees of pathology might be related in a genetic theory" (p. 487).

This paper described learning in terms of a variety of contexts, which was beginning to interest the project. There was an attempt to apply to the natural history description of human beings the various types of learning contexts, such as the Pavlovian, the instrumental-reward, and so on. In this paper Bateson also discussed the growing differences in the project when he described the similarity between orders of learning within the individual and learning contexts in the person's environment. He considers statements about context and statements about learning to be synonymous. "The separation is only maintained by saying that the contexts have location outside the physical individual while the orders of learning are located inside. But in the communication world, this dichotomy is irrelevant and meaningless" (p. 481). He pointed out that the contexts have communicational reality only insofar as they are effective as messages, and the characteristics of the system are in no way dependent upon any boundary lines which we may superimpose upon the communicational map. Bateson considers the communication world a Berkeleian one, but he feels the good bishop understated the case.

In this paper Bateson also expressed his opinion of the emphasis upon control which had been developing in the project. Raising the question of whether science might answer moral or aesthetic questions, he says, "I can best make this clear by considering a matter which you as psychiatrists have thought about many times. I mean the matter of 'control' and the whole related complex suggested by such words as manipulation, spontaneity, free will, and technique. I think you will agree with me that there is no area in which false premises regarding the nature of the self and its relation to others can be so surely productive of destruction and ugliness as this area of ideas about control" (p. 490).

Methods of "control" were discussed in another paper by Bateson, "Biosocial Integration of Behavior," in 1961 (15). He postulates two control processes which maintain stability: calibration and feedback. The heating system of a home fluctuates around a setting on the basis of feedback which activates or turns off the furnace. The setting of the system is calibrated. In this sense habit is an example of calibration while meeting each problem and dealing with it on a trial and error basis is an example of feedback. Continuing to emphasize the stability inherent in a system which has sunk its patterns to the level of habit, Bateson defines stability as the ongoing truth of a statement about a system. He then poses a series of descriptive statements about the family of the schizophrenic and examines their truth over time with a question of whether the truth of these statements is maintained by feedback processes, by calibrations, or by a combination of these processes. He concludes that the only calibrations in these families are at the low level of habit formation in the individual and the highly superficial level of external appearances. The result is a system which, while pathogenic, is yet stable.

In 1959 Haley published "The Family of the Schizophrenic: a Model System," (35) which was an attempt to suggest a way of classifying families into types and also an attempt to show how schizophrenic behavior is adaptive to a particular kind of family system. The point of view taken was this: given a father, mother and child in a room, a potential range of communicative behavior is possible between them, but any particular family will habitually select a certain range of that behavior and confine itself within it. At the most general level, (a) three people in a room will communicate with each other, (b) each will qualify his own communication, (c) each will qualify the messages of the others, and on another dimension, (d) there are a variety of ways the three people can handle blame and (e) there are a variety of ways they will handle leadership. The restricted range which any family will choose in these general areas can be seen as a set of rules which this family habitually follows. The family of the schizophrenic appears to follow rules in each of these areas in this way; each person in the family tends to negate, or disqualify, what he himself communicates; each disqualifies what the others communicate; there is a rule that mother is not be blamed in a way she can accept blame; and no leadership will be assumed in this type of family without a negation of that leadership.

Essentially the premise was suggested that each family member communicates conflicting levels of message—thereby disqualifying what he himself says. From this point of view, the double bind is not an occasional instance but family members follow a consistent pattern of conflicting messages. Further, the response to conflicting levels of messages is conflicting levels of message. If someone indicates, "I like you," while at the same time disqualifying this statement with an indication, "Don't pay attention to what I say," the response is most likely to be incongruent, e.g., an acceptance of the statement, qualified with an indication that it is accepted with reservations.

Given the premise that conflicting levels of message are habitual in these families, it would follow that there could be no stable coalitions (which require affirmed behavior), no clear blame, no clear leadership, and in fact no clear statement of family rules. Any statement of a family rule would be negated.

Further, the paper suggests that just as one message can be qualified by another which conflicts with it, so can any family rule be qualified by another which conflicts with it. Schizophrenic behavior is then described as an attempt to adapt to a set of rules which conflict with each other, at different levels, and so inevitably schizophrenic communication will be manifested as messages which conflict with each other at different levels. The patient who must adapt to the rule that he is not to form a coalition with any family member, and also adapt to the rule that he must disqualify what all family members say, is going to be in an "impossible" situation if mother tells him to form a coalition with father. He can only respond by forming a coalition while indicating he is not. If a rule at still another level is being infringed by that particular response, he must also negate that response. Therefore, it is argued, the incongruences which occur at all levels in schizophrenic discourse are habitual responses adapting to all levels of conflicting rules in the family. The schizophrenic must manifest levels of message each conflicting with each other because, like tumblers fitting into a lock, each of his levels of message adapts to a rule which conflicts with another rule. He must both communicate and disqualify that communication, and also disqualify his disqualification, and so give an appearance of someone who is attempting to negate any comment he makes about any relationship with anyone.

The paper further suggests that the members of this type of family behave in a disqualifying way because of a peculiar sensitivity to having their behavior governed by others. A model proposed is a two-level homeostatic system: at Level I, the family members respond in an error-activated way to any breaking of family rules by other members, and so govern each other's range of behavior. At Level II they each attempt to be the one who sets the family rules, and respond in an error-activated way to attempts by the others to set family rules. Most families reach agreement both about rules for family behavior and rules for who is to set the rules for family behavior. In the family of the schizophrenic, each family member disqualifies any attempt by any other to govern his behavior. Inevitably they give an appearance of conflict and constant disqualification. In this type of family the struggle persists at the second level—*who* is to set the family rules—and so questions of rule breaking or misbehavior cannot be resolved without activating a struggle over who is to make the rules. As a result, the parents cannot discipline the child, or even clearly define limits for him, because each attempt by one of them is met by the other with an indication that he or she is not to make the rules for the behavior of others in the family.

A presentation of a similar description of the family was given by Haley in 1958 and ultimately published in 1960 as "Observations of the Family of the Schizophrenic" (36).

Although the paper more properly might come under the therapy section, Jackson published "Family Interaction, Family Homeostasis and Some Implications for Conjoint Family Psychotherapy" in 1959 (52). This paper began as a joint effort with Haley but was published as Jackson's contribution. It reviews the problems of collecting data on the family and discusses the homeostatic aspects of the family with particular emphasis upon therapeutic implications. The major focus is upon people defining types of relationship and the symmetrical-complementary classification of relationships is used. Ultimately Jackson classified families into four categories: stable satisfactory, unstable satisfactory, stable unsatisfactory and unstable unsatisfactory. This mixture of description in terms of stability and in terms of emotional satisfaction was not appealing to other project members, but as a way of classifying families for therapeutic prognosis Jackson considered it useful.

In 1960, Weakland published "The 'Double-Bind' Hypothesis of Schizophrenia and Three-Party Interaction" (66). Taking off from the statement in the 1956 double-bind paper that the bind may be inflicted "either by mother alone or by some combination of mother, father, and/or siblings," Weakland discusses the double bind in more detail with emphasis upon the concealment, denial, and inhibition inherent in the offering of the bind. He points out that when the bind is inflicted by parents rather than merely by one parent, "the obscuring factors that would seem inherent in the two-person situation may easily have parallels or equivalents in the three-person situation." He then points out the empirical evidence which appears in the work of other research projects: Lidz, Wynne, and Bowen, as well as in the institutional situation described by Stanton and Schwartz.

To summarize the project point of view on family organization, it is clear that within a general framework of agreement there was considerable disagreement. The result was a collection of ideas rather than a homogeneous theoretical presentation. The disagreements centered on (A) the choice of a theoretical model; (B) whether to focus upon aspects of the interaction of a family or the totality of the family organization; and (C) differences in assumptions about the motivation of players in the family game.

(A) The lack of a theoretical model in the family field has always been a major problem. Any description of a family must be hung upon some implicit or explicit analogy, and with the shift from the study of the individual to the study of the family all previous analogies in psychiatry become inappropriate. The preferred model in the project was some form of homeostatic system which involved levels, but debate centered on what form it should take. Bateson preferred to attempt to utilize some modification of Von Neumann's Theory of Games despite protests from other project members as well as his own admissions that the assumptions of Game Theory could not be utilized for describing family behavior. The formal structure proposed of robots interacting in patterns subject to mathematical description was appealing and elegant but the fact that the robots were not learning organisms and that they communicate within a clearly defined series of levels negated the usefulness of the model. In addition, the assumptions about the motivation of the robots could not be used analogously with human behavior and there was an emphasis upon decision making rather than on communicative behavior.

Haley's proposal that the family could be seen as a homeostatic organization with Level I for the rules for behavior in the family and Level II for rules for *who* was to make the rules was opposed by Bateson. He objected to the idea that a family should be described in terms of members attempting to control the behavior of one another. At the higher level of governing process, Haley argued that the struggle was over *who* was to set the range of behavior of family members, and Bateson argued that at that level the settings should be described in terms of the calibrations of habit in the individual, or habitual patterns in the family.

(B) A major dissension in the project centered on what aspect of family organization was to be focused upon for descriptive purposes. Bateson's lifelong preference, in general, was to choose a characteristic sequence and to relate that sequence to a variety of situations in the field of science. Therefore his preference was to emphasize the double bind as a sequence which occurred in schizophrenic families and to generalize that sequence into the field of evolution, biological processes and so on. Other project members objected that he was making the double bind too specific as an etiological factor in schizophrenia and too diffuse and undefined when he generalized into the evolutionary process.

Those who objected thought the aspect focused upon should be the organized patterns of types of families rather than upon a sequence which occurred at times in one type of family. With the emphasis upon family members communicating multiple levels of message, the double bind appeared as one type of interchange. From Bateson's point of view, the organization of the family should be described within the general framework of the double bind, defined as broadly as possible.

(C) As an attempt was made to formulate a theoretical model for family organization, it became more apparent that the behavior of family members must be explained in terms of some kind of motivation. In studying family interaction, it seemed that much of the disagreement about how to describe a family centered in assumptions, largely implicit, about why people respond the way they do. Haley preferred to postulate an oversimplified motive: that people attempt to govern, or influence and control, what is to happen in relation to other people. If family members were assumed to be "programmed" that way, the stability of a family system as the members responded to each other seemed explainable. Other project members had their own preference for explaining the motivation of family members. Weakland (1960) proposed no motivation for parents posing a double bind for a child, but emphasized the motivation of attempting to conceal it once it was done. Bateson similarly preferred to argue that a central motivation was concealment, with punishment threatened if that concealment was breached. He explains schizophrenic behavior as based upon the person expecting punishment for being right in his interpretation of the context of his own message. Bateson also postulates other motivations: that the parents attempt to put the child in the wrong, and that people have an investment in their adaptive behavior and are hurt if that behavior is condemned. Generally, Bateson preferred to assume that people were motivated as had been traditionally assumed: by fear, hate, love, threats of punishment, and avoidance of pain.

It would seem apparent that the disagreements within the project appeared when there was an attempt to look at real people communicating real messages. At the more abstract level, there was surprising agreement. All project members believed the best approach was in terms of some theory of systems with an emphasis upon rules and pattern and upon stability and instability over time. All project members approached the problems in terms of levels: levels of message, levels of rules, levels of governing process. Additionally, all considered it more and more obvious that the schizophrenic's behavior was in some way adaptive to the particular kind of family organization in which he was raised. It was also assumed by all that family members responded in error-activated ways to each other and so governed the behavior of each other, and that the governing process should be described in an hierarchical way.

Documentation of the Double Bind and the Concept of Levels

In this research project the preference of the members was to examine an area of research, discover a way to put a theoretical wedge into the material, make a description with that point of view, and then go elsewhere. There was no particular interest in the labors, or methodology, of statistical documentation. Essentially it was a "think" project where a problem and an idea were brought together and objective validation was for others to concern themselves with. However, in 1959 the project attempted to enter the field of documentation with a grant to experiment with families.

In that year the project divided administratively into two areas of research. A grant was obtained from the National Institute of Mental Health for a family therapy project, and a grant to support an experimental research project was obtained from the Foundations Fund for Research in Psychiatry. With these emphases, the project began to go in two directions which had never before been preferred: the area of clinical research and the area of systematic empirical validation.[2]

The experimental approach developed out of attempts to classify characteristic sequences in the family of the schizophrenic with the use of verbal and nonverbal material. Families had been recorded on tape and film and subjected to study. A standard interview was structured with the hope that differences between the schizophrenic and "normal" family would appear in some categorizable form from the responses to standard questions. The results of this effort were largely inconclusive. Placing families in limited communication networks with measurement of their behavior appeared a more hopeful alternative.

In the application for a grant it was stated, "We were (in the past) seeking for the right *questions* to ask rather than seeking for those questions which could perhaps be readily tested and which might yet be epistemologically inappropriate." Previous attempts to isolate particular characteristics of those family constellations in which schizophrenia occurs had been unsatisfactory. "The particular variables focused upon by investigators have been parts of the total communicational sequence which we refer to as the double bind. The resulting statistical studies have therefore given unsatisfactory results because the investigators were not able to focus upon the larger patterns, and the particular variables ... are perhaps only pathogenic when they occur in conjunction with the rest of a pathogenic pattern." It was stated that the difficulties faced on entering the experimental field centered not only upon the difficulties inherent in a hypothesis involving confusion of Logical Types, but also the particular difficulties inherent in investigating the occurrence of complex constellations of factors.

The general approach outlined was to "so far as is possible engage in rough counting of double bind sequences in family interaction in both normal and suspected pathogenic families." This was to be done by observing families in relatively free interaction and in planned situations involving a simple task. Secondly, there were to be limited communication networks which involve the passage of information or cooperation in joint decisions, with variations of the network to test different hypotheses. The one example given was a situation where the communication was limited to a single direction. The information could be transmitted from mother to son to father, or from father to son to mother. Additionally, the experimenter might be substituted for the child, without the parent's knowledge, to test parental response to altered behavior from the child.

Although it was suggested that many variants and possibilities for experimental structure were available, the application did not list them. It was assumed they would be developed in the course of exploration.

The addition of Dr. Alex Bavelas as a consultant to the project made the experimental program seem possible. His long experience experimenting with small groups could provide a source of ideas for experimental structures for family groups. Additionally, Bavelas had been experimenting with learning situations and had developed a classification of learning contexts which appeared both useful as another way of defining double bind situations and a possible way of developing a classification system for families.

A summary report on the research program was published by Haley, "Family Experiments: A New Type of Experimentation" (41). This report emphasizes what was finally done more than it emphasizes the difficulties which appeared in the course of the attempt. Several original hopes were unfulfilled: the expectation that particular sequences in families could be tested with experiments and given statistical validation was not met, nor was it possible to count double bind sequences because of the complexity of levels involved in any double bind situation. As a result, the emphasis shifted from testing points of theory or specific sequences in family interaction to an attempt to differentiate the family organization of the schizophrenic family from other types of family organization by placing contrasting families in experimental structures. It was also found that experiments created for groups of unrelated people could not be readily applied to families. The design of experiments involving more than one level of communication proved to be more formidable than expected.

Out of the experimental program, according to Haley's paper, came a portrait of a new field of experimentation. Past psychological experiments with individual human beings or animals, and past small group experiments with unrelated people, appeared to be distinctively different from experiments with people who had a history together and a future together. There seemed to be a discontinuous change between past experimentation and family experiments—in theory, in methodology, and in sampling. The sampling problem proved especially formidable in the measurement of patterns in ongoing groups. To measure differences between two types of relationship (in contrast to measurement of differences between the responses of two individuals) required sampling types of relationship; an area without defined characteristics for sampling purposes.

One experiment which appeared to show a difference between the family of the schizophrenic and "normal" families was reported. It was a coalition experiment where family members scored by getting together with one another in coalition. There was apparently no difference between the two types of families when the experiment was a single-level one, but the addition of a signal button so that family members could both invite each other to get together and also push a button to get together brought out significant differences between them. So many explanations of the differences were possible, and the sampling problems were so complicated, that the results were not presented as conclusive.

Instead of achieving a documentation of the theoretical approach of the research, as was hoped, the experimental program resulted in introducing a small wedge into a new field, thereby following a pattern typical of this research project and perhaps inevitable in an exploratory field.

Therapeutic Change and Conflicting Levels

The orientation of the Bateson project was anthropological; the research group preferred to approach a problem by observing natural history situations with as little intrusion upon the data as possible. Such an orientation is antithetical to experimentation, just as it is to a clinical approach where someone attempts to describe his influence upon a system as he intrudes upon it to bring about a change. The goal of an anthropologist is to observe and describe a system, whereas the goal of a psychotherapist is to exert maximum influence.

Although the research group was not interested in a specifically clinical investigation, somehow the subject of psychotherapy was a source of study throughout the history of the project. Rather intensive research was done upon almost all techniques of psychotherapy extant, with recordings and films made of a variety of psychotherapists at work. The last grant obtained was specifically for a study of family therapy, and the practice of psychotherapy was one of the duties of the research team. Bateson, as part of his work in the Veterans Administration hospital, was doing psychotherapy with patients, and when schizophrenia became an object of study, Haley and Weakland began to do therapy with individuals and later with families. In 1956 Haley began a part-time private practice as a hypnotherapist and family therapist, and later Weakland did the same. Jackson continued his clinical practice throughout the research, as did Fry. Although psychotherapy and psychopathology were only two of the many sources of data for the study of communication, the group developed a communication description of psychotherapy and a novel theory about the cause of therapeutic change.

The first papers presented by the research project included the subject of psychotherapy. Bateson (1) and Haley (30) discussed psychotherapy as an attempt to change the metacommunicative habits of a patient by offering a framework where rules for the interchange are the subject of the interchange in a "game" where there is extensive playing with labels. In the original joint paper, (3) a therapeutic bind is discussed and implicit in the discussion was the emphasis upon the therapist arranging the situation so that therapist rather than patient sets the rules. In 1958 in "The Art of Psychoanalysis" (31) Haley described this form therapy as a struggle over whether patient or analyst was to gain an advantage in a relationship by being the one who set the rules for the interchange.

By 1958 the project members were treating whole families, and Jackson described conjoint family therapy and differentiated it from treating family members individually (52). His discussion centered upon the effect of improvement in a member upon the family unit, and the prognosis for different types of family. In his final paragraph he says, "It may be that the peculiar pathologic sticking together that these families demonstrate can be used to keep them in therapy. Perhaps our therapy should be called homeopathic family therapy since we proceed on the notion that the particular communication devices the family uses can be in turn used against them for therapeutic purposes as in the homeopathic idea that 'like cures like'" (p. 140). Although Jackson does not describe these communication devices, he expresses a point of view which the project was developing at that time: the idea that there is a parallel between the formal structure of psychopathology and the psychotherapy which brings about change.

In 1959 Haley published the first of a series of papers on different types of psychotherapy. In "Control in Psychoanalytic Psychotherapy" (33) he suggests that symptoms can be described as the imposition of a double bind. The patient does something which circumscribes the behavior of another person and qualifies this message with an indication that he is not doing it or cannot help it. These conflicting levels of message posed by the patient are met by conflicting levels of message, or double binds, posed by the psychoanalyst. The structure of the psychoanalytic situation is described as a way of putting the patient at a disadvantage as long as he continues with symptomatic behavior. In this paper Haley first published an idea which originated from his observation of Milton Erickson at work. Studying the brief therapeutic techniques of Erickson, it became clear that he handled symptomatic behavior in a patient in the same way he handled resistant behavior in a hypnotic subject—by encouraging it.

When a hypnotic subject resisted, Erickson encouraged him to resist, thereby stepping to a metacommunicative level and defining resistance as cooperative behavior. Similarly, among the many ways Erickson dealt with symptomatic behavior, a characteristic theme was the encouragement of that behavior. When symptomatic behavior is seen as a way of gaining an advantage in setting the rules for a relationship, the encouragement of that behavior means that it not only loses its function but also poses the patient a paradox; the symptom which the patient came to have changed is encouraged. In brief therapy the symptom may be directly encouraged, while in psychoanalytic therapy Haley suggests that the general permissiveness of the analyst, as well as his emphasis upon the patient behaving in his usual ways as subject for study, places the patient in this paradoxical situation. This idea was later generalized into the observation that in all forms of psychotherapy the way to help someone over a problem is to encourage him to have it.

In 1961 Jackson and Weakland published a paper (59) presenting the history and background of the experiences of project members treating families containing a schizophrenic member. They describe the nature of the problem and the family's resistance to change. Suggesting that incongruent messages provoke incongruent messages, they say that when the incongruence is concealed the reply is correspondingly exaggerated, "the typical case for schizophrenic utterance" (p. 41). This exaggerated reply in turn influences others toward further incongruence and concealment. In the three-party situation, when the child "responds in a disturbed way with markedly incongruent messages and ones likely to have some reference to the family relationships" (p. 41), the parents are likely to insist more strongly that there are no differences in what they think and say, rather than admitting differences, and so the problem continues. Additionally, the family members persist in disqualifying each other's communication so that both agreement and disagreement are avoided, and this sort of communication has a paralyzing effect.

Therapeutic tactics to deal with this sort of system are described as attempts to meet the family on its own ground though with a different orientation—toward "positive change" instead of defensive maintenance of a sick system. That is, the therapist himself must employ dual or multiple messages involving such incongruences as will serve to come to grips with the whole complexity of the messages of the family members he must deal with. The therapist uses "explicit" statements that convey concealed and unexpected implicit meanings, he uses "content messages joined with framing statements," and he gives "instructions whose carrying out will constitute a further message." They add, "We have spoken of this elsewhere, perhaps too narrowly, as the 'therapeutic double bind,' the broad principle described here, of using multiple—and often incongruent—messages therapeutically, is what needs recognition, and then further investigation" (p. 42).

It seemed apparent at this time to the project that psychotherapists typically offer incongruent messages to patients and in fact offer behavior similar to that used by family members when they do family therapy. In discussing family therapy, Haley (40) points out that the various schools of family therapy which have developed use tactics which are formally the same as the tactics typically used by family members in disturbed families.

In a series of papers on psychotherapy Haley described the incongruent behavior of therapists in terms of paradoxes. He described psychoanalytic therapy (33), brief psychotherapy (38), the therapy of schizophrenics (39), family therapy (40), and ultimately put this approach into a book (43) which included discussions of other types of therapy. Essentially his argument was that the source of therapeutic change resided in the paradoxes posed patients by therapists rather than in the self-understanding which was traditionally thought to be the cause of change. The paradoxical aspects of "transference" were discussed in "Transference Revisited" by Jackson and Haley (63). Although a variety of types of psychotherapy have developed which do not emphasize insight or self-understanding, all forms of psychotherapy have paradoxical situations as a common factor. These can be summarized briefly here as they were presented in these papers.

In logic, a paradox occurs in such a statement as "I am lying," because the "truth" of the statement is qualified as "false." If one uses this formal structure and generalizes from it, one can also say that a paradox occurs if a "benevolent" statement is qualified as "punishing," or vice versa (such as "I am helping you by kicking you"). Similarly, a "directive" statement can be qualified as "nondirective." From this point of view, the art of psychotherapy is replete with paradoxes when the therapeutic interchange is seen as a process of defining, or qualifying, the rules for the relationship and who is to make these rules.

All forms of psychotherapy typically define the situation as a benevolent one where an expert takes charge and helps a patient over his problems in a relationship which is voluntary on the patient's part. Yet this situation is also defined in quite a conflicting way by other behaviors of therapists who also define the situation as one where the expert does not take charge, the patient is put through a punishing ordeal, the therapist does not deal with the problem the patient wants resolved and even encourages that problem, and the therapist indicates the patient must attend the sessions.

Although most therapists prefer to emphasize the more benevolent aspects of their trade, it is obvious that psychotherapy is a punishing experience. To offer all the unsavory aspects of oneself in psychoanalysis is not pleasant, and the brief therapist may directly prescribe an ordeal for the patient. Similarly, the therapist defines himself as an expert but disinvolves himself from offering expert advice to the patient who asks for it; he prefers to put the patient in charge of what is to happen in his life. Additionally, in some forms of therapy the therapist avoids dealing with the presenting symptom of the patient and indicates the *real* problem is what is behind it. In other forms of therapy, the therapist similarly negates the symptoms as a manipulative force, often by encouraging symptomatic behavior. The elaborate permissiveness (and lack of opposition to symptomatic behavior) of all forms of therapy can be seen as encouragement of symptoms, with certain techniques specifically designed to encourage that behavior. All forms of therapy also imply, directly or indirectly, that the relationship is voluntary, but they also indicate the patient must continue no matter how much he would rather not when he is "resistant." A similar set of paradoxes apply to marriage and family therapy; the addition of people in the room provides variations but no changes in basic tactics. The goal in family therapy is to change the "setting" of a self-corrective system of multiple elements by dealing with all family members at once. It is possible to see individual therapy as an attempt to change a family system by using one member as a lever.

With the enlargement of the description of psychotherapy to include more than just the patient, and with the suggestion that paradox is inherent in various methods of treatment, the project offered a new explanation of the cause of therapeutic change. Not only was it suggested that the process of therapy was the working out of rules of relationship, as was suggested early in the research, but the ways psychotherapists prevent the patient imposing his rules were also described. By the nature of the paradoxes the patient faces, each of his attempts to set the rules for the interchange is met by a counter-move at a metacommunicative level which requires him to behave differently. In summary, the essential paradox faced by the patient in all methods of therapy is this: he is benevolently helped to recover from a problem by being encouraged to continue with it in a setting where he must undergo an ordeal as long as he continues with the problem. From this point of view, insight and self understanding become a *modus vivendi* for therapist and patient dealing with each other rather than the causal factor in therapeutic change.

Summary

When communication is the subject of investigation, all data are relevant and studying the paradoxes which arise in communication leads through strange terrain.

Metaphor

It was in the field of play and metaphor that the project first sought examples of the paradoxes of abstraction. Since metaphor is the very stuff of communication, any data can become relevant, but the peculiarities of metaphor appear more vividly in some circumstances than others: ritual, humor, play, and the tactics of schizophrenics.

One of the major confusions in human life is the difficulty people have interpreting the metaphorical statement or act. For example, the bloody side of the history of Christianity was based upon the question of heresy, and typically the heretical episode was a conflict over whether an idea should be interpreted as metaphorical or literal. An early heresy was the issue whether Christ existed as a man or was a metaphorical statement about the divinity in each of us. Later men were burned alive over the question whether the bread and wine was really the body and blood of Christ or only metaphorically so.

Although it was not always a burning issue, the nature of metaphor has been central to the nature of religious ritual, to art in all its forms, to play and humor, to fantasy and dream, and to the communication of the schizophrenic. When metaphor is used in fantasy and play, it is a rewarding and enriching experience, but when it is important in a power struggle there can be dismaying results. In humor and play, in fantasy, or in that peculiar metaphor the ventriloquist's puppet, the metaphoric device discovers delightful parallels between apparently unrelated phenomena. In a struggle, the same device becomes restrictive and arouses the most violent emotions. The schizophrenic individual manages to use metaphor in a way that enriches language, while he also uses it to deny, and to express the despair of one who feels helplessly caught in a restrictive struggle in an uncertain world.

The investigation of paradoxes in metaphor by the research project found difficulty with discovering the nature of the literal, and with the realization that metaphor is but a term for the analogies by which we perceive and think and deal with one another. Like other important aspects of human life, metaphor is an exasperating subject of study while also a crucial consideration in any procedure for studying other subjects. Whether he is counting responses to a Rorschach card, examining the chemistry of the brain, or describing the universe, the scientist is wrestling with the problem of the nature of metaphor.

Humor and Play

The juxtaposition of messages in a joke, the turn of phrase in wit, the exaggeration of parody and caricature, are playing with Logical Types in such a way that a pronounced emotional effect is produced in the listener. Typically there is a shift in Logical Type so that something which was classified in one way becomes classified in another, with this shift often occurring with a reframing of the context of a single word. When Mark Twain says it is easy to stop smoking, he has done it many times, the "stop" changes Logical Type in midstream. Similarly, in play there is a retyping of messages which, in another context, might be grim in nature. Whether in the war games of children or the bites of animals, when the activity is typed as "play" the unpleasurable becomes pleasurable. Within the framework of rules of a game, activities are acceptable which would be roundly condemned in another framework; for example, the aggressive hostility expressed in competitive play. Introducing the concept of Logical Types into the description of play and humor presents the ultimate possibility of a rigorous description of these ambiguous procedures.

The project observation that the play of animals indicates an ability to metacommunicate raises important questions about animal behavior quite separate from those involved in play itself. For example, questions are raised about the use of animals in research. If an animal can metacommunicate, there is always the possibility that his response to an experimental situation is not merely a response to a planned stimulus but also a metacommunicative comment about his relationship with the experimenter or the context. If the white rat can play, then when he is pressing a lever he may be communicating at more than one level.

Learning

In the course of the research, Bateson's original observation that people not only learn but also learn to learn was extended to the beginnings of a description of learning contexts. Not only does the dog in the Pavlovian experiment develop a fatalist philosophy, but by his participation he encourages the experimental situation to be such that this philosophy is appropriate. The participation of the learner in a learning context is evident in resistance to change. If someone has been regularly exposed to a learning situation in which he must wait for reward rather than take action, he will object to a shift in such a context if it requires him to take action for that reward. His behavior is, in turn, a learning context for his *vis a vis*.

From this point of view it is conceivable that human relations could be described in terms of a typology of learning contexts which include the learner as participant. The contexts structured for experimental purposes are a beginning of such a listing of contexts. The reward or punishment may be contingent upon the instrumental act, contingent upon some random event, and so on. Any particular context may be defined by the participants as one sort at one moment and another sort at another moment. A particularly interesting learning context is the one where reward is contingent upon the subject attempting an act and failing. This sequence occurs typically in hypnosis where the subject faces a "challenge" and is asked to try to resist the hypnotist and fails. Pathological families also appear to enjoy this type of context.

The paradox which can be described in terms of learning contexts is formally similar to that which occurs when a message is qualified by another which conflicts with it. If a mother asks a child not to be so obedient and to initiate more behavior instead of merely waiting, and when he does so she condemns him for behaving so independently, she has shifted from defining the learning context as instrumental to defining it as a Pavlovian and the child cannot have one without the other. Similarly, in the statement "Disobey me," the speaker is saying, "If you obey me I will punish you." But his command is to disobey, and so he is also saying, "If you disobey me I will reward you," but the victim cannot have one context without the other because he is caught in a conflict of levels, or paradox. It was the contention of the project that extreme forms of psychopathology, such as schizophrenia, were the result of a child facing, and participating in, habitual learning contexts which conflicted with one another in a paradoxical way.

Hypnosis

One of the peculiarities in human life has been the appearance of trance behavior in certain individuals. Sometimes in dance, sometimes in divining the future, and often in the healing arts a person will behave as if he is involuntarily driven by forces beyond him and will apparently manifest a variety of perceptual and somatic changes. In many cultures, and for many years in the West, it was assumed that trance was a product of the influence of supernatural forces. Only recently has hypnosis been looked upon as an example of the powerful influence one person may have upon another if both fully cooperate.

The project contribution to hypnosis was a shift in the area of description. Traditionally only the hypnotized subject was described with a consequent emphasis upon his state. By including the hypnotist in the description, it became possible to differentiate the hypnotic relationship from others and to find formal parallels between different methods of induction. Hypnotic behavior, rather than the hypnotic state, was defined as responsive to the peculiar double-level requests of the hypnotist. When the hypnotist asks the subject not to do something, and then requests that something happen, the subject is faced with conflicting levels of message. The only appropriate response for the subject is to do that something while qualifying this message with an indication that he is not doing it. When a subject manifests this type of behavior, he is behaving like a hypnotized subject and is capable of experiencing the variety of subjective experiences of trance. The resistance of the subject is met by shifts to metalevels of direction so that resistance is redefined as cooperation and no move the subject can make is labeled as initiated autonomously. A description of the interpersonal context of hypnosis raises possibilities of drawing parallels with a variety of other phenomena in human life where a person is caught in a type of relationship which produces within him distortions of perception and odd emotional states.

Schizophrenia

Not only has schizophrenia been one of the more peculiar human deviations, but equally peculiar has been the lack of description of schizophrenic behavior. Fifty years of a voluminous literature devoted to schizophrenic thought processes, emotional states, logic, and ego characteristics contain only an occasional anecdote which shows how a schizophrenic actually behaves. Yet the point of the voluminous literature was to explain his behavior.

With a rudimentary description of schizophrenia in terms of Logical Types, the project was able to hypothesize what sort of learning situation would produce an individual who exhibited such a confusion of levels of communication. With this hypothesis, the project was further able to examine the current family interaction of the schizophrenic for evidence of the conflicting levels of message for which his incongruent behavior would be appropriate. Finally, it was possible to refine the hypothesis further by suggesting that the behavior of the schizophrenic is a manifestation of messages which conflict at all levels as a way of adapting to the conflicting rules of a type of family organization. The beginnings of a description of types of family organization was made which included an attempt to differentiate families by experimental methods.

Psychotherapy

There is probably no more confused area in psychiatry than the field of changing people. There is confusion over what needs to be changed, confusion over the nature of the problem and the history of the problem, and confusion over investigation of etiology and tactics for inducing change. Central to this confusion has been the simple assumption that what the patient needs is to understand himself better and become more aware of the ideas he would rather not become aware of. All distortions of perception, emotional distress, and behavioral symptoms are presumed to disappear with such awareness; despite considerable evidence to the contrary and despite the occurrence of change without awareness and awareness without change.

The contribution of the project in this area was the enlargement of the description to include patient and therapist and the introduction of levels into the analysis of the interchange. With this shift, other factors in the interchange appeared more relevant than self-awareness as a cause of change. In particular, the variety of paradoxes faced by a patient in the therapy setting as long as he continued with his symptoms appeared to be causal to change. Additionally, when the patient is forced to change his behavior as a result of therapy, he requires his intimates to change their behavior in relation to him. As a result, he sets up a new network of relationships which require him to persist in his new mode of living. From this point of view, individual therapy uses the individual patient as a lever to change a family system, and family therapy is an attempt to induce change in a system by dealing with all intimates at once. Whether the patient faces a therapist alone or conjointly with his family, he faces a situation which provides him with ways to behave differently and by the imposition of paradox forces him to do so, with a consequent shift in his subjective experiences.

The project began in a period when a social scientist could choose one of two directions: the investigator could concentrate upon trivia with rigorous methodology and produce trivial results (as Bateson put it, "if it's not worth doing it's worth doing well"), or the investigator could move into the abstract realms of questions of identity, human purpose, and existential philosophy. In the trivial area of typical psychology and psychiatry, there was absurd oversimplification. In the abstract area there was an inability to conceptualize the human being in a way which would ultimately lead to the documentation of ideas. The project sought a middle ground which was sufficiently abstract to deal with formal patterns but sufficiently conceptualized to lead to verification of hypotheses. The areas chosen to investigate were those important areas in human life which an academic social scientist would consider too formidable to inquire into: metaphor, humor, schizophrenia, hypnosis, family systems, and psychotherapy. Into these areas the project attempted to bring the communication point of view, the concept of levels, and theoretical concepts from related disciplines. The project drew upon the terminology of artificial languages and the field of semantics, the language of ethology, the ideas of kinesics and linguistics, Information Theory, Game Theory, and ideas from cybernetics about homeostatic systems. The hope was to achieve a rigorous description of important areas in human life. The exasperation came with the absence of adequate analogies to deal with the problems of multilevel patterns in human communication systems.

A Comment by Gregory Bateson

In 1961, when Jay Haley showed this manuscript to me as leader of the research group, I was critical of it and discouraged him from publication. Today I am glad to see it made available in print. This sample of our rages and griefs of long ago may inform with patience or amusement—perhaps even with wisdom—the work of other and newer research groups.

But "Ev'n in our ashes live their wonted fires" and I want to add somewhat to the story as Haley tells it.

First, Haley gives no picture of the great mass of theory and empirical support for theory which the project accumulated. We were not always happy but we were enormously and nontrivially productive. My note scribbled on the front of the 1961 manuscript says *"No mention of work of last two years,"* and goes on to list what immediately came to mind as major achievements:

"Tidying up experimental neurosis." This was the discovery that the so-called breakdown in discrimination in the famous Pavlovian experiments was better described as the induction of psychosis by double bind. Later published in Bateson (21, p. 296).

"u function." This was punning project slang for the bridge between deutero-learning and animal communication: the discovery that almost all of prelinguistic mammalian communication is the labeling of contexts and patterns of relationship. The cat's "mew" denotes a proposed or desired dependency (21, p. 374).

"Learning theory in psychotherapy." This referred I believe to developments of the "therapeutic double bind" to which Haley himself contributed a great deal.

"Array." I cannot now recall to what this referred. Possibly to the idea of mapping double bind sequences onto group theoretical matrices rather than onto the Theory of Logical Types. We never followed this up.

"Perceval." This referred to the editing and republication of *Perceval's Narrative* by Stanford University Press (16). This book, first published in 1838 and 1840, is amongst other things a massive and repetitive documentation of how a

schizophrenic, before all modern psychiatric theory, saw the double binding worlds of his family and two lunatic asylums.

"N. H. I." This referred to the "Natural History of an Interview" work with Fromm-Reichmann, Brosin, Birdwhistell, McQuown, and others in the paralinguistic and kinesic content of an interview with the mother of a problem child. [Finally available in microfilm (Bateson *et al.* (22)].

"Fry-humor." This referred to William Fry's book *Sweet Madness* (29) applying double bind theory to the phenomena of joking and humor.

"Mothers' letters." This referred to Weakland and Fry's paper "Letters of Mothers of Schizophrenics" (70). It is interesting that this paper has provided the take-off point for an experimented study by E. Kim Smith (1972) of stress induced by double bind.

In addition to not giving our joint work sufficient credit, Haley slides too lightly over very real epistemological differences between himself and me. As I saw it, he believed in the validity of the metaphor of "power" in human relations. I believed then—and today believe even more strongly—that the *myth* of power always corrupts because it proposes always a false (though conventional) epistemology. I believe that all such metaphors derived from pleroma and applied to creatura are antiheuristic. They are groping in the wrong direction, and the direction is not less wrong or less socially pathogenic because the associated mythology is in part self-validating among those who believe it and act upon it.

A Comment by John H. Weakland

It appears that, after all their vicissitudes of working jointly, the principal members of the Bateson project share a final point of general agreement—that an account of the project's history may now be useful. Had I written such a history myself, it would probably have been a rather different work in emphasis and interpretation, although consistent with Haley's article in the main. But this did not and now will never happen, and in the circumstances I do not think it is appropriate or useful to comment in detail on either specific agreements or specific disagreements with Haley's account. I would, however, like to make three brief general comments on the paper and the project as I view them.

First, I think this paper is useful because it provides some concrete—even if imperfect and necessarily partial—descriptive account of the way research is actually carried on and how it develops. This has not been done very much, even in the natural sciences—though Watson's account of the working out of the structure of DNA in *The Double Helix* (1968) is an important exception—and probably even less in the social sciences, though anthropologists recently have begun to discuss what field work is actually like. Instead, we more often hear only myths about cooperative dedication to the progressive discovery of truth, guided by the clear rules of scientific method. An account of the Bateson project is, in two respects, a particularly appropriate counterpoint to such simple myths. At many levels, the project itself involved critical inquiry into mythical preconceptions—about language, mental illness, communication, and psychotherapy—and gradual progress toward formulations which are not only more realistic, but also appear more useful. At the same time, as I think Haley's account makes plain enough, this project involved considerable conflict of ideas and personalities, and sometimes confused searches into complex matters, involving a wide variety of concepts and foci of attention. Yet despite this resemblance of scientific research to human behavior generally, its accomplishments were considerable.

Second, while I see our concern with developing a broad communicational view of human behavior as more important than any particular application or test we made of this viewpoint, I do not agree with Haley's characterization of this work as a "think project." Certainly it involved a lot of thinking, and its essential accompaniment, discussion. But it should not be forgotten that this thinking occurred in conjunction with a great deal of examination of data, of many kinds. The fact that these were seldom statistical data is to me relevant in a positive sense. Certainly it is not easier work, for example, to listen closely and repeatedly to a tape of a therapy session, than to hear a therapist's summary of what occurred in that session, based on his memory and conceptual scheme, or to make tabulations based on a number of such summaries. Moreover, I believe that this project involved the most crucial sort of scientific work, the beginning of reformulations of a whole field as broadly discussed by Kuhn in *The Structure of Scientific Revolutions* (1962). When the aim is to get a fresh and fundamental view of any object of study, the natural history method of looking directly at raw observational data is often the most appropriate.

Finally—not least though perhaps least attended to—I think that in the story of this project there is an implicit indication of its inherent limits as well as of its accomplishments. This is useful to note because a similar limitation is inherent in all scientific and scholarly work, and its recognition is superior to a myth of ultimate knowledge.

It is plain in Haley's account, by much illustration and some explicit statement, that we were repeatedly involved in struggles to find or construct an adequate language with which to discuss communication and interaction clearly and precisely—struggles manifest in the wide variety of alternative analytic concepts and angles we used at various times. I believe we achieved partial success in this—that is, considerable improvement over what had gone before—but partial success only. Both what we achieved and its limits are, I think, suggested by one of our most important though little heeded conclusions: that there is *no* simple literal message—*all* communication, in our attempts to deal with each other and the world, descriptively and manipulatively, is metaphoric, complex, metacommunicative.

The basic problem our work faced goes even beyond the obstinate fact that our subject as well as our tool for handling it involved words. The root of the matter is that, for all its variety and flexibility, language is only part of communication and behavior. The concrete whole cannot be comprised within the specialized part—sad as this realization must be to all of us who as scientists or scholars specialize in puffing matters into words. One can at most depict certain slices of the larger reality in words well enough to be helpful, for certain limited purposes—so long as one keeps realizing the account is always only partial.

A Comment by Jay Haley

The history is about ideas and not about the administrative aspects of the research project and so it is inevitably incomplete. I would like to make a comment or two here. First of all, Bateson rightly points out that I overlooked the book on humor by William F. Fry, M.D. (29) as well as the paper on letters of mothers of schizophrenics by Weakland and Fry (70). I would like to emphasize that Dr. Fry was a participant in the project from the days when, just out of psychiatric residency, he joined it as a consultant. In an accident of poor timing the Navy took Dr. Fry off in 1956 which was the year the double bind paper came out and made the project well known. Had he not been gone that year he would have joined the rest of us in writing that article.

Besides the members of the research project, there were many people who made a contribution to our thinking over the years who do not appear in any of the bibliographies of the project. Some of these people were prominent social scientists and others were unknown students. Even though they are mentioned in the history I would like to emphasize again here three men who particularly influenced me among the many who provided ideas to us.

Alan Watts brought the ideas of Zen to the project and since he was a specialist on paradox and we were a project on that subject there was an informal sharing of ideas in the early days of the research. John Weakland and I took a course from Watts on the parallels between Eastern philosophy and Western psychiatry back in the days when he was Director of the American Academy of Asian Studies. I think the focus on Zen offered us an alternative to the ideas about change offered in psychiatry in the 1950s.

In the mid-1950's Ray Birdwhistell was visiting the Center for the Advanced Study of the Behavioral Sciences (where many social scientist visitors became available to us). He was working with Bateson and others on the monumental work, "The Natural History of an Interview" (22). I was privileged to watch Dr. Birdwhistell at work on his kinesic studies of films at that time, and we learned from him how complex communication of body movement can be. As we worked with films of families over the years, he visited us, gave freely of his ideas, and set an example of high standards in the social science field.

In 1953 Gregory Bateson arranged that I take a seminar on hypnosis, although he was not an enthusiast about that subject. He introduced me to Milton H. Erickson, M.D., who was offering the seminar. From that time on Dr. Erickson became an important influence on my thinking. John Weakland and I met with him every year for many years, first on the nature of hypnosis and later on the nature of therapy. Not only was Dr. Erickson offering a new point of view about therapy but his work was so replete with paradoxes that it helped clarify our thinking about that subject.

Gregory Bateson provided a stream of interesting people to the project, and he seemed to know everyone of any importance in a variety of scientific fields. He could also distinguish the lightweights from the heavyweights among scientists as well as he could differentiate the significant idea from the trivial one. Although Bateson is usually thought of as a scientist and teacher rather than an administrator, his skills as a director of a research project should not be overlooked. I do not wish to minimize the difficult times of intense debate that we had, but looking back it seems remarkable that despite precarious financial support he held together a research group for 10 years. This group was not dealing with pedestrian ideas or methodology but with highly charged material examined in innovative ways and so disagreements were inevitable. John Weakland and I also shifted from being students of Bateson to becoming colleagues over that 10 years, with all the problems that can accompany such a shift. Yet he kept us focused upon significant ideas in a way so productive that three group members and two consultants produced some 70 publications.

Few men were ever given the opportunity that John Weakland and I had in that decade. We not only enjoyed each other's company, but we were able to do full-time research on whatever we thought important with Bateson as a teacher and guide. When we were struggling in the dark with unformed thoughts, Bateson offered us an expectation that we would work at our maximum ability, a confident attitude that a problem could be solved, and often an idea to solve it. What more could one ask of a research director?

Endnotes

1. Haley: *1974*. As Bateson rightly pointed out when he first read this history, to say that people "attempted to control" was not a way of describing two individuals relating to one another but was putting a "need" into them as individuals. All description implies motivation, and it was exasperatingly difficult to describe a system motivation when the system was made up of persons.

   This issue of power and control was always a problem within the project. It seemed to me that how much power one person would allow another to have over him was a central issue in human life. It was also a particular issue in our special fields of investigation—hypnosis, therapy, and processes within families, particularly the families of the mad. There was little or no research on power and control at that time, and in fact there seemed to be an avoidance of the subject. The moral issue of whether one should or should not struggle for power seemed to introject itself into the study of the phenomenon.

I was trying at that time to shift from the observation of the individual to the observation of a system and to view a power struggle as a product of the needs of a system rather than the needs of a person. I still prefer that view and am trying to clarify it. I think it is misleading to say that an individual has an inner need to control other people, just as I think it is naive to postulate an instinct of aggression. When we acknowledge that all learning creatures are compelled to organize (they cannot not organize, just as they cannot not communicate as Bateson pointed out many years ago) and that organization is hierarchical, then we must expect confusions in the hierarchy. At times conflicting levels of hierarchy will be defined, and at times the structure will simply be ambiguous. (For example, when a therapist assumes the posture of an expert and puts the patient in charge of what is to happen, the hierarchy is confused.) When the hierarchy is not clearly established, the creatures within it will struggle with one another. An observer watching the action and thinking in terms of the individual as the unit can postulate a drive for power within the person because he is not viewing the situation. I have found it most productive to postulate "needs" in the context of individuals, and I was groping in that direction at the time of the project.

2. *Haley, 1981*: It was in 1959 that the Mental Research Institute was founded by Don D. Jackson, and it was at that time that Virginia Satir joined him. In the minds of many people, there has been a confusion between the Bateson project, or double bind project as it was sometimes called, and the Mental Research Institute. Actually there was never any connection between them except that Dr. Jackson was a part-time consultant on the Bateson project and also Director of the MRI. The Bateson project continued until 1962 quite independent of the MRI and sharing no other participants except Dr. Jackson. In later years I did work at the MRI, as did John Weakland, but that was after the Bateson project finished its decade of existence. Actually Bateson would not allow his project to be part of the Mental Research Institute and so no personnel or projects were shared. Jackson later co-authored the book *Pragmatics of Communication* which was essentially a summary of the ideas of the Bateson project. Bateson objected to it, as did I, because of the implication that the ideas originated with the authors of that book and not with Bateson,

and because the ideas were not summarized accurately. Whether it was the basic ideas, such as the notion that a person cannot not communicate, or the paradoxes, such as the directive to "be spontaneous," the ideas had been formulated over many years by Bateson and his group. The careful formulations of the project members are not presented correctly in that book and those readers interested should turn to the works by the Bateson project members listed at the end of this chapter.

References

1. Bateson, G., "A Theory of Play and Fantasy," *Psychiat. Res. Rep.*, *2*, 39–51, 1955.
2. Bateson, G., The Message "This is Play," in *Second Conference on Group Processes*, New York, Josiah Macy Jr. Fnd., 1956.
3. Bateson, G., Jackson, D. D., Haley, J, and Weakland, J. H., "Toward a Theory of Schizophrenia," *Behav. Sci.*, *1*, 251–264, 1956.
4. Bateson, G., "Language and Psychotherapy, Frieda Fromm-Reichmann's Last Project," *Psychiatry*, *21*, 96–100, 1958.
5. Bateson, G., *Naven*, 2nd edition with a new chapter, Stanford Univ. Press, 1958.
6. Bateson, G., "Schizophrenic Distortion of Communication," in C. Whitaker (Ed.) *Psychotherapy of Chronic Schizophrenic Patients*, Boston, Little, Brown & Co., 1958.
7. Bateson, G., "Analysis of Group Therapy in an Admission Ward," in H. A. Wilmer (Ed.) *Social Psychiatry in Action*, Springfield, Ill., Thomas, 1958.
8. Bateson, G., "Anthropological Theories," *Science*, *129*, 334–349, 1959.
9. Bateson, G., Panel Review, in J. H. Masserman (Ed.) *Individual and Familial Dynamics*, New York, Grune & Stratton, 1959.
10. Bateson, G., "Cultural Problems Posed by a Study of Schizophrenic Process," in A. Auerback (Ed.) *Schizophrenia, an Integrated Approach, A.P.A. Symposium 1958*, New York, Ronald Press, 1959.
11. Bateson, G., "The New Conceptual Frames for Behavioral Research," *Proceedings of the Sixth Annual Psychiatric Institute*, Princeton, 1958.
12. Bateson, G., "Minimal Requirements for a Theory of Schizophrenia," *Arch. Gen. Psychiat*, *2*, 477–491, 1960.

13. Bateson, G., "The Group Dynamics of Schizophrenia," in L. Appleby, J. M. Scher, and J. Cumming (Eds.) *Chronic Schizophrenia: Explorations in Theory and Treatment*, Glencoe, Ill., Free Press, 1960.
14. Bateson, G., Discussion of "Families of Schizophrenic and of Well Children; Method, Concepts and Some Results," by Samuel J. Beck, *Amer. J. Psychiat*, *30*, 263–266, 1960.
15. Bateson, G., "The Biosocial Integration of Behavior in the Schizophrenic Family," and "The Challenge of Research in Family Diagnosis and Therapy, Summary of Panel Discussion: I. Formal Research in Family Structure," in N. W. Ackerman, F. L. Beatman, and S. Sanford (Eds.) *Exploring the Base for Family Therapy*, New York, Family Service Assoc., 1961.
16. Bateson, G. (Ed.) *Perceval's Narrative, A Patient's Account of His Psychosis, 1830–1832*, Stanford Univ. Press, 1961.
17. Bateson, G., Jackson, D. D., Haley, J. and Weakland, J., "A Note on the Double Bind—1962," *Fam. Proc. 2*, 1963.
18. Bateson, G., "Exchange of Information about Patterns of Human Behavior," In W. S. Fields and W. Abbot (Eds.) *Information Storage and Neural Control*, Springfield, Ill., Charles C. Thomas, 1962.
19. Bateson, G., "Communication Theories in Relation to the Etiology of the Neuroses," in J. H. Merin (Ed.) *The Etiology of the Neuroses*, Palo Alto, Science and Behavior Books, 1962.
20. Bateson, G., "Problems of Credibility and Congruence in Applying Computational Methods to Problems of Peace," delivered at the Spring Joint Computer Conference, American Federation of Information Processing Societies, San Francisco, 1962.
21. Bateson, G., *Steps to an Ecology of the Mind*, New York, Ballantine, 1972.
22. Bateson, G., Brosin, H. W., Birdwhistell, R. and McQuown, N., *The Natural History of an Interview*, University of Chicago Library Microfilm Collection of Manuscripts in Cultural Anthropology, Series 15, Nos. 95–98.
23. Erickson, M. H. Haley, J. and Weakland, J. H., "A Transcript of a Trance Induction with Commentary," *Am. J. Clin, Hyp.*, *2*, 49–84, 1959.
24. Fry, W. F., "The Use of Ataractic Agents," *Calif. Med*, *98*, 309–313, 1958.
25. Fry, W. F., "Destructive Behavior on Hospital Wards," *Psychiat. Quart, Suppl.*, *33*, Part 2, 197–231, 1959.

26. Fry, W. F. and Heersema, P., "Conjoint Family Therapy: A New Dimension in Psychotherapy," in *Topic. Prob. Psychother.*, *V. 4*, 147–153, Basel and New York, Karger, 1963.
27. Fry, W. F., "The Schizophrenogenic Who?" *Psychoan. and Psychoan. Rev.*, *49*, 68–73, 1962.
28. Fry, W. F., "The Marital Context of an Anxiety Syndrome," *Fam. Proc.*, *1*, 245–252, 1962.
29. Fry, W. F., *Sweet Madness: A Study of Humor*, Palo Alto, Calif., Pacific Books, 1963.
30. Haley, J., "Paradoxes in Play, Fantasy, and Psychotherapy," *Psychiat. Res. Rept.*, *2*, 52–58, 1955.
31. Haley, J., "The Art of Psychoanalysis," *Etc.*, *15*, 190–200, 1958.
32. Haley, J., "An Interactional Explanation of Hypnosis," *Am. J. Clin. Hyp.*, *1*, 41–57, 1958.
33. Haley, J., "Control in Psychoanalytic Psychotherapy," *Progress in Psychotherapy*, *4*, 48–65, New York, Grune & Stratton, 1959.
34. Haley, J., "An Interactional Description of Schizophrenia," *Psychiatry*, *22*, 321–332, 1959.
35. Haley, J., "The Family of the Schizophrenic: A Model System," *Am. J. Nerv. Ment. Dis.*, *129*, 357–374, 1959.
36. Haley, J., "Observation of the Family of the Schizophrenic," *Am. J. Orthopsychiat*, *30*, 460–467, 1960.
37. Haley, J., "Control of Fear with Hypnosis," *Am. J. Clin, Hyp.*, *2*, 109–115, 1960.
38. Haley, J., "Control in Brief Psychotherapy," *Arch. Gen. Psychiat.*, *4*, 139–153, 1961.
39. Haley, J., "Control in the Psychotherapy of Schizophrenics," *Arch. Gen. Psychiat.*, *5*, 340–353, 1961.
40. Haley, J., "Whither Family Therapy?" *Fam. Proc.*, *1*, 69–100, 1962.
41. Haley, J., "Family Experiments: A New Type of Experimentation," *Fam. Proc.*, *1*, 265–293, 1962.
42. Haley, J., "Marriage Therapy," *Arch. Gen. Psychiat.*, *8*, 213–234, 1963.
43. Haley, J., *Strategies of Psychotherapy*, New York, Grune & Stratton, 1963.
44. Jackson, D. D., "Countertransference and Psychotherapy," in F. Fromm-Reichman and J. L. Moreno (Eds.) *Progress in Psychotherapy*, *1*, 234–238, Grune & Stratton, 1956.
45. Jackson, D. D., "A Note on the Importance of Trauma in the Genesis of Schizophrenia," *Psychiatry*, *20*, 181–184, 1957.

46. Jackson, D. D., "The Psychiatrist in the Medical Clinic," *Bull. Am. Assoc. Med. Clinics*, *6*, 94–98, 1957.
47. Jackson, D. D., "The Question of Family Homeostasis," *Psychiat. Quart. Suppl.*, *31*, 79–90, part 1, 1957.
48. Jackson, D. D., "Theories of Suicide," in E. Shneidman and N. Farberow (Eds.) *Clues to Suicide*, New York, McGraw Hill, 1957.
49. Jackson, D. D., "The Family and Sexuality," in C. Whitaker (Ed.) *The Psychotherapy of Chronic Schizophrenic Patients*, Boston, Little-Brown, 1958.
50. Jackson, D. D., "Guilt and the Control of Pleasure in Schizoid Personalities," *Brit. J. Med. Psychol.*, *31*, part 2, 124–130, 1958.
51. Jackson, D. D., Block, J., Block, J. and Patterson, V., "Psychiatrists' Conceptions of the Schizophrenogenic Parent, *Arch. Neur. Psychiat.*, *79*, 448–459, 1958.
52. Jackson, D. D., "Family Interaction, Family Homeostasis and Some Implications for Conjoint Family Psychotherapy," in J. Masserman (Ed.) *Individual and Familial Dynamics*, New York, Grune & Stratton, 1959.
53. Jackson, D. D., "The Managing of Acting Out in a Borderline Personality," in A. Burton (Ed.) *Case Studies in Counseling and Psychotherapy*, New York, Prentice Hall, 1959.
54. Jackson, D. D. and Weakland, J. H., "Schizophrenic Symptoms and Family Interaction," *Arch. Gen. Psychiat.*, *1*, 618–621, 1959.
55. Jackson, D. D., (Ed.) *The Etiology of Schizophrenia*, New York, Basic Books, 1960.
56. Jackson, D. D., "The Monad, the Dyad, and the Family Therapy of Schizophrenics," in A. Burton (Ed.) *Psychotherapy of the Psychoses*, New York, Basic Books, 1961.
57. Jackson, D. D., Satir, V. and Riskin, J., "A Method of Analysis of a Family Interview," *Arch. Gen. Psychiat.*, *5*, 321–339, 1961.
58. Jackson, D. D. and Satir, V., "Family Diagnosis and Family Therapy." in N. Ackerman, F. Beatman, and S. Sherman (Eds.). *Exploring the Base for Family Therapy*, New York, Family Service Assoc., 1961.
59. Jackson, D. D. and Weakland, J. H., "Conjoint Family Therapy, Some Considerations on Theory, Technique, and Results," *Psychiatry*, *24*, Suppl. to No. 2, 30–45, 1961.
60. Jackson, D. D., "Action for Mental Illness—What Kind?" *Stanford Med. Bull.*, *20*, 77–80, 1962.

61. Jackson, D. D., "Interactional Psychotherapy" and "Family Therapy in the Family of the Schizophrenic," in M. I. Stein (Ed.) *Contemporary Psychotherapics*, Glencoe, Ill., Free Press, 1962.
62. Jackson, D. D., "Psychoanalytic Education in the Communication Processes," in J. Massermann (Ed.) *Science and Psychoanalysis*, New York, Grune & Stratton, 1962.
63. Jackson, D. D. and Haley, J., "Transference Revisited." *J. Nerv. and Ment. Dis., 137*, 363–371, 1963.
64. Jackson, D. D. and Watzlawick, P., "The Acute Psychosis as a Manifestation of Growth Experience," *A.P.A. Res. Reports*, *16*: 83–94, 1963.
65. Weakland, J. H. and Jackson, D. D., "Patient and Therapist Observations on the Circumstances of a Schizophrenic Episode," *Arch. Neur. Psychiat.*, *79*, 554–574, 1958.
66. Weakland, J. H., "The Double-Bind Hypothesis of Schizophrenia and Three-Party Interaction," in D. D. Jackson (Ed.) *The Etiology of Schizophrenia*, New York, Basic Books, 1960.
67. Weakland, J. H., "The Essence of Anthropological Education," *Am. Anth.*, *63*, 1094–1097, 1961.
68. Weakland, J. H., review of E. H. Schein, I. Schnier and C. H. Barker, *Coercive Persuasion*, New York, Norton, 1961, *J. Asian. Studies*, *21*, 84–86, 1961.
69. Weakland, J. H., "Family Therapy as a Research Arena," *Fam. Proc.*, *1*, 63–68, 1962.
70. Weakland, J. H. and Fry, W. F., "Letters of Mothers of Schizophrenics," *Am. J. Orthopsychiat.*, *32*, 604–623, 1962.
71. Whitehead, A. N. and Russell, B., *Principia Mathematica*, Cambridge Univ., Press, 1910.

19

The Effect of Long-Term Outcome Studies on the Therapy of Schizophrenia

INTRODUCTION

Robert E. Wubbolding, EdD

Winston Churchill once remarked that words are the only things that last forever. Jay Haley's words enliven this statement in that to this day his imperishable ideas continue to impact the professions. We would do well to understand his thinking and to act on his injunctions presented in "The Effect of Long-Term Outcome Studies on the Therapy of Schizophrenia," in which he summarized research studies demonstrating significant changes in schizophrenic patients and advocated an optimistic view for therapists treating schizophrenic behaviors.

Antipsychotic Drugs

Haley laments the overuse of drugs, the historic use of lobotomies, and antisocial shock treatments. Though electroconvulsive therapy has radically changed (Harvard Mental Health Letter, 2007), his description of antipsychotic drugs as a "major problem" could apply in 2009. If their use was widespread in 1989, they have become more accessible in 2009, and some would argue that they are now the treatment of first resort for many disorders. If universal health care becomes a reality, could it be that antipsychotic drugs will be more accessible to even more people for lesser cost? Almost certainly, we will see more widespread use of prescribed drugs if the current effort by psychologists to obtain prescribing privileges is successful. One can only wonder if talk therapy will survive in 10, 20, or 50 years. Will social workers, counselors, and others join the bandwagon and seek "parity"? Will they abandon talk therapy and choose to spend only 10 minutes with each patient? Moreover, some contend that the almost effortless access to legally prescribed drugs results in dangerous social messages such as the possibility of achieving happiness and solving problems without both behavioral change and hard work (Breggin, 1999). Drugs are the quick fix. All is well in a few days or weeks. And yet unasked and unanswered is the question "What do *I* need to do to get better?" Talk therapy focused on this question in 1989 and in 2009 this question is even more relevant.

Optimism

Haley points out that research studies demonstrate that patients can be freed of schizophrenia, or at least their plight improved. He states that this fact substantiates his suggestion to jettison any vestige of therapeutic pessimism and adopt the expectation of improvement and possibly a complete return to normality. Making the case for talk therapy, he adds, "Most of the past results seem to have been the result of spontaneous remission of chronic cases in routine hospital custody rather than systematic therapy. Surely, a therapist today can do better than that."

The cognitive therapy schools provide comprehensive delivery systems for implementing talk therapy applied to mental disorders, including schizophrenia. Whether disputing ineffective self-talk or helping patients realize that they choose parts of their behavior, cognitive therapists and reality therapists, like myself, believe that change is possible. Reality therapy, solution-focused therapy, and others emphasize the curative nature of engaging in satisfying human relationships, finding exceptions to problem behaviors, and developing rational core beliefs.

Current Therapies

The point of view of the reality therapist coincides completely with Haley's hopeful perspective. Additionally, reality therapists define behavior as composed of actions, cognition, emotions, and physiology. Some of it is under the control of the person generating the behavior, especially actions. In implementing the principles of reality therapy, therapists believe that human behavior springs from five internal genetic needs: survival or self-preservation, love or belonging, power or inner control, freedom or independence, and fun or enjoyment (Glasser, 1998; Wubbolding, 2000). They help patients clarify specific wants related to the more generic needs. Do they want to live more productive and happier lives? Patients are asked to observe the world around them and to describe in detail what people living "normal" lives do. How they spend their time. How they interact with others in a multitude of settings. What they talk about. What kinds of relationships they have. How they achieve a sense of inner satisfaction or accomplishment. What they do to have a sense of freedom and independence. How they enjoy life and have fun. What they do to avoid scrapes with the law and with the mental health industry. In short, much time is spent discussing what normal people do, followed by helping patients implant in their own minds the desire to adopt similar behaviors.

Reality therapists do not help patients *overcome* problems. They assist them in *replacing* the negative symptoms. This is congruent with the Ericksonian principle that there is not a one-to-one correlation between the problem and the solution. Often, strengthening relationships constitutes the most effective way to deal with a lack of power or inner control. Having fun can ease the pain of being trapped in a problem as well as being dependent on negative feelings.

Consequently, a minimal amount of time is spent discussing hallucinations, delusions, incoherent speech, odd mannerisms, and so on except to ask about the effectiveness of these behaviors and to teach clients to evaluate them. "Is what you're doing helping you or hurting you?" "Is your current behavior getting you what you want?" And the key self-evaluation question is "Do these behaviors bring you closer to other people, or do they erect a barrier?" Gradually, patients learn that they have more control over these actions than previously believed. They search for answers to the seemingly simple question, "Who is important to you, and what can you do to improve the relationship?"

"Normal" Behavior

This direction is similar to choices made by "normal" people in other areas of their lives. People seeking athletic skills associate with successful athletes and choose similar athletic behavioral patterns such as diet, lifestyle, continuous practice, and development of motor skills. Anyone wishing to be rich needs to do what rich people do regarding work, investing and saving, as well as associating with successful individuals and groups. People with deep spirituality and religious commitments exemplify lives that serve as models for people seeking an elevated sense of spirituality.

Schizophrenia as Behavior

Schizophrenia is not a static condition. Nor is it the patient's basic problem. Similar to all mental disorders, schizophrenia is a collection of behaviors generated for a purpose: to impact the external world and to gain a sense of control, that is, the satisfaction of the five genetic needs. Behavioral choices can be effective or ineffective for achieving this purpose.

Behaviors grouped under the rubric of schizophrenia are ineffective attempts to satisfy human needs. The task of the therapist is to help clients replace these less helpful internally generated behaviors with effective ones—behaviors that genuinely satisfy the five needs in productive ways that contribute to patients' environments.

Sporadic Schizophrenic Behavior

Schizophrenia is not an all-pervasive collection of behaviors. At least some patients act normally or sanely at times. Because of this, therapists can employ the Ericksonian concept of utilization, that is, using whatever patients bring with them. Hoyt (2009) defined *utilization* as "attending to the goodness of the person's mind and body using their energy, preferences, point of view, skills and potential" (p. 38). Short, Erickson, and Erickson (2005) added that utilization "is the defining hallmark of Erickson's clinical approach" (p. 185).

The reality therapist implements this principle by helping patients describe in detail what they do, how they spend their time when they are sane, when they are able to resist the urge to act psychotic, and what they are doing when other people don't notice or attend to their craziness.

Case Example

A patient came to me because she heard voices and showed "odd mannerisms." At first, she wanted to tell me about her voices. After all, that is what other therapists wanted to hear about. I told her that I'd listen if she thought it would help, but she has probably told many people about them. She agreed that one more description of them would accomplish very little. We then spent most of the next six weeks conversing about how she could keep her apartment neat and clean, what she could talk about with her neighbors other than voices, her plans for exercise, and her hopes for obtaining a job.

Together we utilized her strengths, her friendly personality, her desire to relate to other people, and her interest in recovering her long-abandoned meticulousness for keeping her home spotless. We utilized what she brought to the therapy and faced her situation with optimism.

In six weeks, she reported that her voices disappeared. As Haley states, "Therapy can be successful if it is assumed that confusion, thought disorder, and bizarre behavior are the result of the social situation [in reality therapy terms: lack of belonging] and stress [in reality therapy terms: lack of feeling effective control], not some unfortunate biological cause which is yet to be found."

Indirect Communication

In many ways, current therapy seems to focus on direct straightforward communication. And yet, there is a subterranean signal often received by patients. The underlying message, the metacommunication, is that you can replace your symptoms, you can improve, but endless talk about how you got to this place—the dogged pursuit of what caused your condition, or even the unflagging discussion of the manifestations of the diagnosis—leads down a "DES" (dead-end street). If you want to be rich, imitate rich people; if you want to be mentally healthy, make choices similar to those of normal people, especially regarding your relationships. This approach operationalizes the optimism advocated by Haley. His message is even more relevant in 2009 than it was in 1989.

Endnote

Additional information on Jay Haley's therapy with psychotic patients can be found in The Second Edition of *Leaving Home The Therapy of Disturbed Young People* (1997), which includes a chapter "A Model Therapy for Psychotic

Young People," (pp. 283–306), with Neil Schiff, and "A Positive Approach with a Psychotic Couple," a chapter in *The Art of Strategic Therapy* (2003).

References

Breggin, P. (1999). *Brain disabling treatments in psychiatry*. NY: Springer Publishing Company.

Glasser, W. (1998). *Choice theory*. NY: Harper Collins.

Harvard Mental Health Letter. (2007). Electroconvulsive therapy. Retrieved April 2, 2009, from https//www.health.harvard.edu/newsletters/Harvard_Mental_Health_Letter/2007/February/Electroconvulsive_therapy.

Hoyt, M. (2009). *Brief psychotherapies: Principles and practice*. Phoenix, AZ: Zeig, Tucker & Theisen, Inc.

Short, D., Erickson, B., and Erickson, R. (2005). *Hope and resiliency*. Norwalk, CT: Crown House Publishing Company.

Wubbolding, R. (2000). *Reality therapy for the 21st century*. Philadelphia, PA: Brunner Routledge.

THE EFFECT OF LONG-TERM OUTCOME STUDIES ON THE THERAPY OF SCHIZOPHRENIA

Jay Haley

According to long-term follow-up studies of people diagnosed schizophrenic, one half to two thirds will become normal and be back in the community after a period of years. With evidence that schizophrenia is reversible, professions involved in social control and those doing therapy face new responsibilities. Therapists can approach psychotic symptoms expecting the person to become normal. The goal is to help people past periods of acute disturbance without doing them long-term harm.

No other malady has proven more interesting and exasperating for therapists than schizophrenia. Generally, there has been a pessimism about achieving a positive outcome in therapy with such cases. Now, research findings provide evidence that such pessimism is not warranted. Therapists can have hope, and even enthusiasm, for doing therapy with people suffering from this diagnosis.

The prejudice about prognosis in schizophrenia has existed since Kraepelin (1896) created the term *dementia praecox*, suggesting that peculiar young people were demented and so would deteriorate like the elderly demented. To this day the prejudice continues as well as the hope that a biological cause of schizophrenia will be found so that treatment failure can be explained as not the fault of those who do the treatment.

There was a period in the 1950's when a new view of schizophrenia developed causing a temporary change in the pessimistic view of the malady. At that time, in every scientific field, the social context began to be emphasized and the family and the hospital were defined as part of schizophrenia. This shift of focus to the social arena led to the encouragement of a family approach in therapy and to new kinds of therapeutic milieus in hospitals. Some therapists found that successful outcome was difficult to achieve, but possible, particularly if the social context did not prevent a return to normality. At that time, there were jokes from wry therapists who said that when they cured a schizophrenic they were not applauded but told there had been a misdiagnosis.

With the introduction of powerful antipsychotic drugs the debate changed. The medication enthusiasts, pleased that they had found a medical treatment to use, began to oppose any psychotherapy and only taught the use of drugs. Despite doubts about the success of the drugs for producing positive outcome, and concern with the permanent brain damage they could cause, it reached the point where doing talk therapy with a person diagnosed schizophrenic, instead of using harmful medication, was almost malpractice. (Simultaneously, there has been a fear among psychiatrists that they can be sued for damages for using antipsychotic drugs. One legal paper suggests that the brain damage be classed as a "mass accident" as if no one is responsible [Appelbaum, Schaffner, & Meisel, 1985].) The ultimate defense of drugs was that the malady was incurable and so maintenance on drugs for a lifetime was necessary. This pessimism was crystallized in the DSM-III, which comments on schizophrenia, "A complete return to premorbid functioning is unusual—so rare, in fact, that some clinicians would question the diagnosis" (American Psychiatric Association, 1980, p. 185). For many years, this view has been taught to psychiatric residents. Social workers have even been persuaded to teach that pessimistic view to the patient's family (Anderson, Reiss, & Hogarty, 1986).

While this expectation of failure was becoming orthodox, simultaneously, a series of research projects were finding that the outcome of people diagnosed schizophrenic did not support such pessimism. An excellent review of long-term research studies in the field of schizophrenia was recently published. Harding, Zubin, and Strauss reviewed a series of long-term follow-up studies which show remarkably positive outcomes in schizophrenia (Harding, Zubin, & Strauss, 1987). They say, "…one-half to two-thirds of more than 1300 subjects studied for longer than 20 years achieved recovery or significant improvement" (p. 479). They add, "The five long-term follow-up studies reported since 1972 have produced such similar results that the confluence of evidence appears to override the differences in their designs" (p. 478).

The argument that achieving normality means the person was misdiagnosed can apply in a few cases, but not with samples of a large size from a variety of studies. The other argument is that schizophrenia is a malady with periods of remission. Therefore, normality can be expected at times, but the fragile person still has schizophrenia underneath. This point is difficult to support when large numbers of cases are followed over many years.

A brief summary of these studies (Harding, Zubin, & Strauss, 1987) might clarify the issue for therapists, who are referred to the review paper and the original studies for details.

1. Manfred Bleuler (1968) did a 23-year follow-up on 208 patients who had been admitted to Burgholzli Hospital in Zurich. He found that 23% of the first admission group had achieved full recovery after 20 years. An additional 43% sustained significant improvement. For Bleuler, recovery meant that a person could be fully employed in gainful work, and that he could resume his former role in society.

   One might argue against such a finding by questioning the diagnosis, which would be difficult with Burgholzli cases, or one could question the nature of recovery. Perhaps being fully employed and resuming a former role in society only means that the schizophrenic masked his or her symptoms as part of a social recovery. That seems improbable with a sample of this size, but if it was only an isolated study the pessimist might not change his or her views.

2. In the United States, there was a 32-year longitudinal study of 269 chronic patients in Vermont's only state hospital (Harding & Brooks, 1984). The cohort selected in the mid-1950s had been ill for an average of 16 years, totally disabled for 10 years, and hospitalized continuously for 6 years. By the 1980s, one half to two thirds of this group had achieved significant improvement or recovery as rated on a variety of scales. Thirty-four percent of the group, which precisely fit the DSM-III schizophrenia subsample, achieved full recovery in both psychiatric status and social functioning, and an additional 34% were significantly improved in both areas. (The authors of the DSM-III would have to question the diagnosis in 68% of these cases.) This rate of improvement is remarkably like Bleuler's 66% results. Accepting these findings in the two studies, one cannot maintain a view that schizophrenia is a diagnosis which indicates an inevitable deterioration because of a hopeless disease.
3. Ciompi and Muller in Switzerland in 1976 examined 289 subjects 37 years after first admission (Ciompi, 1987). They report that 29% had complete recoveries and that between 24% and 33% had only minor residuals, totaling more than half having favorable long-term outcomes. They point out that the favorable outcomes could not be attributed to neuroleptics because their cases were hospitalized before the drug era, as were Bleuler's. They found that favorable outcome indicators were work behavior and positive expectations of outcome. The importance of a positive expectation of outcome has always been considered important by therapists specializing in schizophrenia. The negative view that the person diagnosed schizophrenic is incurable usually leads to therapy failure.

4. In 1975, Huber, Gross, and Schuttler studied 502 subjects an average of 22 years after admission and found 26% had achieved complete recovery and 31% had sustained significant improvement. Again, over half recovered or were significantly improved. There were 13% permanently hospitalized.

One might wonder why these studies, and others like them, have not been emphasized more. These are not results of one or two cases, which might be ignored. There were 1,300 subjects studied for longer than 20 years, and one half to two thirds achieved recovery or significant improvement. Not many "psychiatric disorders" have so good an outcome. These results come from different studies in different countries in a variety of settings, and the results are remarkably similar. Such findings cast doubt about the yet-to-be-discovered physiological cause of schizophrenia, and raise the question whether this malady should not be considered a psychological and social problem rather than one in the domain of medicine. The issue has been obscured by the wide publicity given in psychiatry to any study indicating a physiological cause of the malady, while these positive outcome studies have been largely ignored.

Therapists of people diagnosed schizophrenic face a pleasant challenge today. Therapy should be more successful now than the outcome of the past generation when therapy was less developed, and so a 50% recovery rate should be surpassed. Most of the past results seem to have been the result of spontaneous remission of chronic cases in routine hospital custody rather than systematic therapy. Surely, a therapist today can do better than that.

Guidelines for Therapy

If more than half the patients diagnosed schizophrenic will be fully recovered or significantly improved if they are not harmed, then obviously treatment should not cause harm so the patient has a chance to recover. This seems so reasonable that hardly anyone could object. Yet, when we focus upon specific consequences of that idea, other issues arise. These research results indicate that some obvious changes should be made in both the social control procedures and the therapy approach to schizophrenia.

As we look back over the history of schizophrenia from this more positive point of view, we can only regret the extensive use of lobotomies, custodial shock treatment, and harmful research procedures which were done many years ago. Of those patients damaged, over half might be living normal lives today. Fortunately, a more sophisticated psychiatry with a greater concern for patients' rights exists today.

When we turn to what could be harmful practices today, it would appear that the use of antipsychotic drugs is a major problem. For some time, the evidence has been mounting that the use of antipsychotic medication is dangerous because they do brain damage. From 26% to 40% of people given antipsychotic drugs develop *tardive dyskinesia*, a form of brain damage which produces uncontrollable movements and an involuntary biting of the tongue (Mukherjee, Rosen, Cardenas, Varia, & Olarte, 1982). In almost half those cases, the damage is irreversible and the person will have this behavior forever. The Sandoz pharmaceutical company, which produces these brain altering chemicals, estimates 43% will develop *tardive dyskinesia* in outpatient treatment, and 56% in inpatient treatment (Sandoz Pharmaceuticals, 1981). Since so many people being medicated are young, this can mean a lifetime of brain damage produced by treatment based on the assumption of incurability, which is no longer tenable. Now that a 50% recovery rate from psychosis is acknowledged, it is evident that normality can occur spontaneously after psychosis, but not necessarily after medication. Even the careful use of minimum doses provides a risk which cannot lightly be taken when brain-damaging chemicals are used.

The widespread use of medication has had social effects on therapy independent of the biological effects. Therapy with a person labeled schizophrenic is obviously less effective if the therapist has the negative expectation that the person is incurable because of a physiological handicap. The outcome improves remarkably when the therapist assumes there is nothing basically wrong with the person, and he or she can achieve normality. Therapy can be successful if it is assumed that confusion, thought disorder, and bizarre behavior are a result of the social situation and stress, not some unfortunate biological cause which is yet to be found. If the therapist has the view that the person is basically incurable and will live a handicapped life, never to be truly normal, then the family and everyone in the social context expects the person to be handicapped and not able to function normally. In addition, the medication can have the physiological consequence of preventing normal activity, such as normal sexual behavior. Its use also marks the person in the family as a handicapped person, where normality is not expected; otherwise the person would not be put on the medication. The therapist is placed in the impossible position of trying to encourage everyone to expect and require normal activity while telling everyone the person is a defective person by giving him medicine.

Another unfortunate occurrence with the use of medication in schizophrenia is that psychiatrists in training only learn how to select drugs and how to select other drugs to counteract the side effects of the drugs they have been prescribing. They do not learn how to do therapy with either individuals or their families. For example, suppose a young psychiatrist should be sitting with a person diagnosed schizophrenic and his family, and the schizophrenic says something like, "My head was just cut off." Would the young psychiatrist have been taught to receive that as a metaphor about the situation or as an indication of thought disorder, indicating a need for increased medication?

Since many of this generation of psychiatrists are not learning how to do talk therapy, because of the emphasis on medication in their training, they are not skilled in how to do therapy. Therefore, they often use their authority to argue that therapy should not be done because talking is of no use and drugs are essential.

The effects of long-term institutionalization are well known. If a person is to be able to function outside custody when he or she becomes normal, he or she needs some experience outside the hospital with work and normal social behavior. Outpatient therapy, rare use of custody, and regular recesses to the community are necessary to keep people involved in a rapidly changing world.

The More Positive View

If half the cases diagnosed schizophrenic have been found to recover after a period of time, and an additional number recover after proper therapy of the first acute crisis, therapists should have an expectation of success. Certainly, we should expect better results with therapy compared with 30 years ago.

When we look at ways to avoid harming people who are in a state of excitement or threaten violence, we might find ourselves returning to old-fashioned methods of social control. If powerful, brain-damaging chemicals are to be avoided, it becomes necessary to restrain a person without doing harm. This can mean returning to the use of hot tubs, cold packs and other harmless physical restraints. A major problem is that the harmless procedures require more staff time and so are more expensive. Chemicals used to quiet people are relatively cheap. Some of the new procedures for working with psychotics require more skilled staff. For example, when a person is in an acute state, it can be helpful to talk him or her down in the ways learned to talk down people in a state of excitement from illegal drugs. That can require staff working in shifts until the acute period is passed.

Moments of excitement are rare in psychosis, and most of the time of a person diagnosed schizophrenic is spent in quiet boredom on a hospital ward. It seems more sensible to have outpatient therapy with the family to prevent hospitalization, to provide shelters when client and family must be separated for a few days during times of trouble, and to offer serious job rehabilitation programs to help people support themselves as they become normal.

Since there has been no specialized training in the therapy of schizophrenics for the last 20 years, it seems evident that such training programs should begin. When drugs are no longer used, therapy can be done with these difficult problems only if competent therapists are available. An organization for drug-free therapy with all types of psychological problems is now being formed which will share experiences and skills.

Summary

With the evidence that schizophrenia is reversible and changes to normality over time, our view of therapy must change. After a number of years, perhaps because of changes in the family or the treatment milieu, one half the people with this diagnosis will be functioning normally outside hospitals. Obviously the goal is to get past periods of acute disturbance without doing harm, which means avoiding harmful medical treatment and brain-damaging drugs. If psychiatrists are to continue to be involved in the treatment of psychosis, they need to give up their focus on social control procedures and learn to do therapy with disturbed individuals and their families. Success should not be defined as the person not making trouble; instead, a good outcome is when the person functions normally in the community and is active in school or work. If custody and restraint are required because of extreme behavior, temporary confinement can be necessary in a place where the staff is kindly. Plans should be made with the family to bring the person home promptly and the family should be helped by skilled therapists to organize so that normal behavior is expected and custody is not necessary again. In a way, the field is returning to the therapeutic and social control procedures which were used before the development of antipsychotic medications. In fact, it could be argued that the goal should be to return to the procedures used in the period of moral treatment in the 1840's, when the least harm and the most good was done. At a minimum, professionals dealing with people who have been given this unfortunate diagnosis are obligated not to interfere with their spontaneous recovery.

References

American Psychiatric Association. (1980). *Diagnostic and statistical manual of mental disorders* (3rd ed.). Washington, DC: Author.

Anderson, C. M., Reiss, D. J. & Hogarty, G. E. (1986). *Schizophrenia and the family*. New York: Guilford.

Appelbaum, P. S., Schaffner, K. & Meisel, A. (1985). Responsibility and compensation for tardive dyskinesia. *American Journal of Psychiatry, 142*, 806–818.

Bleuler, M. (1968). A 23-year longitudinal study of 208 schizophrenics and impressions in regard to the nature of schizophrenia. In R. D. Kety (Ed.), *The transmission of schizophrenia*. Oxford: Pergamon Press.

Ciompi, L. (1987, February). Toward a comprehensive biological-psychological understanding and treatment of schizophrenia. The Stanley R. Dean Award Lecture, presented at the Annual Meeting of the American College of Psychiatrists, Maui, HI.

Harding, C. M. & Brooks, G. W. (1984). Life assessment of a cohort of chronic schizophrenics discharged twenty years ago. In S. Mednick, M. Harway, & K. Finello (Eds.), *The handbook of longitudinal research, II*. New York: Praeger.

Harding, C. M., Zubin, J. & Strauss, J. W. (1987). Chronicity in schizophrenia, fact, partial fact, or artifact? *Hospital and Community Psychiatry, 38*, 477–486.

Huber, G., Gross, G. & Schuttler, R. (1975). A long-term follow-up study of schizophrenia: Psychiatric course of illness and prognosis. *Acta Psychiatrica Scandinavica, 52*, 49–57.

Kraepelin, E. (1896). *Dementia praecox and paraphrenia*. Edinburgh: Livingston.

Mukherjee, S., Rosen, A. M., Cardenas, C., Varia, V. & Olarte, S. (1982). Tardive dyskinesia in psychiatric outpatients. *Archives of General Psychiatry*, *39*, 466–469.

Sandoz Pharmaceuticals, Medical Education Service. (1981). Film pamphlet.

20

The Loyal Opposition

INTRODUCTION

Neil P. Schiff, PhD

In December 1999, at the Milton H. Erickson Foundation 20th Anniversary Celebration, Jay Haley was given a tribute in the form of a festschrift for his enormous, paradigm-changing contribution to the field of psychotherapy. Reluctant to receive such an honor because of his inherent modesty and his uneasiness about being a revered figure, and much more accustomed to thinking of himself as the loyal opposition, he gave this paper in the form of a keynote address. Suggesting a contemplative setting and a wise observer, a half a century ago in time, Jay uses the framework of a prediction to trace the ideas and development of family therapy to which he was a seminal contributor. Jay describes this revolutionary mode of thought and practice that emerged in the 1950s, contrary to what might ever have been expected if trends commonplace at the time had continued over the ensuing years. In a broad look at the field of psychotherapy, Jay focuses on a number of critical issues, including the length of therapy, the perception of the unconscious, the relevance of the past, and hypnosis, that function as axes around which one observes the changes Jay, his mentors, and his colleagues helped bring about. He pays homage to the major figures of the time beginning with Gregory Bateson, the British anthropologist and polymath, whose grant to investigate paradox in communication, based in Palo Alto, California, led to the study of psychotherapy and allowed Bateson to bring together the remarkable minds of Jay Haley; his colleague on the project, John Weakland; William Fry as a consultant interested in humor; and the major therapists of the time, Milton Erickson and Don Jackson, who were consultants to the project on hypnosis and the psychotherapy of schizophrenia, respectively, and both of whom worked in ways that were antithetical to the conventional analytic practices of the day. The Bateson project allowed Jay and John Weakland contact with other therapists, who were working in unusual and interesting ways at the time, such as John Rosen and Joseph Wolpe. Most of this study of psychotherapy took place in the fertile intellectual soil of the San Francisco Bay area in the 1950s, where Jay and his colleagues also had contact with such intellects as Alan Watts and Norbert Wiener.

Jay illuminates unexpected changes in the field from long-term therapy to brief therapy, from the perception of the unconscious as a repository of dreadful thoughts and impulses to its perception as a positive force (which was one of Milton Erickson's many unique ideas), and from the theory that the past caused the present to the theory that symptoms are caused by the current social situation, which Jay suggests may have been Bateson's contribution. Jay acknowledges Don Jackson's major influence on the field and asserts that Jackson's inclusion of family members in psychotherapy may have made him the original family therapist who understood early on that family therapy was a sea change in thought, not simply a change in therapeutic technique. Most importantly, Jay then describes the development of certain ideas that became central to his own thinking and are fundamental in family therapy today.

Using a case study involving a woman's symptom, Jay reveals an extraordinary conceptual shift in how he viewed the woman's problem. He moves from thinking about the problem in individual terms to thinking of the problem in terms of a dyad and then, ultimately, to thinking of the problem in terms of a unit of three, the infamous triangle that is now the basic unit of analysis. As he continues to consider his case and learns more about what has happened, he observes that problems seem to cluster at identifiable points in family life and represent difficulty on the part of the family moving from one stage of family life to another. Thus, he discovers the existence and relevance of the family life cycle.

Jay often said that one should choose a way of thinking about a problem that is helpful in making sense of it and guides a therapist in how to intervene, not necessarily wedding oneself to a particular view. Thinking in terms of a unit of three (he would say it takes three people to make a problem) and considering the stage of family life, essentially emphasizing the core social context in which a problem occurs and the primary persons involved in it, comprise a remarkable step forward, made at a time when there was no precedent for such thinking. Jay (Haley,) has remarked, "I think my most significant contribution is breaking therapy down to a practice of specific skills—of simple ideas, skills, and techniques" (Yapko, 2001, p.199). When he cofounded the Family Therapy Institute of Washington, DC, in the mid-1970s, he wrote a simple outline for trainees, which was divided into two parts, "What to Know" (essentially, "how to think") and, second, "How to Do" (in other words, "how to intervene"). An essential aspect of this paper is Jay's description of the development of the former: how he discovered what to think, illustrated in the analysis of his case. As he discovered the family life cycle, which guides one's view of what is broadly normal and therefore a goal at any given stage of family life, and began to think of problems in terms of three people, it became possible to make more sense of the patient's problems, know what functions they served in the patient's social context, know who to include in the therapy, and understand the general goal toward which the therapy should be directed. These ideas and their application are taken for granted now. It is easy to overlook what a large and original conceptual step they represented at the time.

It has been 10 years since Jay delivered this address, and the field now seems to show what might be characterized as a regressive drift back into individual therapy (and thinking in individual terms), which occurs under various guises for a variety of reasons, some ideological, some economic, some simply convenient. I remember Jay remarking wryly one night, when he was at my home for dinner and I was called away to manage a case in crisis, that it was no wonder therapists did not want to do family therapy—it was too much effort. Yet the practical benefit of the originality, independence, and rigor of his thinking endures, embodied in his shift to thinking in units of three and in terms of a family life cycle and explained simply in his writings at a time when he was frequently dismissed. Jay ends his paper on a droll and hopeful note. He reports an unusual case and encourages older therapists to continue to work, suggesting that one is never too old to meet interesting people and intimating, with characteristic wit, the possibility of encountering something quite novel.

References

Yapko, M. D. (2001). Jay Haley on Jay Haley. In J. K. Zeig (Ed.), *Changing directives: The strategic therapy of Jay Haley* (pp. 183–202). Phoenix, AZ: Milton H. Erickson Foundation Press.

THE LOYAL OPPOSITION

Jay Haley

I am honored to receive this tribute. I am also uncertain what to say about it since I have little experience receiving tributes. More often I have received the opposite.

I think it is proper to emphasize at once that a tribute to me also belongs to the leaders and colleagues I fell among over the years. The leaders protected me during controversies and provided ideas that kept me going.

I'd like to pay tribute to my wife, Madeleine, who works with me and makes the effort worthwhile.

I also owe the enthusiasm of trainees who participated in ideas with me. You may have heard what I say here. If so, hearing it twice can make you twice as wise.

I should also express my appreciation for the opponents I had over the years. Those who opposed me forced me to clarify ideas and tasks.

With those tributes to colleagues acknowledged, I face the task of saying something relevant to this meeting. Since hypnosis is well covered in this meeting, I should emphasize the broader field of therapy. There are so many important people and ideas to mention that acknowledgement is too complicated. I have decided to offer a simple structure for this presentation. Simple frameworks are good for complex situations. Suppose in the decade of the 1950s a wise observer was sitting in a comfortable chair before a fire. This observer wished to see if he, or she, could predict what therapy would be like today, 50 years in the future.

There is a change right there. In the 1950s an author only needed to refer to "he" not "he or she" when making a statement. Who would have predicted the significant changes in female rights in the field of therapy in this half century? They even achieved administrative power.

What other changes could one predict would happen in the field of therapy? The 1950s were the decade when family therapy was born. That was certainly a major happening and I will dwell on that. I will cite some cases that forced me to join that movement. But let me begin with another prediction issue.

In the 1950s I was talking with a woman and she said with pride that she had been in therapy, psychoanalysis, for 18 years. What happened was that she got married and became upset at the ceremony. So she went into therapy. After 18 years she divorced her husband. Coincidentally she ended her analysis. When I met her she was considering marrying again and was becoming upset. She was seriously thinking about going back into therapy. There was a therapist ready, willing and enthusiastic about offering her more deep therapy. She would once again have a triangle for a marriage with everything shared with another man.

Long-Term Therapy

Given cases like that in the 1950s, what could we predict about the typical length of therapy in the future? It seems obvious that one could only predict that therapy would be longer and longer because that was what was happening. With nothing to restrain the length of therapy, there would not be a theory of dosage. I recall cases where outcome research could not be finished because the therapy never ended. An obvious prediction would be that therapy would get longer. Would that be so in these modern times?

Brief Therapy

Quite the opposite length of therapy has happened. In the 1950s short-term therapy was condemned as shallow and superficial. One would expect it would continue to be looked down upon as shallow and not deep. Instead, brief therapy has become the fashion. One cannot advertise a training seminar or workshop without having "brief" in the title. As therapy gets shorter the titles get longer. "Behavior therapy" once had to be added as it became popular, like "behavior object relations therapy." Now we have that and "brief narrative cognitive behavior therapy." The prediction that therapy would get longer and longer was undone by adventurous therapists willing to use common sense, and the insurance companies guiding us all to shorter and cheaper jobs. In these years of transition there has been a training problem. Most teachers were teaching the premises of long-term therapy while trainees were doing brief therapy out in the field. They also were required to continue to use an antiquated diagnostic system that did not offer guidance for brief therapists. The diagnosis is so negative. You would not want a friend who could be described in the DSM-IV.

The Unconscious

What about the unconscious? Has it changed from its birth to the new age? The argument has been made that the unconscious was created, or discovered, in the latter half of the last century. It is still used to explain behavior today. Has it changed? One might argue that the unconscious permeated therapy ideology and that it has too many roots in tradition to change. Yet what about the positive unconscious? It seems at the turn of the century the unconscious divided into those who said it was a repository of awful ideas and repressed incestuous impulses and those who said that it was a positive influence and that if one left actions up to the unconscious there would be positive results. The positive unconscious has its origins in the work of Milton Erickson and his hypnotic school, which was quite different from hypnoanalysis. I recall him once saying that if he misplaced a manuscript he did not search for it. He assumed his unconscious had set it aside and would produce it when appropriate. That view created solution-focused therapy.

So the person predicting the future would have to acknowledge that the unconscious underwent changes since 1950. It appears that the positive unconscious is a major contribution to therapy now. It frees therapists who were tapped in the negative ideology.

Privacy

An obvious change is in terms of privacy. In the 1950s therapy was a secret activity. Analysts would not only have a thick door to their offices, but some of them would have two doors so that no one in the waiting room leaning against the door could overhear secret statements. Some even had two waiting rooms so that patients would not see each other in passing. Would one predict a privacy change? It has happened. Now exposure is everywhere. There are one-way mirrors and videotaping sessions. A supervisor or a group of trainees can be watching the therapy action live. The supervisor can telephone into the therapy room. More contemporary, the supervisor can send a message to be picked up by a computer monitor in the therapy room. The therapist can see the message on the screen but the client cannot. It is the least intrusive way of giving supervisory suggestions during the action.

The Past

Whatever the view of the unconscious, therapy primarily has been focused on the past. A person's behavior was explained as caused by past parenting and past traumas. Sometimes whole therapies were conducted without mentioning the present. Would that focus on the past be predicted to continue?

We were all trained in an ideology which says the past is not good for you because of awful repressed ideas and traumas. I, myself, had a birth trauma. When my mother was about to give birth to me, the doctor was late. My father delivered me. He did so while my mother told him he was not doing it right. That argument obviously caused me to have a negative view of doctors and it could have caused me to be interested in family therapy.

I can offer another trauma which happened when I was 18 years old. I was working as a steel driller in a shipyard during World War II and I was drafted. I had to go through an examination to allow me into the army. With other young men I ran about in underwear through different tests. One interview was with a psychiatrist. I worried about that, wondering what he would see about my mental health with his insightful eye. Would my birth trauma eliminate me from the military? When my turn came a young psychiatrist in a white coat said to me, 'Were you ever dropped on your head when you were a baby?" I replied, "Not to my knowledge." He said, "Next." That was my psychiatric examination. This is a true story. I think that trauma created some of my attitudes about the military and even about psychiatry. Yet was it remembered accurately? Did the shock distort the memory? Can it also be that a symptom is caused by a past trauma but that has nothing to do with the cure of the symptom? Cure and cause separated after the 1950s.

Who would have predicted in the 1950s that the birth and other traumas concept as a source of symptoms would last forever? Who could have predicted that the issue of false memories would some day threaten the power of the past? The trauma could be falsely remembered or even be an illusion influenced by the social context of the memory. The past became not trusted. Erickson raised this issue of memories by deliberately changing the memories and so the past of clients. Parents joined in the issue by bringing charges against children and saying their version of the past was false.

I recall interviewing mothers of schizophrenics to get their history of their life with their sons and daughters. I could see a mother in her thinking rewriting the past to make sense out of her offspring going mad. That became the true history.

Of course it was Freud who was most involved in past memories of traumas. He persuaded us and then confused us. I should quote Freud to give some class to this paper. In his 1896 essay "Heredity and the Etiology of the Neurosis," he says, "Going back into the patient's life, step by step, guided always by the structural connection between symptoms, memories and association, I finally came to the starting point of the pathological process, and I had to realize that the same factor was at the bottom of all the cases subjected to analysis, namely, the effect of an agent that must be accepted as the specific cause of hysteria. It is indeed a memory connected with the person's sexual life, but one that presents two extremely important features. The event, the unconscious image of which the patient has retained, is a premature sexual experience with actual stimulation of the genitalia, the result of sexual abuse practiced by another person, and the period of life in which this fateful event occurs is early childhood, up to the age of 8 to 10, before the child has attained sexual maturity.

"I have been able to analyze thirteen cases of hysteria completely. The experience mentioned above was not lacking in a single case; it was present either as a brutal attempt committed by an adult or as a less repugnant seduction, having, however, the same result. In 7 out of 13 cases, we were dealing with a liaison between children, sexual relations between a girl and a boy slightly older, generally her brother who had himself been the victim of an earlier seduction." Apparently 6 out of the 13 were sex relations with an adult.

Freud reports 100 percent had "actual stimuli of the genitalia" in his cases of hysteria. It is rare to have 100% in our field. Perhaps that was because, he said, some of the memories only surfaced with guidance and intense analysis. That raises a question today. Whose memories were they? Are memories created by the client or even by the therapist when enthusiastic for a theory?

One might expect that Freud would suggest there is no incest tabu but only a tabu on revealing incest. One also could expect Freud to call the police, particularly if the liaison was still going on. Had he made a public confrontation in the family, then family therapy might have been born a hundred years earlier. He was dealing with action, not just ideas. Instead, he changed his mind and said that some of the patients were not telling the truth. In that way he changed the past by changing memories. From then on women were said to be creating the memories of such abuse. In my time I can recall daughters being hospitalized routinely when they brought up this accusation, while nothing was done to the father.

Enough of these memories and what might be predicted from them. Let me turn instead to what the person sitting by the fire in the 1950s would predict about the years to come.

In the 1950s it was assumed that the past caused the present, but would the idea ever develop that the present causes symptoms? That did not seem likely. Yet that is now a fundamental tenet of family therapy. Symptoms have a function in the present social situation, which is why that situation must be changed to relieve symptoms. Could Gregory Bateson have proposed that? It is possible, since anthropologists focus on present happenings, unless they are archaeologists.

Having brought up Gregory Bateson, what would the person in the comfortable chair predict about that man? Would anyone predict that this British anthropologist would be thought by many people worldwide, and in the family therapy textbooks, to be a founder of family therapy? Did he present a theory of family therapy which could dominate the field of therapy? There is a basic problem in relation to anthropologists and therapy. The task of a therapist is to intervene and cause a change. The anthropologist's task is to observe and not to intervene and cause a change. (At least that was so in Bateson's generation before anthropologists were hired by the government to provide information for the State Department.) Bateson was an academic anthropologist, even though he opposed academicians, but nowhere in his job description is family therapist. Officially he was ethnologist in the Veterans Administration Hospital where our research project was housed for 10 years, and he published 70 papers. It was John Weakland and I on the staff, and Don Jackson and William Fry as consultants. Let me give what amounts to Bateson's idea of his job description. In "Steps to an Ecology of Mind," he said, "The essays must speak for themselves but here at the beginning let me state my belief that such matters as the bilateral symmetry of an animal, the patterned arrangement of leaves in a plant, the escalation of an armaments race, the processes of courtship, the nature of play, the grammar of a sentence, the mystery of biological evolution, and the contemporary crisis in man's relation to his environment can only be understood in terms of such an ecology of ideas as I propose."

The ecology of ideas here by Bateson is so broad and profound that one overlooks the absence of a description of family therapy or a systems theory which might be applied to it. His writings and lecturing express a fascination with primitive tribes, like the Iatmul and how they bathe their children differently. A major interest was in every type of animal behavior. But where is family therapy? When he interviewed families later in the project, he didn't focus on changing them but rather explored their patterns of behavior and ideas. An anthropologist's task is to learn from the family, not to intervene and change them.

Many people who think of Bateson's interest in family therapy don't know the variety of his major and minor interests. They are unfamiliar with the variety of research he did in the 10 years of our project, as well as his activities before and after. He was pleased that William Fry joined the project and studied humor. He welcomed the study of films. He enjoyed schizophrenia as a set of metaphors. Yet his project focused on the nature of therapy and developed family therapy. Bateson himself did therapy with schizophrenics and alcoholics. While he was not particularly interested in therapy as a scientific endeavor, his project turned to it and all the members studied different approaches to therapy as well as hypnosis, which Bateson also was not too enthusiastic about.

Bateson sought out and ended up with two of the major therapists of the time. One was Milton Erickson. The other was Don Jackson. They became consultants on the project and their ideas were woven into meetings and writings. Both of them represented a minority view and opposition to the ways of thinking of the proper therapy at the time.

What of the ventriloquist we studied with enthusiasm? Bateson became interested in ventriloquism as a form of communication built upon logical types in the form of messages and meta-messages. The ventriloquist doll was speaking but not speaking. The ventriloquist was speaking but not speaking. Bateson liked that potential for paradox. Sometimes a Bateson interest was difficult to defend since it was not about diagnosis or therapy. I would be asked by colleagues why we were studying ventriloquism in this Veterans Hospital. I didn't quite fully understand the reasons, but I learned to answer by looking thoughtful and saying we would soon have a publication to explain it all.

Of course, Bateson would choose an unusual and not a traditional ventriloquist doll. The ventriloquist he studied was a young physician who was a ventriloquist as a hobby. He used a female doll. He sat with his hand up the back of her dress, which made quite a picture. What complicated the communication metaphor was the fact that the ventriloquist by profession was a proctologist.

If Bateson had discussed ventriloquism in terms of family therapy, or individual therapy, or as a framework for family ideas, there would be less confusion about what he was doing. Defending some of his other interests was sometimes necessary. A life ambition of Bateson was to communicate with another mammal. At one point he became interested in the octopus. He was essentially an evolutionist and he wanted to communicate with the octopus as well as try to discourse with otters in the zoo and monkeys in their habitats. The ethnology field was opening up in the 1950s. Many social scientists were out in the field watching every variety of animal just as therapists began to watch family members interacting together. In the 1950s everything happened to shift the focus away from the individual to the social context, whether in the jungle or mental hospitals or families or therapy interviews.

The octopus study was inconvenient because Bateson needed a place to sit and watch them. He also had to bring the small creatures up from southern California and keep them in tanks which he regularly had to fill with salt water from the northern California ocean. It was quite a drive to bring back garbage barrels of seawater, which were heavy. Bateson was looking for a place to put the tanks of octopus so he could study them. He decided the hospital morgue was a good place. It was quiet and not very active, fortunately. He proposed to the research committee of the hospital that he would like to use the morgue to house his octopuses. The research committee was made up of psychiatrists and physicians and psychologists who sometimes had trouble understanding Bateson. Why was the hospital ethnologist studying octopuses? He even wanted to put them in the morgue to study them. Was this significant of something? Members of the research committee would individually come to me and ask why this was proposed. I responded thoughtfully and said it was high-class scientific research and we would soon have a publication which would explain it all. Actually the octopuses were difficult beasts to study, even from the point of view of logical types. They had eight legs and changed color and hid under the sand and squirted black ink to hide behind. So a description of their communication was awkward. The committee voted him the morgue. Apparently they could not understand why it was happening but didn't want to interfere with something that might be important.

Bateson studied the octopus in the morgue for a while, and then he got bored sitting there doing only that. He also found that some of his many visitors were uncomfortable having conversations in the morgue. So he took the tanks and set them up in his living room at home where he could study them while doing other things. He was probably the only anthropologist who kept octopuses in his living room. On the wall above the fireplace was an original painting by Blake that was turning smoky.

Although it is difficult to predict from Bateson's behavior that he would be considered a family therapist, it should not be thought that he was not interested in therapy. As administrator of his project he used his small research funds to examine therapy in different situations. For example, he paid the fare to Pennsylvania for John Weakland and I to study John Rosen and watch his power struggles with people diagnosed schizophrenic. He also paid our way for many visits to study Erickson in Phoenix. This began as a hypnotic exploration and became a focus on therapy. Other therapists were studied, including Joseph Wolpe. We did not study family therapists in the early 1950s because there were none or even the name "family therapy." When the project ended in 1962 Bateson did not study therapy but went off to study dolphins and crabs. I don't think he considered family therapy profound enough to study and he preferred profound evolutionary topics.

There could be other surprises if one were predicting the future in the 1950s. For example, John Weakland and his interests would be difficult to predict. When he came to the project he had been a chemical engineer. One might have expected him to continue to make penicillin, which I believe was his job. One's expectations would be wrong. He wanted to be a sociologist, and he was going for his doctorate. One might not predict it, but he wished to study Chinese films. He wanted to do a dissertation on the relationship between characters in Chinese films and family structure in China. He thought films expressed in metaphor that structure. His dissertation committee objected to his dissertation as planned because it did not have statistics. John refused to change his dissertation plan and he ended up without a doctoral degree. The government complicated John's research at that time by forbidding Chinese films coming into the United States so he did not have access to them. He came to Menlo Park at the invitation of Bateson, who was also studying films. I was too. My first paper "The Appeal of the Motion Picture" was published in 1952. One would not expect him to end up investigating hypnosis and family therapy.

I remember Bateson invited Norbert Wiener, of cybernetic fame, as one of the visitors to our project. We had begun to examine the communication of schizophrenics as an issue of logical types. Bateson explained to Wiener the idea that schizophrenia could be described as a confusion of logical types and so was paradoxical. Wiener immediately understood the idea from a system view and said it was a perfectly logical explanation of the nature of schizophrenia as communication of a social nature.

On that visit Bateson invited Wiener to his home to hold a seminar. We anticipated a brilliant discussion. Unfortunately Wiener was learning Chinese, and John Weakland's wife, Anna, was Chinese. Wiener would only talk Chinese that evening because he wanted to practice it. Most of us did not know Chinese, so we did not learn much about self-corrective systems from that visit of the prophet.

Hypnosis

While skimming over the Bateson project I should at least mention hypnosis. The idea of the double bind developed in the project and the first one I understood was in the process of hypnosis. The hypnotist follows a sequence. First the hypnotist tells the subject to do something voluntarily. After the response, the hypnotist tells the subject to do something involuntarily. That is of course paradoxical. One cannot follow a directive involuntarily. It is most evident with the "challenge." The hypnotist says, "Disobey me." How is it possible to disobey? If he disobeys, he is obeying. It was paradoxes of that kind we were studying in schizophrenia, hypnosis and therapy. When the hypnotist tells the subject to put his hand on the chair, he then follows it with a suggestion that the hand will get lighter and lift up. When that happens the hypnotic response is doing something without doing it because it is involuntarily. Deepening the trance follows the same pattern as the induction.

Therapy has a similar sequence when the therapist influences the client to do something spontaneously, which is a goal of therapy.

Jackson

The therapy of Don Jackson needs to be emphasized. Bateson hired him as consultant to the project when we began to study the therapy of schizophrenics. He was considered the authority on the therapy of schizophrenia on the West coast. As the Bateson project ended, Jackson founded the Mental Research Institute. When it was founded it seemed a fragile and temporary institute. One might predict it would not last and then find that it exists to this day. Jackson was an active man. He not only founded an institute but he was head of psychiatry at the local clinic. He wrote more than 100 papers and several books, including one on the stock market, and he trained most of the local psychiatrists. (We need to be grateful to Wendel Ray for collecting his writings and he soon will have them published for one and all.) He also was a fundraiser and kept me in research funds for several years.

Jackson and I founded *Family Process*. Being ambitious, we wished to make an impact on the therapy field. The question was whether to encourage family therapy papers to be distributed among different journals and reach a wider field.

Or should we open up a journal and collect the better papers in one place? We decided to start a journal and did so. It was a while before there were sufficient papers.

If one were predicting, it would be expected that Jackson would become the grand old man of family therapy, especially because of his work with couples, but he did not become that. Instead he died young. It was an ambiguous death from medication. I knew him well and believe it was an accidental death. In the late 1960s I organized a family therapy meeting in his honor, and there were about 40 participants, most of the family-oriented therapists then existing, and some pretending to be family oriented.

Jackson was properly trained and analyzed at that bastion of psychoanalysis, Chestnut Lodge, where he was supervised by Harry Stack Sullivan. In California he had an individual view but began to see couples and families in his practice. One day he took the couch out of his office and resigned from the psychoanalytic association.

If one is searching for people who were at the origin of family therapy, Jackson headed the list. At the time there were people who realized that family therapy was a revolution in ideas, not a technique of therapy. There were others trying to salvage individual therapy and compromising on the extreme nature of the ideas. Jackson was one of the extremists. As an example, the group therapists ignored family therapy for a period, and then found it was competing and wished to define family therapy as a branch of group therapy. They called a meeting and asked Jackson to speak. It was a large meeting with the major group therapists attending. Jackson said that group therapy was a collection of individuals unrelated to each other, and had nothing to do with family therapy which was an organized structure of people with a history and future together. He said that he didn't think group therapy offered anything new in theory or practice. It just adopted the theory of repression and used the ideas. Then he proceeded to present family therapy as he saw it. A number of family therapists hesitated to take an extreme position, but when on a program with Jackson they did so. With his death, I think the field of therapy became more individual and oriented to artificial groups.

It is interesting how some therapists discovered family therapy because of a therapy situation where they could not overlook the family organization. Of course many learned about the ideas at meetings and went home and tried them. Those of us going around the country and talking about it were surprised at the shock people had at the simple idea of bringing a whole family together in an interview.

Let me give an example from my own experience of learning from a case in an unexpected way.

A young woman was referred to me by a psychiatrist friend in the 1950s. She had a shaking right hand. It was intermittent and was interfering with her work because she would involuntarily throw a pencil or other object. The psychiatrist wished to do the therapy while I removed the symptom, a curious way of thinking we had in those days. I was in practice as a hypnotherapist and brief therapist. I hypnotized the young woman thinking of the problem as an individual one. I suggested her *left* hand begin to shake. She was a cooperative subject. The left hand shook and the right hand stopped shaking. This was cheaper than the neurological tests she had been through. I awakened her and she said, "Now my *left* hand is shaking." I said, "Isn't that better? You don't write with your left hand." She said, "I don't want either hand to shake." I hypnotized her again and suggested her right hand shake occasionally when necessary. I awakened her and we chatted. I asked her what I had begun to ask clients, "What if this gets worse?" She said, "I'll lose my job." I asked, "What if you lose your job?" She said, "My husband will have to go to work." I had a flash of insight. This symptom could be thought of as a two-person problem, perhaps a marital one and not an individual one. I found out that her husband had just come out of the Navy and could not make up his mind whether to go to work or school. Meanwhile she was supporting him. My viewing becoming broader, I said, "How do your parents feel about this?" The young woman said, "They want me to leave him. My mother calls me every day and says I should leave him." The young man could not choose a job because his wife's parents looked down on the level of job he would get. He could not go to school because the parents would not want him supported by the daughter while he goes to school. Still entering a new world, I found I could think of this as a three-person problem. There was a mother-in-law problem and so this could be thought of as a three-person symptom, at least. This case, and others like it, forced me to think beyond the individual. There was one more way of thinking that this case forced upon me. It was a success since the young woman's hand stopped shaking, the husband got a job, and the parents began to support the marriage. I took the credit for the success of the case.

As I thought about it later, I decided the success might have happened if I had never been near the family. What solved the case was the young woman getting pregnant. With that, she could quit work, the husband would have to go to work, and the parents began to support the marriage. They wanted their daughter back, but not with a baby.

It seemed to me the family had reached a stage where the problem could be solved by moving to the next stage of family life. From then on I began to think of symptoms as not occurring randomly but clustering at certain stages of family development. The goal of the therapy can be to help the family to the next stage without the problem being necessary.

Empowering Parents

Returning to predictions, when observed in action in the 1950s parents were described in a negative way. Seeing family members together for the first time, the therapist would tend to be critical of the parents and side with the problem child. They would not even talk on the telephone to parents even if the parents were paying for the therapy. Anecdotes about families would emphasize how wrong parents were. Would that incorrect hierarchy continue? It appears to have changed. Now the training is the opposite. It is on how to empower parents, not how to put them down. With families with severe problems, such as a diagnosis of schizophrenia, there are remnants of the bad feeling among parents who felt they were picked on at one time. They even organized to encourage medication instead of therapy.

Compulsory Therapy

Up to the 1950s it was assumed that a client must seek therapy. It was said that it must be voluntary and a person should really need and want therapy. Some people should reach bottom before they would be ready for therapy. The theories are built on the assumption the person or family seeks therapy. How would a change in that idea be predicted? Would therapists turn people down if they were not enthusiastic about therapy? Has that changed? It could be predicted that voluntary therapy would continue and increase. That is not so, but quite the opposite. Now there is compulsory therapy for increasing numbers of cases. With sex abuse and domestic violence and drug and alcoholic abuse, the courts have discovered therapy and are now requiring it and even designing it in terms of how many sessions for what crime.

The client is offered jail or therapy and sometimes chooses therapy. When in therapy interviews, the client often does not want to be there. The therapist does not want to be there doing therapy with someone who does not want to be there. That is contemporary therapy. One alternative is to put them all in groups and hope for the best.

One problem is that the government is using therapists. Therapists are becoming agents of the State by being used to do something about the deviants the State wants to be different. Being an agent of the State, instead of seeking a personal liberation, is a new development in therapy. Who would have predicted it?

Schizophrenia

Schizophrenia was an interesting malady in the 1950s and a small number of people were doing therapy with them. Medication arrived seriously in that decade and today medication is the alternative to therapy. An interesting finding has been ignored. There have been five long-term studies with large samples and all find that one third to one half of schizophrenics recover and will become normal and back in the community if they have not been harmed (Haley, 1989). This was before neuroleptic drugs so medication did not provide the recovery. It would seem the proper treatment would be to prepare long-term patients to live in the community when they become normal and so teach them to socialize and work during absence from the community. As a man diagnosed schizophrenic said recently, "I haven't worked for eight years. How am I to get some training in the hospital?"

Schizophrenia is out of fashion now, but there are still interesting cases of other kinds. One segment of the population is increasing. That is the older citizens who seem to live forever. They are posing new problems. For example, we had a couple come in who had been married for 63 years. They came in with a marital problem. Who knows the marital problems of that age?

Let me comment on another case that shows that older therapists should not retire but do therapy because of the interesting people one meets. A few weeks ago a middle-aged man and wife came in who were angry at each other. They lived in a house belonging to a grandmother, mother's mother.

The grandmother was 82 years old and supported them. It was revealed that the 82-year-old grandmother was a prostitute. (She didn't like to be called a prostitute and preferred "call girl.") She had always been one and had men who were frequent returns during her career. This activity of grandmother was upsetting to the couple. They didn't like grandmother to have this career, but they liked the financial support she gave them. That gave them one source of their arguments. There was a granddaughter who did not like to visit the house because men would be waiting in the living room. It is obvious that senior citizens in good shape can continue to have a career. Therapists should continue to work when they have the skills and be glad to discover interesting people.

One final prediction. In the 1950s I would never have predicted that I would be given a tribute like this one.

References

Freud, S. (1986). Heredity and the etiology of the neurosis. *Revue Neurologique, 4*, 161–169.

Haley, J. (1952). The appeal of the moving picture. *Quarterly of Film, Radio, and Television*, *4*, 361–374.

Haley, J. (1989). The effects of long-term outcome studies on the therapy of schizophrenia. *Journal of Marital and Family Therapy*, *15*(2), 127–132.

Appendix: Bibliography of Works by Jay Haley

BOOKS IN ENGLISH

(1963/2006). *Strategies of psychotherapy*. Norwalk, CT: Crown House.

(1967). *Techniques of family therapy*. New York: Basic Books. With L. Hoffman.

(1968). *Advanced techniques in hypnosis and psychotherapy: Selected papers of Milton H. Erickson, MD*. New York: Grune & Stratton.

(1969/2006). *The power tactics of Jesus Christ and other essays*. Norwalk, CT: Triangle Press/Crown House.

(1971). *Changing families: A family therapy reader*. New York: Grune & Stratton.

(1972). *Family therapy and research: An annotated bibliography of articles and books published 1950–1970*. New York: Grune & Stratton. With Ira D. Glick.

(1973). *Uncommon therapy: The psychiatric techniques of Milton H. Erickson, M.D*. New York: Norton.

(1981). *Reflections on therapy and other essays*. La Jolla, CA: Triangle Press.

(1984). *Ordeal therapy: Unusual ways to change behavior*. San Francisco: Jossey-Bass.
(1985). *Conversations with Milton H. Erickson, M.D.: Vol. 1. Changing individuals. Vol. 2. Changing couples. Vol. 3. Changing children and families*. La Jolla, CA, and New York: Triangle Press/Norton.
(1987). *Problem-solving therapy* (2nd ed.). San Francisco: Jossey-Bass.
(1991). *Conversations on therapy: Popular problems and uncommon solutions*. New York: Norton. With D. R. Grove.
(1993). *Jay Haley on Milton Erickson*. New York: Brunner-Routledge.
(1996). *Learning and teaching therapy*. New York: Guilford.
(1996). *Leaving Home: The therapy of disturbed young people* (2nd ed.). New York: Brunner-Routledge.
(2003). *The art of strategic therapy*. New York: Brunner-Routledge. With M. Richeport-Haley.
(2007). *Directive family therapy*. New York: Brunner-Routledge. With M. Richeport-Haley.

BOOKS IN FOREIGN TRANSLATIONS

Chinese

(2004). *Problem-solving therapy*. Taipei, Taiwan: Wu-nan Book.
(In press). *Leaving home*. Taiyuan: Hope Publishing House.
(In press). *Uncommon therapy*. Taiyuan: Hope Publishing House.

Czech

(2003). *Neobvykla Psychoterapie. Miltona H. Ericksona*. Praha: Triton.

Dutch

(1963). *Strategieen in de Psychotherapie*. Amsterdam-Utrecht: Erven J. Bijleveld.
(1974). *De Machtspolitiek van Jezus Christus*. Amsterdam: Den Haag.
(1975). *Buitengewone Therapie de Methoden van Milton H. Erickson*. Haarlem: De Toorts.
(1978). *Directieve Gezins-Therapie*. Haarlem: De Toorts.
(1996). *Handboek Therapeutisch Handelen*. Baarn: H. Buitgevers.

Finnish

(1997). *Lyhytterapian Lahteilla. Milton H. Ericksonin Terapeuttiset Menetelmat*. Helsinki: Mieli-Kirjat.

French

(1979). *Nouvelles Stratégies en Thérapie de Famille: Le Problem-Solving en Psychothérapie Familiale*. Paris: Jean-Pierre Delarge.
(1980). *Changements Systémiques en Thérapie Familiale*. Paris: Les Editions ESF.
(1984). *Un Thérapeute hors du Commun, Milton H. Erickson, M.D.* Paris: Hommes de Groupes.
(1985). *Changer les Couples. Conversations Avec Milton H. Erickson*. Paris: E S F editeur.
(1991). *Leaving home. Quand le Jeune Adulte Quitte sa Famille*. Paris: E S F editeur.
(1991). *Tacticiens du Pouvoir: Jésus-Christ, le Psychanalyste, le Schisophrène et Quelques Autres*. Paris: E S F editeur.
(1992). *Stratégies de la Psychothérapie*. Toulouse: Editions Eres.
((2004). *La Thérapie Ordalique*. Paris: Editions IFHE.
(2009). *Directive family therapy*. Paris: Editions du Sevil. With M. Richeport-Haley.

German

(1976). *Direktive Familientherapie*. Munchen: Pfeifer.
(1978). *Die Psychotherapie Milton H. Ericksons*. Munchen: Pfeiffer.
(1981). *Ablösungsprobleme Jugendlicher Familientherapie*. Munchen: Pfeiffer.
(1989). *Ordeal Therapie*. Hamburg: ISKO-Press.
(1990). *Die Jesus-Strategic die Mucht der Ohnmachtigen*. Basel: Aus d. Amerikan iibers von Ulrike Franke-Weinheim.
(1996). *Typisch Erickson Muster Seiner Arbeit*. Paderborn: Junfermann Verlag.
(1999). *Therapie Lehren & Lernen*. Paderborn: Junfermann Verlag.
(2001). *Learning and teaching therapy*. Baarn: H. Buitgevers.

Hebrew

(1982). *Problem-solving therapy: New strategies for effective family therapy*. Tel-Aviv: Publishing House Ltd.

Italian

(1974). *Tecniche di Terapia della Famiglia*. Roma: Astrolabio. With L. Hoffman.
(1976). *Terapie non Comuni. Teciche ipnotiche e terapia della famiglia*. Roma: Casa Editrice Astrolabio-Ubaldini Editore.
(1983). *Il Distacco dalla Famiglia*. Roma: Casa Editrice Astrolabio.
(1984). *Le Strategie della Psicoterapia*. Firenze: Sansoni Studio.
(1985). *La Terapia del Problem-Solving. Nuove Strategie per una Terapia Familiare Efficace*. Roma: NIS.
(1988). *Cambiare I Bambini e le Famiglie, Conversazioni com Milton H. Erickson* (Vol. 3). Roma: Casa Editrice Astrolabio.
Haley, J., & Grove, D. (1995). *Dietro lo Specchio. Problemi ingarbugliati e soluzioni originali nella terapia della famiglia*. Roma: Astrolabio.
(1997). *Formazione e Supervisione in Psicotherapia*. Trento: Edizioni Erickson.
(2009). *Strateghi del potere: Gesu Cristo, lo psicoanalista, lo schizofrenico e altri ancora*. Milano: Raffaello Cortina Editore.
(2009). *Problem-solving therapy*. Rome: Francoangeli.

Japanese

(1985). *Problem-solving therapy*. Tokyo: Kawashima Shoten.
(1993). *Conversations on therapy: Popular problems and uncommon solutions*. Tokyo: Japan Uni Agency.
(1997). *Conversations with Milton H. Erickson, M.D.: Vol. 1. Changing individuals*. Tokyo: Japan Uni Agency.
(2001). *Conversations with Milton H. Erickson, M.D.: Vol. 2. Changing couples*. Tokyo: Japan Uni Agency.
(2001). *Conversations with Milton H. Erickson, M.D.: Vol. 3. Changing children and families*. Tokyo: Japan Uni Agency.
(2001). *Uncommon therapy: The psychiatric techniques of Milton H. Erickson, M.D.* Tokyo: Japan Uni Agency.
(1986). *Strategies of psychotherapy*. Tokyo: Reimei Shobo.

Polish

(1995). *Niezwykla Terapia. Techniki Terapeutyczme Miltona H. Ericksona*. Gdanskie: Gdanskie Wydawnictwo Psychologiczne.

Portuguese

(1991). *Terapia No-Convencional Técnicas Psiquiátricas de Milton H. Erickson, M.D.* São Paulo, Brazil: Surnmus.
(1998). *Aprendendo e Ensinando Terapia*. Porto Alegre, Brazil: Artmed.

Serbian

(In press). *Power tactics of Jesus Christ*. Novi Sad: Psihopolis.
(In press). *Strategies of psychotherapy*. Novi Sad: Psihopolis.

Spanish

(1966). *Estrategias en Psicoterapia*. Barcelona: Ediciones Toray, S.A.
(1972). *Tacticas de Poder de Jesucristo, y otros Ensayos*. Buenos Aires: Editorial Tiempo Contemporaneo.
(1974). *Tratamiento de la Familia*. Barcelona: Graficas Saturno, Andres Doria.
(1976). *Técnicas de Terapia Familiar*. Buenos Aires: Amorrortu editores. With L. Hoffman.
(1980). *Terapia no Convencional. Las Técnicas Psiquiatricás de Milton H. Erickson, M.D.* Buenos Aires: Amorrortu editores.
(1980). *Terapia Para Resolver Problemas*. Buenos Aires: Amorrortu editores.
(1984). *Terapia de Ordalia. Caminos Inusuales Para Modificar la Conducta*. Buenos Aires: Amorrortu.
(1994). *Las Tacticas de Poder de Jesucristo y otros Ensayos*. Barcelona: Paidos.
(1996). *Conversaciones sobre terapia. Soluciones no Convencionales para los problemos de siempre*. Buenos Aires: Amorrortu. With David Grove.
(1997). *Apender y ensenar terapia*. Buenos Aires: Amorrortu.

(2006). *El arte de la terapia estratégica*. Barcelona: Paidos. With Madeleine Richeport-Haley.

(N.d.). *Trustornos de la Amncipacion Juvenil y Terapia Familiar*. Buenos Aires: Amorrortu.

Swedish

(1975). *Psykoterapi-strategi och teknik*. Stockholm: Natur och Kultur.

(1976). *Strategisk psykoterapi. Milton H. Ericksons psykiatriska tekniker*. Stockholm: Natur och Kultur.

(1979). *Familjeterapi*. Stockholm: Natur och Kultur.

(1982). *Flytta hemifian Familjeterapi med storda undomar*. Stockholm: Natur och Kultur.

FILMS

Coming home from the mental hospital (early 1970s).

Heroin my baby (1970s, 50 minutes enacted).

A modern little Hans (1971, 50 minutes). Philadelphia Child Guidance Clinic.

Only on Sunday (1972, 50 minutes). Philadelphia Child Guidance Clinic.

Jay Haley on strategic therapy (1978, 50 minutes). LaJolla, CA: Triangle Press.

Remembering Milton H. Erickson: A conversation with John Weakland (1980s, 60 minutes). LaJolla, CA: Triangle Press.

Strategic-structural therapy: Is there a difference? A conversation with Jay Haley and Salvador Minuchin (1980s, 50 minutes).

Milton H. Erickson: Explorer in hypnosis and therapy (1993, 56 minutes). With M. Richeport-Haley. Williston, VT: Crown House Publishing.

How did you meet him? (1994, 50 minutes). With M. Richeport-Haley.

Dance and trance of Balinese children (1995, 45 minutes). With M. Richeport-Haley. New York: Filmakers Library.

Approaching a crisis: Threats of violence, divorce and suicide (1997, 50 minutes enacted). With M. Richeport-Haley. LaJolla, CA: Triangle Press.

The guaranteed cure: A case of bulimia/anorexia (1997, 50 minutes enacted). With M. Richeport-Haley. LaJolla, CA: Triangle Press.

Jay Haley seminar on clinical hypnosis (1997). With M. Richeport-Haley. LaJolla, CA: Triangle Press.

Remembering Gregory Bateson: A conversation with John Weakland (1997, 78 minutes). LaJolla, CA: Triangle Press.

Whither family therapy? A Jay Haley version (1997, 50 minutes). With M. Richeport-Haley. New York: Insight Media.

Who is Paul Riley? A conversation between Jay Haley and Braulio Montalvo (1997). With M. Richeport-Haley.

Unbalancing a couple (1998, 30 minutes). With M. Richeport-Haley. LaJolla, CA: Triangle Press.

Compulsory therapy: A case of violence (1999, 35 minutes). With M. Richeport-Haley. LaJolla, CA: Triangle Press.

Family therapy at a distance: A case of depression (1999, 55 minutes). With M. Richeport-Haley. LaJolla, CA: Triangle Press.

Jay Haley on directive family therapy (1999, 40 minutes). With M. Richeport-Haley. LaJolla, CA: Triangle Press.

A positive approach with a psychotic couple (1999, 45 minutes). With M. Richeport-Haley. LaJolla, CA: Triangle Press.

Changing a violent family (2000, 43 minutes). LaJolla, CA: Triangle Press. With M. Richeport-Haley.

The boy who can't stop fighting (2001, 45 minutes). With M. Richeport-Haley. LaJolla, CA: Triangle Press.

Brief strategic therapy with couples (2001, 50 minutes). With M. Richeport-Haley. LaJolla, CA: Triangle Press.

How many clients are in one body? (2001, 45 minutes). With M. Richeport-Haley. LaJolla, CA: Triangle Press.

Family therapy in Bali (2004, 30 minutes). With M. Richeport-Haley. LaJolla, CA: Triangle Press.

Index

A

B

G

H

T

U

For Product Safety Concerns and Information please contact our EU
representative GPSR@taylorandfrancis.com
Taylor & Francis Verlag GmbH, Kaufingerstraße 24, 80331 München, Germany

www.ingramcontent.com/pod-product-compliance
Lightning Source LLC
LaVergne TN
LVHW021115300926
849160LV00010B/742

* 9 7 8 0 4 1 5 8 0 5 3 3 9 *